T0355477

The Center of the World

'What is a place? Where is a place? What does a border do to a place? June Howard's luminous study of regional fiction in a national lens bears upon the urgent, trans-local, transnational issues of our time while anchoring them in deep historical and critical perspective. This is a book of critical analysis that reaches successfully way beyond its stated disciplinary aims, to engage the most intimate and simultaneously the most expansive questions in American literary studies.'

Laura Wexler, Yale University

'In *The Center of the World*, Howard offers a fresh look at the complexity of regional writing and its connection to the world beyond local region... Howard's book contributes significantly to our understanding of the role of regionalism.'

Leah Blatt Glasser, *American Literary Realism*

'The panel found much to admire in this thoughtful, humane and reflexive discussion of the continuing relevance of local/regional fiction. It calls readers to appreciate the many connections between place, nation and the world in works of 'local color' and for them to see the relevance of those linkages for shifting conceptions of race, class, gender and nationality. Examining the 'entanglement' of place and time and power, and the politics and place of knowledge production, it is an important book for our Trump/Brexit-dominated times.'

British Association for American Studies Book Prize Committee

Lucy Humphrey's sculpture, a two-ton acrylic sphere filled with water, inverts the horizon and evokes the interconnection of local and planetary perspectives. *Horizon* is shown here installed at the 2013 Sculpture by the Sea exhibition, between Bondi and Tamarama Beaches in Sydney.

OXFORD STUDIES IN AMERICAN LITERARY HISTORY

Gordon Hutner, Series Editor

Family Money
Jeffory A. Clymer

America's England
Christopher Hanlon

Writing the Rebellion
Philip Gould

Living Oil
Stephanie LeMenager

Antipodean America
Paul Giles

Making Noise, Making News
Mary Chapman

Territories of Empire
Andy Doolen

Propaganda 1776
Russ Castronovo

Playing in the White
Stephanie Li

Literature in the Making
Nancy Glazener

Surveyors of Customs
Joel Pfister

*The Moral Economies of
American Authorship*
Susan M. Ryan

After Critique
Mitchum Huehls

*Realist Poetics in American
Culture, 1866–1900*
Elizabeth Renker

The Center of the World
June Howard

Unscripted America
Sarah Rivett

Forms of Dictatorship
Jennifer Harford Vargas

Anxieties of Experience
Jeffrey Lawrence

White Writers, Race Matters
Gregory S. Jay

*The Civil War Dead and
American Modernity*
Ian Finseth

The Puritan Cosmopolis
Nan Goodman

The Center of the World

REGIONAL WRITING AND
THE PUZZLES OF PLACE-TIME

June Howard

OXFORD

UNIVERSITY PRESS

Great Clarendon Street, Oxford, OX2 6DP,
United Kingdom

Oxford University Press is a department of the University of Oxford.
It furthers the University's objective of excellence in research, scholarship,
and education by publishing worldwide. Oxford is a registered trade mark of
Oxford University Press in the UK and in certain other countries

First published 2018
First published in paperback 2022

Impression: 1

Published in the United States of America by Oxford University Press
198 Madison Avenue, New York, NY 10016, United States of America

British Library Cataloguing in Publication Data

Data available

Library of Congress Cataloging in Publication Data

Data available

ISBN 978–0–19–882139–7 (Hbk.)
ISBN 978–0–19–287169–5 (Pbk.)

frontispiece: Lucy Humphrey, Horizon, www.lucyhumphrey.com Photo: Patrick Fileti.

Printed and bound by
CPI Group (UK) Ltd, Croydon, CR0 4YY

For my colleagues

{ PREFACE }

This is a book about writing about particular places. It is also a book about how such writing shapes the ways we inhabit and imagine, not only neighborhoods and provinces, but also the world.

Simultaneously, equally, localities and regional writing are fully themselves, and are shaped by their borders and forces beyond their borders. Simultaneously, unpredictably, particular places shape the "beyond." My argument is that the local and the national and the global, the place and the planet, are never disconnected. I multiply terms deliberately here; let me mark all their meanings and relationships as provisional, to be investigated in the pages that follow. I hope to interrupt the familiar process of arraying such categories on a scale from small to large, and to reveal how habitually we correlate places with particular times.

I set out to study the local color fiction in the latter nineteenth and early twentieth centuries, mostly—not only—in the United States. *The Center of the World* is still very much about that topic. But, step by step, I have adventured far beyond the confines of my (perhaps any) scholarly specialization. Reading the regionalism of the past, I found myself continually drawn to recent publications—place-oriented fiction is often considered old-fashioned, but it is a vital part of contemporary literature. Pursuing questions that interested me entailed crossing national borders, and seeing them as features of the landscape rather than limits. The more I read, the more I found authors of every era—writing to and from and about many particular places—challenging me to think flexibly about the scale of their work. And my investigations converged, to a degree that sometimes seemed almost uncanny, with big issues in cultural and social theory.

I have come to see the way my inquiry unfolded, not as odd, but as entailed by the continuing vitality of regionalism—multiplied by the stretch between my endemically post-structural skepticism and my determinedly historicist orientation. During the time I worked on this book (quite a lot longer than I intended), I have been just one of many scholars analyzing how categories of identity and difference, conflict and solidarity, intersect with place—one of many mapping the movements of literary works and ideas—one of many struggling to find non-teleological ways of writing about modernity. I found that I could not answer my questions about "local color" without taking on those problems.

Let me propose a broad description of the puzzles I found myself engaging: how can we recognize both the inevitably situated nature of story-telling and knowledge-making, and the way they enable connection between people, between distant places, and across time? My best answer is expressed in the particular pages that follow. To put what I have learned abstractly, as writing a preface requires: as far as I can see, we are both the creatures and the creators of our horizons.

In the course of shaping this inquiry into a book, I have come to understand that I am writing as much about time as about space and place. A horizon is defined by where the sun rises and sets. On my reading, its circularity (as we rotate to look at it or it moves with us) already evokes the spinning globe. Also commonsensically, but more metaphorically, "horizon" indicates mental limits. To say that someone wants to broaden their horizons is everyday discourse. Organizations have "planning horizons" of a year, or two, or five years—the process often, not always, provokes comments on the need to see farther. In the specialized realm of philosophy, the term invokes pretty much the same puzzle; for phenomenologists, delimiting horizons both makes meaning possible on the ground, and implies the possibility of expansion. From the perspective of a literary scholar: metaphors (intrinsically and metaphorically) broaden horizons, making connections that violate literal and logical boundaries, to say nothing of national borders.

The phrase "the center of the world" evokes the puzzles that interest me so effectively and thoroughly that it came to seem inevitable as a title. I do not specify "American literature" as a topic, because doing so always somehow seemed to imply that the United States is the center of the world. It is not, of course. It is the ground I stand on, where I write from, enabling and obstructing me at the same time. The *national* haunts the regional and the global, just as *race* does—and they haunt my title. Let me take the risk of being reductive, to reduce the risk of being misunderstood: what I am saying is that claims of centrality are always right, and always wrong. Studying regionalism has taught me that the center of the world is everywhere.

That does not emancipate me from dealing with the determinate relations of place. Like so many regionalist authors, I am committed to decentering yet must engage terrains of power that are never flat and rarely tilt in only one direction. I hope that both the received definitions of local color and regionalism, and the phrase "the center of the world," will have changed their meanings for the reader by the time we reach the last page of the book.

The first chapter, titled "From the Ground Up: Thinking about Location and Literature," discusses conceptual questions explicitly and considers past and present studies of my topic. It begins by moving between the way we talk about place in ordinary language, and specialized usages, in order to generate a fresh concept of "region." Its claim that we should think both relationally and substantively may seem simple, but it is hard-won. Those categories are mobilized in a survey of American literary regionalism and its reception—an approach that enables me to identify through-lines in scholarly reading, and work past the current stalemate between critics seeking deep authenticity and those who are sure they have found shallow tourism. I test received opinion against the available empirical evidence about the circulation of regional writing. And I move temporality to the center of the discussion; borrowing a term from Bahktin, I develop an account of the *chronotope* of this distinctively modern form and track back to the insights of Raymond Williams. I end the chapter with a brief explanation of why I have framed this study as an exploration of genre.

The second chapter, "Local Knowledge and Book-Learning," shifts into the mode of literary history. The figure of the schoolteacher, who personates the contested connection between the particular place and the world beyond, plays an important role in local color fiction in the nineteenth century—and powerfully persists. The one-room schoolhouse, in particular, is a site where provincial and metropolitan or cosmopolitan knowledges meet. The presence of teachers in this body of work has been noticed before, of course. But their profound significance for the form emerges only on the conceptual landscape established in the first chapter. This—I believe—is the value of genre criticism, which is best understood not as classification but as a pressure on interpretation that enables us to see patterns. I offer a series of readings to demonstrate that the one-room school and its teacher appear in texts by many different authors, over a long period, and to show how our understanding of those works is altered by recognizing this pattern. I attend to enormous differences across racial lines in what schooling means, and the force of counter-examples. I conclude by expanding my horizons, and considering the implications of this work for college and university teachers. I point out that we have more in common with schoolteachers than we usually acknowledge. As other scholars have suggested, the cultural work of regional writing continues; here I offer a concrete and immediate, even urgent, example of how acknowledging the importance of the places we live might shift our perspective.

The third and fourth chapters analyze works by two writers who have been important in my inquiry: Sarah Orne Jewett and Edith Eaton. These chapters are interpretive, but not only interpretive; my understanding of regionalism was developed in dialogue with these authors. I am not "applying" a theory or "demonstrating" my argument, but unfolding the implications of my approach and continuing—with their help—to interrogate the premises of literary analysis and social theory.

Jewett has played an important role in discussions of local color fiction from their beginnings. Since this research originated in my period specialization, in some sense it was always as much about time as about place. In Chapter 3, "The Unexpected Jewett," I argue that despite Jewett's participation in her own construction as a canonical local colorist, there is much to be gained by reading her in our contemporary frameworks and even against the grain. I take the opportunity to reconsider my own past work, and to assess where Jewett criticism stands today. What do we know about how she thought about race—and how should our conclusions on that point shape what we think about her? I turn to Jewett's own accounts of her project, and read a particular story closely. I argue that we can best understand Jewett's work by taking her religious belief seriously, and joining her in imagining the collapse of racialized nationality, the everyday, and the infinite into a transfiguring moment. The center of Jewett's world is the New England village, reimagined as a woman-centered, radically Christian democracy.

Edith Eaton has entered the canon of literary regionalism more recently. She achieved a public voice in the early twentieth century, mostly but not only under the explicitly-of-color name Sui Sin Far; was subsequently neglected; and has now been rediscovered. In Chapter 4, "World-Making Words, by Edith Eaton and Sui Sin Far," I offer a sketch of her life and works, attending closely to how recent research has changed our thinking and to how she is raced and placed in literary history. Eaton was able to get stories about profoundly subordinated immigrants from China to North America into print, both as news and as fiction. Her success as "Sui Sin Far" depended on her connection to "Chinatown"; I argue that understanding the history of that strange, global locality helps us to understand this doubly-named author. Also, no readers including scholars have adequately recognized the ways she locates herself in literary tradition. I try to do so in close readings of three stories by Sui Sin Far, and go on to show that Edith Eaton challenges and claims multiple national literatures, imagining writing beyond their horizons.

The fifth and final chapter, like the second, ranges across time and offers many examples. In fact it is broader, because I consider stories on screens as well as in print. Probably it has always been best to understand works in any medium by thinking about media, in the plural; in "Regionalisms Now" I take on this challenge. I think beyond the moment of a work's production (the central focus of my past research) and consider circulation and reinvention. It would not be tenable, given my approach to literary kinds, to suggest that there "is" a current genre that lineally descends from local color. Genres are not entities; the notion of tradition is utterly implicated in the problems this book examines; contemporary culture is fractionated. Yet writers continue to be fascinated by place, and to use and transform the formal resources offered by the authors they have read. The project of narrating place still, today, projects temporality; the texts I choose to write about offer (interesting, immanent) theories of place-time. The categories that I have generated through my study of the past prove useful for understanding the present. I attend most closely to the work of Wendell Berry and Ernest Hebert. I leverage the insights of many writers, from V. S. Naipaul and John Berger to D'Arcy McNickle and Ursula Le Guin.

I hope it is already apparent that I use "local color" to refer to a specific kind of late nineteenth-century literature, and "regionalism" to refer more broadly to place-oriented writing (including local color). I precipitate those terms out of the provisional, although I leave the difference between writing and literature suspended. I do know that literary scholars sometimes position "local color" and "regionalism" as opposites. I first encountered those categories as a student who wanted to understand literary genres in the United States at the turn from the nineteenth to the twentieth century. When I looked them up in handbooks, local color was described as limited and quaint—regionalism, instantiated by Faulkner, as more ambitious, even (puzzlingly) "universal." When the comparison was with realism, regionalism shifted into the stigmatized position. The looking-up has moved online, but versions of these appraisals are circulating today. Every element of their received wisdom implicates the issues I examine. Through a category like "quaint," places are located in time, and value is assigned through location—both generally, and in literature's generic system. In "From the Ground Up," I begin with everyday usages, with the goal of bootstrapping us into an analytic relation to the play of our attention and the place of authority. I also discuss the sources of "place-time," which appears in my title. I took the liberty of inventing it, late in my writing, as a shorthand term that nods to physics and acknowledges both materiality and social construction.

Writing this book, working from many and varied sources, I have tried to write accessibly. By that I mean both making an effort to be clear, at the level of the sentence, and explaining the sources and stakes of my claims. I remain a passionate proponent of interdisciplinarity, but the very success of that project has made it more difficult to know who one's audience is, when to stop reading, where to stop writing. I hope for readers who range across many fields, and these puzzles matter beyond the academy. Teaching, interdisciplinarity, and public engagement are (I believe) more closely connected than usually acknowledged; we are beckoned to many horizons. Let me say, dear reader: boundaries between kinds of writing seem increasingly unclear. This is mostly—but I hope not only—an academic book. My point of entry to attention is a university press with a very long history, and a broad reach. Like the regional writers I center in this study, I have reflected on how publishing places me on the landscape of power. My academic coordinates allow me long thoughts that sometimes produce long sentences; important matters sometimes turn on a fine point. And I know that background explanations themselves may become dull. In the end, "accessibility" requires location to be meaningful. Someone has to be able to get somewhere. My awareness that different kinds of knowledge, from everyday to expert, are constantly clashing and combining has shaped both the content, and the style, of the book.

{ ACKNOWLEDGMENTS }

I have been fortunate beyond measure in my conversation partners during the time I have worked on this book. I have dedicated it to my colleagues, to say thank you and to put front and center an acknowledgement of how utterly I am indebted to my community of inquiry. I do particularly mean my co-workers on the Ann Arbor campus of the University of Michigan. I also mean "collegiality" in its broadest and strongest sense, including both people who have moved on to other places and scholarly friends who actually work elsewhere and have never had an office next door except in my imagination. I delight in Wikipedia's explanation of the term: "Colleagues are those explicitly united in a common purpose and respecting each other's abilities to work toward that purpose." Remarkably, my daily experience has lived up to that somewhat utopian description more often than not.

I want to acknowledge the collaboration of Kiara Vigil in my work on Gertude Bonnin. The contributions of Sarah Ruffing Robbins, Dottie Webb, and Laura Aull are mentioned in the text. These particular colleagues were once, I am proud to say, my students. Their influence, and that of other students, is not confined to the points where it comes up. I am grateful for the opportunity to think things through in the classroom with so many wonderful undergraduate and graduate students. Outside the classroom, I owe warm thanks as well for the research assistance of Katherine Lennard, Jesse Carr, and Rachel Miller.

My ongoing conversations with Sandra Zagarell have informed my perspective on regionalism for a very long time; I am especially grateful for what she has taught me about Jewett. Ernie Hebert kindly agreed to an interview that helped me a great deal at a key moment in my thinking about regionalisms in the present day. I want to thank Mary Chapman for sharing her research and for not asking, but motivating, me to rewrite much of Chapter 4 at a moment when the book was accepted and, I thought, almost done. Even during the busiest times, Joshua Miller generously honored our pact to serve as "first readers" for the books we were working on—giving me both excellent advice and confidence. Gordon Hutner has been a key interlocutor ever since I decided this work needed to become a book, and its three readers for Oxford University Press were wonderfully generous and insightful. Jim Dean has constantly inspired me to write from the ground up, asking me very hard questions and helping me—every single day—to find my way to workable, hopeful answers.

The University of Michigan has provided material support for my research in many ways—from a salary to live on and the research account associated with my Thurnau Professorship (awarded in recognition of my teaching), to a crucial sabbatical term and complementary funding that enabled my appointment as a Fulbright Scholar in 2013. I owe thanks as well to the Danish Fulbright Commission; I was not able to work much on this book while teaching at the University of Southern Denmark in Odense, but I learned a lot from my colleagues and my students. I am grateful to those who have engaged with me at the many talks about regionalism I have given during my work on this book, and remember responses at the University of Copenhagen, and the University of Coimbra in Portugal, as especially thought-provoking. Longer ago, the hook that has kept me writing about this topic was set at a conference panel on "The Schoolteacher as Border-Crosser," organized by Sarah Ruffing Robbins for the 1999 American Studies Association Convention in Toronto. Frances Smith Foster was the presiding spirit (her encouraging note about my paper stayed on my bulletin board for years) and the discussion helped me see what the horizons of this work might be. Most recently, it heartened me to participate in great conversations about regionalism at the American Literature Association's conference on the topic in New Orleans in September 2017.

It is completely conventional, I know, to say that I have been thinking about regionalism for too long to be able to offer individual thanks to everyone who has helped me; it is also completely true. I will just say again: thank you, colleagues and students.

The third section of Chapter 3 is a revised version of a portion of "Unraveling Regions, Unsettling Periods: Sarah Orne Jewett and American Literary History," which appeared in *American Literature* 68 (365–84). Material from "Sui Sin Far's American Words," published in *Comparative American Studies* 6:2 (144–60) in 2008, appears in the third and fourth sections in Chapter 4; it is reprinted by permission and I supply here the reference to the journal's website required by Taylor and Francis: www.tandfonline.com.

I am grateful to these individuals and institutions for permission to reproduce images: the Association of European Border Regions; Air Science Consultants, Inc. DBA Skywatch Weather; the Earth Science and Remote Sensing Unit, NASA Johnson Space Center; Wallace J. Nichols; the Regents of the University of Minnesota; Jon de Mello, C.E.O., The Mountain Apple Company; the St. Louis Art Museum; the University of Michigan Press; Historic New England; Joe Mabel; the Clements Library, University of Michigan; the Special Collections Research Center, University of Chicago Library; the Library of Congress; Counterpoint Press; Ernest Hebert; Working Dog Productions; and Yale University Press.

{ CONTENTS }

List of Figures   xix

1. From the Ground Up: Thinking about Location and Literature   1

2. Local Knowledge and Book-Learning: Placing the Teacher
   in Regional Story-Telling   48

3. The Unexpected Jewett   97

4. World-Making Words, by Edith Eaton and Sui Sin Far   121

5. Regionalisms Now   161

   In the Place of a Conclusion   218

   Endnotes   223
   Bibliography   227
   Index   245

{ LIST OF FIGURES }

1.1   Map from the website of the Association of European Border Regions (2017). Members are indicated in red, non-members in green, with mixed red and green for partial and planned members. The online version of the map can be varied to show, for example, large-scale cross-border collaborations as well. Reproduced by permission.   5

1.2   Example of a weather map of the United States by Air Science Consultants, Inc. DBA Skywatch Weather. Used by permission.   6

1.3   Photograph of the Earth taken from Apollo 17 on December 7, 1972. Image courtesy of the Earth Science and Remote Sensing Unit, NASA Johnson Space Center. Photography AS17-148p22727, available from the website http://eol.jsc.nasa.gov.   9

1.4 and 1.5   Publicity materials for the Blue Marbles Project. Used by courtesy of Wallace J. Nichols. Information about the Blue Marbles Project is available on the website http://www.wallacejnichols.org/130/blue-marbles/html.   10–11

1.6   World Map: Hobo-Dyer Equal Area Projection. Copyright 2015 www.ODTmaps.com. Used by permission. For maps and other related teaching materials contact: ODT, Inc., PO Box 134, Amherst MA 01004 USA; 800-736-1293; Fax: 413-549-3503; Skype: ODTInc; Email: odtstore@odt.org; Web: http://manywaystoseethe world.org.   12

1.7   Upright Human Body, Space and Time. From Yi Fu Tuan, *Space and Place: The Perspective of Experience* (copyright University of Minnesota Press, 1977), p. 35. Reprinted by permission.   36

1.8   The cover of Israel Kamakawiwo'ole's album *Facing Future*, released in 1993 by Mountain Apple Records. Reproduced courtesy of Jon de Mello.   37

1.9   Hecataeus' world map, 500 BCE, as rendered by Jona Lendering (modified slightly for this publication), courtesy of Livius.org.   43

2.1   Winslow Homer, *Snap the Whip*, published as a centerfold in *Harper's Weekly*, September 20, 1873.   49

2.2   Winslow Homer, *The Country School*, 1871; oil on canvas; 21 ¼ × 38 1¼ inches; Saint Louis Art Museum, Museum Purchase 123:1946.   49

2.3   Mary Keithan's Michigan *One-Room Schoolhouses*, published in 2008, offers a selection from her several hundred photographs of one-room schoolhouses across the state and includes information about the Michigan One-Room Schoolhouse Association, founded in 1993 and still active as of 2017. Cover reproduced by permission of the University of Michigan Press.   50

2.4   Frank Beard, "*First Acquaintance with Flat Creek*," from Edward Eggleston,
       The Hoosier School-Master: A Novel (New York: Orange Judd and Company,
       1871), p. 10.   52

2.5   Frank Beard, "*Old Jack Means, the School Trustee*," from Edward Eggleston,
       The Hoosier School-Master: A Novel (New York: Orange Judd and Company,
       1871), p. 13.   54

2.6   Frank Beard, "*Hank Banta's Improved Plunge-Bath*," from Edward Eggleston,
       The Hoosier School-Master: A Novel (New York: Orange Judd and
       Company, 1871), p. 36.   54

2.7   Frank Beard, "*Bull*," from Edward Eggleston, *The Hoosier School-Master:
       A Novel* (New York: Orange Judd and Company, 1871), p. 75.   56

2.8   Frank Beard, "*Jeems Phillips*," from Edward Eggleston, *The Hoosier
       School-Master: A Novel* (New York: Orange Judd and Company, 1871), p. 48.   60

3.1   Portrait of Sarah Orne Jewett with book (undated). Reproduced with
       permission from Historic New England.   99

3.2   Sarah Orne Jewett at the age of eight. From Francis Otto Matthiessen,
       "*Sarah Orne Jewett*," published by Houghton Mifflin in 1929.   119

4.1   Edith Eaton's grave, Mount Royal Cemetery, Montréal. Photograph
       by the author.   122

4.2   "The Chinese Sacred Lily, or Oriental Narcissus," from
       The Geo. H. Mellen Co. Illustrated Catalogue of Bulbs, Roses and Plants,
       Innisfallen Green Houses, Springfield, Ohio, 1899, p. 11.   127

4.3   The cover of the original edition of *Mrs. Spring Fragrance*, published by
       A. C. McClurg and Company of Chicago in 1912.   128

4.4   Acknowledgements page, and facing blank page, from the original edition
       of *Mrs. Spring Fragrance*, showing its "Chinese" decorations.   128

4.5   The title page of Eaton's "The Son of Chung Wo," published in Leslie's
       Illustrated Weekly in 1910, demonstrating the use of a "chop suey" typeface.   129

4.6   Portrait of Edith Eaton, published in the *Independent* in 1909.   132

4.7   Historic Chinatown Gate, Seattle, Washington, about two weeks before its
       formal unveiling, February 8, 2008. Photograph by Joe Mabel.   134

4.8   Cover and back page of the "Guide Book to the Joss House" distributed
       by the Wah Mee Exposition Company at the Chicago World's Fair, 1893.
       Reproduced with permission from a pamphlet in the collection of the
       William L. Clements Library at the University of Michigan.   135

4.9   Frontispiece and first page of the "Guide Book to the Joss House"
       distributed by the Wah Mee Exposition Company at the Chicago
       World's Fair, 1893. Reproduced with permission from a pamphlet
       in the collection of the William L. Clements Library at the
       University of Michigan.   135

4.10 The Ferris Wheel and Chinese Theatre (on the left) on the Midway Plaisance at the World's Columbian Exposition in Chicago. Photograph taken by E.R. Walker in 1893. Reproduced by courtesy of the University of Chicago Photographic Archive [apf3-00088], Special Collections Center, University of Chicago Library.   136

4.11 The Robert Louis Stevenson monument in Portsmouth Square, San Francisco. Reproduced from the 1907 book *Stevensoniana: An Anecdotal Life and Appreciation of Robert Louis Stevenson*, ed. Sir John Hammerton (facing p. 308).   154

4.12 *Cuba Libre, c.*1898. Attributed to F. W. Guerin, St. Louis. From the Library of Congress, https://www.loc.gov/item/2005688946.   158

5.1 Map of Port William, from Wendell Berry's *That Distant Land*. Drawn by Molly O'Halloran and reprinted by permission of Counterpoint Press.   179

5.2 Genealogy of Port William families, from Wendell Berry's *That Distant Land*. Drawn by Molly O'Halloran and reprinted by permission of Counterpoint Press.   180

5.3 Saints Peter and Paul Church in the North Beach neighborhood of San Francisco. Photograph by the author.   188

5.4 Map of the Darby region, reproduced courtesy of Ernest Hebert.   191

5.5 "Cooty's Cabin," reproduced courtesy of Ernest Hebert.   191

5.6 The Indigeneous northeast: a network of waterways. From Lisa Brooks, *The Common Pot: The Recovery of Native Space in the Northeast*, p. xvii (copyright University of Minnesota Press, 2008), p. xvii. Reprinted by permission.   199

5.7 Publicity poster for *The Dish*, 2000. Reproduced by permission of Working Dog Productions PTY LTD.   211

5.8 "Wheat Strips on Plateau," from *Taking Measures across the American Landscape* by James Corner (author) and Alex S. MacLean (photographer) (Yale University Press, 1996), p. 128. Reprinted by permission.   214

{ 1 }

From the Ground Up

THINKING ABOUT LOCATION AND LITERATURE

That one lives at the center of the world is the world's profoundest thought.
—WENDELL BERRY, *Whitefoot*

[T]he particular mix of social relations which … [define] the uniqueness
of any place is by no means all included within
that place itself.

—DOREEN MASSEY, *Space, Place and Gender*

What Is a Region?

Everyone knows what a region is.

It's an area, a section, a domain, a district. A province, a neighborhood, a territory, a vicinity, a locality … a place.

A word that means all those things is not a very precise tool for thinking with.

Expert knowledge is more informed by—indeed sometimes captive to—
everyday understandings than we usually realize. In previous work, I argued this
was so for "sentimentality," and I have come to think it is pervasively true of
scholarly terms. We can't get the "real" out of "realism," or the "modern" out of
modernism and modernity. Regionalism is a form of realism and decisively
engaged with the nature of the modern. My clarifying effort will have to work
through confounding complexities, from crowding semi-synonyms to the discon-
tinuities of genre—to a way of thinking about this term that is useful for my
specialist enterprise, and also explains the continued relevance of particular places
in so many efforts to understand life in the twenty-first century.

In other words: what I seek to do, in this chapter, is to articulate region as
a *concept.*

In *Travelling Concepts in the Humanities* Mieke Bal offers a lucid, eloquent
explanation of what that means. Concepts look like words or labels, but they are,
instead, "miniature theories," implying a "systemic set of distinctions" (22) and rooted

in specific scholarly conversations. She analyses the concept of the concept, its history, its specific role in the humanities, in careful detail. And she argues that to be productive they should be understood not only as requiring ongoing critical reflection, but also as interacting *with* rather than being applied *to* the cultural objects being studied. In the humanities, although we do not always explicitly or effectively defend our doing so, we construct knowledge in dialogue with the works we study. I suspect the somewhat peculiar status of literary studies in the university is linked with this truth. For at least the last half-century, theories and insights from our field have exercised enormous influence across the academy. Yet colleagues in other disciplines find our methods disconcertingly flexible, and rarely accord our work the status of science (indeed they sometimes seem to privately believe that we are simply speculating). Beginning by analyzing *region* enables me to be rigorous. As Bal shows, the clarification of concepts now does much of the work once done by disciplines, and it can make the difference between a "muddled multidisciplinarity" and a "productive interdisciplinarity" (25). The conviction that claim is correct underpins the reflections I offer below.

We need the grip that refining "region" as a concept will give us, because it is not only a vague and powerful word in everyday speech, but also a technical term in an astonishing variety of disciplines. Literary scholars have borrowed from many of them and offered summaries of the powerful body of work theorizing *place* (amply represented in my bibliography). For me, the most useful thing about looking across these cacophonous conversations is that a common theme— or more precisely, a fundamental tension—does emerge. We are constantly shifting between what I call *substantive* and *relational* understandings of region. I will take that distinction—arrived at after considerable study and thought, despite its seeming simplicity—as a guide in sorting through multiple disciplinary takes on region. In the next section, I will show that it can also move us beyond unhelpfully polarized debates in literary scholarship.

To begin by stating it simply: when we talk about regions, we talk about particular places. Say (for example) "the Midwest," and certain landscapes, cities, and states come to mind, weighty and substantive. Yet a relational element is always implicit, because every region is defined by its location in a larger system; "the Midwest" depends on opposing terms like "New England" and "West," and on overlapping ones like "Great Lakes." That is true even if one is gazing out a window in Michigan—as I am while writing these words.

The substantive view of region invokes the real. Does anyone really doubt that there is a there there? But already we are involved in the massively recursive processes that constitute that real. Putting it less simply: the iterated insistence on the simple fact of location marks an aporia. As we have known since Saussure, in language there is only difference, without positive terms. The way the relational shadows the substantive is in some sense a version of how, in general, common sense is unsettled by theory. But it is not *only* that, and that is not the only thing to say;

nor is the relational at work *only* in representation. As the geographer Doreen Massey puts it in the passage I have used as an epigraph, "the particular mix of social relations which…[define] the uniqueness of any place is by no means all included within that place itself" (5). It does not matter where you are. If you gaze around looking for traces of other places you will find them, frozen in commodities produced elsewhere or written on the ground as pavement leading away. Or, in the case of the trees outside my window, standing substantial and quiet but embodying by their very presence an intricate history of land-use decisions made at multiple sites.

I am saying, then, that although the substantive and the relational approaches to region constantly pull apart, may seem opposed in a given account, they can never be separated.

The balance does shift as any given discussion progresses. For quite a long time scholarly usages have been shifting toward the relational. The increased emphasis on the social construction of categories—gender, race, nation, and so on—is visible not only in the "soft" fields of literary and cultural studies but also in adjacent ones like history and anthropology, and across the social sciences. Remarkable work like that of the humanistic geographer Yi-Fu Tuan, which fully acknowledges both the substantive and the relational aspects of place, brings disciplines together. And certainly many scholars of literary studies, in any decade, have acknowledged the material and institutional, remembering that narratives are neither arbitrary nor easily malleable, and that they take hold and have effects. But I think it is uncontroversial to note that, whether we call it constructivism, post-structuralism, anti-foundationalism, or something else, the trend—punctuated by course corrections—has been broadly away from treating anything as solidly existing and toward an interest in how it is made.

The relational is also fundamental to approaches to region in the social sciences and policy studies—something especially worth noting in a book of literary scholarship, given the humanist tendency to think of everyone else as excessively substantive. In international relations, a discussion that focuses on region is about the interdependence of neighboring states, often focusing on how economic, political, and cultural connections mesh. In urban planning, a region is understood quite specifically as a metropolitan area and its hinterland. We can turn to a classic of anthropology for a particularly vivid statement of this received view: big cities are defined "by their capacity to import and export people, products, images and messages. Spatially, their importance can be measured by the quality and scale of the highway and rail networks linking them with their airports." This is Marc Augé, who returns to the substantive in the next sentence—and then wonderfully reinscribes the relational in it: cities' "relation with the exterior is being written into the landscape at the very moment that so-called 'historic' centres are becoming increasingly attractive to tourists from all over the world" (vii). I would add only that that tourism has been around for a very long time, so that "moment" may be understood as spanning centuries.

Regional*ism* always means pretty much what it does in literature—a big idea that is shared by enough people to be considered a movement. But outside literature it is less often advocacy for a particular place than a call for attention to relationships. A regionalism more or less by that name emerged in the period after the Second World War, its most consequential result the formation of the European Coal and Steel Community in 1951—which was designed, as stated explicitly in the Schuman Declaration, to unify production and make war between France and Germany "not merely unthinkable, but materially impossible." That organization became the European Economic Community in 1958. Another wave of advocacy, "the new regionalism," began in the 1980s, and in 1993 the EEC became the European Union. The very fact that the EU's roots in coal and steel are mostly forgotten marks the success of a regionalist project in shaping the globe. The North American Free Trade Agreement (NAFTA) took effect in 1994; the African Union was formed in 2001 and began to function the next year. In today's economic and political landscape, we take the importance of these regional organizations for granted. Yet their power is constantly renegotiated. The EU in particular has been intensely challenged since the global financial crisis of 2008. There was a break between the period when every news outlet seemed full of anxious (even panicky) discussions of the difficulties of the common currency the euro, and the coverage of European tensions over the Syrian refugee crisis and immigration generally. But now "Brexit," the 2016 British vote to leave the European Union, may even test the federation's viability. The entailed prospect of Scottish voters revisiting and reversing their 2014 decision to remain within the United Kingdom demonstrates at once the persistent and pervasive tension between nationalism and regionalism—and the impossibility of fully separating them.

European federalism has led to an increased emphasis on regionalism in a more local sense as well. The Maastricht Treaty that created the EU provided for the establishment of a Committee of the Regions, which held its first plenary session in Brussels in 1994. This "assembly of regional and local representatives" must be consulted on many matters, and is committed (according to its mission statement) to both integration and diversity. It works to involve local and regional authorities in European governance, aspiring both to respond to "the challenges of globalisation" and to ensure that "decisions are taken and applied as close to the citizens as possible and at the most appropriate level." The ambition of the project is striking—and so is the ambiguity of its place-keeping term: how close to the ground is "appropriate"? The privilege now accorded the local is clear—although it's equally clear throughout public discourse that this valuation has not dispelled the countervailing habit of representing many places as parochial, backward, in fact *not* to be trusted with decisions.

There is also an Association of European Border Regions, formally instituted in 1971 with the goal of lowering barriers and enhancing cooperation in regions striving to stay connected across national boundaries. (See Figure 1.1.) It is pleasing that its formation was first discussed at a conference in Basel, Switzerland—a

FIGURE 1.1 *Map from the website of the Association of European Border Regions (2017). Members are indicated in red, non-members in green, with mixed red and green for partial and planned members. The online version of the map can be varied to show, for example, large-scale cross-border collaborations as well. Reproduced by permission.*

city whose airport offers exits to three different nations. Their website vaunts: "95 out of the approximately 163 working border and cross-border regions have become members of AEBR." The numbers, the *scale* of the issue, are surprising. The emergence of a federal system in Europe—unevenly and perhaps now insecurely, but persistently, expanding—has profoundly enabled such initiatives, allowing advocates to affirm connections despite deeply vexed histories. Such cross-border connections are important in the Western hemisphere, as well. Of course, the supranational region is available in everyday usage—we easily say "Latin America." We indicate border regions that cross national boundaries, as in "Great Lakes"—although within the U.S., it seems easy to forget that four of the five have Canadian shorelines. Studies of the U.S.–Mexico borderland—let us say

Aztlán, and gloss it as the Southwest—have been extraordinarily productive. So has the new Southern studies, in books like *Look Away! The U.S. South in New World Studies*, which views that region through its links with Latin America and the Caribbean. I am working towards a perspective, articulated in the last pages of this book, that includes the Global South as well.

It is intuitive to think of the local, regional, national, and global as a set of concentric circles, each one getting larger and containing the others. What we see here is quite different, and it is a key point for the concept of region: the national often *interrupts* the regional. Both social solidarities and imagined places emerge on many sites, and they are not organized into a tidy geometry of scale. I might equally say that the regional challenges the national, and many examples will follow. But since the eighteenth century, the nation has tended to push the other categories around—certainly conceptually, although something similar might be said about events. A great deal of powerful scholarship over several decades has shown us nations as imagined communities, and as historically contingent, but it is not easy to visualize the globe without a four-color Westphalian grid over it. Thinking through region helps.

This is a particularly important move for Americanists, I think. Many studies of regionalism in the large and powerful United States construe it as internal to the nation. The weather map that still appears in newspapers, and can be found frequently on the Web, may stand in for that habit of mind. (See Figure 1.2.) It is easily read because it is so familiar—a drawing of the outline of the forty-eight contiguous states, with or without Alaskan and Hawaiian appendages, is instantly recognizable

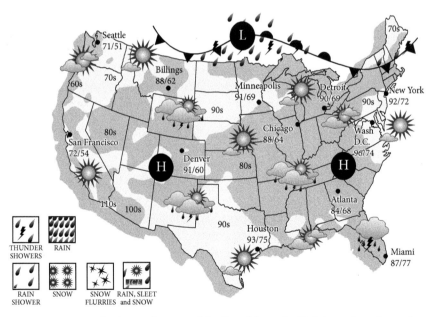

FIGURE 1.2 *Example of a weather map of the United States by Air Science Consultants, Inc. DBA Skywatch Weather. Used by permission.*

as "America". I have often traced it in the air in front of students, who have no trouble identifying it (as they occasionally point out—when I forget and draw it from my own perspective, they even recognize it backwards). It requires some work to recognize, instead, the peculiarity of the image and see the image as a truncated part of the continent somehow floating in space. Ontario, Sonora, and so on are erased—an especially peculiar thing to do when representing meteorological forces that certainly pay no heed to national boundaries. The success of a project in social life is marked, as many have observed, by its becoming invisible. So I am trying here to defamiliarize place categories that we take for granted; I want to make the very image of the world map, with every bit of land tucked tidily inside a national boundary, seem strange.

While pursuing this inquiry I have spent a fair amount of time looking at and thinking about maps. They propose a relation between elements presented on a flat surface, and might themselves be considered compact theories; as the geographer Denis Wood puts it, they are "engines that convert social energy into social space, social order, knowledge." He argues persuasively that maps "as we know them" (*Rethinking*, 6–7) arise in conjunction with the modern state, are oriented to organizing its interests. But I have also studied idiosyncratic maps (see Harmon, *You Are Here,* and Harzinski), and artists' maps (see Harmon, *The Map as Art*), and Wood's own remarkable maps of Boylan Heights, North Carolina, in *Everything Sings.* Those works question the nature of mapping, turn it to new purposes, undertake projects of counter-mapping (Wood's term). Indigenous people's representations of space also open up a vast prospect of alternatives. Peter Nabokov's account of the functions of American Indian cartographic discourse, for example, is capacious: images from this archive may depict "terrestrial or cosmological environments," working "as a mode for cross-cultural argument, a mirror for collective self-expression, a rhetorical device for staking out social or diplomatic positions, or a visualization technique often used in conjunction with oratory or storytelling for the charting of proper behavior or spiritual development" (241). These maps are a record of dispossession, but also let us glimpse a way of thinking outside the cadastral. The way centers work in Native representations of time and space has also played a role in forming my perspective.

I will work out my view of region in terms of literature, for the most part. But I want to insist that its consequences for social life in general are potentially profound. In the U.S., we might think of the environmentalist suggestion that political boundaries be reconfigured to conform to watersheds. Or consider China—the largest state in the world, in terms of both population and land mass. Whether it is, whether it even *could* be, effectively governed as a single unit has been a question for a long time. Currently, top-down state power successfully insists that all of China run on the same time as Beijing (replacing the five time zones in effect from 1912 to 1949). Visualizing China as a democracy almost requires thinking in terms of federalism. This is certainly not a suggestion that is welcomed by the government currently in power—but so I think, and surely the members of the European Committee on Regions would agree. Protesters against the World Trade

Organization and participants in one of the Occupy movements are not so visible as they were for a while—but we might also imagine them joining this conversation. Anarchists are not opposed to governance, as long as it is *self*-governance. So that crucial question of scale arises again. How close to the ground *can* decisions be made?

In contemporary politics, of course, the word to conjure with—whether one is enthusiastic or alarmed—is less often regionalism than globalization. Equally of course, the movement of trade, ideas, armies, individuals across vast spaces is not new. Neither is the image of the spinning world that subtends the discourse of globalization—in fact, it is very old. Denis Cosgrove's *Apollo's Eye* traces "the historical implications for the West of conceiving and representing the earth as a unitary, regular body of spherical form" (ix), moving from ancient Greek and Roman representations to the twentieth century. In a nice and important distinction, he notes that his sequence of chapters does not propose "a linear or progressive historical narrative, although such a narrative is always implicit, and often explicit, in the ideas of the globe and globalization themselves" (xi–xii). But he shows that it is "from images of the spherical earth that ideas of globalization draw their expressive and political force" (ix).

Photographs of the earth from space first became available in the early 1960s, and are now commonplace. In her *Sense of Place and Sense of Planet*, Ursula Heise provides a vital analysis of the more recent history of this figure, and vividly describes the power of the iconic "blue marble," taken in 1972 by the astronauts of Apollo 17: "Set against a black background like a precious jewel in a case of velvet, the planet here appears as a single entity, united, limited, and delicately beautiful" (22). (See Figure 1.3.) I will say frankly that I love this image—but that should not prevent, it should if anything invite, analysis. As Heise points out, its use especially in the environmental movement embodies a tension, an often "anti-technological rhetoric relying on an image produced by advanced technology" (23). And certainly we should recognize that its serene, appealing integrity erases political and cultural differences and the play of power across that blue surface.

Although we cannot find any past moment when human beings were not in movement, arguably the speed of global connections and their pervasive penetration into everyday life constitute an unprecedented phenomenon. Similarly, it seems to me that within my lifetime there has been a change in how we *imagine* the global. A NASA archivist is cited as "plausibly" speculating that the blue marble is the "most widely disseminated image in history"—it is telling this impossible-to-prove claim was made, and is regularly quoted; it is only one of many testimonies to the image's reach and power (see Monmaney, Lazier). Within a few years of the photograph's making, a children's program called "The Big Blue Marble" and promoting international understanding (including a "pen pal" club) appeared on North American public television. There is a project to animate our appreciation of the planet by passing blue marbles through the hands of every person on earth. (See Figures 1.4 and 1.5.) Businesses from bookstores to a maker of biomaterials use versions of the name "Blue Marble." NASA continues to use it for subsequent

FIGURE 1.3 *Photograph of the Earth taken from Apollo 17 on December 7, 1972. Image courtesy of the Earth Science and Remote Sensing Unit, NASA Johnson Space Center. Photography AS17-148p22727, available from the website http://eol.jsc.nasa.gov.*

generations of their freely distributed images of Earth (they are not photographs, but laboriously composed representations of massive data sets). One was chosen as default wallpaper by Apple, in fact. The jewel-globe seems to be on its way to commonsensical invisibility. The image is both ubiquitous and intimately present—it is out there, and in the palm of the hand.

In scanning the Internet, I have been struck by the increasing frequency of images that show the globe not in space, but in human hands. (Readers are invited to do their own image searches.) Think too of the application Google Earth, which can be used on one's desk or lap or, often, on a cell phone in the palm—it is both intimate and interactive. The reader has probably had the experience of beginning with a spinnable blue marble, and zooming vertiginously but enjoyably down to a current location. (Anyone who has not should take a break and do so, because no still image can capture the sensation.) These figures may imply that we

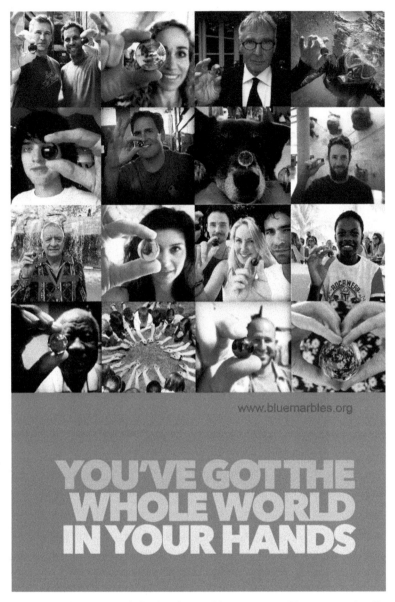

FIGURE 1.4 *Publicity materials for the Blue Marbles Project. Used by courtesy of Wallace J. Nichols. Information about the Blue Marbles Project is available on the website http://www. wallacejnichols.org/130/blue-marbles/html.*

have a responsibility to the globe—but in any case they powerfully embody the juxtaposition of the global and the local that is another commonplace of our day. The slogan "Think global, act local" is sometimes attributed to the early twentieth-century Scots town planner Patrick Geddes (an early proponent of regionalism), sometimes to David Brower or Jacques Ellul or Yoko Ono. It scarcely matters; the

FIGURE 1.5 *Publicity materials for the Blue Marbles Project. Used by courtesy of Wallace J. Nichols. Information about the Blue Marbles Project is available on the website http://www.wallacejnichols.org/130/blue-marbles/html.*

juxtaposition seems to be (paradoxically) everywhere. As Heise demonstrates, much environmental advocacy has been based on attachment to locality, to particular places. But there is a widespread effort to imagine positions that value both, visible both in social movements and—my focus here—in intellectual work. Heise's own eco-cosmopolitanism is among them.

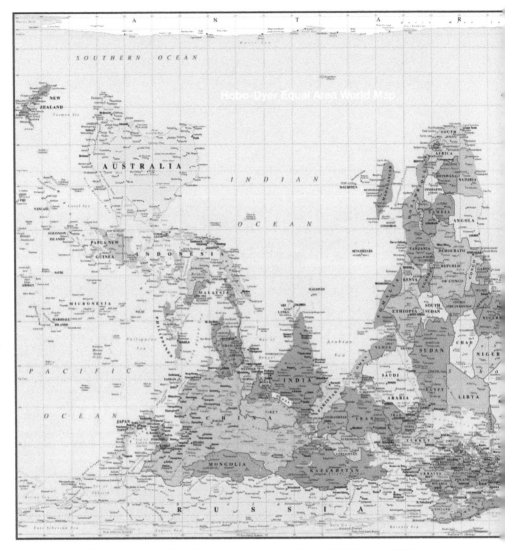

FIGURE 1.6 *World Map: Hobo-Dyer Equal Area Projection. Copyright 2015 www.ODTmaps. com. Used by permission. For maps and other related teaching materials contact: ODT, Inc., PO Box 134, Amherst MA 01004 USA; 800-736-1293; Fax: 413-549-3503; Skype: ODTInc; Email: odtstore@odt.org; Web: http://manywaystoseethe world.org.*

Cosmopolitanism—being a "citizen of the world"—seems to follow from the global perspective. It is a very old idea, but an appealing one for me and most modern intellectuals. It is also vital, and easy, to critique it as a false universal—as "The Class Consciousness of Frequent Travelers," to cite the title of an essay by Craig Calhoun. As he put it in a later piece, "the privileged specificity of our mobility" should not be mistaken for a better attitude: "the genuinely attractive ethical orientation toward a common human community of fate can be undermined by an unattractive self-congratulation and lack of self-critical awareness of privilege"

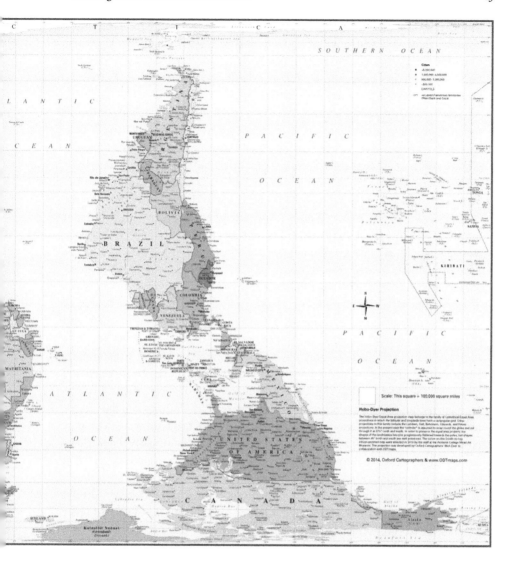

("Cosmopolitanism in the Modern Social Imaginary," 106). Embracing the notion that the world is in our hands should not prevent us from noticing the lack of racial diversity in those images from the Internet, and the dominance embodied in their conventional orientation. As advocates for the Global South remind us, from the perspective of space the North Pole is not necessarily the top of the world—yet a south-up map looks strange to many of us. (See Figure 1.6.) Calhoun points out that experiences of diversity and mobility do *not* mean that one knows the world as a whole. Only those comfortable in international airports and hotels think so— refugees and migrant workers, who also travel a lot, generally don't. At the same time that we take the vision of the blue marble seriously, we must not disregard but engage the solidarities that—on the ground—bind people together. The imagined global democracy that subtends and animates the notion of the "citizen of the world" must (again in Calhoun's words) "put down roots in the solidarities that organize most people's sense of identity and location in the world" ("Class Consciousness," 893). Both in architecture and in literary studies there has been a call for critical regionalism; this is a call for critical cosmopolitanism. My project— I hope—inhabits the place where they converge.

How then are we to think about these terms—global, local, national, regional—all apparently orbiting around one another? Before I consider the usability of region, specifically, as a concept, I want to make a brief excursion into the rigors of geography—arguably the homeland of the concept. My source text is a volume titled *Regionalism in the Age of Globalism*, produced by a collaborative research project between a German and a North American university (Universität Bonn and the University of North Carolina). This is (deliberately) not the usual reference point for a study of American literature, but its introduction by Lothar Hönnighausen asks questions that should by now seem familiar, and resonant: why has the European Union created the Committee of the Regions? Are region and regionalism "concerns of the past rather than of the present or future" (xiii)?

Geographers' received opinion, in the formulation of Robert Ostergren, recognizes three categories of regions: the "instituted," the "objectively denoted," and the "naively perceived" (2–4). As the word's Latin root "regere"—to direct or rule— suggests, region indicates not only physical space but also political structuration. For a very long time, human beings have organized territories to be ruled and managed. The most familiar regional divisions are those of governments. Regions are also instituted by other organizations, however—by churches and businesses, for example. Denoted regions, on the other hand, are created for analytic purposes, whether by scholars or by planners. They abstract and simplify the world by classifying it, as (he points out) every investigator must do. Ostergren suggests that these denoted regions are themselves of two kinds. "Formal" regions are uniform according to some criterion—his example is one defined by religion, its "precise extent... determined by how great a dominance of Lutherans is required in order to be included" (3). "Functional" or "nodal" regions are tied together by people's movements, so that "all places within the region experience more spatial interaction with the same central place or node than they do with any other" (3). Here his examples are the circuits traced by shopping trips and newspaper circulation. This distinction in effect repeats the division between substantive and relational approaches to region—the formal defines a place by what it is, identifying some substantial quality and mapping by that standard; the nodal defines it by its connections, mapping its relationships to other places. It is encountering this pattern repeatedly that has led me to identify this issue as foundational.

These two kinds of regions are explicitly and purposefully created; those in Ostergren's last category, "perceived" regions, are informally and much more unevenly constituted. That does not make them less important. Of course perceptions shape, and are shaped by, the impacts of officially and analytically bounded areas. Indeed, for several decades now scholars have paid enormous attention to the power of "imagined communities." Benedict Anderson's influential phrase, and the work on the cultural dimensions of nation-building that has followed it, reminds us that it is a scholarly fiction to imagine that the instituted can precede the perceived. Or vice versa—in a modern world in which expert knowledge is constantly inserted into public discourse, denoted regions are also always being transformed into "naïve perception." The recursion between the categories is constant. But in a book that approaches the problem of region through literature, the danger is paying not too much but too little attention to the "state" part of the nation-state, losing one's bearings in an imagined realm of imagined communities.

Let us think about how each of Ostergren's three categories applies to my home place: Michigan. It is lines drawn by an instituted government that make me, without ambiguity, a resident of the state. From this perspective there is no chance that I actually live in Ohio, or Indiana; even if I divided my time between two houses in different states, the terms of my membership would be regulated by formal policies. But the very fact that I mention neighbor states marks the relational nature of place, even for instituted regions—we explain where we live by making a difference, saying where we are *not*. "Michigan" exists as a denoted entity, as well—there is no shortage of scholarly studies of topics from the auto industry to the zebra mussel that use it as a category. And it is certainly a perceived place. I don't live far enough north to say that "you're a Michigander when you define summer as three months of bad sledding," but I might make the unfair joke that our four seasons are "almost winter, winter, still winter, and road work." And I do characteristically point to the palm of my right hand, or the back of my left, to explain where in our mitten-shaped state I live. Of course, some of my fellow Michiganders aren't sure my city, Ann Arbor, is actually part of the state ("have you been to Europe? No, but I've been to Ann Arbor"). All these details point strongly to the substantial aspects of my home place. But they also reveal the relational. For example, that last joke is made because my university town's connections with other places in the world are organized differently from those of other cities—both in terms of demographics and tastes, they are highly visible. They are not necessarily stronger—I could go on to discuss the Polishness of Hamtramck and the Arab-American presence in Dearborn, or the history of the Detroit neighborhoods called Greektown and Mexicantown.

In the realm of the denoted and perceived, I do in fact simultaneously inhabit other regions. Researchers studying the zebra mussel are likely to organize their work with reference to the Great Lakes area—a large "denoted" region that crosses multiple state borders, demarcated by the physical presence of a group of freshwater seas. I also live in the Midwest, a perceived region that is less clearly defined but widely used, and with a now-peculiar name that implies the history of the settler-colony that grants my passport. I think too of my colleague Michael Witgen using the Ojibwe place-name Anishinaabewaki, in a talk in Ann Arbor—looking up and explaining, "That's where you all are, by the way." Meanwhile, the Michigan Humanities Council officially encourages our collective story-telling, and is funded (like other states' councils) primarily by the federal government—and it collaborates with the Midwest Arts Council. I can be said from various perspectives to live in North America, the Western Hemisphere, the West, the global North—and, of course, on Earth. The discourse of the "blue marble" presents the world as unified exactly *because* it is particular, limited, finite (I will come back to the question of what a "world" is in Chapter 4). From the perspective of space, the planet is humanity's particular place in the galaxy and universe—our province.

Contemplating this intertwining, and particularly the peculiar notion of Earth as a region, brings me full circle to the task of refining the concept. By now my opening point, that "region" is best understood as entailing both the substantive and the relational, has (I hope) demonstrated its grip by enabling me to analyze complex claims. Place in general has this double aspect, of course. I do not want to claim that only one term could serve for this discussion. Indeed, we might be talking about "section" had it not acquired unpleasant associations through the trauma of the U.S. Civil War. But "region" is well positioned to do that work. I hope it can also disrupt the habit of arraying place categories into an overly abstract hierarchy of scale—as I have suggested, concentric circles exist in geometry, but not history—at the same time that it engages the particularly fraught relation of region and nation that has emerged in this section. As we examine exertions of power by one region over another, the boundary between nationalism and imperialism is not fixed and clear but exactly the opposite. We see this in the situation of Scotland and Catalonia, for example, and for North America Jennifer Greeson demonstrates the point eloquently and persuasively in *Our South*. As we move into literature, that tension takes us quickly to the topics of progress and civilization, to modernity, and eventually to the mutual entanglement of time and place.

Surveying the Literature

The story of the local color movement in American literature has been told many times—or, more precisely, many stories have been told, constructing continuities of many kinds. In discussing fiction I use "local color" and "regionalism" almost interchangeably—the shade of difference acknowledges that the former was more commonly used in the nineteenth century, the latter in the twentieth and since. I offer a brief narrative here, to conjure up the cultural landscape and to serve readers with all levels of familiarity with the topic. There is an enormous body of critical writing on regionalism as a genre (to say nothing of the voluminous studies of the various authors I discuss). I am thoroughly indebted to that work but will not try to summarize it in detail. Many other critics do such reviews—and I do not wish to offer a map, like the one in Borges's story "On Rigor in Science," with a scale of a mile to the mile. I concentrate rather on developing an account of our scholarly conversation in terms of the concept of regionalism I have developed. Subsequent sections of this chapter will carry the argument forward in my own terms.

One place to start, following an American Studies tradition, is with the prescient French observer Alexis de Tocqueville. During his travels in America, he crossed part of Michigan in an uncovered cart that followed "scarcely cleared paths in the middle of immense forests of green trees" to deliver bundles of mail to cottages serving as post offices (290). He marveled at how many letters Americans sent and received, at the informed interest in national affairs shown by people who were (to his eye) living in a wilderness, and at the number and circulation of newspapers. In the third decade of the nineteenth century, then, the United States could already be considered a place where thought circulated with amazing rapidity. After the Civil War, the rate of increase in the volume of printed matter produced and distributed in the United States surged even higher. More publishers produced more copies of more books, and they cost less to buy. The number of magazines being published, according to estimates by the historian Frank Luther Mott, more than tripled in the fifteen years between 1865 and 1880.

It takes a leap of imagination to grasp the power that print must have had a century and a half ago, before the other media that constantly compete for later generations' attention had come into existence. Knowledge of other places came either by word of mouth or from words on paper. So did stories. Magazines printed far more fiction than they do now; by Mott's calculations, in the early 1870s a third of their pages were filled with serialized novels and short stories, and that percentage increased in the decades that followed. New technologies for printing illustrations meant that more and more images were circulating through that medium too. Not everyone had access to printed materials, of course. It is no easy matter to establish literacy rates, but it is estimated that in 1850 almost 90 percent of the white population (of both genders) could read. By 1900 that rate was almost 94 percent—although statistics on the non-white population were not collected, and by self-report only about 54 percent of that group was literate (Kaestle et al., 25). For people of all classes print was becoming inescapable—in making purchases, in traveling, at church, on the job, and at leisure. Historical studies of reading practices suggest that those who could not read might still listen to stories read aloud and thereby actively participate in the communal literary culture of a specific place, as well as of the nation and the world (see for example McHenry).

Literary histories of local color often begin with the publication, in the new California magazine *Overland Monthly* during the summer of 1868, of an anonymous story entitled "The Luck of Roaring Camp." Locally, this tale of a mixed-race, mysteriously blessed child born to a prostitute in a Gold Rush-era mining camp was controversial; in the East and elsewhere in the country it became enormously popular and was praised by critics as well. By the fall, everyone knew that the author of the story was also the editor of the magazine—Bret Harte. Originally from Albany, New York, he had been a journalist and writer in California for over a decade. But the fiction and poetry he published over the next two years exemplified the rapid circulation of some printed material and thought. Harte's writings sold copies of the *Overland Monthly* both in the West and in the East, ensuring its success, and the stories were sometimes reprinted all across the country within days of their appearance. (It took slightly longer for his work to appear in England.) Soon Harte accepted an offer of $10,000 to write exclusively for the distinguished Boston magazine *The Atlantic Monthly* for a year. Harte was neither the first nor the biggest literary celebrity of the era (Charles Dickens's reception in America can be compared to that of the Beatles), but the lavish contract itself was news, and his railway trip across the country with his family generated publicity at every stop. Their host for their first week in Boston, the eminent author and critic William Dean Howells, wrote later that Bret Harte's journey from the Pacific to the Atlantic had been "like the progress of a prince, in the universal attention and interest which met and followed it" (290).

Harte's explosive national success is a useful entry point because it marks a moment when the writerly strategy of focusing on particular places became highly visible. The term "local color" was certainly already in use—a search in the "Making of America" database of books and journals published from roughly 1840 to 1900 produces hundreds of examples, the earliest in 1838 in a *North American Review* article about De Quincey's *Life of Raphael*. It meant very much what it means in everyday speech today—vivid, place-bound detail—and often (as in that first example) referred to the visual. The increase in references to literature after 1868 is quite visible, although the other senses do not disappear. By 1886, James Lane Allen could open an article titled "Local Color" like this: "One everywhere meets with this phrase in current criticisms of fiction" (13).

For Harte, the most salient source of this kind of writing was Western humor, an oral tradition that entered into print in the 1830s and 1840s through sketches and anecdotes appearing in newspapers and "sporting" journals catering to men's interests. Mark Twain's early publications also emerged through this form. Years later, looking back at his own place in literary history, Harte described this humor as distinctively American, praised it as irreverent and original, and implied its link to later fiction by writing that it "voiced not only the dialect, but the habits of thought of a people or locality" ("The Rise of the 'Short Story,'" 3).

But we could choose another beginning point, in quite different publication sites. In 2010, Josephine Donovan published a book that argues convincingly for connections between the early nineteenth-century Irish and Scottish "national tale," French *romans champêtres* (rural novels), and *Dorfgeschichte* (village tales) in Germany and Switzerland. More commonly cited in literary histories is the influence of English writer Mary Russell Mitford's popular *Our Village*, first published as a book in 1824 (followed by further installments for the next decade and frequently reprinted). Washington Irving's *Sketch-Book* (1819–20) is also often mentioned. Harte did not acknowledge either these more distant sources or the sketches of village life that appeared throughout the Northeast, during the 1820s and 1830s, in annuals, gift books, magazines, and occasionally in book form as well. But their intensely local focus and episodic form, foregrounding atmosphere and a web of relationships rather than plot, links them to many later regional fictions. For that matter, humble characters engaged in everyday activities, often speaking in dialect, could also be found in the domestic fiction of the mid-nineteenth century. For example, Susan Warner's immensely popular novel *The Wide, Wide World* (1850) weaves long passages of quotidian detail into its didactic and dramatic narrative; her character Aunt Fortune would be quite at home in a local color story.

These bodies of work, oriented strongly although not exclusively to women's concerns, are influential sources for New England local color writers. Harriet Beecher Stowe stands at the confluence of these traditions and, indeed, others: she makes Cotton Mather a precursor of regionalism when she cites his history of Christianity in New England, *Magnalia Christi Americana* (1702), with its "wonderful stories" of "the very ground I trod on," as one of the books that shaped her imagination (Fields, 28). Like Mark Twain, Stowe is often discussed as a major author without reference to regionalism, but her work, like his, is deeply informed and engaged by it. Stowe had published New England sketches before she became the author of the nineteenth century's most successful didactic novel, *Uncle Tom's Cabin* (1852), and her 1862 novel *The Pearl of Orr's Island* was set in an actual location on the Maine coast. That novel contributed crucially to the development of local color, and subsequent works such as *Oldtown Folks* (1869) helped to confirm folkloric material, humorous rural characters, and dialect as conventions of the form.

We might also look to the South. For example, James Pendleton Kennedy's portrait of plantation life, *Swallow Barn*, was published in 1832, and republished in the early 1850s. Jennifer Greeson characterizes the Louisiana author George Washington Cable as "the most-read U.S. fiction writer of the 1870s and 1880s" (261); she does not cite her evidence for thinking so, but the unsupported claim itself indexes his stature. Joel Chandler Harris's *Uncle Remus* books were also very popular; the first was published in 1880 and "Brer Rabbit" is one of the few local color characters familiar to a wide readership today.

From Harte's opening reference to French Pete and Kanaka Joe, to Harris's affirmation of the origins of his tales in African folklore, these texts offer reminders— not always heeded by readers and critics—that regions are not contained by the nation. For that matter, as Greeson reminds us, "the Reconstruction South crossed and recrossed the border between domestic and foreign" (260). National reconciliation between North and South is one of the key historical processes of the era of local color, one that many authors engage. The continuing, dynamic reconfiguration of ethnic, racial, and national identities is another. A third is the continuing development of networks of communication and transportation, which quickly left the rapid circulation that astonished de Tocqueville behind in the dust.

Between the end of the Civil War and 1890 the miles of railroad track in operation in the United States more than quadrupled. Perhaps the most visible symbol of integration between East and West was the completion of the transcontinental railroad in 1869. During the war Congress specified that its tracks be "standard gauge" (originally set by the British, eventually international); by 1886 all United States railways, even in the South, conformed to that width and interconnected. Not only goods but also people circulated; inhabitants of rural areas migrated to the cities, African-Americans moved from the South to the North, and millions of immigrants arrived from eastern and southeastern Europe. Labor organization also scaled up; in 1877 the first national strike stopped the trains and deeply alarmed the privileged classes. Or, as we consider the complex transformations and national integration that characterize the period, we might think of an institution very much taken for granted today: time zones. The conventional date for their adoption in the United States is 1883, when the various railway companies finally agreed on a standard and—after the November 18 "day of two noons"—most of the urban population came under its sway. But they were no more a new idea or a finished product than local color was an invention out of whole cloth: Greenwich Mean Time dates to the seventeenth century (it was primarily an aid to marine navigation), and the U.S. Congress did not enact the Standard Time Act until 1915. (I will return to the question of how we imagine and organize *time* later in this chapter.)

The sketch I am presenting here is inevitably shaped as much by my reading of literary history and criticism as by encounters with primary texts. By its nature, because we must have a ground to stand on, such a narrative not only simplifies and shapes but also builds on the very categories it is establishing. I am referring to regions as if they existed without being (partly) constituted by the cultural work of regional story-telling; I am mentioning some writers and eliding others who would change the story. Rowland Robinson and Philander Deming or Mary Austin would interrupt the alignment of male writers and the West, female writers and the Northeast, that I have suggested; Alice and Phoebe Cary would bring in the Midwest, the relation of prose and poetry, and collaboration. As Judith Fetterley and Marjorie Pryse point out, to put New England at the center is to forget that "Stowe was living in Cincinnati when she wrote 'Uncle Lot' and Cary's *Clovernook* sketches represent life in Mt. Healthy, a rural community just north of Cincinnati" (11). Joaquin Miller, poet of the Sierras, or the Hoosier James Whitcomb Riley might also remind us to consider verse—and so on. The reader may reasonably ask, at this point, why undertake to write about genre at all? The answer is in part, of course, because we must—but I will also return to that question at the end of this chapter, and specify the *kind* of coherence I am proposing. To get there, let us first consider how refining the concept of region might allow us to analyze those inescapable, indispensable literary-historical stories.

Contemporary comments and most twentieth-century scholarship on local color fiction treat it as representing particular places. Whether we think of Perry Westbrook's close study *Acres of Flint: Writers of Rural New England, 1870–1900* (1951), or of Jay Martin's broader literary history *Harvests of Change: American Literature 1865–1914* (1967), these are *substantial* accounts of how writers portray regions. That does not, however, mean they ignore circulation—Martin, for example, observes that these authors frequently found it necessary to write from elsewhere—but embedded in the very expression "elsewhere" is the presumption that authors are from, and *of*, the region they write about. Over time, the status of the genre clearly declined, as it was increasingly positioned as a minor form in a literary world that valorized complexity, irony, urbanity. Then from the 1970s feminist literary scholarship animated a new kind of attention to regional writing. Attuned to social construction and power, this body of work recognizes the vitality of subjugated knowledges; "minor," in quotation marks, becomes an honorific. Yet, frequently focused on recovering women's experience, this body of work is often strongly substantive as well. In *New England Local Color Literature: A Women's Tradition* (1983), Josephine Donovan writes of Stowe's *Mayflower* sketches: "they depict authentic regional detail, including authentic dialect, authentic local characters, in real or realistic geographical settings" (50). This concern with authenticity is embedded in the conventions and reception of the form, and as Jeff Karem has shown, forms a continuity with the reception of ethnic literatures in the twentieth century that opens a connection to the present. This original and deservedly influential work has been followed by others—Kent Ryden's *Landscape with Figures* comes to mind—that strive to articulate the substance of regional identity. There are of course many more such efforts, not only about New England but also about other regions. Recently, in my own vicinity, Jon K. Lauck's *From Warm Center to Ragged Edge: The Erosion of Midwestern Literary and Historical Regionalism, 1920–1965* is an appropriate indicator of the impressive scholarly energy being mobilized in the Society for the Study of Midwestern Literature and the recently founded Midwestern History Association.

Received opinion in literary scholarship has now, however, shifted decisively to the *relational*, in interpretations that focus on the connections between local color writing and locations beyond the region. In her remarkable essay on "Nation, Region, and Empire" in Emory Elliott's 1991 *Columbia History of the American Novel*, Amy Kaplan writes: "Regionalists share with tourists and anthropologists the perspective of the modern urban outsider who projects onto the native a pristine authentic space immune to the historical changes shaping their own lives" (252). Richard Brodhead's 1993 *Cultures of Letters* includes a powerful chapter that reads regionalism as oriented to a privileged metropolitan and national audience, arguing that it *tells* "local cultures into a history of their supersession by a modern order now risen to national dominance" (121). Stephanie Foote's 2001 book *Regional Fictions* develops an account of the "cultural work" of regionalism in relation to national identity. Each of these accounts is persuasively nuanced, much more complex than the version of this argument that has become the received view. Criticism today sometimes starts from the premise—which, despite my admiration for the works I have just mentioned, I will oppose—that regionalism simply *is* literary tourism, an elegy, a commodified outsider account.

The turn toward the relational continues, in scholarship that situates regionalist writers on a broad landscape. Titles tell the story: Tom Lutz's *Cosmopolitan Vistas: American Regionalism and Literary Value* appeared in 2004, Philip Joseph's *American Literary Regionalism in a Global Age* in 2007, Jason Arthur's *Violet America: Regional Cosmopolitanism in U.S. Fiction Since the Great Depression* in 2013. That perspective also informs valuable work linking this literature with other disciplines—for example, Michael Elliott's *The Culture Concept* and Brad Evans's *Before Cultures* with anthropology, Jennifer Greeson's *Our South* and Hsuan Hsu's *Geography and the Production of Space in Nineteenth-Century American Literature* with geography. I would not venture to say that it results from the general "cultural turn," from the contemporary resurgence of regionalist fiction (discussed in Chapter 5), from other factors, or from all of the above—but these works take the form very seriously, valuing it as (at minimum) historically significant. From my perspective, scholarly debates have often become unhelpfully focused on whether local color and regionalism (and for that matter realism) are the same or distinct, written by insiders or outsiders, nationalist or subversive, empathetic or exploitive, and so on—which often become entangled with questions of what the critic does and does not consider admirable. Grounding my account in a concept of region as necessarily both substantive and relational, I am working to get past these oppositions—but I would not by any means claim that I am the first to recognize both elements. Many of these works do, implicitly and sometimes explicitly. I think particularly of Douglas Reichert Powell's *Critical Regionalism*, which is strongly based in his home place of Johnson City, Tennessee, but also adopts its title term from architecture—another field in which tugs of war over this network of concepts have been going on for decades. Dalia Kandiyoti's *Migrant Sites* links regionalism with what she calls diaspora literature, showing that the spatial imagination through which immigrants produce senses of place includes figures of both enclosure and movement.

Arguably, attention to both the substantive and the relational has been there from the earliest discussions of American literary regionalism. The classic location is Hamlin Garland's 1894 manifesto *Crumbling Idols*. He writes:

> *Local color in a novel means that it has such quality of texture and back-ground that it could not have been written in any other place or by any one else than a native.*
>
> It means a statement of life as indigenous as the plant-growth. It means that the picturesque shall not be seen by the author,—that every tree and bird and mountain shall be dear and companionable and necessary, not picturesque; the tourist can not write the local novel.   (53–4)

The emphasis—it is in the original—on the substantive could hardly be stronger; the contrast with the view of regionalism as literary tourism is stark and explicit. Yet Garland does also make broader connections—just before this passage, he writes that "local color means national character" (53). He is writing against the influence of established and English standards, yet he opens the chapter by praising the local color of Homer and Chaucer, and asserting that Norwegians and Russians are "almost at the very summit of modern novel writing" (49–50). In addition to the traces of the complementary perspective in this text, Garland is the author of "Up the Coulee," a story from *Main-Travelled Roads* (1891) that offers a powerful immanent analysis of how the *relation* of regions constitutes them. (It has frequently been analyzed; I have been most influenced by Carrie Tirado Bramen's reading in *The Uses of Variety*.)

"Up the Coulee" is the story of McLane brothers, born (like Garland) on a farm in Wisconsin. Howard, the elder, leaves home and is successful in the East; he neglects to think much about those he leaves behind, even when his father's death leaves his younger brother Grant fixed in place by responsibility for the farm and family. The action takes place during Howard's first visit home after many years. In the opening, he admires the landscape, finding it "dear and companionable" but also clearly exercising an articulate aesthetic sensibility developed elsewhere. His cultivated perceptions enable him eventually to appreciate—along with the reader—the tragedy of Grant's life, which is not just his material deprivation but also what wearisome labor has made of him. Grant is heroic—named after the general, his face described in the story's last words as "scarred with wrinkles that had histories, like saber cuts on a veteran, the record of his battles" (87)—but he is also broken; it is too late for him to make a new start. "Up the Coulee" constantly represents region, race, class, gender, power, and culture as deeply bound together, and it links to my work in multiple ways. For example, Grant's wife Laura regrets giving up the freedom she experienced as a schoolteacher—an element that will take on new resonance in the context of Chapter 2. What I want to emphasize here, however, is the way in which Howard is both an insider and an outsider. Garland's affirmation of the perspective of the native is complicated by thinking in terms of the *return* of the native. My allusion to Thomas Hardy's 1878 novel is deliberate. I am not concerned here with questions of influence—rather, with the way figures like Howard and Clym Yeobright enable a perspective that is both substantive and relational, that values both the provincial and the cosmopolitan and reveals each as incomplete. As Bramen puts it, "Local color is neither the authentic voice of the subaltern nor the mouthpiece of the metropolitan elite, but a locus for a variety of ideological positions that articulate the relation between city and country for a local and/or a national audience" (125).

The intellectual history that follows from this discussion is both deep and broad, and is being pursued by many scholars. For example, in a 2014 essay Jonathan Schroeder dives deep by tracing the origin of the term "local color" to its source in neoclassical theories of painting, and also situates it in "the long aesthetic history of the detail" (553). He argues for understanding local color as a form of realism. In another recent article, Christine Holbo explicates Hamlin Garland's critical thought and his many influences and connections, and proposes him as a modernist—in her larger project adding sentimentality into her synoptic reading of the system of literary genres. Indeed, Bramen, Schroeder, and Holbo are all interested in the history of how difference (in their respective terms, variety, pluralism, and perspectivalism) comes to be understood as positive, and as a distinctively American value. I might put it: how does the center become movable? In the end, the goal of progressing through these complexities and distinctions is—as Fredric Jameson shows in *The Antinomies of Realism*—to understand the capabilities of form, and its relation to social life.

As I survey this literature with my gaze fixed on that horizon, I find myself frequently turning back to the work of Raymond Williams. It is good to remember, as we trace trends and turns, that diverging impulses and recognitions are built into strong scholarship of any period. The eloquent and influential *The Country and the City* (1973) is certainly relevant; he also writes directly about regional fiction in a little-known essay from 1982, "Region and Class in the Novel" (collected in *Writing in Society*). There Williams suggests that the category dates to the late nineteenth century, and after a *Keywords*-like, conceptual investigation that links region to subordination, he observes that what is striking

> is the steady discrimination of certain regions as in this limited sense 'regional,' which can only hold if certain other regions are not seen in this way. This is in its turn a function of cultural centralization; a modern form of the 'city-country' discrimination. It is closely connected with the distinction between 'metropolitan' and 'provincial' culture, which became significant from the eighteenth century. Yet this is no longer a distinction of areas and kinds of life; it is what is politely called a value-judgement but more accurately an expression of centralized cultural dominance. (230)

In the modern era, we cannot talk about place without talking about inequality. In some sense that may always be true—or at least, it has always been true so far in human history. Subordination is not exactly rare, and time and space are constitutive elements of human experience—it is hard to imagine an artifact of expressive culture that could *not* be analyzed in terms of those categories. But it is differently, crucially true in the nationalizing, colonizing, globalizing world of the fictions I am investigating. Bramen appropriately titles her chapter "The Uneven Development of American Regionalism." Regional writing as a modern genre is about a landscape that is always already tilted by power.

I argue throughout that we should take regionalist writers seriously, that we should listen to them more carefully and give them more credit for sophistication than scholars usually do. (Brodhead's work is brilliant—its blind spot is that he takes up one attitude to Henry James, and a very different one to Charles Chesnutt and Sarah Jewett.) That does not mean, however, that all writers who occupy this terrain excel, or even that they correlate the substantive and relational effectively. In Williams's words: "there is indeed a kind of novel which is not only set in its own place but set in it as if there were no others." As he points out, this is "at least as likely to be true of a New York or California or Home Counties novel as of the more readily perceived type" (230)—that is, one set in Wisconsin or Michigan, in Wessex or Wales. The difference is whether importance is taken for granted or founded on a particular claim, paralleling and intersecting the difference between white/ unmarked and racial/ethnic literature (see Karem, and I will return to this point in Chapter 4). The "encapsulation," the "fly-in-amber" (231) quality that Williams criticizes is the risk that regionalism constitutively incurs. Let us call it—using, as so many critics have, an adjective that correlates space and time—being "quaint." Mobilizing the friction of the particular, local fictions slow things down and gain time to consider multiple perspectives. They may acknowledge or contest the metropolitan claim to the future—often, they do both. But everything is still on a slant.

Williams is vexed by regional and working-class novels that treat those experiences as encapsulated, and neglect relation. But he is not writing against the forms themselves. In fact, he is—unusually for him—writing openly as a regionalist, a Welsh novelist. Like Garland, he was both a fiction writer and a critic, although his reputation rests on his accomplishments in the latter field. Williams tells us that he wrote *Border Country* "seven times" as he tried to find the right balance between "internal processes" and "wider pressures" (*Writing in Society*, 231). His concern to convey both the substantial, distinctive quality of place, and the way it is constituted by connections, is visible throughout the trilogy. For me, its most powerful and unexpected aspect is its representation of the effort and cost of distilling human experience into abstractions, whether for the labor union or for the university. In the words of his most sympathetic character, the historian Matthew Price: "The techniques I have learned have the solidity and precision of ice cubes, while a given temperature is maintained. But it is a temperature I can't really maintain; the door of the box keeps flying open" (9). This passage is surely evocative for anyone who attempts to practice interdisciplinary scholarship. As I have said already, my investigation of local color writing has converged with my effort to puzzle through contemporary theory and understand the enterprise of knowledge making itself. In Chapter 2, the relation of place and knowledge will come to the fore.

Just now, I want to turn in a more empirical direction. Bramen writes, rather ambiguously, "a local and/or a national audience"; a question about the circulation of this literature is embedded in that slash. Whether we should see the genre as focused on the local, or toward the national and beyond, has been central to the criticism for a quarter-century. Let me, to move forward, explore that question directly.

The *Local* Local

One of the key elements of the current view of local color as literary tourism has been the observation that it circulated in national magazines. That is correct, and important. It does not follow, however, that local color *only* circulated in the "quality" magazines and *only* reached an educated and elite audience. *Atlantic Monthly*, *Harper's Monthly*, *Scribner's*, and *Century* are the most accessible magazines for scholars, certainly—they are the ones most often preserved, most often mentioned in literary histories and prominent authors' biographies. But there is an unfortunate tautology in arguing that the genre is defined by the places where we find it, without looking to see if it can be found elsewhere.

In this section I will argue against the claim that "[in] nineteenth-century America regional writing was *not* produced for the cultures it was written about" (Brodhead, *Cultures of Letters*, 122). Brodhead's positive arguments are incorporated throughout, and his account does address the trajectory of authors like Harte and Stowe and Edward Eggleston (a key figure in Chapter 2), recognizing that nineteenth-century cultures of letters are complexly related and change over time. But this negative assertion is far too sweeping. And it is too often repeated as taken-for-granted truth in subsequent scholarship, without fresh investigation and in more reductive forms. Let us examine the evidence for the contrary case.

A small scholarly exercise immediately exceeds the received view. I begin with Sarah Orne Jewett in order to address the strongest version of the case for a national and elite orientation—she is an important author in virtually every account of the genre, and Brodhead devotes an entire chapter to her in *Cultures of Letters*. If we look at Clara and Carl Weber's bibliography of her printed works, we see that she certainly did publish, frequently, in the magazines mentioned above. Yet reading on, we find the names of much less familiar periodicals: *Sunday Afternoon, Good Company, Pocket Magazine, The Congregationalist, The Berwick Scholar, California Illustrated Magazine*. And we find unexpected names: *The Independent* (often), *Ladies' Home Journal, McClure's, Harper's Bazar, Cosmopolitan*. Indeed, Jewett published her first story in the weekly story paper *The Flag of Our Union* ("Jenny Garrow's Lovers," 1868). The uncollected "A Financial Failure" appeared in the *Boston Sunday Globe* (1890), "Told in the Tavern" in the *New York World* (1894). Jewett's writing for children complicates the picture further. Already, the circulation of her work presents itself as quite varied.

Acknowledging these unexpected sides of Jewett (discussed at greater length in Chapter 3) just scratches the surface of the mass of writing about locality that circulated and has now disappeared or sits, mostly inert, in the print record. Literature is, as Franco Moretti has famously characterized it, a slaughterhouse; most published works are read—if at all—briefly. Consider Richard Malcolm Johnston. His "Goosepond School" appeared in 1857 or 1858 in Porter's *Spirit of the Times*, a sporting paper published in New York, and was widely reprinted in papers in his home state of Georgia—where his first book was published during the Civil War, and unsurprisingly did not receive much circulation. However, his work was reprinted during the vogue for local color and his career revived; late in life Johnston became a successful author with Harper's publications and a national circulation. In a sense that first story—which continued to be his best known and which I discuss in Chapter 2—migrated from one culture of letters to another. So Johnston was far more successful than most writers—although few know his name today.

Even fewer know most or any of the women writers of the Adirondacks that Kate Winter includes in her 1989 anthology *The Woman in the Mountain*, which ranges from the mid-nineteenth century to the contemporary. Yet even the earliest and most obscure of them, Lucia Newell Oliviere, born in 1855, actively published journalism during her lifetime, and occasionally fiction and poetry; her daughter got a collection of her poems into print soon after her death in 1927. Or, "Cully Gage" seems almost unknown outside of Michigan—that is the pseudonym used by Charles Van Riper for his tales of the Upper Peninsula in a series of *Northwood Readers*, published beginning in 1977 by Avery Color Studios, Inc., in Gwinn, Michigan. Each of these scattered and disparate authors has interested and moved me, and I think this book offers a framework that connects their work. (Oliviere's "The Stage Driver," for example, speaks directly to the role of book-learning in the relation of locals and outsiders that I will discuss in Chapter 2.) But this selection is also arbitrary, from an immense set of possibilities—and that is precisely the point. My primary purpose here is to index the sheer volume and variety of writing about particular places, and how variably it circulates.

The researcher Charles Johanningsmeier has accumulated empirical evidence more specifically opposing the paradigm that equates regionalism with Northeastern, white, high-bourgeois hegemony. In 1997 he published both a monograph on the distribution of fiction through newspaper syndicates in the late nineteenth century, and an article on Jewett's and Mary Wilkins Freeman's active participation in that market. As he points out in the former, "The increase in production and readership of American newspapers between 1860 and 1900 were phenomenal; newspapers became a part of the lives of almost every American.... Given that the vast majority of daily and weekly newspapers included syndicated fiction, the readership for these materials was quite large" (2). In the latter Johanningsmeier shows that Jewett and Freeman "were not at all shy about forwarding their own interests in the world of print," and that between 1884 and the end of the century, their stories were distributed to at least twenty, and possibly as many as 140, newspapers across the continent (58). Given the low cost of newspapers, syndicated stories reached an audience that included all classes. Johanningsmeier calculates, based on stated circulation and a conservative estimate of two readers per copy, that Wilkins's stories in the *Boston Sunday Globe* in the winter of 1891–2 had a potential audience of 300,000. And they also appeared—at least—in newspapers in Toronto, Detroit, and St. Louis (72 and note). Again, our sense of how these works circulated is substantially expanded.

In his recent research Johanningsmeier is documenting regional writers' wide availability in public libraries. He has examined a large group of library "finding lists" from the 1870s to the early 1900s. In that period, as standards emerged but the card catalog was not yet fully established as an institution—the newly formed American Library Association enabled uniformity when it specified the size cards should be in 1876, and the Library of Congress made printed cards available for sale in 1901—many libraries had local printers produce annual lists of their holdings. These were rarely saved, but Johanningsmeier has nevertheless located and examined 178 finding lists; over 80 percent are from the Northeast and Midwest, where most public libraries were located, with some from the West, and a very few from the South ("Realism, Naturalism, and American Public Libraries," 3–5). Without detailed charge records, available in only a few cases, readership cannot be directly demonstrated through this lens. But Johanningsmeier also has substantial evidence supporting his case that librarians were responding to patrons' demand in ordering multiple copies of a journal like *Harper's Monthly*, and that the audience of what he calls regional realism was not exclusively elite. He analyzes photographs of libraries, for example: "The ubiquity of magazines and newspapers in public library reading rooms of this period is indicated not only by finding lists but also by the many surviving photographs of such rooms and accounts of their dispersal therein. One sees in these photographs many people reading periodicals as well as numerous unbound newspapers or magazines on tables or in racks and bound volumes of magazines on the shelves" ("Welcome Guests," 275). Indeed, Johanningsmeier thinks that working-class men, not usually visualized as an audience for the *Atlantic* and *Harper's*, frequently used the reading rooms. His vision of the American reading public, like de Tocqueville's, is democratic.

Regional fiction in book form is well represented on the finding lists as well. Johanningsmeier specifically mentions the popularity of Bret Harte, Edward Eggleston, Mary Hallock Foote, Mary Hartwell Catherwood, and Mary Noailles Murfree. Or, taking Jewett as an example again: after its publication in 1877, 128 of the 178 libraries he studied (72 percent) had *Deephaven* in their collections. After its publication in 1896, 86 (again, 72 percent) had *The Country of the Pointed Firs*. Johanningsmeier points out that, contrary to the view that the audience of local color was elite and urban, half of these libraries were in cities and half were in "rural areas or small towns and cities." And contrary to the view that those depicted were excluded from the audience of local color stories, "in Maine itself, of the fourteen post-1877 libraries surveyed, twelve (86%) carried *Deephaven* and all ten (100%) of the post-1896 libraries acquired *The Country of the Pointed Firs*" (10). Johanningsmeier argues, "Not only did libraries make the elite monthly periodicals available to a socioeconomically and geographically diverse group of readers, but they also made works of this subgenre widely available in other less-well-known periodicals and in book form" ("Realism, Naturalism, and American Public Libraries," 9). His findings are fully consistent with Christine Pawley's intensive study of reading in the late nineteenth century in Hamlin Garland's home town—Osage, Iowa—which shows a local community "inextricably connected" to other places through multiple, criss-crossing print networks addressing "the nation, Iowa, the Catholic church, or Protestant America." On her account these were also productive, both in the sense that inhabitants interpreted what they read and created distinctive meanings, and in the sense that they created print artifacts themselves. As she puts it, "Print culture in Osage mediated participation in several broader cultures which had national reach but which also provided opportunities for creation of local variants" (4–5).

Nancy Glazener uses a different approach to provide, in *Reading for Realism*, a rich view of the reading formations indexed by particular magazines. Her focus is primarily on a group of magazines, led by *Atlantic Monthly*, that explicitly reviewed literary works and discussed literary standards, and functioned, in words from her subtitle, as a "*U.S. Literary Institution, 1850–1910*." (I agree, although as I argued in *Publishing the Family* we should also make distinctions among those magazines.) Glazener provides strong empirical support for the powerful role of periodicals in solidifying conventions at the moment of the vogue for local color. Her readings support the case for the genre's contribution to national unity, and embrace of racist and ethnocentric ideas—but she does not claim to offer a complete account. Glazener acknowledges that readers had diverse reactions. Her chapter on regionalism considers magazines outside the group, and finds that although some journals outside the Northeast, such as *Overland Monthly*, remained bound to an *Atlantic*-like understanding of the literary, others like the Boston-based *Arena* undertook to "write the rural" in a very different way. The fine-grained particularity of this analysis enables complexity.

In a recent book, Emily Satterwhite works more directly on reception, by examining fan mail sent to regionalist authors. Her focus is "Appalachian-set" fiction, which deserves more discussion than I have given it so far. Her framework is relational, an orientation visible for example in the nice distinction she makes by defining her object of study in terms of where novels and stories are *set*. She does not use "'Appalachian literature,' which encourages the assumption that fiction about the region is also fiction *of* the region" or even an expression of the land, "somehow *by* the region, as Hamlin Garland proposed"—referring to his assertion in *Crumbling Idols* that in Southern fiction "the cotton-boll has broken into speech" (11, quoting Garland, 62). However, when she reads the fan letters, and maps the places from which they were sent, the result contradicts the view of local color as oriented to the national *literati*. Rather, her "maps provide empirical evidence that fans of regionalism lived in and near the region being represented and in a wide range of rural and metropolitan locales" (13). The sample size is not large, but the accumulation of examples makes a powerful case for seeing the audiences of regionalism as multiple.

Satterwhite's findings do not reverse the reigning paradigm and ground the form in substantive regional roots or subjugated knowledge. Rather, she demonstrates that different groups of readers interpreted and valued the same fictions differently. For example, Mary Murfree's work appealed to both urban elites, and privileged residents of her own rural region. Satterwhite memorably shows that although when it was revealed that the vigorous stories of the Tennessee mountains signed by "Charles Egbert Craddock" were in fact by a young lady, readers in Boston and New York were shocked because they had identified the author with his (in fact, her) rough characters—admirers in Appalachia had accurately estimated the writer's class position and had only to rethink his/her gender. The cosmopolitans who hosted Murfree in the wake of her success listened to her, but saw her as a representative of the exotic. On the other hand, Appalachian readers of the quality journals focused on her elite social standing, took pride in her accomplishments, and appreciated the attention she brought to the region because they felt it confirmed and enhanced their own status.

Turning to the mid-twentieth century, Satterwhite discerns four groups who wrote fan letters to Harriette Arnow. Three of them treat Arnow's characters from the Kentucky hills with condescension: urban highbrows in the Northeast, Midwestern professionals who live in areas receiving Appalachian migration, and elites from Kentucky and rural areas of other states. The fourth group, who sometimes distance themselves from and sometimes identify with the characters, is composed of out-migrants from the rural South. Satterwhite's research, drawing on reviews and scholarly interpretations as well as letters, extends beyond my limited concern with audience here. She argues that there are commonalities across

Appalachian-set fiction since 1878: it constructs the region as resistant to modernity and the site of authentic, and prominently *white*, community. I will return to her work in Chapter 2, and I too hope to show that discussion of this genre can usefully extend to the present.

The picture emerging here shows regionalist writing circulating in highly varied kinds of publications, to multiple audiences, for almost two centuries. It *can* accommodate the recognition that the genre was crucially built into the historical formation of high culture in late nineteenth-century America, as local color circulated in the national magazines and solidified conventions for representing places and did important "cultural work." We see authors reacting in the gravitational pull of that urbanizing, standardizing, modernizing era. Moving to the city felt like leaving the local; so Edward Eggleston (for example) does not imagine that the provincials he portrays are part of the conversation, and uses real names in his fiction—he learns better, as I will show in Chapter 2. And as Satterwhite and others point out, in some sense to write is intrinsically to take up a certain distance from everyday life; anyone writing about a region stands at least metaphorically outside of it. On the other hand, Jewett's letters record that she read her work aloud to locals, including an eccentric dressmaker who figured in a story (Donovan, "Jewett on Race," 405–6). She wrote explicitly and eloquently about her project of mediating between different kinds of people (which I will discuss at greater length in Chapter 3). The fact that many authors announce their project as representing the region, have a deep connection to local life, or both, should not end discussion of how to position them. But there is, I think, conclusive evidence that we should not reduce this body of work to the tendentious configuration "literary tourism."

In other words, this empirical discussion has converged with the concept of region developed earlier. That category, I suggested, entails both the substantive and the relational. The particular location is constituted through connections. In a sense it is not surprising that so much literary scholarship has been focused on the ways in which local color takes the perspective of the "insider" or the "outsider," since both the sense of place and the view from elsewhere are foundational to the form. But the either/or debate is not productive, and understanding the genre requires taking both aspects—or more precisely, the full range of positionings along a continuum which sometimes explodes beyond a mere line into many dimensions—into account.

Taking Alexander Posey as a counter-example shows how much more capacious a view of regionalism is enabled by considering both the substantive and the relational. Posey was a member of the Creek nation, born in 1873 at a ranch in what is now Oklahoma. In 1902 he was editing the Eufaula newspaper the *Indian Journal*, and began to write and publish humorous letters purportedly addressed to him by a full-blood named Fus Fixico. His political satire clearly had an affinity with other dialect writing of the period—another newspaper editor linked him explicitly with Mr. Dooley and Uncle Remus (Littlefield and Hunter, 22)—and his work gained considerable attention. As articles about Posey appeared, the Fus

Fixico letters were reprinted; newspapers in New York, Philadelphia, and St. Louis asked him to become a regular contributor (19). He had previously been urged to submit his poetry to eastern magazines, and declined—"arguing that he wrote for a local audience and that eastern audiences would not appreciate his local references." Similarly, he kept the Fus Fixico letters local, "citing his concern for territorial issues and characters and his belief that eastern readers would probably not understand him" (40).

The excerpt from Posey's work below is one that needs relatively little annotation. The emphasis here falls on *relatively*, for it is accessible only in comparison to other passages—the reader needs to know that the allotment process is under way at this moment, that Tams Bixby was the acting chairman of the Dawes Commission, and that he had a distinctive signature.

> Well, so I was had no paper to write news on it hardly this time but some old slick wrapping paper what the clerk was twist up 'round some things I was buy with due bills in Eufaula last Saturday. Maybe so, that kind of paper was no 'count for nothing but kindling, but I was had no other kind a paper except Creek deeds what Chief Porter and Dawes Commission was scribble up signing they names to it, like they was just learning how to make letters so you could read it. They was one name signed to it that was look like a thousand-leg that was freeze to death in winter time. I was show it to some lawyers in Eufaula and they say, maybe so, Tams Bixby was sign his name that way.   (73 [Letter 12, March 6, 1903])

Posey purposefully chose to limit his writing's circulation—the Fus Fixico letters are the antithesis of "literary tourism." But his perspective engages the full range of connection "From Nation to Neighborhood" (I take the phrase from the title of an essay by Philip Deloria). An account of regionalism as a genre needs to be able to accommodate this *local* local—an emphatically particular, yet not narrow or "encapsulated," body of work.

Posey's control of *both* local dialect and Standard English is crucial to his accomplishment. He was of course among people who spoke in many different ways, in Eufaula and the nearby territories—there is variation in every community. And Posey was certainly not unique, there or anywhere, in being able to code-switch. Let me acknowledge here as well that dialect appears in many kinds of writing, not only in regionalism. But during the late nineteenth-century vogue of local color, and since, it has been understood as one of the defining features of the genre. I will close this section by reflecting on how profoundly the politics of language, and the possibilities for narrating, shape both local relations and translocality. To consider the role of dialect in local color writing is to be forcefully reminded that the form inhabits the tilted landscape of power. Speech classifies people. It places them—us—relentlessly, in many systems, all of them characterized by inequality. But discourse is material; it is always producing relations, not just reporting or reflecting or even reproducing them. As Bakhtin and many since have argued, language itself contains the traces of contestation. At this level, too, regional writing is best understood relationally rather than in terms of (pure) authenticity or (simple) subordination.

The inclusion of local speech was one of the key ways local color offered to provide *knowledge* of a region. Well into the nineteenth century, the systematic study of language and its deployment in literature were not distinct. In the *Biglow Papers*, James Russell Lowell, like Posey, blended political satire with writing in the vernacular—in his case, several varieties of Yankee dialect. His work was admired and influential; it helped to inspire Edward Eggleston's *Hoosier School-Master* (as we will see in Chapter 2). Only later, with the professionalization of academic work and the emergence of linguistics, did such meticulous rendering of varieties of English come to seem like something utterly different from scholarship.

Traffic between the expert and vernacular continues, of course—specialists refined "dialect" into a term of art, but it continues to be used (as I have been using it so far) more broadly; they invented "code-switch," and it is increasingly making its way into everyday speech (see for example Thompson). But we take the separation of kinds of knowledge-making so thoroughly for granted that it is an effort to imagine a time when it was not obvious that language study and story-telling occupy different realms.

Expert knowledge about language now diverges sharply from common-sense knowledge, even—in fact especially—that of the educated public. In the everyday of the mass media and the university, "good English" is a virtually unquestioned value. Those of us who, truthfully answering the question "what do you do?", give an answer that elicits the recognition "so you're an English teacher," know how self-righteous, and/or defensive, people are on this topic. Yet from the perspective of linguists, Standard English is a socially privileged dialect, not an intrinsically superior language. Over time, in any language, usage does what it will—despite misguided loyalty to prescriptions against splitting infinitives or using "hopefully" as a sentence adverb. Remarking at a social gathering that "all dialects are equal" is likely to provoke contradiction, yet that is not a controversial claim but received scholarly knowledge. The profoundly stigmatized Black English Vernacular is not a careless or devolved version of Standard English, but an independent dialect that both preserves older forms (for example, "aks" rather than "ask") and offers additional nuance (for example, in verb tenses that distinguish between the present and the habitual). The value attached to varieties of any language has nothing to do with capabilities of expression or speakers' intelligence, and everything to do with power. As teachers, we recognize that our students gain an important advantage by mastering Standard English, and do our best to help them do that. It is a sad fact that this is generally understood as correcting their mistakes, not as instructing them in code-switching. No classroom, however "multicultural," is equal when students fear—or are—being judged by how they speak (see Curzan). Both as scholars and as teachers, we should appreciate the academic witticism that "a standard language is just a dialect with an army," and the enormous role schools have played in the modernizing, nationalizing project of standardizing language and knowledge (a central topic of Chapter 2).

The familiar pattern of dialect fiction is a narration in Standard English, with unconventional spelling visually announcing the difference when local characters speak. Such speakers are often although not always explicitly portrayed as provincial, perhaps quaint, even ignorant and backwards. Implicitly, the convention itself conveys and confirms subordination, which is often recursively reconfirmed by its correlation with differences of class and race. It is also in some sense entailed by the very medium of print, which is inexorably oriented to circulation and thus to the standard. And attitudes to non-standard speech are deeply connected—as Gavin Jones and Joshua Miller have shown for different periods—to attitudes about national unity and diversity. Yet authors deploy dialect in many ways, including against the grain of the pattern. In *A Hazard of New Fortunes* (1890), for example, William Howells writes the character Lindau's lines with a heavy German accent, virtually imprisoning him in a marginalizing orthography. Yet when he and Basil March begin speaking German together, Lindau is promoted to Standard English— and soars into cosmopolitan, utopian eloquence. Posey's Fus Fixico speaks directly to the reader, although one could argue that quotation marks are implied by the way his letters are embedded in an English-language Indian newspaper. More directly within the local color tradition, the complexity of Charles Chesnutt's frame narrative in his collection *The Conjure Woman* (1899) provides a striking example of writing against the tilt of power. The book is double-voiced. It can be read in terms of the familiar pattern privileging the narrator. But today, for critics reading in context, it belongs to the formerly enslaved dialect-speaker Uncle Julius, whose stories are the substance of the volume. Perhaps the most obvious passage undermining the frame narrator, the white entrepreneur John, is in "The Grey Wolf's Ha'nt"—when he reads a dry philosophical account of metamorphosis to his sympathetic wife Annie, and then utterly fails to recognize its connection to Uncle Julius's following tale of shape-shifting. Much more recently, James Still's stories of Appalachia are dominated by regional voices. Sometimes that is because so much of the story is speech (as in "These Goodly Things" or "Bare-Bones"), sometimes because it is first-person narration (as in "The Scrape" or "Hit Like to 'a' Killed Me")—sometimes both (as in "A Master Time").

It is a considerable effort to imagine the immense popularity of dialect writing in the late nineteenth and early twentieth centuries, because (as anyone who has taught Chesnutt's conjure stories in the undergraduate classroom knows) it is so heartily disliked today. For contemporary readers, words spelled unconventionally to suggest non-standard pronunciation seem to present an almost insuperable obstacle to understanding—and certainly to enjoyment. Nadia Nurhussein's recent book on American dialect poetry helps a great deal here. She argues convincingly that we are wrong to think the silent reading of dialect poetry was ever easy. Rather, it was a self-consciously sophisticated exercise of literacy, requiring "an intense focus—of reader and writer—on an unusual printed text" (17) and more akin to modernist experiments than we realize today.

Nurhussein also recovers in detail the far more accessible practices of performance that conveyed this verse aurally to many enthusiasts. In its moment, she suggests, the fascination of the form inhered in the way it expressed the shifting balance between orality and literacy in a period when more and more people learned to read, more and more skillfully. The eras seem less different when we consider that in the later twentieth and early twenty-first centuries, readers continue to invest effort and respond powerfully to densely realized, distinctive language that seems to create a world. The impact of *A Clockwork Orange* clearly has much to do with "Nadsat," the invented argot in which Anthony Burgess's narrator speaks. More speculatively, I think of the way the philologist J. R. R. Tolkien's invented languages subtend the solidity of Middle-earth. Nurhussein points out as well that over the course of the twentieth century poets came to rely not on orthography, but on syntax, to represent dialect (8); this is true as well of Still's very readable stories. If we ask what contemporary forms might continue the performance tradition, we are faced with an immense selection of examples from radio, film, and television that foreground the aural apprehension of distinctive speech. I will evoke just one; the pleasures and the insights of the Baltimore-set cable television series *The Wire* depend crucially on its precision in capturing the many ways people talk in a particular place.

Turning to American literature written in languages other than English would expand this discussion even further. The continent's literature is massively multilingual (see Sollers). To mention just one example: Peter Conolly-Smith has written about local color serials by Johann Rittig and Caspar Stürenburg that appeared in the German-language newspaper the *New Yorker Staats-Zeitung* in the late nineteenth century. As Patricia Okker notes in the volume in which his essay appears, studying such authors reminds us of the transnational character of such works. In whatever language or medium they appear, they depended on and addressed not only the ethnic community in a particular place, but also the larger network of immigrants from those nations in the United States, and connections to particular places abroad. I will turn back to this topic briefly in Chapter 4.

At each turn of this exploration, I have found that the local is not abolished as it is taken up into regionalism. From this point forward I will take it as established that the genre is most productively understood not as an insider or an outsider discourse, but as incorporating both possibilities and engaging questions of the relationship between places. In the next section, I go on to investigate the implications of the adjectives that keep cropping up in descriptions of local color and regional writing. "Quaint" and "backwards" bring to the surface the correlation of *time* with place and power. Here is another point where expert and everyday views of language differ; it is commonly believed that dialect is vanishing, that modern media cause the speakers of a given language to sound more and more alike. Specialists tell us that by their nature languages are constantly changing, and that—empirically—regional variation in American English is not decreasing. That information has difficulty making headway into public knowledge, however, because the association of provincial places and speech with the past has extended roots in commonsensical thinking about place and the notion of modernity itself.

Telling Time

Mikhail Bakhtin invented the term "chronotope" for "the inseparability of space and time" as expressed in literature. He derived it from science, explicitly mentioning Einstein's theory of relativity at the beginning of an essay originally written in the late 1930s. My understanding is that the notion of a space-time continuum allows mathematical models of the universe to be radically simpler and more elegant, from the level of the subatomic to the supergalactic. In her marvelous and difficult *How the Universe Got Its Spots: Diary of a Finite Time in a Finite Space*, Janna Levin shows how this fundamental insight works through topology, as space and time are curved together. The universe is not, on this model, infinite. It is (in her phrase) really big, but rather than extending emptily in all directions forever, it is made up of particular spots. The puzzles of place are, in other words, as fundamental as it gets. This section will argue the point that Bakhtin made when he added a final section to his essay in 1973: correlations of time and space are "the organizing centers for the fundamental narrative events of the novel. The chronotope is the place where the knots of narrative are tied and untied" (250). Even—"every entry into the sphere of meaning is accomplished only through the gates of the chronotope" (258). The term "place-time" that appears in my title was designed retrospectively to evoke the impossibility of separating social construction, materiality, and temporality in considering either location in general or any particular spot.

The chronotope of regionalism entails an orientation to the past. This is visible from the beginning of my discussion of the concept, for example when Hönnighausen asks: "are region and regionalism concerns of the past rather than of the present or future" (xiii)? In the nineteenth century and beyond, the convention was for local color stories to be set back a generation or so. That is not necessarily so today—the regional mysteries I discuss in Chapter 5, for example, are often set in the present—but I will argue in this section that the orientation to the past remains implicit in how local communities are represented. In this literary space-time continuum, particular places figure previous eras. To demonstrate this, let me begin with another fundamental condition of existence, one more accessible and immediate than physics: the human body.

In his classic *Space and Place*, Yi-Fu Tuan maps how our intuitive understanding of time is projected from an upright individual body. "The future is ahead and 'up.' The past is behind and 'below'" (35). He also correlates those orientations with the sacred and profane, respectively (see his diagram, Figure 1.7). The fact that this is generally true in Western culture is perhaps best demonstrated by a counter-example reminding us that this is a social construction, and that it is

UPRIGHT HUMAN BODY, SPACE AND TIME

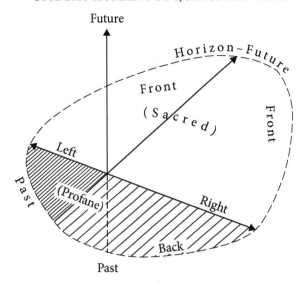

FIGURE 1.7 *Upright Human Body, Space and Time. From Yi Fu Tuan,* Space and Place: The Perspective of Experience *(copyright University of Minnesota Press, 1977), p. 35. Reprinted by permission.*

possible to think differently: in Hawaiian culture, the future is imagined as not in front of us, but behind us. This is of course quite logical—we can look back at the past, but we cannot see the future. For most people it is a mind-twisting experience to think like this, rather than seeing ourselves marching forward into tomorrow. The cover of Israel Kamakawiwoʻoleʻs album *Facing Future* helps by providing a vivid illustration (see Figure 1.8). Iz, with his back to us, is confronting his future; his look at the land, sea, and sky, and our look at him, are already entering the past. In English, "facing" and "confronting" pull us into paradox by reinserting the correlation of the front of the body with the future. In Hawaiian, that paradox does not exist; the directional phrase for "behind" is already embedded in the term for future time, "ka wā ma hope" (see the Ulukau Hawaiian Dictionary online). Cultural studies scholars will think, as well, of Benjamin's Angel of History, facing the catastrophe of the past and present, blown backwards into the future by the storm of progress.

The embodied figuration in which we perpetually journey forward in time is both distinctively modern and frequently manifest in everyday speech. It informs what I have come to think of as the vernacular poetry of the remote. Phrases like "back of beyond" or "the middle of nowhere" are evocative, and some expressions have revealing origins as well. In American English, the kind of place represented in local color writing is often called "Podunk"—dismissive slang for a small, backwards town. The term has a deep history, originating in Algonquian (it means a marshy place); it becomes the name of a tribe and (many times over) a place name.

FIGURE 1.8 *The cover of Israel Kamakawiwoʻoleʻs album* Facing Future, *released in 1993 by Mountain Apple Records. Reproduced courtesy of Jon de Mello.*

It was given literary life by Samuel Griswold Goodrich (better known as Peter Parley) in 1840, and has constantly recirculated since. Mark Twain, whose house in Hartford was within a few miles of the Podunk River, once wrote that people even knew about something "in Podunk, wherever that may be" (294). Today there is an ePodunk.com website, which "provides in-depth information about 46,000 communities across the country," taking a somewhat defensive tone about "the power of place" (displayed as a slogan), and offering as one of its notable features the chance to email images of vintage postcards. Or—the "boondocks" or "boonies" originated in the Tagalog word "bundok," which means "mountain" and colloquially indicated places distant from coastal cities, difficult to get to and to move around in, a usage picked up by American soldiers in the Philippines in the early twentieth century.

I asked audiences for talks I gave in five European countries during 2013 for their equivalents to "Podunk" and "the middle of nowhere." The results are also evocative. To cite only a few examples: my Danish students offered "der ude hvor kragerne vender," "so far out the crows turn around and fly back" (the most poetic, to my ear), and "over syvende kartofel-række," "beyond the seventh potato row." Portuguese colleagues suggested "onde o diabo perdeu as botas," "where the devil lost his boots," and "os cus de Judas," "out Judas's ass"; my Swiss brother-in-law, "au diable vert," "at the green devil." Icelandic students who attended a talk in Copenhagen contributed "út í rassgati," "out the ass"'; an Australian I met later that day, "out woopwoop." The association of remoteness with the profane as opposed to the sacred—whether the potato, the devil, or the ass—seems to dominate. I cite these examples partly out of pleasure in the sheer creativity of vernacular constructions of place, to show slang as (in Michael Adams's phrase) "the people's poetry." But I also want to accumulate a sense of how consistently a word like "backwards"—and, I am speculating, its equivalent in other languages—constructs around itself a nexus coordinating the body, time, and space, and thus begins to tie the knots of narrative.

The profane is also (let me paradoxically call it) to the fore in a widely used twentieth-century American idiom for a remote, backwards place: "Bumfuck, Egypt," sometimes abbreviated (presumably to avoid voicing the obscenity) as "BFE." It seems to appear first in the military, perhaps during the Second World War, certainly by the Vietnam War. In those years I think "Egypt" would have evoked stereotypes of the archaic (think pyramids) as well as the remote. That has been overridden by the widespread, increasingly racialized Euro-American hostility to the Arab world, and its conflation with Islam and other Muslim countries—one current variation is "Bumfuckistan." I will not undertake to establish the origins of the figure, but folk etymologies illuminate its cultural significance. In a discussion of the phrase on a messageboard on snopes.com, one poster—clearly military or ex-military—writes: "It is Bum F*** Egypt. And used to describe the worst place you could be OR where you are when you don't know where you are. Also describes where the Sargeant is going to ship your dumb ass to if you don't immediatly get your s*** together." Another poster (responding to the question, why Bumfuck, Egypt as opposed to "Blowjob, China or Doggystyle, Brazil"?) links it to Appalachia: "I immediately think of 'Deliverance'—small, isolated rural area, cut off from the rest of the world, not much to do ... you know the rest. Although the term has been around longer than the book or the movie. I think that particular sex term is used to emphasize the fact that you don't want to be there, because you'll probably be anally violated." I am simultaneously tempted to apologize to readers offended by my using these words at all, and to RangerDog and Cervus for transporting their casual keystrokes to an academic book. Like dialect characters, they are positioned at a disadvantage—or (more precisely) allowed the advantage of frank, vivid speech and at the same time subordinated and subsumed. Is this not an effective demonstration of the way figures of place plunge us into politics?

Places are material, but also persistently associated with ideas and tendencies, and valued differently—always depending on perspective, and changing over time. I doubt one could position London in relation to Rome without writing several books; even Brooklyn to New York might take more than one volume. What would we say about San Francisco and Palo Alto, or Shanghai and Nanjing? Or Havana and Miami and Mumbai? These are the names of cities, of course. They invoke the non-concentric complexities of region, nation, and globe that I have discussed. And certainly they invoke correlations with time—to answer any one of those questions would certainly require considering those cities' associations with antiquity and national history, and with modernity. But for thinking about regionalism, we need also to consider how each of these cities is defined in relation to remote and rural places, whether in its region and nation or crossing those boundaries.

All of these topics are larger than my project, of course. Raymond Williams's extraordinary *The Country and the City* is in effect a history of English literature— in fact, of England and its colonies as well. As he points out, this opposition is "one of the major forms in which we become conscious of a central part of our experi- ence and of the crises of our society"; its "persistence has a significance matched only" by the importance of its variability (289). The association of the city with being forward-looking, the country with being backwards, is pervasive. But the contrast does not mean only one thing; as Williams writes, "People have often said 'the city' when they meant capitalism or bureaucracy or centralized power, while 'the country'... has at times meant everything from independence to deprivation" (291). Far from thinking of all instances as the same, I see this book as a contribu- tion to the ongoing project of analyzing the multiple meanings of the country/ city opposition.

Williams calls the strongest pattern he finds "the escalator"—the repeated referral backwards of an image of rural life as organic and virtually unconflicted, unified as a human community and in a harmonious relation to nature. There are many versions of this figure, in *The Country and the City* and beyond. It is associ- ated with nostalgic memories of childhood, with the notion of a "golden age," and of course with the pastoral. Bakhtin's chronotope of the "idyll" may be ranged here as well. He writes that it takes many forms, from "ancient times to the present" (224), but its most general feature is "the immanent unity of folkloric time. This finds expression predominantly in the special relationship that time has to space in the idyll: an organic fastening-down, a grafting of life and its events to a place, to a familiar territory with all its nooks and crannies, its familiar mountains, val- leys, fields, rivers and forests, and one's own home" (225). His discussion of the eighteenth- and early nineteenth-century provincial novel as idyll is as close as Bakhtin comes, in this classic essay concerned mostly with earlier works, to modern literature.

It is again helpful to think in terms of both the substantive and the relational. We can imagine an everyday life of ontological plenitude, seeing infinity in a grain of sand and the golden age in substantial shepherds. Among the writers I am studying, Sarah Orne Jewett and Wendell Berry do so most powerfully, and indis- pensably through their spiritual orientations (for both, Christian belief). Yet even in Hesiod, the pastoral is an alternative to a more sophisticated—although suppos- edly lesser—life. And American regionalists, Jewett and Berry included, are con- stantly reckoning with how places are connected. Throughout the literature we call modern and contemporary, the country may be represented and substantial—but it is always, necessarily, in relation to the city. For this industrializing, colonial (perhaps post-colonial and even post-industrial) world, let us say that the *engine* of the figure is contrast and critique. "Chronotope" is an evocative rather than a precise term, but here, we see how the paradox inherent in the concept of region converges with a pattern in space-time.

To appreciate the specific cultural power of this pattern requires another circuit through broad questions, to defamiliarize—from the ground up—the way we constantly project the past onto locations. Is it not odd, for example, that we commonly speak of some places as older than others? The geological age of the surface does vary. The Big Island of Hawai'i is young, made of lava that solidified less than a million years ago—and at Kilauea one can sometimes watch rocks form. The oldest are thought to be in Canada's Northwest Territories and the Jack Hills of Western Australia, where scientists tell us there are zircons that have held their shape for over four billion years. But the difference between one million and four billion years is not on a human scale, and that is not what we mean when we talk about a place being old; rather, we are reacting to the salience of a site's known human history. Indeed, what is noticed is most often the history of one's own racial or ethnic group, erasing not only the non-human (both geological and biological) but also the stories of other peoples.

Or—think how powerfully places where we once spent time remind us of eras in our own lives. In the first volume of *In Search of Lost Time*, Proust famously associated involuntary memory with a tea-soaked madeleine, but what its taste evokes is precisely a place of his childhood—a very particular place: "the good people of the village and their little dwellings and the church and all of Combray and its surroundings, all of this, acquiring form and solidity, emerged, town and gardens alike, from my cup of tea" (48). For all of us, revisiting particular buildings, streets, or vistas conjures up the personal past. Svetlana Boym's brilliant *Future of Nostalgia* portrays that "historical emotion" as "coeval with modernity itself. Nostalgia and progress are like Jekyll and Hyde: alter egos. Nostalgia is not merely an expression of local longing, but a result of a new understanding of time and place that made the division into 'local' and 'universal' possible" (xvi). To return to Bakhtin's figure: space and time are curved together in everyday and literary narrative, as well as physics.

The next step in registering the significance of the correlation of time and space in regional writing entails engaging the fraught notion of *modernity*. Craig Calhoun's concise definition, "the self-conception of an era idealizing change and especially progress" (*Critical Social Theory*, 291), is clarifying. Figures like "the back of beyond" and "the middle of nowhere" position remote places as not only distant but behind the times—old-fashioned, boring, unimportant, and so on. In modernity, the claim to the future is a trump card. It can be contested by a counter-claim—as, for example, Marxism challenges capitalism. Such debates are resolved in one sense by their ability to persuade; in another, we must, ultimately, wait and see. Or the claim can be challenged by an appeal to a different set of values rejecting the appeal of progress, often although not necessarily "traditional." In some sense the most ambitious question of this book is how we can think outside the framework of Western modernity, while still coming to terms with it as an immensely consequential phenomenon—I am trying to do just that, and imagine alternate ways of thinking. The task is recursively complicated by the recognition that the power of "tradition" is itself a modern formation. Cultural historians have shown us that many practices we think of as long-established are recent inventions. (See Hobsbawn and Ranger, *The Invention of Tradition*.) For the work I am doing, the most relevant example is the exhibition catalogue *Picturing Old New England*, which shows—in extraordinary, beautiful detail—how our images of the Pilgrims, the village green, and so on were created in the late nineteenth century.

More immediately, what I want to do is call attention to how much it matters that both "backwards" and the more polite adjective "quaint" are located by recursion between the spatial and the temporal. In a sense this does not so much need demonstrating as defamiliarizing, precisely because it *is* common sense. Harold Ross did not need to explain what he meant when he combined condescension to the old-fashioned and the hinterland with disdain for women, and said that the *New Yorker* would not be published for "the old lady in Dubuque." Another example from the magazine world of the 1920s mobilizes the connection to time more explicitly. Henry Luce's biographer Alan Brinkley writes that even in the early years when its circulation was small, *Time* magazine was "an important force in journalism" because "it reached men and women in all parts of the country and promised to rescue them from isolation and provincialism and prepare them for the cosmopolitan world. 'Can you afford to be *labelled* as a man from Main Street?' an early advertising leaflet asked potential *Time* subscribers. 'Can you afford to *be* a man from Main Street? Civilization moves forward on a thousand fronts,—business, art, politics, science, religion. You have only to ignore it, and you slip back again centuries in time. But can you afford to live in the dark ages?'" (138). (The "Main Street" figure refers to Sinclair Lewis's bestselling 1920 novel.) In other words, it circulated between places—that is precisely what magazines do—but announced its affiliation with the center. I have chosen conspicuous examples, from famously antagonistic publishing institutions. But this vocabulary of civilization, and the particular way it correlates time and space in a figure of modernity, can be found anywhere and everywhere today.

"Civilization" is also a term we tend to take for granted, one that has been returning to its former prominence in public discourse. It is easy to forget how fundamentally it implies a *sense of direction*, forward and upward, so that a phrase like "the pinnacle of civilization" seems natural. (That is actually a rather precarious and peculiar figure, leaving no place to go but down.) This is another keyword, of course, and I will not digress far into the details of its intellectual history. But reading Brett Bowden's *Empire of Civilization* on precisely that topic, it is striking how closely notions of a cultivated person and of an enlightened or advanced society are linked; as Tuan shows us, the orientation is mapped onto and through the individual body. Scholarly practitioners of evolutionary biology and history may disclaim teleology, but the assumption that we are ascending remains pervasive (which means that it often silently subtends expert knowledge as well). One need not be a naïve advocate of "progress" to be carried along in this current of thought; the normative implication of "modern" and "civilization," and their recursive entangling of space and time, are at work as soon as the terms are used.

Reading Bowden, it is clear that the consequences of the idea of civilization—for the development of international law, for example—can scarcely be overstated. He argues convincingly that "the dominant architects of international society continue to be informed and influenced by a faith in the Enlightenment ideal of progress and humankind's universal linear march toward...a modernity that is universally liberal democratic, market capitalist, and cosmopolitan in appearance" (2–3). Many discussions of "globalization," its critics have shown, assume this model. His goal in tracing this intellectual history is not only to show the interconnected development of ideas about civilization, with their "devastating consequences" (228) for societies deemed in need of civilizing, but also to appeal to readers to think differently. It is possible to focus on the way "cultural groupings have overlapped and freely borrowed from one another" (231) rather than on the clash of civilizations, and to relinquish vaunting claims about hierarchy in favor of respectful dialogue. As Bowden says: the West needs a new theory of history (230). I often hear political positions casually described as "progressive"—which I believe anchors them in a chronotope that undermines any aspiration to inclusive justice. The stubborn project of this book is to avoid that pitfall by thinking through the particular.

I have come a considerable distance from the notion of local color. But a key point in Bowden's story is the continuity between the subordination of particular places in nation-building, and in imperial projects. As he points out, the English "honed the techniques they employed in the Americas and elsewhere in the centuries prior, through conquest and expansion into the Celtic lands of Wales and Ireland" (132). The discourse of civilization is deployed within nations—including the United States—as well as globally. It informs the projects carried out in the schools, discussed in Chapter 2, for example. I want to be clear: there are many histories here, and I am not equating them. But I am saying that this broad intellectual history is relevant to appreciating what it means when, in a regional mystery published in 2013, Bell Elkins—an Appalachian native who has returned to her home town—is told by another character that it is time for her to " 'pack up and come back to civilization' " (Keller, 246).

As discussed in the first section of this chapter, the local and the global are by no means distant ends of a continuum. How can we think "local" without thinking "limited"? think about the global, without making it—in Anna Lowenhaupt Tsing's words—"a claim to explain everything in the world at once" (*Friction*, ix)? Her *Friction*—as its subtitle says, *An Ethnography of Global Connection*—is about

FIGURE 1.9 *Hecataeus' world map, 500 BCE, as rendered by Jona Lendering (modified slightly for this publication), courtesy of Livius.org.*

a particular place, the Indonesian rainforest. But on that site, as she shows, an extraordinary range of actors undertake projects—from local entrepreneurs to United Nations funding agencies, from North American investors to village elders to diversely affiliated scientists and environmental activists. What happens in these "zones of awkward engagement" (xi), as she calls them, is not what anyone planned. She shows us the way the same events or claims mean different things to different people, the way in which ideas and images are changed when they are transported to a new location even when they appear the same. We see, precisely, friction—the light and heat generated by contact. The topic of *Friction* might seem remote from my own, but the book has been with me throughout the process of writing this one. It offers a way of thinking differently about the local and the global, a way forward through—not around—the paradoxes of place.

In some sense, for each of us, the center of the world is wherever we are. One figure for this claim might be the world map that (it is said) Hecataeus of Miletus created in the fourth or fifth century BCE—where Miletus occupies the center spot. (See Figure 1.9.) Yet to say "each of us is at the center" is precisely to generate a paradox. My long view of this theme can only be impressionistic, but I think for example of the reflections the modern writer Marguerite Yourcenar gives to the

Roman emperor Hadrian: "Both the man and the stars which are the objects of his gaze roll inevitably toward their ends, marked somewhere in the sky; but each moment of that descent is a pause, a guide mark, and a segment of a curve itself as solid as a chain of gold. Each movement in space brings us back to a point which, because we happen to be on it, seems to us a center" (156). This perspective has been articulated many times (I have already mentioned Native American maps as a place where one can find it), and I will return to versions throughout the book. In Chapter 3 I discuss Jewett's reference to Dunnet Landing's "childish certainty of being the centre of civilization." In Chapter 5, I will return to the notion in my discussion of Wendell Berry. His close and tender account of the experiences of a mouse, in a book for children, provides one of my epigraphs: "Like humans, she lived in the little world of what she knew, for there was no other world for her to live in. But she lived at the center of her world always, and of this she had no doubt" (11). Each of these examples both affirms the claim of centrality and contradicts it, by putting it in perspective.

Henri Lefebvre, in his magisterial volume *The Production of Space*, links the concept of the center to time: "Centrality as a form implies simultaneity, and it is a result thereof: the simultaneity of 'everything' that is susceptible of coming together—and thus of accumulating—in an act of thinking or in a social act, at a point or around that point. The general concept of centrality connects the punctual to the global" (332). The translation is formal and perhaps difficult, but precise. A paraphrase, in the terms I have been using, might be: the creative, world-making moment that constitutes a place depends on and implies the space-time continuum.

On this view, as Lefebvre goes on to say, the center is "movable" (332). In modernity, however, the landscape tilts. Gravity—power—exerts itself. Lefebvre asks: "What makes present-day society different in this regard? Simply this: centrality now aspires to be *total*. It thus lays claim, implicitly or explicitly, to a superior political rationality (a state or 'urban' rationality)... Despite countervailing forces, some subversive, some tolerable—and tolerated on various grounds (liberalization, flexibility, etc.)—the centre continues effectively to concentrate wealth, means of action, knowledge, information and 'culture.' In short, everything" (333–4). In short, everything!—yet the city, modernity, (Western) civilization, do *not* consume and replace everything. The local and particular persist, whether tolerated or not. Totality is an idea, an aspiration—and, as Lefebvre says, irrational and illegitimate. I would add that it is visibly destructive, perhaps even insane. But the accumulated power of the center is material and real, on the (always still-particular) ground.

The phrase "the center of the world" affirms the spot we inhabit as irreducibly important. But its claim depends on surrounding places, which simultaneously constitute the center and incubate challenges. The substantive is always, immediately, haunted by the relational. My title runs the risk of seeming totalizing in order to embrace this paradox. The "we" may be seen as arrogant, or vulnerable; it plants its feet on the ground, but it also speculates. (What spot do we inhabit? *You* tell *me*.)

Why Genre?

It is ambitious, perhaps even foolhardy, to write about regionalism in general. After all, my topic is a literary form defined by its concern with the particular. But genres necessarily exist at some level of generality. Does that provide a warrant for my approach, or deepen the difficulty? Genre criticism is widely practiced, yet it has long been and it remains an unfashionable approach. In 2013, I sat in a very big ballroom at the Modern Languages Association Convention, at a session organized by the association and chaired by its president, with the impressive title "The Twenty-First Century MLA: Reimagining the Order of Things." A panel of distinguished scholars discussed plans for reorganizing the organization's divisions and discussion groups, to rise to the challenge of our future. Their presentations were organized under established headings like "Regions" and "Period." One of them—a past editor of *PMLA*—dismissed her topic of "Genre" as a misguided, obsolete category.

I have some sympathy for this point of view. My work depends on thinking about literary kinds, and I consider the approach valuable. Yet I often find the way generic terms are defined and mobilized in scholarship to be muddled or wrong-headed. Even in very fine work, moments of classification tend to close down rather than open up interesting questions. So although I have written on this topic elsewhere (*Publishing the Family*, "Sand in Your Mouth"), it seems worthwhile to close this framing chapter by saying something about my assumptions. If there is—as recently claimed (see Rosen)—a resurgence of genre criticism, all the more reason to be explicit about what distinguishes my approach.

It is impossible to do cultural interpretation without using terms that identify kinds—at least, no one to my knowledge has managed it. Yet whatever our intellectual formation, as scholars we inhabit an intellectual universe that is sophisticated and skeptical about classification. Genre necessarily functions as a system—there is only difference, without positive terms. The assertion at the MLA session was that crediting the existence of such a system became impossible after Derrida's essay "The Law of Genre," published in English in 1980. (Or rather, it was always impossible, and he pointed that out.) And indeed my work has been shaped by the recognitions he educes there. To put commonsensically and declaratively what he demonstrates on the page: entities are defined by contrast, and inextricably involve each other. Every separation becomes an invagination.

But after we have accepted the insights of Saussure and Derrida, there is still no way of analyzing the artifacts of expressive culture without positing kinds. I am saying something similar to David Perkins's ironic and paradoxical un-affirmation in *Is Literary History Possible?*: "we cannot write literary history with intellectual conviction, but we must read it" (17). We do genre criticism despite its impossibility. And we *can* open the trap, by conceiving forms not as fixed sites in a closed, abstract system but rather as nodes in loose and constantly changing social arrangements. For the period I am working with, there are not only philosophical but specific historical reasons to avoid thinking of genres as pure or even as unambiguously bounded. Prose fictions of the modern era are capacious compendia—whether printed or electronic books, they are what Henry James called "large loose baggy monsters." In these commercially circulating forms elements of all sorts are constantly appropriated and reappropriated; they are characterized by what I have usually called, following Fredric Jameson, generic discontinuity. The conventions and themes we associate with any given genre traverse a variety of works rather than constituting a category that contains them. This is not, I want to suggest, generic "hybridity," despite the excellent work that has been done using that term. It implies a prior state of purity and a misleading analogy to the biological, warranting a notion of separate kinds by locating it in science when (according to my understanding) biologists actually see speciation as a complex and ongoing process. The recognition that genres are mixed should be a premise, a beginning point, not a conclusion.

This view of genre has not been fully incorporated into standard practice in American literary studies. That is presumably why genre criticism seems to suffer from an especially acute version of the legitimation crisis that afflicts literary studies in general. Yet it is not new—it has been powerfully articulated for several decades, and its power is enhanced by the sophisticated treatment of genre as a social contract that has emerged in the scholarship of rhetoric and composition. John Frow offered an excellent textbook exposition in 2006, restated for specialists in his contribution to the special issue of *PMLA* devoted to "Remapping Genre" in 2007. On this view—which is also mine—it does not make sense to assert a definition of a form, or to ask of any modern fiction, "does this belong to that genre? or not?", as if the literary system were a series of pigeonholes and the problem was to find and properly label the right one. Rather, we need to ask: what is the intellectual history of this term, and what is usage doing with it now? How does it move between discursive domains? How is its value assigned through differentiation? We need (to put it another way) to refine a concept, follow it over time and across places and institutions, study its capacity for generating narrative. As Frow puts it, "Rather than asking, what kind of thing is this text? we should be asking something like, what kind of world is brought into being here" (" 'Reproducibles,' "1633)? My previous books were primarily concerned with what the analysis of form could show us about literary works' moment of production; here I include their subsequent circulation as well, which enlarges my horizons and raises the stakes. Genre criticism can, I think, tell us a great deal not only about literary kinds but also about the world.

Let me return to the particular and end this chapter with an example. Mary Wilkins Freeman's *The Jamesons* was serialized in *Ladies' Home Journal* in 1898 and 1899, then published as a book by Doubleday, McClure. This short novel was reprinted for the first time in 2000, in Sandra Zagarell's edition of Freeman's stories (and has since become easily available). This is a work by an author strongly associated with regionalism, and it has many of the characteristics discussed so far. It is the tale of a small New England village; it includes dialect and accounts of local practices; it is centrally concerned with women's lives; the structure is somewhat episodic, a kind of narrative of community (the term is Zagarell's), although it does include a marriage plot.

The Jamesons is particularly interesting in terms of the debate over whether local color is empathetic or touristic, an insider or an outsider narrative. As Zagarell points out, the narrator is a native, whose gaze is turned on a family of summer visitors from New York. The comic opening is about local knowledge, as Mrs. H. Boardman Jameson misreads what she sees—and the fire department gets involved. Her landlady says: "My house is not on fire, and has not been on fire. I am getting tea, and the kitchen chimney always smokes when the wind is west. I don't thank you, any of you, for coming here and turning my house upside down and drenching it with water, and lugging my furniture out of doors" (83). The cognitive advantage of the villagers continues throughout; Mrs. Jameson's patronizing attitude and efforts to reform Linville are absurd, although the long-suffering locals indulge or resist them with unfailing courtesy. For example, she does not manage to persuade her neighbors that hens should (for hygienic reasons) sit on hard-boiled eggs. Just one of her projects succeeds, one that invokes the quaint past: at her suggestion, Linville holds a celebration of the centennial of its founding. The process of recreating a colonial kitchen, organizing a procession and banquet, reveals the New England past as an urban fantasy—virtually a tourist attraction, to which Mrs. Jameson seems to have invited "every celebrity whose grandfather ever drove through Linville" (139). On the other hand, the event also reconciles the locals and the summer people and resolves the novel's marriage plot. *The Jamesons*, as Zagarell shows in more detail in her analyses of the novel, turns local color conventions upside down. That is also to say that it deploys them, and puts them into question.

It is beside the point to ask if this is satire or regionalism. As soon as we have asked the question, it is both. I imagine that readers expect to find Sarah Orne Jewett in the pages that follow (and you will). The appearance of W. E. B. Du Bois, Edith Eaton, and Wendell Berry is probably not surprising—but what about Alexander Posey, Catherine Marshall, and Ursula Le Guin? The challenge is not to decide who is in and who is out. It is to rise to the challenge of writing literary and cultural history, and to learn from the pressure that classification exerts on literary production and interpretation—and that new works and changing interpretations exert on classification.

Each of the following chapters works from this understanding of genre. Each inquires into what narrative knots are being tied by authors, into how the chronotope of regionalism is being mobilized to make worlds. Here too I attend to both the substantive and the relational—to particular works and the distinctiveness of the form, and to the systems within which they take on shape and significance.

We live in the center. But we make knowledge in the middle, by considering relationships. Chapter 2 turns to a specific element of regional writing in the United States—representations of the classroom as an in-between place, connecting country and city, local and global, provincial and cosmopolitan. Studying those stories has changed not only how I think about literary history, but also how I think about my own location as a teacher of literature.

Local Knowledge and Book-Learning

PLACING THE TEACHER IN REGIONAL STORY-TELLING

Teachers and schools—especially, the one-room schoolhouse—appear again and again in regionalist writing. They play a key role in linking localities to distant sources of information, to visions of the nation, and to cosmopolitan projects. These connections are not depicted as one-way. Rather, they are full of friction (both in the word's ordinary meaning, and in Anna Tsing's particular usage evoked in Chapter 1). Negotiation over competing kinds of knowledge, collaboration between insiders and outsiders, and struggles over affiliation pervade and shape this body of work. The schoolteachers in these stories deserve our attention—because there are so many of them over such a long period, and because they are so interesting.

The concept of region and understanding of regionalism articulated in Chapter 1 has enabled me to recognize this topos; equally, studying it helped me develop that analysis. This chapter functions as something like a proof of concept, but it is more than that. I propose revising American literary history to include the schoolteacher as a key figure in regional writing. The image of the one-room schoolhouse has fascinated Americans at least since Winslow Homer's widely popular *Snap the Whip* and *The Country School* in the 1870s (see Figures 2.1 and 2.2).[1] It still does—in literary fiction, and in photo essays and children's books that continue to appear (Figure 2.3 is an example). News media periodically run stories about surviving examples. It is important to continue to revise our understanding of American literature—and also important to recognize that this constellation of conventions and concerns continues into our own moment.

Appropriately, my study of schoolteachers in regionalism began in conversations with a student. Many years ago Dottie Webb and I talked the topic over at length; we each pointed to examples, and considered what the ubiquity and neglect of the figure might mean. Her role in this research underscores the point that teaching is fundamentally collaborative, and also serves as a reminder that literary scholars and other humanists *are* almost always teachers. Much of the time, we spend much of our time at that work. Yet as another former student, Laura Aull, later demonstrated in her research, literary scholars rarely identify themselves as teachers in their publications or cite their work in the classroom as a warrant for

FIGURE 2.1 *Winslow Homer,* Snap the Whip, *published as a centerfold in* Harper's Weekly, *September 20, 1873.*

FIGURE 2.2 *Winslow Homer,* The Country School, *1871; oil on canvas; 21 ¼ × 38 1¼ inches; Saint Louis Art Museum, Museum Purchase 123:1946.*

their knowledge—even when editing an anthology of American literature that includes instructors' guides and suggested assignments. I do so deliberately, throughout this book. The ground of this inquiry has been the academy. That term can indicate a school, or a scholarly society, and the story I want to tell inheres in the double meaning. Both for the writers I am studying and for me the classroom

Michigan One-Room Schoolhouses

Mary Keithan

FIGURE 2.3 *Mary Keithan's* Michigan One-Room Schoolhouses, *published in 2008, offers a selection from her several hundred photographs of one-room schoolhouses across the state and includes information about the Michigan One-Room Schoolhouse Association, founded in 1993 and still active as of 2017. Cover reproduced by permission of the University of Michigan Press.*

is a contact zone between kinds of knowledge, always a particular place, always looking towards whatever horizons may be in view. In this chapter I will move through a series of examples, beginning with a story that was one of the early runaway successes of the local color movement but is now little read. I examine how the topos is mobilized in the work of writers of different regions and races, and conclude with contemporary writers. Finally, I will return to the fact that the occupations "schoolteacher" and "professor" sound quite different to us because of the specific historical ways in which different academies and their faculties developed, and reflect on what it means that "higher education" is so much less oriented to the local than primary and secondary schools. My examination of schoolteachers in regionalist fiction will also prove to be an exploration of what place can mean to a professor; the relation of local knowledge and book-learning is vital to both.

Here is the pattern. Teachers in local color are often literally from someplace else. There are many scenes of their arrivals and departures. Even when teachers are locals, they have been altered by education. They offer access to books that carry traces of other times and places. In one-room schoolhouses, especially, they are loyal to standards that originate elsewhere and are shown correcting grammar and behavior, in effect enforcing metropolitan speech and manners. Teachers represent the power—meaning both the promise and the danger—of distant knowledge. What they stand for above all is broadened horizons and opportunities for the students that they are teaching. (Or they are satirized for failing to offer that—which still implies the expectation.)

At the same time teachers are deeply, inescapably involved in the community. They depend on their salaries. Thus they inhabit the economic system of the region, being paid by the community rather than just spending money they've brought with them (as tourists do). They "board" at students' homes, sharing their circumstances and afforded almost no privacy—readers get uncomfortably intimate descriptions of meals and sleeping arrangements. Teachers care about their students, struggle to earn respect from them, their parents, and the surrounding community. They become involved in local romances.

Teachers are, in other words, both (somewhat) powerful and (somewhat) vulnerable. They are both insiders and outsiders. Often, they struggle internally because they feel pulled in both directions; the question of their affiliation may become an open question in the community. They stand between inside and outside, between local lore and book-learning. They create, in the classroom, a mediating locality. The schoolteacher is not just one possible choice among the cast of characters in any given town. Like regional writing itself, the figure of the schoolteacher negotiates between provincial and metropolitan, between local and translocal knowledges.

Beginning: Edward Eggleston, Indiana, and the Nation

Although their presence has not been the focus of much attention, schoolteachers are present in the works often mentioned as the origins of local color. At the opening of Harriet Beecher Stowe's "Uncle Lot" (1855), for example, the hero James Benton is the schoolmaster of the New England village of Newbury. Bret Harte's stories of the Gold Rush, collected in the meteorically successful 1870 volume *The Luck of Roaring Camp*, included "Mliss" and "The Idyl of Red Gulch," in which a male and a female teacher (respectively) are privileged, respected figures who are tempted into dangerous relationships with locals and in the end must leave the community. And, although both the fact and the book itself are mostly forgotten today, the second striking success of the local color movement was the tale of a schoolteacher.

Edward Eggleston's *The Hoosier School-Master* is set in rural Indiana during the 1850s. It was published in *Hearth and Home*, a magazine that combined articles on agricultural and domestic topics with literature, during 1871. Originally imagined as a three-installment serial, it was so popular that the author—who was also the editor of the magazine—extended it to fourteen. A book edition was brought out before the end of the year; it sold well and was immediately pirated in England and translated into Danish, French, German, and Swedish (Randel 126–7). The retrospective setting suggests an alignment with the critical view that local color is elegiac, and indeed much writing about the one-room schoolhouse—over many decades—mourns its loss or celebrates its survival. The movement to consolidate schools that began in the 1840s accelerated after the Civil War, and one encounters the assumption that one-room schools were disappearing in the late nineteenth century. But they remained part of everyday experience for many people for a very long time—in 1913, there were over 200,000 one-room schools, attended by *one-half* of all American schoolchildren (Gulliford, 35). For the stories I am about to discuss, the placement of these classrooms in the past needs to be thought of not just as historical information, but as a topos, an element of a chronotope that coordinates time and space in a distinctively regionalist way.

The Hoosier School-Master, like many other regionalist tales of teachers, begins with a scene of arrival (Figure 2.4). Ralph Hartsook has walked ten miles to try to get the school at Flat Creek, "mentally reviewing his learning at every step he took, trembling lest the committee should find that he did not know enough" (11). But the trustee he visits, Jack Means, measures him instead "by the standard of muscle" (12). Flat Creek needs a new teacher because the big, tough local boys have beaten up and driven off the last three—and in Means's estimate, Ralph just isn't strong enough for the job. This encounter between the aspiring teacher and the local dramatizes their differing values, as Ralph's expectations are violated at every turn. He is dismayed not only by Means's lack of respect for learning, but also by

FIGURE 2.4 *Frank Beard*, "First Acquaintance with Flat Creek," *from Edward Eggleston*, The Hoosier School-Master: A Novel *(New York: Orange Judd and Company, 1871), p. 10.*

the trustee's conviction that "thrashing" the students is indispensable. Ralph is a sympathetic sort, who would prefer to make the students want to please him, practicing "disciplinary intimacy" (to use Richard Brodhead's concise term). Moreover, when he (it is implied) makes a faint inquiry about the possibility of a committee evaluating his qualifications, Means pauses in the midst of a long speech to say, "Any other trustees? Wal, yes. But as I pay the most taxes, t'others jist let me run the thing" (15). The standard of money invoked here is the equivalent of the standard of muscle—in each case, we are confronted with the fact that naked power rules the Flat Creek school district.

Means does hire Ralph, because he thinks he has "pluck" (15)—a quality that emerges as a mediating value. (And there have been no other applications.) Ralph does immediately demonstrate courage on a hunting expedition, climbing a tree to shake down a raccoon—although partly out of ignorance, as he does not realize how fierce those animals can be. Means has stipulated, like all too many later employers, that Ralph is not entitled to compensation—if he gets injured, it is his own problem because "Flat Crick don't pay no 'nsurance" (15). And Ralph is in real physical danger quite frequently—from the raccoon, from his students' fists and feet, and from tricks played on him, such as the loosening of a board in the floor in order to dump him into the cold water that collected underneath the cabin that serves as a schoolhouse (17–20). Frank Beard's illustrations to the first edition clearly put Jack Means in his place as a yokel, and evoke the dynamic scene of the one-room schoolhouse at the moment of that dangerous "plunge" (see Figures 2.5 and 2.6).

Crucially, Ralph quickly finds a way to impress the trustee and his family with his education: "Out of all the books he had ever read he told story after story. And 'old man Means,' and 'old *Miss* Means,' and Bud Means, and Bill Means, and Sis Means, listened with great eyes while he told of Sinbad's adventures, of the Old Man of the Sea, of Robinson Crusoe, of Captain Gulliver's experiences in Lilliput, and of Baron Munchausen's exploits... The hungry minds of these backwoods people, sick and dying of their own commonplace, were refreshed with the new life that came to their imaginations in these stories" (17–18). ("Backwoods" and variants will appear regularly in this chapter; they should evoke Chapter 1's discussion of embodied figuration and its link to temporality.) Ralph earns enough respect that he is able to form an alliance with Jack's son Bud, the largest and strongest boy in the school—and therefore does not have to fight the others. Because he has also won the affection of Shocky, one of his smallest and least fortunate students, he is warned about the planned ducking and is able to maneuver the perpetrator into stepping into his own trap (he comes down with a "serious fever" [42]). Much of the pleasure of the novel derives from the diverse ways in which the underdog Ralph's quick wits give him an advantage in contests with his students and, later, adults who plot against him. Pluck, intelligence, and kindness combine to enable Ralph to win over some students, gain ascendancy over others, and succeed in Flat Creek.

FIGURE 2.5 *Frank Beard*, "Old Jack Means, the School Trustee," *from Edward Eggleston,* The Hoosier School-Master: A Novel *(New York: Orange Judd and Company, 1871), p. 13.*

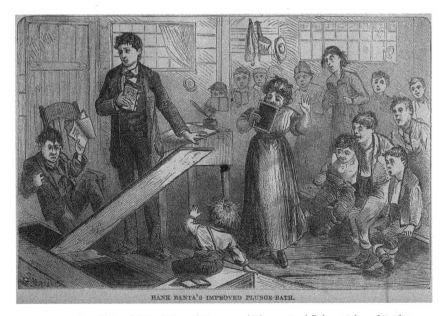

FIGURE 2.6 *Frank Beard*, "Hank Banta's Improved Plunge-Bath," *from Edward Eggleston,* The Hoosier School-Master: A Novel *(New York: Orange Judd and Company, 1871), p. 36.*

These examples from the opening pages of the novel show that Ralph is—to reiterate my general characterization of teachers in local color fiction—to some degree powerful, but also vulnerable. He has walked ten miles to get the school not because he is on a mission to civilize the residents of Flat Creek (although as it turns out he does serve them well), but because he needs the salary that they will pay him. His uncomfortable boarding arrangements are described in excruciating detail. At the Jones's, for example, Ralph must share a bed. The father of the family tells him how to find it: "jest climb up the ladder on the outside of the house. Takes up a thunderin' sight of room to have a stairs inside, and we ha'n't got no room to spare. You'll find a bed in the furdest corner. My Pete's already got half of it, and you can take t'other half. Ef Pete goes to takin' his half in the middle, and tryin' to make you take yourn on both sides, jest kick him" (66). (Pete takes three-fourths of the bed, the roof overhead leaks, and the covers are "insufficient.") Ralph thinks his own thoughts, but he has to eat at the common table—at the Jones's, the fare is "floating islands of salt pork fished out of oceans of hot lard" (81). At the Means's he is subjected to the unwanted attentions of Miranda, their oldest daughter—infatuated, she shows it "by ogling him, by blushing at him, by tittering at him, by giggling at him, by snickering at him, by simpering at him, by making herself tenfold more a fool even than nature had made her" (26–7). And he falls in love with the family's bound girl Hannah (who turns out to be Shocky's sister). In short, he is *involved*. Eventually, accused of being part of a gang of robbers, he is in real danger of being lynched.

The passage about Ralph's story-telling—drawing on the cosmopolitan literary conglomeration of Sinbad, Robinson Crusoe, and Baron Munchausen—is a striking moment. It sounds a note that is pervasive in local color fictions about teachers: through what he has learned from books, Ralph opens up a wider world for his listeners, as less explicitly he does in the schoolroom as well. I would venture to say that most literary scholars have at some point been eager consumers of horizon-broadening fiction or poetry, and hope to pass that taste on to their students (unless professionalism gets the upper hand in graduate school). We tend to believe that, as Wallace Stegner put it, "Anyone who reads…is to some extent a citizen of the world" (254). I have already, in Chapter 1, qualified that investment in cosmopolitanism; and from that perspective it is crucial that Ralph does not display his book-learning *as* erudition, but translates it into locally appropriate story-telling. In other words, he is not invoking the prestige attached to cultural knowledge—he is *teaching*.

Ralph's willingness to learn from his surroundings is key to his success. When his first day of teaching goes badly, he perseveres—taking the Means's bulldog as his model. "He remembered Bud's certificate, that 'Ef Bull once takes a holt, heaven and yarth can't make him let go'…He would be a bull-dog, quiet but invincible." This is not merely a passing thought but a strategy that is described in detail: "In the morning Ralph got out of bed slowly. He put his clothes on slowly. He pulled on his boots in a bull-dog mood. He tried to move as he thought Bull would move if he were a man. He ate with deliberation, and looked everybody in

FIGURE 2.7 *Frank Beard, "Bull," from Edward Eggleston,* The Hoosier School-Master:
A Novel *(New York: Orange Judd and Company, 1871), p. 75.*

the eyes with a manner that made Bud watch him curiously. He found himself
continually comparing himself with Bull" (20–1). In subsequent crises as well,
Ralph finds inspiration in thinking of Bull. (Beard's rendering of the dog is shown
in Figure 2.7.) Far from thinking that his education holds the solution to all his
problems, let alone all the problems of Flat Creek, he connects book-learning
with the local.

In *The Hoosier School-Master*, the values at play are continually figured in
geographic terms. The prestige of New England as the location of American cultivation is simultaneously evoked and put into question through the Hawkins family,
who hail from Massachusetts. Squire Hawkins came to the region as the school-
master, married an uneducated but wealthy girl, and is now a prosperous landowner
and justice of the peace. But he is an absurd figure, described as an "agglomeration"
of odd clothes and ineffectual "patches"—a dirty wig and spectacles that both
keep slipping off, a misaligned glass eye and badly fitted false teeth, whiskers
dyed "a frightful dead black, such as no natural hair or beard ever had" (43–5).
Squire Hawkins's book-learning is one more motley patch—a pretentious
decoration disconnected from local knowledge. Listening to his grandiloquent,
error-filled speech, "Ralph concluded that some Yankees had taught school in
Hoopole county who would not have held a high place in the educational institutions of Massachusetts" (45). The squire's daughter is also half-educated, and
absurd in her constant references to her Eastern connections. "Like many other
people born in the celestial empires (of which there are three—China, Virginia,

Massachusetts), Miss Martha was not averse to reminding outside barbarians of her good fortune in this regard" (92–3). This offhand observation employs a vertiginously complex irony, implying the provincial and even superstitious nature of such inflated self-regard through linking it to China, relying both on recognition of the antiquity of Chinese civilization and on disparaging attitudes towards it. Martha's constantly used catchphrase "when I was to Bosting" is also complex; Boston's cultural capital is treated as a cultural fact, and at the same time Martha's grammar and pronunciation undermine her pretensions. As when Jewett characterizes Dunnet Landing's certainty of being the center of civilization as childish, what is at stake in geographical hierarchy, and who occupies the pinnacle, are put into question.

One manifestation of Bud Means's desire to gain refinement and religion—as he puts it on two occasions, "to git out of this low-lived, Flat Crick way of livin'" (122; see also 118)—is his courtship of Martha Hawkins. It is characteristic of the way the novel simultaneously mobilizes and critiques regional hierarchy that this choice is not wrong, even though it is based precisely on her satirized identification with New England: "I thought, not bein' Flat Crick born herself, she might help a feller to do better" (118). Martha is a good soul, despite her affectations, and Bud's aspirations are admirable. Ralph makes a decisive difference when he reinterprets the *place* of Christianity for Bud:

> 'Do you think that Jesus Christ would—would—well, do you think he'd help a poor, unlarnt Flat Cricker like me?'
> 'I think he was a sort of Flat Creeker himself,' said Ralph, slowly and very earnestly.
> 'You don't say?' said Bud, almost getting off his seat.
> 'Why, you see the town he lived in was a rough place. It was called Nazareth, which meant "Bushtown."'
> 'You don't say?'
> 'And he was called a Nazarene, which was about the same as "backwoodsman."'
> And Ralph read the different passages which he had studied at Sunday-school, illustrating the condescension of Jesus, the stories of the publicans, the harlots, the poor, who came to him. And he read about Nathanael, who lived only six miles away, saying 'Can any good thing come out of Nazareth?'
> 'Just what Clifty folks says about Flat Crick,' broke in Bud.   (123–4)

Ralph's book-learning is precisely what makes this scene possible, yet—as in his story-telling in the scene with the Means family, and in contrast to Squire Hawkins's patchy pretensions—it is integrated with everything else he knows. Ralph interprets his Book in a radically democratic way by connecting Nazareth and Flat Creek—two peripheral villages that can each be understood as the center of the world. And his pedagogy enables Bud to enlarge his own reading, to become able to reimagine places through their connections.

The term "book-learning" (or, often, "larnin'") is a constant reference point in *The Hoosier School-Master*—as it will be throughout this chapter, and in the rest of this book. As Eggleston's other critics have noted, it is characters' bookish or local language that most clearly locates them in the landscape of the novel. For example, Hannah is marked out as an appropriate partner for Ralph, despite her low social status, both by her victory in the public spelling contest held at the school, and by the fact that they are the only individuals who do not speak dialect— Hannah's words like his are spelled correctly on the page. Her English origins, her genteel womanliness, and how they combine in her pallid embodiment—one of the illustrations is titled "Hannah with a white, white face" (186)—reinforce the connection. The biopolitics of nationalism and knowledge are more complexly and ambivalently mobilized in the humble figure of John Pearson. He is a Kentuckian whose nonstandard pronunciation is explicitly noted, a veteran who lost his leg in the War of 1812, a drinker, a skeptic who does not attend church and claims that all human behavior is motivated by selfishness. He and his wife are also among the most benevolent and virtuous characters in the book. They cared for Hannah and Shockey's father in his last illness, despite Pearson's purportedly disliking him as a "Britisher" (96), and took in the little boy to prevent him being bound out (that is, basically, enslaved at the age of seven until he turned twenty-one). Pearson is a brave and vital ally in Ralph's battle against the gang of thieves that plots against him. He is a dialect-speaker who is also an American patriot, an irreligionist who practices Christian charity, an unbookish basket-maker whose embrace of psychological egoism seems to suggest exposure to Bentham or Spencer. Characters are located by their speech, but not only by their speech.

Ralph Hartsook is, certainly, the central representative of book-learning in *The Hoosier School-Master*. In the culturally pervasive terms always acknowledged but only partially adopted by the narrative, Ralph's education and eloquence align him with a Northeastern perspective that is implicitly racialized and privileged. I disagree, however, with Edward Watts's argument that the book's title is an oxymoron, and his suggestion that Ralph's tales of Sinbad, Crusoe, Gulliver, and Baron Munchausen implicitly parallel his own adventures "among the heathens of the colonized world" (180). Watts conflates "metropolitan," "Yankee," and "national", but Eggleston does not. And as I have already suggested, Ralph's characteristic gesture is not simply to affirm attitudes from elsewhere, but to create a mediating space in which they can be connected with the local. In fact, he is a local himself. The narrative directs our attention principally to his status as a stranger in Flat Creek—so much so that it comes as something of a surprise when, well over halfway through the novel, Ralph retraces the journey that opened the book and visits his aunt in Lewisburg, just ten miles away. The reader may wonder, retrospectively, how he could possibly have missed learning "how ugly a customer a raccoon can be" (17)—Ralph's double nature is such a powerful structural feature that it becomes a fault line in the narrative. Like Howard MacLane in "Up the Coolly," and like many other teachers in local color narratives, Eggleston's protagonist is both an insider and an outsider.

Edward Eggleston himself might be characterized in the same way, as both an insider and an outsider, especially at the moment in his life when he wrote *The Hoosier School-Master*. He was indeed born and raised in rural Indiana; in 1871, at the age of thirty-two, he had just moved to Brooklyn. As he was growing up in Vevay County, Eggleston's time was divided between his family's farm and life in town; he heard both French and English spoken, as the region had been settled by francophone Swiss immigrants. His household was full of books but, especially after his father's death, the family struggled financially. As a young man Eggleston traveled to Virginia (one of those "celestial empires") for an extended visit with his extended family. He was employed for a few weeks as a schoolteacher, near his home in Indiana—but he could not endure it and resigned. (The novel is drawn primarily from his brother's more extensive experience.) Later he worked at many different jobs, in Indiana and in Minnesota—laboring behind a plow, preaching the gospel, selling soap, performing a stereopticon show. He loved the prairie landscape, but when he moved to the city he was fascinated by that as well, and wrote light essays about Chicago life, published in a newspaper as "Our Saturday Feuilleton." Such perspectives could not guarantee that he would portray communities as internally diverse, or notions of place as imaginatively active—but they gave him the opportunity to do so.

One index of Eggleston's position at the cusp of changes in the public sphere is the fact that he naively gave some characters in *The Hoosier School-Master* the names of actual people in his home region. As he wrote much later, "it did not seem likely that the story would have vitality enough to travel all the way to Indiana" ("Preface," 23). To be fair, the circulation of *Hearth and Home* was small. But the serial's success—in the context of the voracious development of the national print culture—took everyone by surprise, and the serial was reprinted in many newspapers in the west. The character Jim Phillips is described as "a tall, lank, stoop-shouldered fellow who had never distinguished himself in any other pursuit than spelling" (48), and humorously illustrated (see Figure 2.8). His original, "seeing his name in print in the *Vevay Reveille*, stormed into the office intent upon thrashing the editor; he was pacified by an appeal to his pride as champion speller and in time came to bask in the glory of being in a book" (Randel, 126). And, Eggleston wrote, a young man "bearing the surname I had given to one of the rudest families in this book had to suffer many gibes while a student at an Indiana college. I here do public penance for my culpable indiscretion" (1892 edition, 23). Sarah MacLean Pratt's 1881 *Cape Cod Folks*, based on her experiences teaching school in a village called Cedarsville, also provoked reactions from represented locals (see Webb). She gave new names to urban characters based on real individuals, but did not see the villagers as potential readers

48   THE HOOSIER SCHOOL-MASTER.

This brought the excitement to fever-heat. For though Ralph was chosen first, it was entirely on trust, and most of the company were disappointed. The champion who now stood up against the school-master was a famous speller.

Jim Phillips was a tall, lank, stoop-shouldered fellow, who had never distinguished himself in any other pursuit than spelling. Except in this one art of spelling he was of no account. He could not catch well or bat well in ball. He could not throw well enough to make his mark in that famous Western game of bull-pen. He did not succeed well in any study but that of Webster's Elementary. But in that he was—to use the usual Flat Creek locution—in that he was "a hoss." This genius for spelling is in some people a sixth sense, a matter of intuition. Some spellers are born and not made, and their facility reminds one of the mathematical prodigies that crop out every now and then to bewilder the world. Bud Means,

JEEMS PHILLIPS.   foreseeing that Ralph would be pitted against Jim Phillips, had warned his friend that Jim could "spell like thunder and lightning," and that it "took a powerful smart speller" to beat him, for he knew "a heap of spelling-book." To have "spelled down the master" is next thing to having whipped the biggest bully in Hoopole County, and Jim had "spelled down" the last three masters. He divided the hero-worship of the district with Bud Means.

FIGURE 2.8 *Frank Beard, "Jeems Phillips," from Edward Eggleston,* The Hoosier School-Master: A Novel *(New York: Orange Judd and Company, 1871), p. 48.*

and left theirs unchanged. Angry letters, debates in print, and eventually legal action ensued. (There is also a much later and rather different instance in the 1940s, Zelma Cason's lawsuit against Marjorie Kinnan Rawlings.) Locals are not necessarily imagined into the national public—but those folks sometimes announce themselves.

The way Eggleston is poised at the intersection of multiple cultural systems is striking, although certainly not unique—rather, his complex position indicates how many overlapping transformations were under way at this moment in the nineteenth-century United States. His regional affiliation was revealingly complex. He maintained his ties to Indiana throughout his life although he traveled extensively and lived in many other places. Even within New York, he divided his time between the City and Lake George. On each site, I would argue, he was both insider and outsider. Eggleston's professional identity was complex as well. He had a long, intermittent career as a Methodist minister, as well as publishing prolifically in many genres. And from 1879 on, his best energies were devoted to writing American history. There was nothing unusual or even notable in a clergyman being a versatile man of letters, of course. But it was a long journey from the pious frontier youth who disapproved of worldly literature to the professional author who lobbied so hard and well for the international copyright that his colleagues arranged for one of his books to receive the first registration under the new law, who was one of the organizers of the American Historical Association, and was elected, at the very end of his life, to a term as its president.

According to his biographer William Randel, Eggleston had read very few novels when he composed *The Hoosier School-Master*; he later "confessed" that his only knowledge of plot construction had come from reading seventeenth-century French drama (123). He knew enough, however, to embed in the text coordinates for the nineteenth-century "cultures of letters" that Richard Brodhead has delineated. The narrator addresses several different imagined readers, warning against inappropriate expectations; we see both the developing distinctions among narrative kinds, and the fact that they are not yet fully developed and distinct. In the early chapter "The Struggle in the Dark"—about Ralph's dark night of the soul—the sensationalism of the story-papers is characterized in considerable detail:

> you, friend Callow, who have blunted your palate by swallowing the Cayenne pepper of the penny-dreadfuls, or of a certain sort of Sunday-school books, you wish me to make this night exciting by a hand-to-hand contest between Ralph and a robber. You would like it better if there were a trap-door. There's nothing so convenient as a trap-door, unless it be a subterranean passage. And you'd like something of that sort just here. It's so pleasant to have one's hair stand on end, you know, when one is safe from danger to one's self. But if you want each individual

hair to bristle with such a "Struggle in the Dark," you can buy trap-doors and subterranean passages dirt-cheap at the next news-stand.   (77)

Ralph's struggle remains spiritual—but exciting confrontations and narrow escapes do arrive later. When Ralph walks Hannah home after the spelling school, the narrator gestures briefly toward what Brodhead calls the domestic culture of letters—"You, Miss Amelia, wish me to repeat all their love-talk" (59)—and declines to accommodate that expectation as well. He does implicitly acknowledge an affiliation with that discourse as he goes on to address a very different reader: "And you, my Gradgrind friend, you think me sentimental" (59). The allusion (to Dickens) is literary, but Eggleston is not yet able to appeal confidently to the discourse of high culture—it is too early in the decade and too early in Eggleston's initiation into metropolitan values.

In some sense Eggleston is already writing social history here—he is, implicitly, analyzing the social life of reading. The novel contributes to language study, as well, through its careful representation of dialect. (As noted in Chapter 1, the project had not yet separated from literature; see Jackson.) Not long before, Eggleston had sent a list of "Hoosierisms" to James Russell Lowell, who both as the author of *The Biglow Papers* and as a professor of languages at Harvard was a great eminence in the field; as his biographer puts it, Lowell's "cordial reply was an incentive to continued work in dialect" (Randel, 105). Twenty-one years later, in the 1892 Library edition of *The Hoosier Schoolmaster*, the author added extensive notes on the usages in the book's dialogue, claiming and enhancing its contribution to scholarship. And he wrote a new preface in which he tells the story of the book's "origin and adventures" (5), including the fact that it was partly inspired by his reading Taine for the first time and an account of pirate publications informed by his later work on copyright. Placing the book as part of the movement of "provincial realism" (7) reminds us that readers interested in useful information (Gradgrinds and otherwise) might well have been reading his work for its credible accounts of American regional language and folk life. As I have argued elsewhere, our training makes it difficult for professional readers in the twenty-first century to recognize the fluidity of boundaries between literary, amateur, popular, and professional work, and how much everyday readers—both in the past and the present—value literature as a source of knowledge.

The continuities between Eggleston's literary and later historical work are easily visible (as others have noted). Just as he applied himself to understanding distinctions in the realm of fiction, he became an ardent student of the rigors of historical method. Eggleston is admired by historians today precisely for the way he combined literary sensibilities and professionalism. He was a prescient advocate for social and cultural history, aspiring to bring American history to life for a broad audience by writing well and portraying manners, customs, and language, focusing on how people experienced life rather than on politics and war. He was devoted to detail, undertaking meticulous archival research, and resisted teleological and simplifying narratives even though he aspired to narrate the full sweep of American history. These are dauntingly ambitious goals. Eggleston was drawn constantly on and back, researching the complex sources of the topics he wanted to understand. Already in 1881, his biographer tells us, he was writing to his daughter: " 'New Eng. history & all colonial hist. is a horrible labyrinth' ... In 4000 words of rough draft he had gathered the Pilgrims in England, persecuted them, and shipped them across the Channel. 'I hope to reach the settlement of Boston in the course of ten or fifteen years of work' " (Randel, 162). Indeed, the project was unrealizable, and the volume and scope of his publications never came close to his aspirations. Yet both the vision and the scholarship of *The Transit of Civilization from England to America in the Seventeenth Century*, a book Eggleston published in 1901—that is, after twenty years of research, and one year before his death—have been praised by historians like David Hall and Philip Gura. His popular textbooks are being reprinted and praised, as well.

From the perspective of this chapter, Eggleston is also prescient in his first novel as he addresses, implicitly but effectively, key issues in the history of education. His interest in dialect is part of this exploration, since schools are one of the sites in which the significance of language variation is negotiated. More directly—how much power should rest with local boards of education? What kinds of qualifications should teachers have? These are topics that were debated over and over as common schools emerged during the nineteenth century, and continue to be controversial today. In the twenty-first century, the debate has so far been framed through federal legislation. The emphasis on assessment of student learning in the 2001 "No Child Left Behind Act," and on teacher and principal performance evaluation and common standards in the 2009 "Race to the Top" fund, have had enormous impact, mostly in the direction of standardization. With "high stakes" assessments, teachers have little choice but to teach to the test. With $4.35 billion at stake, many states acted fast to embrace national education standards (see Lewin).

There has also been a powerful reaction against these measures. To judge by comments on the Amazon website, home-schooling parents are an enthusiastic audience for Eggleston's history books for children. (Given his anti-slavery and anti-imperialist politics, Eggleston would not have been pleased by some of their reasons for liking his work.) A different example: Mike Rose's *Why School? Reclaiming Education for All of Us* makes an eloquent case for moving in a different direction, in a small book with a cover depicting a one-room schoolhouse, and concluding with reflections on the continued relevance of such schools to our discussions of education. Discussions of curriculum and assessment are fraught and consequential precisely because they invoke situated and competing knowledges. Indeed, the public school as idea and institution is intertwined not only with the emergence of standard languages but also with the project of building a national citizenry, and with the very notion of modernity (discussed in Chapter 1).

Turning South: Education and Liberation

RICHARD MALCOLM JOHNSTON

The tales mentioned so far offer positive portraits of teachers. On the other hand, the Southern story "The Goosepond School" by Richard Malcolm Johnston paints the schoolmaster Israel Meadows as irredeemably cruel and ignorant. The story initially appeared under a different title in 1857, in the sporting journal *Porter's Spirit of the Times*; both its style and its site of publication exemplify the link between the movement and Southwestern humor discussed in Chapter 1 (see Mott). It was quickly reprinted in many Georgia newspapers and magazines, was central to several later collections of Johnston's stories of "Middle Georgia," and always remained his most popular story (Hitchcock, 50). His first collection, *Georgia Sketches*, added a second schoolhouse story, "How Mr. Bill Williams Took the Responsibility." Volumes published in Baltimore in 1871 and 1874 took the title remembered today, *Dukesborough Stories*, and the second edition included "Old Friends and New," a long story which added a kind, well-educated teacher to the Dukesborough cast of characters. Finally, an enlarged 1883 Harper paperback collection—the first publication that carried Johnston's name rather than the pseudonym Philemon Perch—brought him, late in life, national recognition as a literary man. The publication history of the story, in other words, indexes both the local and the national orientation of regionalism.

"The Goosepond School" is a drama of the one-room schoolhouse in which the balance of power between teacher and student is even more unstable than it is in *The Hoosier School-Master*. The opening of the story shows Israel Meadows terrifying his students, maintaining power over them by constant physical abuse; only the biggest, eighteen-year-old Allen Thigpen, is exempt from whipping because of his intimidating strength. Much of the action of the story focuses on the dilemma of Brinkly Glisson, who endures the teacher's beatings not because he is physically afraid but because he does not want to disappoint his widowed mother, who yearns for him to get an education. But Meadows is an imposter, with "a considerable amount of the wisdom of this world which comes to a man from other sources besides books" but only elementary skill at reading, writing, and arithmetic. Although he has represented himself as an educated man from South Carolina, he was born nearby and has "never been to school a day in his whole life" (14). An illegitimate son who had recently been caught continuing the family business of receiving stolen property, he got the school to earn money while his mother sells their homestead in preparation for their going west. His mercenary motives are the source of Brinkly's difficulties—the boy is promoted to the geography class, even though he does not read well enough to understand the book, to entitle Meadows to an extra tuition payment for an advanced topic.

Geography is the implicit terrain on which the characters' struggles play out. At the opening of the story, we hear over and over Brinkly's efforts to learn his "jography" (9) recitation—he speaks of "is-lands and promonitaries, thismuses and hemispheries" (19). We learn of the widow's pride "when she bought the new geography and atlas with the proceeds of four pairs of socks which she had knit with her own hands. What a world of knowledge, she thought, there must be in a book with five times as many pages as a spelling-book, and in those great red, blue, and pink pictures, covering a whole page a foot square, and all this knowledge to become the property of Brinkly!" (25). Equally to the point is the local geography with which Allen Thigpen confronts Meadows: "I've heern a man—a travelin' man—who stayed all night at our house on his way to Fluriday, say he knowed you. You ain't from South Calliner; I wish you was, but you ain't; you're from Columby County, and I'm ashamed to say it" (35). This place-intensive statement exposes not only Meadows's deception but his limited horizons. His world is small, and he thinks "a couple of days' journey" (11) has made him safe. Even with mispronunciations, even anchored to the humble, necessary detail of the socks, the Glissons understand more about geography because they take it not as a ground for cynical maneuver but as a vision of the wider world.

Brinkly eventually rebels, and triumphs because after learning Meadows's true origin Allen no longer accords him the authority of a schoolmaster and stops the other boys from assisting him. Still later, Brinkly does gain access to the wider world—in "Old Friends and New" the new teacher, George Overton (who hails from one of Eggleston's "celestial empires," Virginia), singles him out as a promising student and sponsors the fulfillment of his mother's hopes by sending him to college. But even in "The Goosepond School" Brinkly's honorable behavior is presented in terms derived from book-learning; when he wins his victory over the schoolmaster, his face shines "with those *gaudia certaminis* which the brave always feel when in the midst of an inevitable and righteous combat!" (31).

In the later story "Old Friends and New," George Overton comes to Dukesborough to study law with a local gentleman, agreeing in return to teach at a school built on his property. The gentleman's son is thus enabled to have the democratic experience of attending a one-room public school without the risk of encountering a teacher hired by trustees who could be fooled by someone like Meadows, or the rough-and-tumble contact zone we see in other stories in this chapter. The teacher himself does not feel endangered either; the "consciousness of having a very superior education...had precluded all apprehension of unfitness for the small duties of a country schoolmaster." As he begins his job, however, he intuitively recognizes that book-learning is not sufficient, and "all at once he felt a seriousness that was surprising to himself" (149). The story pays close attention to classroom interactions; Overton practices disciplinary intimacy, striving to repair the damage that Meadows has done and at one point overcoming a student's resistance simply by insisting that the boy sit on his lap. "People were surprised and somewhat disappointed to find how well their children advanced without the stimulus of the whip; indeed, it was soon found that this discipline was needed at home less than formerly. This did not look exactly right, and some people shook their heads. But the teacher was so handsome and gentlemanlike, and the children loved him so well and studied so hard, that even the oldest seemed to think that they might wait awhile and see what it would all come to" (172). Overton also exemplifies the topos I am studying by becoming involved, in one of the story's multiple plots, in a local romance—he gives private Latin lessons to the lawyer's daughter, and they fall in love over Virgil. But little genuine risk is entailed, and by the end of the story the complex relations of authority have been sorted out in tediously orderly fashion.

The stories discussed so far in this chapter are from what might be called the emergent period of local color, with the genres of the village sketch and Southwestern humor both represented. "A New England Sketch" was first published in 1855, and "The Goosepond School" in 1857, but their settings reach back further into the past. Stowe was working from her memory of already old stories she had heard as a child, and Johnston's autobiography indicates that his story is based on a school he attended at the age of seven, which dates it to 1829. Harte's tales and Eggleston's look back to the middle of the nineteenth century are among the first successes of the local color movement just before and after 1870, and are widely read through the late nineteenth century. Yet as we look later, and beyond the nineteenth into the twentieth century, it is easy to find representations of schoolteachers with similar elements. Indeed, I will be arguing later in this chapter that many of the key elements of the topos can be found in quite recent works (and I extend my argument to the present, and multiple media, in Chapter 5). We have already seen how different the thematic implications of such works can be, and— obedient to the approach to genre I sketched in Chapter 1—I would not argue that such works "are" necessarily local color. But as they narrate relations between local knowledge and book-learning, they illuminate both the stakes, and the range, of literary regionalism.

CHARLES CHESNUTT, W. E. B. DU BOIS, CONSTANCE FENIMORE WOOLSON

Charles Chesnutt's first novel, *Mandy Oxendine*, unpublished during his lifetime, offers a striking example both of long-term continuity in how the teacher is portrayed, and of the enormous range in how similar elements can be deployed. This work is set in the 1880s and was composed during the 1890s (the exact date is not known, and later changes may have been made to the version found in his papers that appeared in 1997). More than twenty-five years after *The Hoosier School-Master*, Chesnutt begins his story with a scene of arrival in which a teacher meets a trustee, and goes on to describe his ups and downs in a one-room schoolhouse and his rejection of whipping as a disciplinary strategy. In some sense the world described is bigger—Tom Lowrey arrives in Rosinville, North Carolina, not on foot but on the train. Jefferson Pate, who meets him and explains that he is the "only colored member er de school committee" (5), is thoroughly deferential to the light-skinned college student who has come to teach the community's African-American children. But we soon learn that Tom was born nearby, making him a returned native; he has chosen this school because the woman he loves, Mandy Oxendine, is living in the area. Although the novel is set many decades after "The Goosepond School," we encounter a similar expectation that local worlds are so self-contained enough that moving can conceal one's identity. Mandy is passing as white, without even changing her name: "the distance of seventy-five miles from their former home was a barrier as wide as the ocean between their past and their present life; for there was no railroad and no well established travel between the two places" (28).

The action of the novel is finally most concerned with Mandy's romances and the consequences of her passing, culminating in an elaborately plotted murder mystery—or to put it more analytically, with sexual danger inflected by class, race, and religion. But it is always interested in education and modernity. Mandy is attending the nearby white school at Snow Hill. She and her mother debate whether or not to attribute significance to breaking a mirror—Mandy says, "Mammy, you're too superstitious. Our teacher says them ole-timey signs an' omens an' conjurations don't mean anything, that it's foolish an' sinful ter believe in 'em" (68). In this passage and the novel as a whole, no credit is given to such traditions. Academic knowledge is passionately admired; Tom Lowrey has "gone away to an institute in a distant part of the State, where Northern philanthropy had provided opportunity for the higher education of colored youth. There the gates of a new world were unlocked for him. He learned of great nations that had lived and died, of great civilizations that had flourished and decayed, of great philosophies and great religious systems that had been swept away by advancing knowledge as fogs obscuring the light of truth; of great literatures, that had flowered and faded, and perished, leaving only a few of their choicest blossoms, to be forever the delight and the inspiration and the despair of mankind" (29). Yet we also know from Chesnutt's other works, especially his conjure stories, that he recognized "superstitions" as an expression of the community's subversive wisdom, and like Mandy's mother he critiques the limits of the system embodied in "readin' and writin', and cipherin'" (68). As I noted in Chapter 1, in "The Gray Wolf's Ha'nt," for example, both the frame narrator John and his sentimental wife Annie utterly fail to see the relationship between the philosophical account of transformation that he is reading and Uncle Julius's juxtaposed oral tale of shape-changing. Each is captive to one side of the opposition between abstract book-learning and local—thus concrete, affective, and vivid—knowledge.

The drive for African-American education, motivated both within that community and from the North, is a powerful element of Reconstruction history and continues into this post-Reconstruction period. The opposition between advocacy for higher learning and industrial education is familiar, and Chesnutt of course stands, here as biographically, with W. E. B. Du Bois against Booker Washington. Both Chesnutt and Du Bois affirm both the "intoxication of learning" (*Mandy*, 29) and the claims of locality. Indeed, I would argue that understanding either of them entails an effort to embrace that balancing act. Du Bois offers us an eloquent development of the topos of teacher as mediator in his essay "A Negro Schoolmaster in the New South," published—to "raves," his biographer tells us (Lewis, 232)—in the January 1899 *Atlantic Monthly* (the version cited below), and then republished as the fourth chapter of *The Souls of Black Folk* (1903). Here the autobiographical element present in all the works I have discussed so far is expressed directly. But particularly in its context in the book, it is clear that there is nothing idiosyncratic about the experience. We see Du Bois standing, like other teachers, between an intensely imagined locality and the inspiring city of intellect—both insider and outsider, in each world.

Du Bois begins with a gesture that combines the conventions of the folk tale and the personal narrative: "Once upon a time I taught school in the hills of Tennessee..." He accurately invokes the power of geography: those hills are "where the broad dark vale of the Mississippi begins to roll and crumple to greet the Alleghanies." And he deploys the power of the talented tenth, by definition racialized, by aspiration classed, and unambiguously gendered: "all Fisk men think that Tennessee—beyond the Veil—is theirs alone, and in vacation time they sally forth in lusty bands to meet the country school commissioners." Yet in the sentence that concludes this opening paragraph, it beckons to readers across race, class, and gender by returning emphatically and evocatively to the personal: "Young and happy, I too went, and I shall not soon forget that summer, ten years ago" (99).

Du Bois is clearly vulnerable at the opening of his essay. He is on foot, like Ralph Hartsook, seeking a school that will hire him. He is repeatedly refused: "I feel the deep weariness of heart and limb, as ten, eight, six miles stretch relentlessly ahead; I feel my heart sink heavily as I hear again and again, 'Got a teacher? Yes.' So I walked on and on" (99). In the remote neighborhood where he is finally hired, he enters into intimate relations with the locals; we learn what he eats, whose house is clean and whose is dirty, how sleeping arrangements are managed. Unlike Eggleston, Du Bois is consistently concerned to demonstrate the humanity and dignity of the locals. At one house, the Burkes's, he was at first "a little alarmed at the approach of bedtime in the one lone bedroom, but embarrassment was very deftly avoided. First, all the children nodded and slept, and were stowed away in one great pile of goose feathers; next, the mother and the father discreetly slipped away to the kitchen while I went to bed; then, blowing out the dim light, they retired in the dark." At another home, "they all went outdoors while the teacher retired, because they did not boast the luxury of a kitchen" (101). He is also frank about the difficulty of his situation. The rough schoolhouse and the challenges of his teaching are described concisely but closely, and contrasted with the "New England vision of neat little desks and chairs" (100) that haunts him.

As in so many other local color stories, these provincial parents are skeptical about the value of "book-learning"—Du Bois uses exactly that word. Like Ralph, he draws on exactly that learning to persuade them: "I put Cicero pro Archia Poeta into the simplest English with local applications, and usually convinced them—for a week or so" (101). There is no local romance, in the sense of a marriage plot, but he does fall in love with the people of the place, at large. This teacher's deepest vulnerability is how much he comes to care about them. He returns years later to learn what has become of his students and their families, now decisively an outsider; but their stories are told to him, and he retells them as an insider. His account of their sorrows—the early death of the vibrant Josie whose yearning for education first brought him to the community, the frustrated aspirations of others—is wrenching. And the chapter concludes with a sentence that is a reminder of the common situation the urban and educated Du Bois shares with the rural and illiterate: "Thus sadly musing, I rode to Nashville in the Jim Crow car" (104).

Du Bois is, above all, *involved*—with individuals, and through them with a community. The story of his two summers as a schoolmaster enables him to declare his affiliation with Black folk, but he never loses sight of particular people. And although this would seem to be the back of beyond—he walks until he is "beyond railways, beyond stage lines, to a land of 'varmints' and rattlesnakes, where the coming of a stranger was an event and men lived and died in the shadow of one blue hill" (99)—Du Bois also shows the place as crossroads for forces of change. It is emblematic in its isolation, "shut out from the world by forests" and "beyond the Veil" (99), but also connected by its orientation to the nearby town, by the networks of religion and economy, and above all by the locals' thoughts and aspirations. His own presence as teacher reflects and activates the yearning for broader horizons. Nor does he take for granted the unity of a face-to-face community—in fact, he is explicitly concerned with how a lived world is constituted. He writes, "I have called my tiny community a world, and so its isolation made it; and yet there was among us but a half-awakened common consciousness, sprung from common joy and grief, at burial, birth, or wedding; from a common hardship in poverty, poor land, and low wages; and, above all, from the sight of the Veil that hung between us and Opportunity" (102). What is the connection between fully attending to local truths, and fully awakening—which implies looking beyond them as well? Du Bois asks, "all this life and love and strife and failure,—is it the twilight of nightfall or the flush of some faint-dawning day?" (104). In the context of *The Souls of Black Folk*, the question opens to the broadest horizons of Du Bois's social theory, and questions I am working to address as well.

This is a divided world. So is Richard Malcolm Johnston's, of course, and that of every other author I have discussed. In "The Goosepond School" the Black world is invisible; we never see inside the white schoolhouse that Mandy Oxendine attends. There is nothing symmetrical about these occlusions, however. The power that resides on the other side of the Veil makes Black teachers far more vulnerable than white ones. In *The Hoosier School-Master* Ralph Hartsook is falsely accused and briefly in danger of lynching. In *Mandy Oxendine*, the noose is actually around Tom Lowrey's neck. Ralph is saved by his own clever maneuverings and his trustworthy ally Bud Means; Tom escapes only by a lucky, implausible coincidence. And let us remember that in the penultimate chapter of *Souls*, a schoolmaster is lynched. In "Of the Coming of John," John Jones is fundamentally transformed by his education and his experience of the North (the complexities and implications of that process, and the famous passages invoking Wagner, are beyond my scope here). When he returns to his remote Georgia home he has become alien enough that his community's pride turns to puzzlement. His teaching is beset by the familiar difficulties: it is "a long, hard pull to get things started in the rickety old shanty that sheltered his school. The Negroes were rent into factions for and against him, the parents were careless, the children irregular and dirty, and books, pencils, and slates largely missing" (260). But he makes progress—until his struggles are foreclosed by his clashes with the white Judge and his son. His school is arbitrarily shut down, as a threat to white supremacy. By the end of the chapter, after he defends his sister against sexual predation, he faces the mob and the "coiling twisted rope" (263) with no hope of rescue.

The horror of this moment is profound, although opinions differ about whether it is amplified or diminished by the melodramatic tone and virtually allegorical structure of the tale. For my purposes the key point is that the teacher's vulnerability here reaches its extreme point—and that his aspirations, his defiance, and his death are all the direct result of education. This is a Promethean view of the schoolmaster.

If one were tempted to generalize about the politics of local color, the contrasts among stories about education in the South during and after Reconstruction ought to provide a sufficient deterrent. For example, in striking opposition to Du Bois's work, Constance Fenimore Woolson's "King David" (1878) narrates the failure of a Yankee schoolmaster to connect with his students or improve them and their lot in any way. Where the author stands is debatable, but within the story racialist and racist claims portray that outcome as inevitable (see Rioux). The former slaves' passionate yearning for education is represented—initially, *everyone* comes to school. But they are compared to parrots, tortoises, and dogs, and the local planters' view that the freedmen have no "capacity for anything save ignorance" (111) is not questioned. A lesson is learned, but only by the teacher: "What a sight was that when the pale Caucasian, with the intelligence of generations on his brow, asked for the prayers of these sons of Africa, and gently, nay, almost humbly, received the pressure of their black, toil-hardened hands as they passed out! They had taught him a great lesson, the lesson of a failure" (122). Chesnutt's later stories about white teachers, "The Bouquet" (1899) and "The March of Progress" (1901), offer yet a third contrasting orientation, focalizing the story through both Black and white characters, engaging difficult emotional and ethical issues across the color line, and asking the reader to generate a mediating perspective.

In the latter story, for example, the African-American people of Patesville have newly gained control over the appointment of a teacher for their own school. The committee's choice is between Henrietta Noble, a white woman from New England who came South after the war to teach the freedmen and has stayed for fifteen years, and Andrew J. Williams, one of her former students. In familiar terms, he "had studied diligently, had worked industriously during his vacations, sometimes at manual labor, sometimes teaching a country school, and in due time had been graduated from his college with honors. He had come home at the end of his school life, and was very naturally seeking the employment for which he had fitted himself." The "progressive element of his people" supports him; as one of his advocates says, "the march of progress requires that we help ourselves" (424). But the story focuses rather on Miss Noble's vulnerability. She has no community beyond her African-American students and their families—the white Southerners have ostracized her, and when she visits her original home she has become a stranger. Those around her know that she is in ill health, but not that she has spent all her savings on medical treatment in New York; she badly needs her job. It falls to the humblest member of the school committee, Abe Johnson, to speak up—at the last minute and in dialect—on her behalf: "Fer fifteen long yeahs I has watched her incomin's an' her outgoin's. Her daddy was a Yankee kunnel, who died fighting fer ou' freedom. She come heah when we—yas, Mr. Chuhman, when you an' Br'er Cotton—was jes sot free, an' when none er us did n' have a rag ter ou' backs." He details her contributions, singling out individuals and mentioning specific times when she helped them, and asks how, when she has grown old and gray serving them, they can "talk erbout turnin' 'er out like a' old hoss ter die!" (426). Miss Noble is chosen; but ironically, the good news is too much for her weak heart— and with her death, progress marches on and Mr. Williams gets the job.

Many elements of "The March of Progress" are unambiguous. Education is prized; Abe Johnson attributes much of the progress of the community to their children being taught "sense an' manners an' religion an' book-l'arnin'" (425). The familiar topos of the teacher in local color—her engagement in the community, her links to knowledge and values located elsewhere, and her profound vulnerability— emerges clearly. Other elements are perhaps less straightforward. The tale has a satirical dimension, as the role of self-interest and self-deception in the political process is revealed. Yet the reader learns that precisely because the story is focalized partly through the erring committee members, who respond to Abe Johnson's eloquence and correct themselves. Although Chesnutt begins the story in a comic tone addressed to a white audience ready to condescend to colored people (the story was published in *Century*), his narrative shows an African-American citizenry deliberating seriously and effectively, and setting aside racial solidarity to do justice to a white woman. This community, like any group of human beings engaged in politics, is fallible—but public debate produces the right result in the end. This kind of double discourse, opening conventionally and open to a racist reading but swerving decisively toward a transformative one, is familiar to readers of Chesnutt's work.

An ambiguity that is less easily resolved—that perhaps cannot be resolved at all— resides in the tale's title. What are we to think of the "March of Progress"? Du Bois poses a similar puzzle when he incorporates his magazine essay on his teaching experiences into *The Souls of Black Folk* and retitles it "Of the Meaning of Progress." The assumption that enlightenment and prosperity naturally advance—indeed, unembarrassed boosting and boasting—is virtually normative in American public discourse during the same years that Jim Crow laws and lynching were constantly on the rise. For African-Americans in the post-Reconstruction era no reference to progress can be more than a step or two away from bitter irony. But also, Du Bois questions any affirmative view of change when he revisits the scene of his school-teaching summers and writes: "My log schoolhouse was gone. In its place stood Progress, and Progress, I understand, is necessarily ugly." In Chesnutt's Patesville, progress seems to be a juggernaut that crushes Henrietta Noble in its path. These stories—like so many of the teachers in local color—occupy multiple viewpoints simultaneously, valuing both the local and the metropolitan and struggling to find a balance between them. They neither reject the notion that history has a direction, nor reach a conclusion about its nature. Thus Du Bois writes, "How shall a man measure Progress there where the dark-faced Josie lies? How many heartfuls of sorry shall balance a bushel of wheat? How hard a thing is life to the lowly, and yet how human and real! And all this life and love and strife and failure,—is it the twilight of nightfall or the flush of some faint-dawning day?"

Education and Conquest: Zitkala-Sa and Gertrude Simmons Bonnin

There is no ambiguity about the meaning of progress in three autobiographical stories that a writer signing herself "Zitkala-Sa" published in *The Atlantic Monthly* in 1900. This next example, in a series that already extends over almost half a century, shows again the substantial endurance of the topos of the teacher as mediator, and how differently it is deployed in different historical circumstances. These essays (which did not appear in book form until 1921, in the collection *American Indian Stories*), are often discussed as regionalist, particularly by feminist scholars (that choice has also been criticized[2]). The arc of my argument about the nineteenth and early twentieth centuries closes with this work by the Yankton Sioux author Gertrude Simmons Bonnin.[3] It does not directly represent the one-room school-house—yet the models of education Bonnin deploys, and the historical framework required to understand them, tell us a great deal about the significance of the topos of the teacher in regionalism.

In *To Remain an Indian: Lessons in Democracy from a Century of Native American Education*, K. Tsianina Lomawaima and Teresa L. McCarty trace a history of Indian education and also (as their subtitle indicates) draw conclusions about how "Native visions for an Indigenously rooted and inspired education hold a promise for schools and a promise for a nation that can look cultural difference in the face, not as an enemy but as an ally" and offer a model for "meaningful, challenging, locally controlled education for all Americans" (170). They begin by challenging the equation of education with schooling, and direct attention to the cultural pattern of respect for the agency of the learner, and the embedding of instruction in the everyday institutions of indigenous societies (differently in different tribes, but in each case systematically). This is quite precisely what we see in Zitkala-Sa's "Impressions of an Indian Childhood." The essay's recurring theme is how the protagonist is instructed—constantly by her mother, and also through her fascination with the legends told by elders at the evening meal. (Bonnin's first book, in 1901, was *Old Indian Legends*.) When the little girl has "lessons" (21) in beadwork, she is expected to create her own designs, and her mother holds her to a high standard—yet the "quietness of her oversight made me feel strongly responsible and dependent upon my own judgment" (20). Her mother models the fundamental importance of respect and courtesy in human relations; the white teachers the narrator Zitkala-Sa encounters later are measured against this standard, and fall short.

Education is also the end—one might say the doom, or fall—toward which the story is moving. At its conclusion, drawn by the "big red apples" promised her by missionaries, the protagonist persuades her mother to send her east to school. At this moment it is not the tree of knowledge, but literal apples and curiosity, that tempt her. She writes that "it was not yet an ambition for Letters that was stirring me" [41]). The fact this line appeared in the *Atlantic* inscribes the success of that ambition into the story—and certainly it matters when we read in the context of Bonnin's life. Within the narrative, however, it is clear that the mother consents only because she believes her daughter "will need an education when she is grown, for then there will be fewer real Dakotas, and many more palefaces" (44). The essay that appeared the next month, "The School Days of an Indian Girl," narrates Zitkala-Sa's experience in boarding school, and shows that her mother was correct when she said, "I know my daughter must suffer keenly in this experiment" (44). Her pain is not caused by the cruelty of an individual, like that of the students at Johnston's Goosepond School, but stems more directly from the oppressive nature of the institution. Her story indicts the entire system of Indian schooling.

The suffering caused by the Indian boarding school, especially the off-reservation schools like Carlisle Industrial Indian School and those that followed it, has become the focus of a substantial literature. Zitkala-Sa/Bonnin's story includes the teachers' indifference to her misery, abusive corporal punishments, and the purposeful erasure of Native languages. In these essays, concluding with "An Indian Teacher among Indians," her experience is portrayed as profoundly traumatic and destructive. Yet her account is relatively mild compared to the secondary literature. Zitkala-Sa did not have access to the horrific statistics about the incidence of tuberculosis and trachoma in those schools—which would no doubt have been effectively deployed by the activist Bonnin. And I imagine that the historical person we seek through those names knew a great deal about what those numbers meant, and grieved. Richard Henry Pratt, the founder of Carlisle, famously advocated the policy "Kill the Indian...and save the man." The institution he creates is engaged in—using the title of another history (by David Wallace Adams)—*Education for Extinction.* There is a terrible accuracy in this equation of genocide and cultural assimilation.

Scholarship also reveals the struggles of Indian families and communities to shape the education of their children, and the children's resistance and resilience.

Zitkala-Sa's stories include an example of the latter, the often-quoted passage in which, instructed to mash turnips, she complies so forcefully that when the jar is lifted its bottom falls out: "I whooped in my heart for having once asserted the rebellion within me" (61). The incident takes on added significance when read in the context of her success as a resisting author, and—even more so—her subsequent career as a political activist. Gertrude Simmons was supposed to learn English—but not so well that she could criticize her schooling in the pages of the *Atlantic Monthly*, let alone lobby Congress, and co-found the National Council of American Indians. As Kiara Vigil notes, writing and speaking were central in the kind of political work that she did (181). Her life also provides supporting evidence for Brenda J. Child's argument that, because students from many tribes lived and worked together and formed close bonds, the off-reservation schools contributed to the formation of pan-tribal alliances and a sense of Native identity.

The understandable focus on the horrors of the boarding schools has obscured not only the complexity of their impact, but also the importance of the other models of Indian schooling that existed alongside them. There *were* also Indian day schools, and a few Native children attended public schools. We do not have completely reliable information, but Adams cites these numbers for government-run institutions in 1900: 7,403 students enrolled in off-reservation boarding schools; 9,604 in reservation boarding schools; and 5,090 in day schools. There were also 246 Indian students in public schools, and 4,081 in a variety of mission, private, and state schools (320). There had been and were, in other words, a substantial number of children attending educational institutions near their homes—no doubt, sometimes, one-room schoolhouses. As all these histories make clear, precisely what is at stake in the shift from day schools to distant boarding schools like Carlisle is that a classroom close to home is a mediating site. It connects the local and the national, rather than being fully under control of teachers and school authorities. The day school, from the point of view of white policy-makers, was just not doing its "civilizing" work. Even the reservation boarding school was not far enough from the influence of parents and community to have the desired effect. Zitkala-Sa is not writing about the one-room schoolhouse, but her work stands on the ground I have been exploring, making it clear how much is at stake in the classroom and demonstrating that different historical experiences can produce utterly different representations of the schoolteacher figure.

In her third *Atlantic* essay, Zitkala-Sa becomes "An Indian Teacher among Indians." The biographical record tells us that her stories track Gertrude Simmons's life closely (not exactly, but the points of variation are not relevant here). She was born on the Yankton Sioux reservations in 1876, and during her childhood attended two boarding schools, first the Quaker institution White's Manual Labor Institute in Wabash, Indiana, and then the Santee Normal Training School in Nebraska. Unusually, she went on to further study, at Earlham College in Indiana (another Quaker institution). Illness cut her studies short, and she took a position as a teacher—although the essay does not specify, it was at Carlisle. Zitkala-Sa/

Simmons has succeeded in school and attained the relatively powerful status of teacher, but the constant emphasis of her publications is on her vulnerability. Her studies, her unhappiness, and her compromised health are always linked; her schooling, her forced assimilation, make her sick.

In Zitkala-Sa's first essay, she is an Indian learner—it portrays the Native education that the school in her second essay is designed to prevent. Her third essay is nominally about teaching, yet there is no scene, no description of what it is like for her to be in a classroom interacting with students. The story is instead about "solving the problem of my inner self" (97), which requires that she confront the counterfeit nature of her official education and return to the status of learner; she leaves her post and embarks on an independent course of study. The essay concludes with a bitter verdict on the Indian school—in a remembered scene that foregrounds not the Indian teacher, but white visitors smugly satisfied by the misleading sight of "docile and industrious" (98) Indian children at their books. Few pause to ask, she tells us in the last sentence of the essay, "whether real life or long-lasting death lies beneath this semblance of civilization" (99). Progress is a disease not just for Zitkala-Sa herself but for her people.

Rejection of schooling does not necessarily mean the rejection of book-learning, however. That does appear: in Zitkala-Sa's second essay, when she is unhappy on a visit home, her mother tries to comfort her by offering "the only printed matter we had in our home"—the Bible. She accepts it courteously to avoid offending, but lays it aside unread: "my enraged spirit felt more like burning the book, which afforded me no help, and was a perfect delusion to my mother" (73). A space opens here between print and religion, which from "Uncle Lot" to *The Hoosier School-Master* and beyond have been allied. Of course religion and progress are also often opposed in the discourses of modernity (I will examine an instance of that rupture at the end of this chapter). The Book of Christianity is useless, toxic, to Zitkala-Sa at this point in her life. (Another of her *Atlantic Monthly* articles is "Why I Am a Pagan," which appeared in 1902, but later in life she converted to Catholicism and even sent her son Ohiya to a boarding school run by Benedictine sisters.) The problem was in fact that the schools did not have *enough* books. All schools for Indian students were designed to turn them away from local knowledge, and the central purpose of the off-reservation boarding schools was to block access to it—but they also locked the door to the library of Western learning.

The model of the Indian school was industrial education; it trained boys to be laborers, and girls to be domestic servants. It not only disregarded students' human needs and disrespected their culture, but also systematically underestimated their intellectual abilities. It was allied with Hampton and Tuskegee, not Fisk (Hampton, of course, like the institute in Indiana Simmons attended, enrolled both African-American and Indian students). Schools can open horizons, but they can also deliver the news that the student is going nowhere. A study by Bernadette Lear shows the literal library at Carlisle as the site of contestation. The famous Meriam Report in 1928 deplored the inadequacy of the books provided.

Yet some administrators and teachers, and the students themselves, worked to expand access to worldly knowledge. As Lear puts it, "books and reading enabled Native children to enact *and defy* the school's expectations, sometimes as part of a literary 'underlife' which existed outside of officially sanctioned curriculum and social activities" (167; emphasis in original). Conquest did not fully prevail. Zitkala-Sa/Simmons/Bonnin, and other Indian students and teachers, wrested knowledge from the gatekeepers of the institution and turned it to their own purposes.

Zitkala-Sa's autobiographical essays conclude, as I have noted, with her embarking on an arduous course of independent study. She is clearly reading Euro-American books—she does not return to Sioux lands but sites her work in "an Eastern city" (98). Reading today, however, I observe that she is embracing the learner-centered, inquiry-based model of Native education that Lomawaima and McCarty describe. We know from the biographical record that Simmons was (again unusually) studying the violin. I move here between interpretation and biography, as literary history so often does. These stories deploy the affecting figure of the educated Indian caught between two worlds—after the protagonist has bitten the apple, she is expelled from the primitive paradise into which she was born but has no secure place in modern civilization. Zitkala-Sa's work has often been read in that way.

What recent studies of Gertrude Simmons Bonnin tell us is that she used such conventions—and everything else that came to hand—to insert a counter-narrative into public discourse. She was challenged from all sides. Her *Atlantic* essays, and later a *Harper's* story in which she depicted a white-educated boy returning to his tribe as a missionary and failing catastrophically, were attacked in a Carlisle newspaper. Yet she managed to maintain her relationship with Pratt for quite some time. (Vigil analyzes the advantages of their relationship for both parties.) She moved in a world of Indian impersonators, and in 1918, after she testified before a Congressional subcommittee in native dress, her authenticity was questioned. But as Cari Carpenter argues, when Bonnin performed her Indianness in public "her challenge was not to maintain her connection to an American Indian identity but rather to fine-tune the public persona that was most amenable to her activist work" ("Detecting Indianness," 140). She was always Sioux, and always a mediator.

In the series of narratives I have discussed since turning South to examine "The Goosepond School," the figure of the schoolteacher is mobilized in ways that register, with exquisite historical sensitivity, the distinctive situation of different groups. There are considerable commonalities, which I will review at the beginning of the next section—it is vital to my literary-historical argument to see those strong connections. But differences are also key—the way Johnston can leave racial identity unmarked but Chesnutt or Du Bois cannot, the turn to concern with authenticity and its link to community that surfaces even in Zitkala-Sa's first essay when her mother anticipates that there will be few "real Dakotas" (44) in the future. These stories *not* about the one-room schoolhouse show us what happens in the classroom as not only a connection or a contest between knowledges, but as, in some historical situations, a struggle to the death. We do know how much schools matter. We see it, writ small in the bitter politics of local school board elections, and writ long in the push and pull between districts, and state boards, and federal powers. The stakes are never higher than in Gertrude Simmons Bonnin's work.

I have been looking in some detail at the implications of particular works at particular moments. But I am most concerned, in this chapter, to track the figure of the schoolteacher over time—to follow the warp rather than the weft of the fabric of discourse. Let us continue on into the twentieth century.

The Topos Persists

The topos of the vulnerable yet powerful teacher, connecting the intensities of local knowledge with the risky prospects of book-learning, continues on into the twentieth and the twenty-first century. Sometimes the elements I have analyzed so far repeat in remarkable detail. There are scenes of arrival. Scenes of negotiation about positions in schools, and of negotiations in classrooms. Emotional connections with students and local romances. Emotional and physical threats to the teacher. All persist in American fiction.

Perhaps the most widely read examples in the twentieth century are set in Appalachia: *The Thread That Runs So True*, a 1949 memoir by Jesse Stuart, and Catherine Marshall's 1967 bestseller *Christy*—a novel based on her mother's life that (although almost unnoticed in the academy) remains popular and influential. I also consider more recent bestsellers, Frank McCourt's memoirs (like Bonnin's work, *not* about the one-room schoolhouse); and I discuss two literary fictions: Raymond Kennedy's *Romance of Eleanor Gray* (2003) and (in a final sustained analysis) Ernest Gaines's *A Lesson before Dying* (1993). I could choose other examples. It would be challenging to parse how *A Jest of God* (1966), one of Margaret Laurence's Manawaka novels that focuses on a schoolteacher, connects but contrasts—or how Daniel Black's 2005 *They Tell Me of a Home* both foregrounds and backgrounds the teacher. (Something would have to be said about Manitoba and Arkansas, and the literary-historical formations we call Canadian and African-American literature, as well.) The examples I have chosen are the ones that carry my argument in the most direct line.

JESSE STUART AND FRANK MCCOURT

Jesse Stuart's account of his years in Kentucky schools, *The Thread That Runs So True* (1949), is a classic both in its region and in the field of education. Stuart was born in 1906 in Greenup County, Kentucky, the son of impoverished tenant farmers. His father could not read or write, and his mother had only a second-grade education. He became a teacher, later a principal and school superintendent, and a prolific and successful poet, short story writer, and novelist; he is a much-loved figure in Appalachia and especially in his home state. Education is a central theme of his work, and over the course of his life he gave hundreds of talks to teachers' organizations all over the country (*Jesse Stuart on Education*, 2). Stuart's biographer Ruel Foster describes the favorable reception of *The Thread That Runs So True*: "Reviews in newspapers all across the country seconded the praise of Dr. Jay Elmer Morgan, founder and president of the National Education Association, who ... [called it] the best book on education written in the last fifty years." Writing in 1968, Foster reports that the book not only sold well initially but "has continually increased its sale each year. Its readers have mailed thousands and thousands of letters to Stuart. Even today his mail carries eight to ten letters a day from people who are ignited by his interest in teaching" (27). That was written more than forty years ago, but the book seems never to have gone out of print, and is still available today. Readers are still writing appreciative responses, although now on Amazon. com—not frequently, but consistently.

Stuart's memoir echoes *The Hoosier School-Master* in many ways. The book's first sentence is another scene of arrival: "Monday morning when I started on my way to school, I had with me Don Conway, a pupil twenty years of age, who had never planned to enter school again" (1). The new teacher, like Ralph Hartsook, is boarding with a trustee and enlists the muscular son of the house to protect him. At this isolated rural school, in a place he calls Lonesome Valley, he is seen as an outsider, although (again like Ralph) he comes from nearby. Almost immediately he must fight an enormous student who has beaten up previous schoolteachers (the most recent, in this case, Stuart's sister). One difference is that he wins this and subsequent battles, and earns local respect, through strength as well as pluck. During the course of the book he faces many discomforts and dangers, from the hardships of his boarding arrangements to being pelted by rotten vegetables and eggs to a very serious attempt on his life. Stuart is vulnerable but also powerful, not only winning his fights but also winning his students' affection and making a real difference in their lives. There are scenes of him rising to the challenge of teaching children of many different ages in the one-room schoolhouse, and of his students at subsequent schools triumphing in academic contests against larger and better-equipped schools.

Eggleston's *Hoosier School-Master* implies that good teaching means connecting book-learning with everyday life; Stuart is explicit and emphatic on that point. In the opening section, he and Don Conway measure and use arithmetic to calculate the number of bushels in a local man's wagonload of coal, and tell him that he has underestimated it; the man takes it to be weighed and realizes that for years he has been selling forty-three bushels for the price of twenty-five. In another memorable scene, Stuart and his students settle a dispute between two men over the size of a field; each had stepped it off, but one is tall and one is short. Stuart writes, "I have often thought that if a little simple learning and arithmetic hadn't been applied here, one of these men would have killed the other before a lawsuit was filed in court. My students were seeing the practical appliance of simple learning to everyday problems" (52). He resents teaching from dull textbooks, and when he gives writing assignments does not use the books' topics but tells his students to "write about the things they knew about: people, places, things, and adventures in Lonesome Valley" (58). This is not only a matter of making academic topics seem relevant—the connection goes both ways, as his students' games at recess inspire Stuart to create a successful pedagogy based on active play for his youngest students. Stuart's commitment to dialogue may be compared to the now better-known pedagogy of Paulo Freire; throughout, he demonstrates his respect for local knowledge and culture. Indeed, his admiration for the abilities of his students—and, when he becomes a principal and supervisor, the dedication of his teachers—is matched only by his frustration with the school system. There *are* things about Kentucky he wants to change.

The power of *The Thread That Runs So True* lies in the way it combines vivid local detail with a passion for education. Stuart tells his teachers that despite their low pay and poor working conditions, even though they are not always treated respectfully, they should "walk proudly, with their heads high, and to thank God they had chosen the teaching profession—the mother of all professions; that they were members working in the front line of American democracy, that they were the ground roots and not the brace roots of American democracy. I believed this deep in my heart and brain. That the teaching profession was the greatest profession of them all" (202). Throughout his long life Stuart returned to writing about his experience in the schools. The theme of education runs through Stuart's fiction as well. His often-reprinted story "The Split Cherry Tree" (first published in *Esquire* in 1939) portrays, from the first-person perspective of a student, a farmer from the hills angrily confronting his son's teacher. But the professor treats him with respect, and he is won over to believe in the value of higher education (which here means high school). The two men first find a common footing through their masculinity—they recognize each other's courage and sense of duty. (Much more could be said about the gender politics of the story.) They become friends—on the basis of the common belief in progress, so at the story's conclusion they are not equals on level ground. The father says to his son, "I am as strong a man as ever come out'n th' hills…But I'm behind, Dave."[4] This linking of space and time is familiar, and the association of the Appalachian mountains with the past is particularly powerful and ambivalent, as I will go on to discuss. Stuart is carried, not so much by his advocacy for education as by the power of the chronotope itself, into an uncharacteristically uncritical view of the centralized school and modernity.

It is worth stopping to note that I have been tracing the figure of the schoolteacher through a series of fictions, and Stuart is deploying it in a memoir. It tells us something about the reach and power of this topos that, when Stuart reached for a way to tell his story, these conventions from local color came to hand. The uniformity with which the works in this series include an autobiographical claim is also striking—I did not deliberately set out to find examples of the porous boundary between fiction and life-writing. But different kinds of writing claim different kinds of authority, and those of regionalism tend to be close to the ground. Readers and reviewers *have* questioned the accuracy of many of these works (including those of the next writer I will discuss). But that is not my concern. We should note as well that when he published *The Thread That Runs So True*, Stuart avoided Eggleston's mistake and changed the names of people and places—a clear indication that he was concerned with broad truths rather than exact fidelity to what happened, as well as of his better knowledge of the world of letters. Considerations of authenticity and authority are woven throughout this volume. But what matters here is the topos of the teacher as insider and outsider, as mediator between different kinds of knowledge. In much of Stuart's work, it takes on an almost utopian cast.

That is so as well in my most recently published example—although prospects for the teacher transforming not only his students, but also the system, are dimmer. One of the most widely read life-writers of recent years, Frank McCourt, by his own account becomes an adult who knows himself, and has something to say to others, through his experience as a teacher. McCourt's memoir of his impoverished Irish childhood, *Angela's Ashes* (1996), written after he retired from twenty-seven years in New York City public high schools, was a bestseller and won many awards including the Pulitzer Prize. He writes about his own schooling in that book, but does not become a teacher until the story's continuation in *'Tis* (1999). *Teacher Man* (2005) focuses on that experience. Perhaps I should call these counter- or semi-examples, for these are texts like Bonnin's focused on institutions that diametrically oppose the one-room schoolhouse.

Both the second and third volumes of McCourt's trilogy were bestsellers, although more modestly successful than *Angela's Ashes*. In them he portrays the massive buildings and mean classrooms of urban schools. McCourt is emphatically not a local, not from the next town or the next county or even the next state; his brogue marks him immediately as a foreigner (despite his American birth). Nor is he in physical danger—he worries about the "blackboard jungle," but faces only drudgery and constant embarrassment. But his self-portrait connects with the topos because his refusal to conceal his vulnerabilities proves to be his most valuable resource. McCourt reacts to everything humanly and spontaneously, earning the close attention of his students and reproofs from his supervisors. (The most remarked-on instance is when, on his first day, he picks up and eats a thrown sandwich [*Teacher Man*, 15–19].) He is challenged by his students and tells the truth—that, for example, he never attended high school himself. The story is, again and again, about how the classroom comes *alive* as a site of contact and transformation for both teacher and student. Memorably, McCourt recognizes the creativity mobilized when they forge notes excusing their absences, and asks them to write in that genre. As the Amazon.com reviewer Shawn Carkonen puts it, he is "a kindred spirit with more questions than answers." Most crucially, McCourt finds many years' accumulation of unmarked compositions in the closet of his first classroom, and has his students read and transcribe them; they are fascinated by these traces left by their predecessors (in some cases literally their parents), and begin to take an interest in writing their own life stories. He tells them his own story—he is, he says again and again, saved by the students' confronting him, recognizing him, asking him for his life. Thus McCourt's long memoir dramatizes its own conditions of possibility in the classroom.

CATHERINE MARSHALL AND RAYMOND KENNEDY

Looking at the work of Stuart and McCourt suggests that the kind of story about teachers I have been tracking spoke to twentieth-century and continues to speak to twenty-first-century readers. That is confirmed by Catherine Marshall's *Christy*. It was a bestseller, and later the basis for a short-lived television series (1994–5)—which led to its return to the bestseller list for a time—and a series of TV movies.[5] It helped to establish the genre of evangelical romance. The annual awards for excellence in Christian fiction established in 1999 are, in fact, named the Christy Awards—honoring Marshall for her many books (including the famous biography of her minister husband, *A Man Called Peter*) but of course with a special nod to *Christy*. The Awards website calls it her best-known work, "estimated to have been read by more than 30 million people."

The novel, set in 1912, tells the story of Christy Huddleston, a nineteen-year-old girl who is inspired by a talk at a church conference to volunteer to teach at a mission in the Smoky Mountains. When Christy arrives in her one-room schoolhouse, a scene that has become familiar to readers of this chapter unfolds. She faces a crowd of students of many different ages, including hostile older boys larger than she is. Some of the elements seem to come almost directly from *The Thread That Runs So True*—her concern over the unsanitary communal drinking gourd, for example, and her distress at the amber splotches on the fresh white schoolhouse paint caused by students spitting tobacco juice. She is endangered on that first day in a quite original way, however—by marbles heated in the stove and left where she will pick them up—but like Ralph Hartsook she is saved by a student who loves her at first sight.

There is a great deal that precedes this scene, however, and shapes readers' responses to it. The first-person narrative of Christy's first year at Cutter Gap is introduced by a prologue set in the present day of the novel's 1967 publication, also in the first person, in which Christy's daughter tells the story of the visit there that led her to write the book. This doubled first-person framing both claims and disclaims the truth of the narrative: "Suddenly, I understood how the story should be written—through mother's eyes, as I had seen it all along. Only, from the beginning, my imagination had taken hold of the true incidents and had begun shaping them so that now, after so many years, I myself scarcely knew where truth stopped and fiction began" (7). This is an even more vertiginously complicated authenticity than Eggleston basing *The Hoosier School-Master* on his brother's experience. Indeed, the narrative's claim to authority is both more individual and more cosmic. It repeatedly suggests that someone else's words have the capacity to lead a character to listen for the voice of God—and that He may speak directly to them. Taken on its own terms, the novel's warrant is in the reader's response.

The novel's complex framing also ensures that its opening is layered with scenes of arrival. The present-day trip segues into the story of Christy's first journey from her home in Asheville (North Carolina) to Cutter Gap (Tennessee). She arrives at the nearest town by rail, and has her determination tested when no one is there to meet her and everyone she talks to advises her against going on. But she persuades the postman to let her accompany him up into the mountains, and her long, difficult walk through the snow is described in detail. It includes her first encounters with the mountain people, and a dramatic delay while Bob Allen, who was to have collected her from the train but instead met with a serious accident, undergoes life-saving surgery on the kitchen table of a mountain cabin. When she finally falls exhausted into bed at the mission, we have been carried four full chapters into the novel.

I think it matters that Christy travels with the postman, who metonymically suggests the power and the limits of both communications circuits and the federal government. During their first conversation Mr. Pentland dramatically recites a slogan Christy has not heard before: "Neither rain—nor snow—nor heat—nor gloom of night—will stay these couriers from the swift completion of their appointed rounds" (39). This rings in another truth-claim—the author has done historical research. Those lines (minus the declamatory dashes) are a translation from Herodotus inscribed on the façade of the main post office in New York City, which was indeed built in 1912. Satterwhite's study of fan letters shows that readers were convinced that the novel was a truthful source for learning about the region (144). To me it seems unlikely that a postman in Appalachia would already have heard them, or been told them by "the gov-ment in Washington" (39)—they have no official standing with the U.S. Postal Service—but perhaps Marshall's investigation turned up some evidence mine did not. In any case the effect of the passage, and the opening as a whole, is to call attention to this particular place as connected to the nation, but also to its remoteness.

These opening chapters are also layered with expressions of affiliation and distancing gestures. Christy's daughter cannot visit the community of Cutter Gap, only its site (often called the Cove), for it has become part of the national park and is now inhabited by "Forest rangers and tourists" (2). Yet she knows these scenes intimately through her mother's stories. Christy is also from the Appalachians, and she feels called and connected to the mountain people; yet as someone from the flat lands she speaks, dresses, thinks differently. Indeed, she is told that "Back in the Cove they don't take much stock in foreigners," and when she replies, "I'm an American citizen, born right in these mountains," she learns that anyone not from the Cove is a foreigner (25). Like Ralph Hartsook and so many others, she is both an insider and an outsider. Emily Satterwhite shows that Marshall occupied the same position—a native, but also a scholar, of the Appalachians. When a correspondent offered to introduce her to locals, she "bristled" and insisted on her roots in the region—but she also had to admit she needed the help (144).

Marshall relies heavily on Appalachian stereotypes. Indeed, according to Satterwhite, *Christy* (along with James Dickey's *Deliverance*) has helped carry them into the twenty-first century (131). These mountain people are barefoot, impoverished, dirty, ignorant, superstitious, suspicious of flatlanders, and carry on murderous feuds. The equation of space and time, with travel up into the "backward" hills as entering the past, cannot get any more explicit. "I had a strange otherworldly feeling. It was as if, in crossing the mountains with Mr. Pentland, I had crossed into another time, another century, back to the days of the American frontier…Ours was the century of progress, everyone said—electric lights and telephones and steam locomotives and automobiles. Yet in this cabin it was still the eighteenth century. I wondered if all the homes in the Cove were as primitive as this one" (43). Quickly, however, we learn that there is a positive dimension to the insularity and rusticity of the "highland" people as well. Cutter's Gap is a close community, preserving traditions like communal work days and old knowledge like ballads and quilt patterns. Their archaic English is beautiful and connects them to spiritual tradition, as well. Christy reflects, while reading the Bible aloud at a mission-sponsored Sewing Circle, that "the language of Scripture did not sound strange to these women because the King James translators had been closer to the Cove speech than was present-day English. Every day I heard 'aye' and 'verily' and 'at cock-crow' and 'thrice' and 'brutish' and 'noisome' and 'hireling'" (188). The notion that Appalachian backwoods speech is this kind of survival is of course widespread, although it is indefensible according to linguists (see Montgomery).

The benighted locals turn out, however, to need assistance even in claiming their own past. The Cutter Gap mission led by the Quaker Alice Henderson is reaching them precisely by teaching them to value their traditions. One example: as so often, local knowledge is particularly valued when it can produce marketable crafts. Weaving is "almost a lost art in the Cove," but at the sewing circle the women are encouraged to restore an old foot-loom and use plants to dye what they make, with the promise that they will be able to get badly needed "cash-money" for their wares (190–1). The novel certainly does contain affirmations of the need for negotiation between local knowledge, and information and authority that come from a distance. We are frequently alerted, for example, that the mission's minister David Grantland—who is from Pennsylvania, and has just graduated from the seminary—is insufficiently respectful to the natives, and mentions abstruse conversations he had at school much too often. And Christy learns much from the intuitive spiritual insights of Fairlight Spencer, a mountain woman who becomes her close friend. But her central mentor is Alice Henderson, another arrival from Pennsylvania who strikes a better balance between attention to the local and book-learning—which here, as so often, includes knowledge of the Book. Christy's reflection on how receptive the mountain women are to the Bible arises because Alice has chosen exactly the right stories, ones that resonate with the women's lives. Again, the charitable visitor is giving the natives access to their own experience. The local and the educated characters do not stand on equal ground.

Like the other teachers in this chapter, Christy is clearly both vulnerable and powerful. She is at emotional risk, filled with uncertainty about both her calling and her competence. She is in physical danger again and again—when she must cross a slippery log bridge on her first walk up to Cutter Gap, from the hot marbles and threatened assaults by violent men, and at the conclusion of the novel when she comes very close to dying of typhoid (caught while nursing one of those big dangerous boys in her classroom). She also clearly has resources, both educational and personal. Despite her self-doubts she is successful in her teaching, successful at connecting with the mountain people, and quickly attracts the liking and respect of all the other central characters. In the image of a slender girl rising to great challenges, the figure of the threatened yet resourceful schoolteacher blends seamlessly with the romance heroine.

Christy is well-named—the novel is not a narrative of community, but follows its protagonist. Like many of the reformers in settlement houses, Christy is only somewhat successful in her work for social change—but very successful at finding personal transformation. The question of how the local ought to be connected to the wider world remains, however, central to the resolution of the story. Christy has two suitors. (Actually she has more—she is very attractive to the mountain men, including one of her students—but only two are treated as real possibilities.) The obvious, and wrong, choice is David Grantland. The right choice is Neil MacNeill, the doctor who operated on Bob Allen.

Christy (and we) met Dr. MacNeill as he was saving a life by his knowledge not only of modern medicine, but also of how to talk appropriately to his patient's family about the procedure and manage their participation (for example, accepting their driving an ax into the floor under the table where he operates to reduce bleeding). He proves in fact to *be* a local, telling Christy when she visits his home, "I was born in this cabin. So were my parents and my grandparents. So you see— I'm a hillbilly." She responds, quite pertinently, "You don't talk like one" (140). Benefactors he met while his uncle was guiding a vacation hunting trip made it possible for MacNeill to attend college, and then medical school. He is also—we learn in a lengthy story told by Alice Henderson—the scion of the aristocratic Scottish family that brought the mountain people here. Dr. MacNeill's authority derives both from the past and the modern—both from inside and "outside" (140).

There is no evidence that Marshall was thinking of Hardy, but what she portrays is the return of the native. It is equally unlikely that she was referencing Garland's "Up the Coulee," but Dr. MacNeill is both Grant and Howard McLane. Small wonder that he is moody and unpredictable. He is also a brilliant solution to the problems the novel poses. His skepticism and distance from the church have worried Christy throughout the novel. But the "stiff-necked" (557), educated doctor—doubly insulated against belief because he is not only a modern but a mountain man, and they expect religion to be confined to the women's pews on Sundays—turns finally to prayer. He surrenders, as Christy is close to death, to the power of love and to God's will. She has put herself at risk for her students but also for him—she saves his soul, and their connection pulls her back into life. The "staying power" Satterwhite recognizes in the novel (131) has a great deal to do with its address to believing readers. I suggest that it also derives from its connection to regionalism, and from its effective use of the topos of the teacher as a mediator between times and places.

Raymond Kennedy's 2003 *Romance of Eleanor Gray* deploys that topos as well. Kennedy was a native New Englander, and his work is always linked to the region—his appearance in this chapter is unsurprising. But his work is generally considered dark and even "absurdist," and he missed popular success while being admired by other writers—so Catherine Marshall and he make an unusual pair. Yet there are some striking parallels between *Christy* and *Eleanor Gray*.[6] The novel's action takes place in 1910, and its protagonist is a girl who has bravely left her family to teach school in the rural Berkshire hills of Massachusetts. It begins with a scene of arrival in which she travels to her new job—with the local postman, in fact. *The Romance of Eleanor Gray* is fundamentally shaped by the equation of temporality and geography, in New England rather than Appalachia. As she travels to her school Eleanor thinks: "The day-long journey struck her at times as a kind of regression, as though she were traveling backward in both time and space, retreating mile by mile from the crowded electrically lighted world of her growing-up years in Fall River to some remote agricultural outpost, where—how should she put it?—where time had stopped, where tilling and planting and harvesting—and milking and wood gathering and other such rudimentaries—had probably not changed in centuries" (2). No critical perspective on this reaction is developed; in fact Kennedy endorses it, in an interview printed in the book.

Eleanor's situation offers another version of the topos of the schoolteacher as mediator between different worlds. Its familiarity, I would argue, helps make it almost plausible that she immediately engages the admiration and affection of her new community, despite the fact that her behavior is often odd and invasive as she becomes obsessed with a former student at the school, Evangeline Sewell. The themes remain regional—Evangeline is from a still more remote area, and this regression beyond regression works in the same way as for example Jewett's successive removals, in *Country of the Pointed Firs*—to Dunnet Landing, then to Green Island, then to the pennyroyal grove. But Kennedy's novel becomes increasingly difficult to read in terms of the topos that concerns me. That is not because Eleanor's schoolhouse has two classrooms (with the lower and upper grades separated), or even because so little attention is devoted to her teaching, but because it is almost wholly focused on her interior life. The story behind the story is that Evangeline has been made pregnant by the other teacher in the school. But Eleanor is not interested in being a mediator, and soon the narrator seems to lose interest in those issues. Disengaging from the topos of the teacher is not, of course, necessarily a fault in the novel. It does, however, mean that it loses connection with a long-inhabited realm of meaning, and on my reading it does not locate another. And, indeed, the novel has had (at least so far) little impact.

ERNEST GAINES

I close my series of examples with two novels by a writer who has been both widely read and critically praised: Ernest Gaines. His early work was somewhat coldly received, Jeff Karem argues, because it did not fulfill the expectations placed on African-American fiction in the 1960s. *The Autobiography of Miss Jane Pittman*, published in 1971, was his breakthrough, its success in print enlarged by the award-winning 1974 film. Education is thematized at various moments in the novel, from Jane's attendance at a freedmen's school (67) through the series of teachers in the one-room schoolhouse on the Samson plantation. Miss Jane's memories mark out the various forms that the failure of education can take. The first teacher is too focused on uplift, driving students away by insisting on ties, hair ribbons, and toothbrushes (160–4). The second is out for himself, exploiting the students and their families, and is driven out of the parish (164–5). The third becomes a tragic mulatta figure (166–207). Finally, Jimmy, a local boy who had helped his elders with reading and writing, who carries their hopes, participates in the Civil Rights movement; when his mother says, "I wanted him to be a teacher or something," Miss Jane replies: "He is a teacher" (254). Jimmy is both vulnerable and powerful, though that formulation is scarcely adequate: he is shot to death, but the community is transformed as others are inspired to join the movement. I would certainly not argue that the *Autobiography of Miss Jane Pittman*'s success resulted from its inclusion of multiple images of schoolteachers—but they may be taken as a metonym for Gaines's shift to engagement with established topoi.

If *Miss Jane Pittman* suggests the continued relevance of the figure of the teacher, in 1993 *A Lesson before Dying* demonstrates that the topos I have been tracing can still form the core of a powerful and widely read novel. It was nominated for the Pulitzer Prize, won the National Book Critics Circle Award, and was an Oprah's Book Club selection. It became the basis for both a film and an off-Broadway play. After its success, Gaines's publisher reprinted all his fiction in paperback. Certainly education is not all that this novel is about—it is deeply engaged with the politics and ethics of capital punishment, for example. But the situation of the schoolteacher as insider and outsider, the value and limits of different kinds of knowledge, are central—and not only central, but also deeply reconsidered, reworked, renewed. Seeing the novel placed in this long tradition helps us, I believe, to understand why it is so compelling, and to appreciate its achievement.

A Lesson before Dying is set in rural Louisiana in 1948. It is narrated by Grant Wiggin, who has returned from his college education to teach in a one-room school on the plantation where he was raised. Grant is most certainly a local—he attended that very school himself, and as he watches his students can remember doing the same things. When he walks through the plantation cemetery, he sees the graves where his ancestors have been buried for the past century. Grant's local knowledge oppresses him; he knows what each family will bring to the Christmas program, he "had heard the same carols all my life, seen the same little play, with the same mistakes in grammar. The minister had offered the same prayer as always, Christmas or Sunday. The same people wore the same old clothes and sat in the same places" (151). Grant wants to leave, has left, and returned because he cannot escape his commitment to the aunt who raised him and to the community.

Grant's Tante Lou expects that loyalty; the other Black elders respect it and take advantage of it, although some of them—especially the community's religious leader—suspect that he is no longer one of them. At one point, when Grant disclaims knowledge of God and sin, he seems so alien that Reverend stops addressing him directly: "'My Lord,' the minister said, looking at me as if I were the devil himself. 'Listen to the teacher of our children'" (182). The whites who surround them are even more suspicious. At the plantation's big house—dating from the antebellum days of slavery (17)—he is tolerated for his aunt's sake, but treated almost as an outsider. "I was too educated for Henri Pichot; he had no use for me at all anymore" (21). Sheriff Guidry tells him he is "too smart for your own good" (49). Grant himself feels like an alien. And he has before him the consequence of such estrangement from self and community whenever he thinks about his teacher Professor Antoine, who died at forty-three, consumed by "hatred for himself as well as contempt for us" (62). Again the teacher is both insider and outsider; Gaines takes that tension to an extraordinarily painful level.

A Lesson before Dying does not begin with a scene of arrival, but read in this context its opening words epitomize Grant's paradoxical location. He cannot arrive, because he has always been there, but he is never fully present—any more than he is fully absent. These lines are indeed a trope, brilliantly twisting the figure we have seen before: "I was not there, yet I was there. No, I did not go to the trial. I did not hear the verdict, because I knew all the time what it would be. Still, I was there. I was there as much as anyone else was there" (3).

The passage refers to the murder trial and guilty verdict that motivate the action of the novel. Jefferson, a young man from the plantation, has been unjustly convicted. His white attorney defended him by arguing that he is not a man, not a human being who can be held responsible, but a boy, a fool, a thing; in words that resonate throughout the novel, he says, "I would just as soon put a hog in the electric chair as this" (8). Grant is challenged—indeed, required—by his aunt and

Jefferson's godmother Miss Emma to visit Jefferson in jail and in the short time before his execution to teach him to (as Miss Emma puts it) "make him know he's not a hog, he's a man" (21).

The opening situation of the novel epitomizes the failure of education. Professor Antoine's bitter prediction to Grant and his fellow students seems to be holding true: "he told us then that most of us would die violently, and those who did not would be brought down to the level of beasts. Told us that there was no other choice but to run and run" (62). He considers both his own teaching and Grant's to be "just a waste of time … You'll see that it'll take more than five and a half months to wipe away—peel—scrape way the blanket of ignorance that has been plastered and replastered over those brains in the past three hundred years" (64). Jefferson has sat in that same one-room schoolhouse, and learned nothing. The novel contains many scenes of Grant teaching, both in school and when he visits Jefferson in jail. There are detailed descriptions of his classroom, and how he divides the class in order to teach six grades. At times he seems uncomfortably like Professor Antoine; he is frustrated by his students, arbitrary, even cruel. And as he talks with Jefferson, it becomes clear that the struggle to reach this unwilling student is a version of his teaching writ large. His other students are also trapped, in effect imprisoned—by their ignorance, by an unequal school system, by the racism that surrounds them.

The novel is threaded through with images of immobility that compress multiple meanings. At the trial Jefferson's godmother is "as immobile as a great stone or as one of our oak or cypress stumps. She never got up once to get water or go to the bathroom down in the basement. She just sat there staring at the boy's clean-cropped head" (3). In one sense Miss Emma embodies the determination and endurance of the women of the community. Both she and Grant's Tante Lou are large women who exercise the stubborn power of resistance, implicitly asserting "we shall not be moved." Yet in another sense, they lack active power, and flexibility. Almost immediately this first image of immobility is echoed by an account of Jefferson's frozen panic at the crime scene—"He wanted to run, but he couldn't run. He couldn't even think" (5). And later, the obese school superintendent who can barely get out of his car to do the required inspection, who cannot be bothered to remember Grant's name and ignores his requests for books and chalk, who treats the students like animals, embodies the massive, destructive inertia of the system of segregation.

Within his community Grant, occupying the honored role of the teacher, is relatively powerful. And he is uniquely mobile—not only has he been to college, he owns a car and often drives to the nearby town for a drink and to visit Vivian, the woman he hopes to marry, who is also a teacher. But he is also vulnerable, in many ways. The menace of white-on-Black violence is omnipresent. It is lightly touched, but we learn from the account of the crime focalized through Jefferson in the opening pages of the book that the white shopkeeper—who felt menaced by two young Black men demanding wine on credit—shot first. Grant's educated speech and his refusal to abase himself make him seem menacing to white folks, too. As he negotiates for access to Jefferson, and he repeatedly visits him in jail, he walks a knife's edge of risk between dangerous defiance and humiliating himself.

Grant's physical vulnerability also points toward the emotional and spiritual dangers he faces. His destructive, and self-destructive, former teacher warns him, both explicitly and by being a monitory example. Grant tells his aunt: "Everything you sent me to school for, you're stripping me of it...The humiliation I had to go through, going into that man's kitchen. The hours I had to wait while they ate and drank and socialized before they would even see me. Now going up to that jail...Maybe today they'll want to look into my mouth, or my nostrils, or make me strip...Years ago, Professor Antoine told me that if I stayed here, they were going to break me down to the nigger I was born to be. But he didn't tell me that my aunt would help them do it." Tante Lou and Emma do not want to ask this of him—but "they ain't nobody else" (79). Being his community's most successful son is a heavy burden for Grant, trapped between the irresistible force of racism and his "immovable" (14) elders. "I clamped my jaws so tight the veins in my neck felt as if they would burst. I wanted to scream at my aunt; I was screaming inside. I had told her many, many times how much I hated this place and all I wanted to do was get away. I had told her I was no teacher, I hated teaching, and I was just running in place here" (15). The novel's figures of immobility are not peaceful; rather, in the image of "running in place," stasis and flight paradoxically entwine.

The school itself is immured inside the old system—it is on the grounds of the plantation, and housed in the church. In these stories of schoolteachers we have seen religion and education connected and contrasted in many ways. Here they occupy the same ground but are disconnected and—as personified by Reverend Ambrose and Grant—even hostile. The minister is (in the description focalized through the teacher protagonist) "not educated, hadn't gone to any theological school; he had heard the voice and started preaching" (100–1). He has known Grant since birth, but is no longer at ease with him. Grant wants to keep his distance from religion, yet he must spend his days in the church—the pulpit and altar looming behind his desk, pictures of Jesus and the minister on the wall. His teacher's desk itself is a table that holds collections or communion on Sundays. This is an intimate estrangement.

Reverend Ambrose demonstrates his power as a preacher in a conversation, late in the novel, in which he asserts that the "reading, writing, and 'rithmetic" (215) Grant teaches are not enough. He tells Grant that book-learning has left him ignorant about his own people and himself, that his gloom is self-indulgent. "'You think you the only one that ever felt this way?' he asked. 'You think I never felt this way? You think she never felt this way? Every last one of them back there one time in they life wanted to give up.'" Grant claims that he does not "owe anybody anything" (216) but Ambrose reminds him that his education was made possible not only by his aunt's hard work, but also by the lies she told to free him into his opportunities. "That's how you got through that university—cheating herself here, cheating herself there, but always telling you she's all right. I've seen her hands bleed from picking cotton. I've seen the blisters from the hoe and the cane knife. At that church, crying on her knees. You ever looked at the scabs on her knees, boy? Course you never. 'Cause she never wanted you to see it. And that's the difference between me and you, boy; that make me the educated one, and you the gump" (218). The minister is only a supporting character, but in this chapter he has the last word; his powerful defense of situated, everyday knowledge against book-learning is left unanswered.

Of course, in some sense Reverend Ambrose is simply annotating Grant's inability to run away; he voices an obligation that Grant is already—albeit reluctantly—honoring. And although I have emphasized Grant's antagonism toward the community especially as the novel progresses, there are other moments. There is the detailed empathy of the moment when Thelma, one of the owners of the Rainbow Club in Bayonne, gives him money to help buy Jefferson a radio, saying "Here"—I quote one sentence from a longer paragraph: "It was the kind of 'here' that let you know this was hard-earned money but, also, that you needed it more than she did, and the kind of 'here' that said she wished you had it and didn't have to borrow it from her, but since you did not have it, and she did, then 'here' it was, with a kind of love" (174). Critics, in particular Herman Beavers, have written eloquently about the tension between the individual and the community in Gaines's work; I will not offer anything like a full account here. To do so would require dealing with aspects of the novel I have not mentioned, such as Grant's developing friendship with the white deputy Paul. But clearly the lesson of the novel entails reckoning with both creative dissent *and* collectivity. As early as 1973, Gaines put his point as directly as it can be put, telling an interviewer that "you must stand individually in order to stand with the crowd. Or in order to be able to lead, you must be an individual" (*Conversations*, 63). In *A Lesson before Dying*, Vivian straightforwardly asserts the special role of the teacher in this complex drama. Grant proposes that they "pack up and leave," and she knows that some people do that. But "'we can't,' she said. 'We're teachers, and we have a commitment'" (29).

Grant at first replies to Aunt Emma's request that he teach Jefferson by telling her that it is too late. Her request is, quite precisely, the opposite of industrial education. No one doubts that Jefferson will be executed within a few weeks or months. There is no point in teaching him useful skills for the job market, or how to be a good second-class citizen. This is education for its own sake. And Grant's project is also explicitly *not* to save his soul (although others will try)—that would be instrumental in a different way. When Grant understands that Emma wants him to teach her godson that he is not a hog but a man, to help him find and affirm his humanity, he is not sure how—after failing to reach Jefferson in the classroom—he can do that. He asks Vivian, "What do I say to him? Do I know what a man is? Do I know how a man is supposed to die? . . . Am I supposed to tell someone how to die who has never lived?" (31). Vivian, weeping, asks him to try—"for me"—"For us" (32). This is just one of the many moments of profound identification between

Jefferson and the narrator. To put it less subtly than the novel does: all lessons, for all of us, are lessons before dying.

Grant does gradually reach Jefferson; through his teacher's recognition, the student learns to recognize himself as human. Grant gives him a notebook and pencil, and Jefferson records his thoughts, addressing them to "mr wigin." His misspelled and mostly unpunctuated paragraphs are incorporated directly into the narrative—directly evoking the familiar local-color contrast between Standard English narrative and dialect voice. It is perhaps a risky strategy for asserting Jefferson's full humanity, but on my reading (and other critics') it is highly successful. The "Jefferson's Diary" chapter is nine pages long (out of the novel's total of 256), but it compels attention. It makes Jefferson more fully present to the reader at the moment of his execution, which takes place offstage. What we have instead is Paul's report of Jefferson's "transformation" (254), and Grant's reaction. I do not want to make the novel seem too optimistic and uplifting; Jefferson is dead, Grant is not transformed, the world is not transformed. But neither are they the same. It is hard to know what is changing, but as Vivian has said, "Something is" (141). The last image of the novel is Grant entering the school to tell his students the news: "I went up to the desk and turned to face them. I was crying" (256). This is a moment of new power, and newly chosen vulnerability. If the classroom can come alive as a site of commitment and recognition, of negotiation between different kinds of knowledge, movement and change may be possible.

Teachers and Learners

Genre criticism proves its worth—I hope readers will agree—when it opens up interpretation like this. By reading *A Lesson before Dying* through the figure of the schoolteacher, we understand it more deeply. This is not only, or always primarily, a matter of grouping it with similar works—differences are equally important, and still not sufficient. Rather, it is a matter of seeing the book's complex implication in, and contribution to, a network of meanings. Genre criticism can also open up literary history, of course. It should enable us to apprehend how that system is working and changing. But that is a matter for another chapter; I want to conclude this one by reflecting on how we are implicated in that network.

I am a teacher. I imagine that most of the people who will read this teach, in fact. Throughout this book, my investigation of regionalism converges with my effort to understand place and power as categories that matter to me personally and politically—indeed, practically, and spiritually, and in every other way I can think of. Literature is, after all—as Kenneth Burke famously put it—equipment for living. I take it for granted that scholarly work is motivated by, intertwined with, our own stakes in an issue—but also that the point of its protocols is to disengage from a narrow standpoint, enlarge our perspective enough to arrive at unexpected conclusions. My point here is not epistemological, although (it should be clear)

I have considered that aspect of the topic. I want to specify our connection to these issues because I think that academics often fail to recognize it; reading higher education into this continuing story can help us to place ourselves.

The history of professionalization has separated schoolteachers from university professors (as I noted at the outset). The pay, working conditions, demographics, and status of the two groups differ. To put it bluntly, professors are more privileged: better paid, better treated, more often male (both groups are still mostly white). The difference is perhaps clearest in the areas that define an occupation *as* a profession: control over accreditation, standards for practice, evaluation. Many academics, especially those of us active in professional organizations, are concerned about the erosion of the distinctive governance practices of higher education. The growth in the administrative sector, and in the hiring of contingent-contract instructors who are de facto excluded from participation in decision-making, is shifting the balance of power away from the faculty. And of course some teachers, especially those represented by unions, are better off than some college and university instructors, particularly those off the tenure track. But compare even professors' diminished situation with that of schoolteachers. They face an extraordinary level of surveillance, often in the context of arbitrary, non-negotiable instructions from school boards and officials. And, in the public schools especially, they have less and less to say about curriculum. Arguably, one of the reasons for the repeated failures of school reform is that it is in the charge of politicians and principals—teachers are rarely consulted, and programs are developed in willful ignorance of classroom realities.

Yet the basic work of schoolteachers and professors is similar. The principles of learning and teaching do not change; the very students sitting in college classrooms were in high school classrooms only a few months or years ago. I hope that my readers have to some degree seen themselves in the schoolteachers in these stories, as I do. Professors also are both powerful and vulnerable, as we face our students. We are the experts; we hope to hold open the door to broader opportunities and horizons. We also care, often very much, what they think of us. Those student evaluations matter—for promotion, for merit raises, and simply, importantly, for the sake of job satisfaction and self-respect. Graduate students and young colleagues sometimes ask me if teaching really counts, for getting tenure; I say (speaking for my own institution) yes—but also that the real reason to work hard at it is its intrinsic importance, both for our students and for us. It's hard to be happy in your daily life as a professor if you don't feel you are doing a good job in the classroom.

Russell Berman devoted his presidential address at the 2012 MLA Convention to "Teaching as Vocation." He proposed recalibrating our sense of the importance of teaching in the profession, undertaking public advocacy for education, and "making common cause with teachers throughout the education system; attacks on K-12 teachers are attacks on us." I applauded to hear it affirmed, at such a central site in our profession, that "We are all teachers."

Berman also acknowledged, however, "the scandalous open secret of American higher education: the greater the importance of teaching in one's job description, the less the compensation and job security" (453–4). (AAUP numbers indicate that the change in the academic labor force is not that there are more teaching-intensive jobs; it's that fewer of them are on the tenure track.) This is true among individuals and also across institutions. Steven Vanderstaay wrote in the *Chronicle of Higher Education* some years ago that he was told, and came to believe, that he was being snubbed at a professional gathering because his name tag located him at a university "with a direction in the title"—a "*regional* institution." He defends the quality of life at his institution—pointing out, among other things, that campuses like Western Washington University are on pristine, beautiful sites because of "their beginnings as normal schools, strategically located in out-of-the-way places where the need for teachers was greatest." Once again, the school is proposed as the site of connection between periphery and center. And I would argue that the papers at every professional convention make it clear that lively and important scholarly work is constantly accomplished at teaching-intensive institutions all across the country. The hierarchy that Berman and Vanderstaay deplore is part of the pattern that engages me throughout this book.

Facing the classroom, we face towards the local. Often, our aspirations turn elsewhere—we are pulled away towards book-learning and book-writing, or towards a more metropolitan place. I have been haunted for years by another *Chronicle* article, by Eric Zencey, on "The Rootless Professors." He argued that academics' disconnection is the result not only of the mobility entailed by the job market, but also of an entrenched attitude of condescension to the parochial and provincial. He suggests that we end up teaching disrespect for the local, and implicitly promoting an uncritical nationalism, because we fail to convey our own sense of citizenship in the "world city"—that is, cosmopolitanism—as a vivid alternative. There are many specific grounds on which one might dispute or qualify Zencey's polemic—and he might well agree that in the years since he wrote, the place-specific environmental education he's arguing for, and programs for community engagement, have increased. Yet I find it hard to resist the force of his critique, as a general description of the academic habitus. My readers will make their own assessment.

The charge that they turn students away from their communities is made against children's schools as well, of course. We have seen an extreme version of that process in Zitkala-Ša's stories—and the history—of Indian boarding schools. In Chapter 5, we will see the Kentucky writer Wendell Berry celebrate situated knowledge absorbed from the community, and indict classroom learning as alienating and destructive. Una Mae and Gregory Reck write that a persistent theme of "writings on Appalachian education is that schools have always been and continue to be an integral part of the exploitation of rural Appalachian peoples," "participating in the denigration of regional lifestyles" (19)—and quote a parent who fears that without local control of the schools the children may become (in a telling phrase) "citizens of nowhere" (24).

Examples of this criticism could be multiplied indefinitely. The separation is damaging not only because it may turn students away from the local but also because it makes it more difficult for them to connect with the learning offered to them in the classroom. In a sequel to her influential *Other People's Children*, Lisa Delpit recounts how her small daughter considered topics like her grandmother's visit when she was asked to write sentences as homework, but in the end produced, for example, "The boy is tall" because sentences are "stuff you write but you never would say... This teacher had, I am sure inadvertently, taught that sentences were meaningless, decontextualized statements you find in workbooks and on the blackboard... Written work in school was not connected to anything real, certainly not to real language. As all good, experienced teachers know, there are many ways to make school feel like it is part of real life" (59). Local knowledge, she asserts, can and should be integrated with book-learning. We might turn to Jesse Stuart and Paulo Freire as exemplary educators who spent their lives advocating that point. A striking recent example is the movement embodied in *Quality Education as a Constitutional Right*, the 2010 volume that emerged from Civil Rights leader Robert Moses's Algebra Project and campaign for the transformation of public schools. It includes eloquent appeals for culturally responsive pedagogy, for teachers to recognize the specificity and value of what students already know and to incorporate it in the curriculum. The emphasis on literacy and education in the African-American struggle we have seen already continues, and so does contestation over the role of the teacher and the curriculum.

Although the form it takes is so variable, this is a structural tension—because schools are—always, among other things—instruments of nation-building. Once we have de-naturalized how regions are incorporated into the nation, that process can never be wholly separated from colonialism. I have been telling this story of national formation throughout, and we can trace it far beyond. Eugen Weber's *Peasants into Frenchmen*, examining as its subtitle tells us *The Modernization of Rural France, 1870–1914*, is a classic and archivally rich account. As he puts it: "The school, notably the village school, compulsory and free, has been credited with the ultimate acculturation process that made the French people French—finally civilized them, as many nineteenth-century educators liked to say. The schoolteachers, in their worn, dark suits, appear as the militia of the new age, harbingers of enlightenment and of the Republican message that reconciled the benighted masses with a new world, superior in wellbeing and democracy" (303). This is a national pedagogy, which teaches that "The fatherland is not your village, your province, it is all of France" (333). Weber argues that not just the patriotic curriculum but the very maps provided by the state to hang on classroom walls were an "assault against provincialism" (334), offering the outline of the nation as an alternative to lived community.

The school system in the United States, of course, has always been and remains far more decentralized than the French system—it is, as represented in the stories discussed in this chapter, profoundly oriented to the local. Angela Sorby writes that she sees American schools as a kind of "impossible synthesis, dependent on local communities for funding and direction but linked to a larger national agenda" (28). This somewhat exceptionalist objection is not enough, however— we must also resist Weber's teleological vision of modernization. Indeed, the resonance it gives the image of the school to see it on this large canvas is fundamentally linked to the constant undertow back toward a conceptual framework in which the West pulls the rest of the world into the future. So let me be clear here, on points discussed at greater length in Chapter 1: I reject any notion of uniform, unidirectional (let alone inevitable) change—as fiercely as I do the usual meaning of the term "civilization," and for similar reasons. That way of correlating space and time is ethnocentric, and allied with gendered and class-based elitism—and it prevents us from thinking clearly. I have not been able to do without the term modern, although I try always to use it carefully and critically; of course, as part of our era's self-conception it is an important element of my object of study. Weber writes that French students were instructed to "Believe in progress with a sincere and ardent faith" (331)—is that not also true in American schools today? Anti-modern views were, and are, available as well; debunkings of all kinds abound. But the view that schooling is a route both to prosperity and fulfillment, and to the wide world and inclusion in the future, remains "common sense."

To see education as a path forwards and up is to be on the landscape of "No Child Left Behind" and "Race to the Top"—which have (I believe, with many others) only intensified inequality. As an educator I try to remember that the system entails exclusion when it offers inclusion—some fail or drop out, some succeed and go on; some go on, and on, and become professors. We can embrace the aspirations for democratic schooling expressed by thinkers like Mike Rose and Roger Moses—but also have a historically informed skepticism about what Harvey Graff calls the "literacy myth."[7] It becomes more possible to hold both thoughts when we think in less vertical terms, seeing the school, instead, in the way the regional fictions I have been examining represent it: as a crossroads. These stories are often precisely about the on-the-ground negotiation that goes on in classrooms and school districts. (Weber's own account shows school attendance suffered until parents and students could see that the skills offered were actually, practically useful—the resemblance to the Recks's account of the high dropout rates in Appalachia is noticeable.) This effort to look two ways at once is not necessarily a paradox, although it may result in an oxymoron—the same impulse is in Anthony Appiah's "rooted cosmopolitanism," I think. So too in Craig Calhoun's critique of actually existing cosmopolitanism he does not abandon broad horizons when he makes his "plea for the importance of the local and particular" ("Class Consciousness," 871), pointing out that relations between groups "involve the development of local hybrid cultures, accommodations, collaborations, and practical knowledge" (893). Schools, whether in out-of-the-way locations or in the center of the city, are places where worlds connect.

Teachers have some—although only some—say about whether that happens productively or hurtfully, purposefully or chaotically. We work in a system. And, importantly, students have something to say too. The notion of the learner as an empty vessel, passively accepting knowledge, has few defenders these days, at any level from early childhood education to higher education. The conventional terms "early" and "high" map the system onto progressive time, and hierarchical space. (So do the names "No Child Left Behind" and "Race to the Top.") But we are capable of thinking less teleologically and less vertically. The classrooms of teachers in (let us call it) the K-22 system look much more connected on the view expressed by John Dewey in *Democracy and Education* in 1916, and later affirmed by Mike Rose: "The child of three who discovers what can be done with blocks, or of six who finds out what he can make by putting five cents and five cents together, is really a discoverer, even though everybody else in the world knows it" (153). If we think of what goes on in the classroom as discovery, the role of teachers changes too—what we are doing is creating ways for students to learn. We often (although I would not venture to make this claim for the pre- and elementary school teachers Dewey evokes) remake our own knowledge as well. As Freire writes, this does not necessarily mean that students correct our mistakes—but when we decline to be "*bureaucrats of the mind*" and "open up to the students' *guesses*, their innocence, and their discrimination" (32), we rediscover our curiosity, enter into a fresh engagement in inquiry. This constructivist view of learning and teaching entails seeing knowledge as situated—that is, as always in some sense *local*.

I learned the term "scholar-teacher" from another former student, Sarah Ruffing Robbins—her influence runs all through this work. When (many years ago now) I taught a session at her summer program for high school teachers in Atlanta, the participants—who were both our students and engaged in educating me—embraced it warmly. The term acknowledged their sense of affiliation with the academy and their eagerness for the kind of knowledge that professors produce, as well as their commitment to students. It positioned them, with Sarah and with me, as inquirers in the classroom. I have used the term on forms where I am asked to put my occupation, ever since, and it resonates even more powerfully for me in the context of this chapter.

This chapter ranges from insights derived from my experience as a scholar-teacher to a significant disciplinary claim. American literary history needs to reckon with the figure of the schoolteacher, and with how that figure links knowledge systems and invokes the fraught problem of scaling-up to modernity. Thus my argument has consequences across the fields of cultural studies, and recursively helps me understand the processes of knowledge-making that have sustained this project. It is continuous with my perspective on regionalism to write (echoing but modifying Berman's phrasing): "we are all scholar-teachers."

{ 3 }

The Unexpected Jewett

A chapter on Sarah Orne Jewett is a predictable element of a book on American regionalism.

As I read Jewett, however, what I find is often unexpected. I work from multiple sources and motives in this chapter. I am grounded in the classroom, in my own and my students' responses over many years of reading and teaching Jewett's fiction. Necessarily, deeply, I am informed by scholarship—by powerful interpretations and charged debates. This is a polarized field; critics I admire write bitterly against each other, and I sometimes find myself cast as an antagonist. I have taken the opportunity to rethink where I stand in those debates. I am also thinking through what it means to read Jewett in relation to the account of regionalism I propose in this book.

The place of an essay on a single author in a book about genre should not be taken for granted. On the view of literary classification I argue at the end of the first chapter, authors do not define forms, either by their manifestos or in their works. Rather, they are participants—with readers of many kinds, including editors and publishers—in the ongoing, iterative conversations that constitute literary institutions. Nor is what they make contained or explained by forms, of course. Analyzing Jewett's work in terms of genre should not mean closing off interpretation by labeling, but opening it up by making connections. I think of my discussions of Jewett and (in Chapter 4) Edith Eaton as sharing ground with microhistory, an approach I have written about and practiced elsewhere: through the focus of these two careers I approach large questions on delimited grounds, without answers given in advance. In the end I am most interested in work that talks back, in the way I discuss in Chapter 1 (following Mieke Bal). Jewett's (and Eaton's) does.

I have chosen these authors because each of them has been an important interlocutor for me as I have worked on regionalism. I could have chosen others, but Jewett and Eaton have amply repaid my attention, and the differences between them have proved interesting as well. Jewett's career begins at the moment of—and contributes to—local color's ascendance. She has always had a prominent role in accounts of the genre, and the debates over her work are consequential for American literary scholarship, especially as feminist criticism has reshaped it. Eaton belongs to the next generation, and she was in multiple ways a marginal writer. She both accommodates herself to and challenges classifications—forms, and also racial categories—and I will suggest that reading her work can also change our understanding of literary history. These chapters are not of course full accounts of these authors, but they offer new perspectives, and they redirect and advance my argument about the form.

In the next section I evoke the figure of Jewett, concisely characterizing the author for readers whose specialties lie elsewhere, and indicating how I, specifically, see her. Then I turn more directly to Jewett's own words. How, in her explicit statements about her project and in her fiction, do the concept of region I have proposed, and the categories of local knowledge and book-learning, play out? That discussion is followed by an extended interpretation of Jewett's story "A Late Supper." My first efforts to understand the relation of the local and the translocal were on the site of Jewett's work, and this story taught me a great deal. Here the role of religion in connecting people and places (a topic that appeared repeatedly in Chapter 2) becomes central. In Jewett's fiction the right relation of country and city can only be achieved through that mediation.

That is *not* a statement about the genre of regionalism. Form is a shaping force, recursively shaped by what writers do with and to it. But relation to form is the beginning, not the end, of interpretation—it leads me to an analysis of Jewett's distinctive ground. She does, in turn, teach us something about the capabilities of the chronotope.

Turning to the Author

Sarah Jewett presented herself as a local color writer. She was born in the small town of South Berwick, Maine, to an extended family with deep roots in the Piscataqua river region. She was also a cosmopolitan woman, who was widely read and in adulthood spent part of each year in Boston and made multiple trips to Europe. She visited the American South and the Caribbean as well (Patrick Gleason has recently shown the importance of those travels). Jewett described herself as "made of Berwick dust" ("Old Town," 609) and she also had quotations from Flaubert posted above her writing desk. (Figure 3.1 is an undated image of Jewett reading.)

Jewett never gave any indication that she felt the conventions of local color as a constraint, or that she was torn between her orientation to the local and her access to the wider world. She *was*, as we will see, constantly interested in how people in particular places think about time and space, and negotiate difference. Acknowledging that orientation is something very different from what we see in the long record of critical condescension to Jewett. She and her work are constantly portrayed as diminished by provincial, ladylike limits. F. O. Matthiessen opened his 1929 biography of Jewett with this sentence: "The first thing she could remember was a world bounded by the white paling fences around her house." In his influential literary history of the turn into the twentieth century, published in

FIGURE 3.1 *Portrait of Sarah Orne Jewett with book (undated). Reproduced with permission from Historic New England.*

1967, Jay Martin wrote that Jewett built a "fictive fence" (143) around her birth-place, citing Jewett's sketch "From a Mournful Villager": "People do not know what they lose when they make way with the reserve, the separateness of the front yard of their grandmothers." It does not (yet?) go without saying that this is a gendered disrespect. The attitude has been amply debunked—I will simply take for granted that Jewett is an important writer. Yet these comments also invoke the risk that regionalism constitutively runs—what Raymond Williams calls "encapsulation." Attention to the substance of the local can become (or be taken by inattentive readers as) neglecting relation, and writing about a place "as if there were no others." I write against the expected, quaint and ladylike Jewett. But I also want to register the grounds for that grievous reduction, to incorporate rather than merely refute it.

In Chapter 1 I began to detail the ways in which Jewett's body of work is more varied than generally acknowledged. That narrowing is partly the result of choices she herself made in submitting different pieces to different kinds of publications, and assembling collections of stories. Although her stories were variously reprinted in periodicals and collections, the only selected volume published by Houghton Mifflin during her lifetime is titled *Tales of New England* (1890), and its table of contents reads accordingly. She considered packaging her stories about Irish immigrants into a book to be called *Transplanted Shamrocks*, but they only appeared together in 1996, in a valuable edition by Jack Morgan and Louis Renza. Her stories about French-Canadian residents of the region are also left out of the canonical Jewett, and erased in claims like Richard Brodhead's that Jewett "wrote about one thing: the life of countryfolk in Maine coastal villages" (*Cultures*, 150). "The Gray Mills of Farley" was published in *Cosmopolitan*, hardly an obscure venue, but did not appear between hard covers until the *Uncollected Short Stories of Sarah Orne Jewett* appeared in 1971. Jewett's treatment of the problems of industrialism in that story has proved interesting to critics, and its inclusion in Michael Davitt Bell's Library of America volume of Jewett's work arguably made it canonical. But intriguing uncollected stories like "Stolen Pleasures" and "An Everyday Girl," respectively about an employee at a machine shop and a girl working in a hotel, remain virtually unread.

It is difficult, and probably not useful, to draw a line between Jewett's choices about what and where to publish, and the impact of advice she received from others, whether friends, fellow authors, editors, or publishers (for her, categories with a great deal of overlap)—including the powerful information received when a piece is rejected. Jewett would, I think, have eagerly subscribed to the notion of the social text, and the understanding of authorship as fundamentally collaborative, that now prevails in editorial theory. After her death Annie Fields, the partner in her "Boston marriage," edited Jewett's letters for publication and deleted intimate nicknames—persuaded by Mark Anthony DeWolfe Howe that they would be misunderstood. But critics have retrieved those elements of her correspondence, and indeed are suggesting that we reevaluate the place of the epistolary in literary history (Gaul and Harris). Scholars who study and edit letters, examine unpublished manuscripts, locate and study uncollected work, recover the dialogue of the social text. We are now familiar with the love poems that Jewett did not publish. We know that Jewett was a woman who loved women, and as Josephine Donovan has written, that better understanding of Jewett's life "should lead us to reevaluate the... image of Jewett as a passionless 'spinster,'... upon which much mistaken critical evaluation has been founded" ("Unpublished," 26). Jewett lived and worked in the midst of complex and changing social expectations—and she wrote not so much for, as in, a literary marketplace. Being able to place her work about place in magazines was recognition; we may see it as entailing misrecognition as well, but there can be no question that for her it meant both earning money and reaching readers.

Against the image of the quaint and ladylike Jewett—let us remember that she was a highly successful author. She published from a very early age. Some verses and a story appeared locally when she was just fourteen. At eighteen she placed a story in a Boston newspaper, and had the courage to send her work to the most distinguished literary journal in America. William Dean Howells, then assistant editor, accepted her third submission, and Jewett was twenty when she first appeared in the *Atlantic Monthly*. Her first novel, *Deephaven*, appeared when she was twenty-eight; she would publish nineteen books during her lifetime. Jewett was not a professional author in the same sense that Edith Eaton was—her family was well off and she did not need to earn her own living. But it mattered a great deal, both for her sense of self and for her situation, that her publications made her financially independent. (We will see the echo of that concern in my discussion of "A Village Shop," below.) She worked very hard at her writing, amidst family responsibilities, frequent illness, a busy social life, and travel. She published consistently and successfully until the carriage accident on her fifty-third birthday, from which she never fully recovered. It may still for many readers and critics be unexpected to see Jewett as—the image is Charles Johanningsmeier's—a shrewd businesswoman, but she was that. She was also certainly a literary artist, increasingly as that category became available to her through shifts in the marketplace for stories. And she felt a sense of vocation—she believed that her work (including her writing for children) mattered, that it did good in the world.

The Jewett we read today is unpredictable because we take into account both work that circulated widely *and* work that did not—letters, unpublished manuscripts, uncollected stories. It was fascinating to learn in 2014 that an alternate final chapter for *Country of the Pointed Firs* has been available since the 1930s in two folders marked "Miscellaneous pages" at Harvard's Houghton Library. Melissa Homestead and Terry Heller have now meticulously transcribed the manuscript and published it, with a brilliant essay on its context and implications. Their complex argument affirms the value of reading across both versions, but complements many feminist readings by showing that the ending Jewett rejected would have directed attention more conventionally to heterosexual romance, rather than the power of friendship, a topic I will soon turn to. Its attention to lines reflecting on a bequest to Mrs. Todd that appears in the unpublished chapter, showing Jewett "thinking through questions of money, class, and social aspiration" (340), also complements the critical turn to consideration of Jewett's engagement with large intellectual and historical issues, such as the materials of anthropology (Evans) and economics (Strychacz). Such accounts take Jewett very seriously, and they also implicate her in the ideologies of her day in a way that has provoked disagreement from other scholars.

Controversies over fraught topics like Jewett's thinking about race, which began elsewhere, are now frequently refracted through a story that appeared in *The Atlantic* in 1900, "The Foreigner." As Patrick Gleason notes in his 2011 *Legacy* article, it is surprising that any of her Dunnet Landing stories were out of print until 1967. Yet it is unsurprising that the one that remained unread for so long depicts (as he puts it) "the secrets behind Mrs. Todd's herbalist powers and empathic connections" as rooted in "a history of racial exclusion and sexual threats to the homogeneity of that small maritime community" (24). "The Foreigner" is a remarkable story, one that has been opened up by critics in an equally remarkable way. Following other powerful interpreters, Gleason offers biographical and historical context, and reads the text closely, to show that this ghost story is haunted by racial otherness and by Jewett's ambivalent endorsement of empire. He shows how Jewett's biographers quote her letters selectively and misleadingly to present her as innocent of racism. It may once have been easy to see imperialism as an uncomplicated or exclusively masculine ideology or practice, but no longer. As Gleason writes, citing the powerful work of Amy Kaplan, Anne McClintock, and Anna Brickhouse,

"Jewett emerged from a literary community that had for decades already encoded representations of national expansion in the language of domesticity, and the supposed border between the foreign and the domestic was itself a fiction emerging from the discourse of American exceptionalism" (42).

It is because Jewett did *not* build a fictive fence around her region, because her work attends to the local without being "encapsulated," that these prospects open up. I will continue to engage with the fraught topic of our (that is, my own and other scholars') affiliation with and distance from Jewett in the sections that follow, and will show it as seamlessly connected with Jewett's own concerns. I hope, however, it is already clear that, writing as an historically minded feminist, I continue to read this author in dialogue with what we know about her period, but certainly not as an inert example of obsolete attitudes. Her voice is, precisely, unexpected.[1]

Standing Between

Jewett's *Deephaven* was persistently, although not permanently, popular; it was published in 1877, and reprinted four times in the next twelve years. Then, in 1893, Jewett wrote a preface for its fifth appearance—in a full-dress new edition with new illustrations that was published (in 1894) simultaneously in a large, numbered gift format and in an ordinary, less expensive size.

In this much-cited document she articulates her project as a writer—and specifically as a regional writer—explicitly and eloquently. She distances herself from the book itself, in some ways—she even finds it "callow," writing that there are sentences that make her feel "as if she were the grandmother of the author of *Deephaven* and her heroines" (8). She places her motives in the specific historical context of the beginning of tourism in New England. Today "tourist" is often viewed as a negative category, implying superficial and exploitive consumption of the antique, the underdeveloped, the exotic. Jewett sees the emerging practice in an unexpected way: "crowded towns and the open country were to be brought together in new association and dependence upon each other. It appeared as if a second Harvey had discovered a new and national circulation of vitality along the fast-multiplying railroads that spun their webs to bind together men who had once lived far apart" (2). Jewett is alluding to William Harvey's seventeenth-century account of the motion of the heart pumping the blood. For Jewett, whose father and grandfather were doctors and who considered becoming one herself, medical knowledge tends to be powerful. Circulation and the railroads knit smoothly into the categories I have been using to engage local color. But it would be a stretch to suggest that as Jewett evokes spiders she is also thinking of the industrial looms located not far from her home. (Or—even more—of not only Arachne but Anansi.)

Jewett imagines what we call tourism as invigorating national unity and creating social—and potentially, spiritual—connections. But the possibility of misrecognition, rather than connection, haunts her vision of encounters between the city and

the country. It motivates her project. Snippets of the paragraph below are familiar—
I give it in full. It is more germane, so considered, to the question of what form
can do to mediate between islands of experience, and to the relation of Maine and
the wide world as Jewett sees it. (In our still more connected world, the reader is
invited to instantly access the Sarah Orne Jewett Text Project, based at Coe College,
to read, or reread, the whole as a context for my argument.)

> The young writer of these Deephaven sketches was possessed by a dark fear that
> townspeople and country people would never understand one another, or learn to
> profit by their new relationship. She may have had the unconscious desire to make
> some sort of explanation to those who still expected to find the caricatured Yankee
> of fiction, striped trousers, bell-crowned hat, and all, driving his steady horses
> along the shady roads. It seemed not altogether reasonable when timid ladies
> mistook a selectman for a tramp, because he happened to be crossing a field in his
> shirt sleeves. At the same time, she was sensible of grave wrong and misunder-
> standing when these same timid ladies were regarded with suspicion, and their
> kindnesses were believed to come from pride and patronage. There is a noble
> saying of Plato that the best thing that can be done for the people of a state is to
> make them acquainted with one another. It was, happily, in the writer's childhood
> that Mrs. Stowe had written of those who dwelt along the wooded seacoast and by
> the decaying, shipless harbors of Maine. The first chapters of "The Pearl of Orr's
> Island" gave the younger author of "Deephaven" to see with new eyes, and to
> follow eagerly the old shore paths from one gray, weather-beaten house to another
> where Genius pointed her the way.   (3–4)

Despite the extended, heated debate over reading Jewett's writing as touristic or
empathetic, she is very clear about where she stands: between.

Let us note that this is a *mutual* misunderstanding. The line about the selectman
being mistaken for a tramp is frequently quoted without what follows. That appro-
priation follows the modulation of the passage, which suggests that Jewett's initial
address is to townspeople—but it is clear that the locals are also addressed, and
also need to educate and enlarge their sympathies. Jewett's stance is partly a matter of
her biographical position as someone who is both locally rooted and committed,
and (by the standards of her day) cosmopolitan. But it is by no means only that. She
chooses to inhabit the role of mediator. And she does so by explicitly positioning
herself within a tradition of regional writing, both as a critic of stereotypes and as
a disciple of the greatest American woman writer of the nineteenth century.

In Chapter 2 I suggested that schoolteachers often play the role of the mediator
in local color fiction. I believe it indicates the value of this account of the genre that
it adds resonance to the much-discussed "Schoolhouse" chapters (3–7) of *Country
of the Pointed Firs*. Making this connection does not require any profound change
in existing interpretations. They amply discuss the way the narrator's decision to
rent the schoolhouse for her writing at least temporarily divides her from the community of Dunnet Landing. They comment as well on the ambiguity embodied
in the role of Captain Littlepage, whose name evokes and perhaps also belittles

book-learning. In the dialogue in this section, the narrator behind the narrator—let us call her Jewett—does not allow either speaker to complacently occupy a secure knowledge, or correlate the two of them with a binary between the local and the translocal. The issues play out *between* them.

The narrator, certainly, belongs to the wide world, and Captain Littlepage is a local. Yet she is, as we know, "a lover of Dunnet Landing" (377, in Michael Bell's Library of America edition which I cite for works it includes), and he is a much-travelled sea captain who in the funeral procession where we first see him is "the one strange and unrelated person in all the company" (384). The narrator is in the schoolhouse precisely to write, presumably for publication, and she occupies the teacher's seat throughout—although she playfully tells the much older captain that he should have "the place of honor" (387). He too is oriented to book-learning—his first words after entering the schoolhouse are a quotation from *Paradise Lost*. Mrs. Todd even believes he has "overset his mind with too much reading" (387). Captain Littlepage is also, however, given a powerful speech about the importance of thinking from what one sees, rather than from the page. He says, "a community narrows down and grows dreadful ignorant when it is shut up to its own affairs, and gets no knowledge of the outside world except from a cheap, unprincipled newspaper. In the old days, a good part o' the best men here knew a hundred ports and something of the way folks lived in them. They saw the world for themselves, and like's not their wives and children saw it with them. They may not have had the best of knowledge to carry with 'em sight-seein', but they were some acquainted with foreign lands an' their laws, an' could see outside the battle for town clerk here in Dunnet; they got some sense o' proportion" (390–1). Much as he loves literature Captain Littlepage is ambivalent about print culture; the newspapers misinform, and "Lord help" the crews of ships whose captains read about medicine (391), presumably because they were doctored out of books. But he is an unequivocal advocate of cosmopolitanism—in an unexpected form, since he locates it not only in a village, but in the past.

Jewett stands between the townspeople and the country people, and between different kinds of knowledge. She is accurately understood as an artist who renders the local, yet her work is always enabled by distant sources. Sarah Way Sherman's account of the key role of the Demeter-Persephone myth in her work is the most salient of many examples. Jewett's letters are full of her thoughts about whatever she has been reading (and there is always something)—she writes affectionately, often irreverently, about authors, treating them as companions. It is very clear in Jewett's life and writing that she *loved* books—let us take that commitment as given. She also makes available a critique of book-learning that aligns her with the skeptical perspective sketched in Chapter 2. One explicit example is in "The Courting of Sister Wisby"—a story that we know Jewett read aloud to a local audience, and that was sent to the educated subscribers of *Atlantic Monthly* in 1887 (Donovan, "Jewett on Race"). Mrs. Goodsoe says, "there's win'rows o' young doctors, bilin' over with book-larnin', that is truly ignorant of what to do for the sick, or how to p'int out those paths that well people foller toward sickness. Book-fools I call 'em" (*King*, 57–8).

A story in which that critical view is more deeply conveyed by the narration itself is "A Village Shop," published in 1888 in *The King of Folly Island*. It is not surprising that unlike "Sister Wisby," which was collected in the same volume and reprinted in *Outlook* in 1894, it did not have a previous magazine publication, and has received little critical attention—it is a story that does not fit the canonical Jewett very well. This is the unexpected and almost unread Jewett; despite its occasional humor, the story is very dark. That quality seems connected to its affiliation with Hawthorne, and particularly *The House of Seven Gables* (the connections will be apparent in my summary). Perhaps he influences the story's mood; I also suspect the connection to an illustrious author licenses Jewett to strike unusually negative notes.[2]

The story is focalized through Esther Jaffrey, one of the last descendants of an old and distinguished family in the village of Grafton. She and her mother put all their resources into supporting her brother Leonard at Harvard; "their pinching economies, and the cheerful sacrifice of their own comfort...reckoned as nothing in their pride and joy at furthering the interests of Leonard Jaffrey, the only son and last hope of his house and name" (230). Esther is the Jaffrey who has ability and energy, but subordinates herself to a man who proves to be a disappointment, an indolent "book-worm" (235). "He was absolutely without any original thoughts or gifts, he was unproductive from the beginning, yet with unquenched appetite he devoured the wisdom and imagination that were stored between his book covers. Unsated, unflagging, unforeseeing, he became at last a perfectly unavailable treasury of other people's knowledge, like some lake that has no outlet" (244–5). This description of book-learning is as bitter as any passage in Jewett's work.

Esther, after her mother's death and her brother's return home, manages to keep the household afloat by taking the shocking step of opening a small shop in the room he had expected to use as a study. Leonard simply stuffs his bedroom with books; again, the textual detail conveys distaste and even danger. Looking at his room, "it was impossible not to be reminded of certain shell-fish whose covering thickens with age. No wonder that a suggestion of brown leather bindings followed him in his rare progress into the outer world, for here there were hundreds shelved in crowded lines, piled in small toppling precipices against the wainscoted walls, and stacked in sliding hillocks here and there on the uncarpeted floor. Leonard Jaffrey himself could find his way among them, even in the dark, like a soft-pawed pussy cat; the noise of a fallen book was the only sound that roused his anger. There was apparent danger for a stray visitor, as if in time this floor and walls of experienced volumes would suddenly close in and stifle the room's occupant" (264). He is moved from his accustomed ways only when a local farmer, John Grant, motivated by loyalty to the Jaffrey family and a desire to help Esther, places his daughter with them as a student and boarder. Leonard makes love to the girl, and they become engaged.

The narrator endorses Esther's outrage, although also chides her for the unworldliness which prevented her from seeing what was happening. Part of the shock is that Jaffreys do not marry Grants—there is the merest hint that the sympathy between John Grant and Esther could become something more, but neither would consider violating the established order to explore the possibility. But most importantly, as Esther argues, the romance is a betrayal of the trust between teacher and pupil. Equally serious—Leonard is so irresponsible that he is unconcerned about how he will support a wife, let alone a future family. A *deus ex machina* arrives at this point: a wealthy former resident has given Grafton a great deal of money to create a public library, and the town's selectmen arrive to ask Leonard to become the librarian, with a generous salary. This would seem, according to the "coupling convention" (the phrase is Ann DuCille's), to be a happy ending. Yet the story suggests nothing to diminish the unpleasantness of the way Leonard has taken advantage of Nelly, and it refrains from imagining a successful outcome for her marriage to a middle-aged man "with as much energy as a barnacle," "the most unproductive man of letters in New England, with no apparent value either social or commercial" (236). And nothing diminishes the injustice of Esther's situation. Yet she makes her own, unconventional happy ending; when Leonard says that now she should give up the shop, she replies fiercely, "*Never!*" (290; emphasis in the original). Like Jewett, she cherishes her ability to earn an income, which indexes a profound independence.

Jewett's negative portrayals of book-learning are linked to masculine power and complacency, as here and with Parson Dimmick in the "Poor Joanna" section of *Country of the Pointed Firs*. Certainly not all educated male characters are tarred with that brush—Dr. Leslie, in *A Country Doctor*, is a powerful counter-example, bringing his immense learning to bear with kind, careful attention to individuals and situations. About that kind of knowledge Jewett discriminates; local knowledge, on the other hand, she consistently works to elevate. I have chosen this description from "Law Lane," a story that appeared with "A Village Shop" in *The King of Folly Island* (after appearing in the new *Scribner's* in 1887). "The thump of a flat-iron signified to an educated passer-by that this was Tuesday morning; yesterday having been fair and the weekly washing-day unhindered by the weather" (115). *Education* here means both knowing local customs (that Monday is washing day) and intelligently observing local conditions (thus being able to estimate the impact of something like rain).

Jewett's careful analyses of the *kinds* of knowledge demonstrate both the necessity of correlating book-learning and local wisdom, and the cognitive function of emotion. The latter is most compactly expressed in her eloquent parenthetical remark, in a letter to Elizabeth McCracken at the end of her life, that "I always insist that love isn't blind: it is only love that sees!" (Fields, *Letters*, 230). The work of Terry Heller, which I have already quoted and will quote again, has helped me see the significance of that statement. So has Alain Badiou's argument that love is a "truth-procedure." The project of helping people understand each other is common in authorial ideologies, of course, and the topic is well covered in Jewett criticism. I want in this chapter to show that Jewett's mediating work takes on additional resonance in the context of an understanding of regionalism as both substantive and relational, and that it can be connected with the topos of the schoolteacher. I also want to attend to Jewett's distinctiveness, and specifically to how central love and spirituality are to her vision of the proper relation of the country and the city.

Jewett dramatizes how knowledge works—its on-the-ground entanglement with location and with emotion—constantly, throughout her fiction. Sarah Way Sherman writes about this topic with great insight in her critical biography, and Marjorie Pryse and Judith Fetterley make it central to their *Writing Out of Place*. A classic location for this reading of Jewett is the "Green Island" chapter of Jewett's best-remembered novel, which Marcia McClintock Folsom analyzes in her extraordinary article "'Tact is a Kind of Mind-Reading': Empathic Style in Sarah Orne Jewett's *Country of the Pointed Firs*." She unfolds Jewett's affirmation that "Sympathy is of the mind as well as the heart" (414), showing in detail how Jewett establishes a chain of sympathy that blends the cognitive and the affective. In the conversation between the narrator and Mrs. Todd, at the opening of the chapter, they respond to each other's unspoken thoughts; as they cross the water, Mrs. Todd annotates the landscape for the narrator, translating observations into local meanings. As Folsom says, "Mrs. Todd's ability to grasp a whole situation through intense and active interpretation of a glimpse or a detail indicates her complete familiarity with her world, and also the unbroken wholeness and integrated expressiveness of that world" (70).

One element that Folsom does not address is the vertical ordering of one set of signals. The narrator asks Mrs. Todd the meaning of the flag flying above the spruces, and is told that it invites the big schooners to come in for herring (presumably for bait); when the catch is poor, "they just fly a little signal down by the shore, an' then the small bo'ts comes." In the next sentence, we see a kind of flag flying still lower; Mrs. Todd says, "look!...mother sees us, she's wavin' somethin' out o' the fore door!" She wonders affectionately, "How do you suppose she knows it's me?", but of course Mrs. Blackett interprets the signs that are visible from her point of view with corresponding intelligence, and greets her daughter. In some sense these signals progress from high to low, from large to small scale—yet Jewett subtly unsettles any correlation with significance. When she asks about the flag, their young assistant Johnny Bowden regards the narrator with "contemptuous surprise" (405) at her ignorance. It is of course precisely his boyishly limited horizons that lead him to overestimate the role of this piece of information in the scheme of things and misunderstand the situation. The narrator is not offended, the reader is amused—and intricately wound, by participating in this play of perspectives, into Jewett's project.

The tradition of reading Jewett as distinctively skilled in enlisting empathy goes back a long time. In Elizabeth McCracken's 1904 book *The Women of America* (based on travels undertaken for and originally published in *Outlook*), she writes admiringly about Jewett in the chapter on women of letters. "In journeying about the United States, I was more than once amazed to find, not that Miss Jewett's books were more widely read than those of any other woman of letters in America, but that they were read with a certain fullness of appreciation by persons to whom their peculiarly local background was utterly unfamiliar" (205). McCracken reads this reaction in terms of national unity and goes on to recount giving away her copy of *Country of the Pointed Firs* to a woman who is drawn to it; replacing it, and giving it away again; and then giving it away a third time. She describes these women from different regions as reading Jewett with a deep sense of personal connection. One writes, "I had no idea people in Maine were so much like people out West, at heart" (209). Another feels for the first time that she understands what New England is "really like," because "Reading that book is very much the same as being there" (211). The third (a "State of Maine woman" herself) "feels like I was talking with old friends" (214). McCracken represents a chain of sympathy that is very much in Jewett's spirit, and when she sent a copy of her book to the author, Jewett embraced the link by carrying it on: "My last copy of your delightful book was just going to my friend Madame Blanc-Bentzon in Paris when you put this one into my hand!—You see that I have—unconsciously, too!—been behaving with it as some one else did with a certain book called 'The Country of the Pointed Firs'" (Fields, *Letters*, 227–8). She cites the same "reminder" from Plato as in the *Deephaven* preface, enlisting McCracken as a contributor to the project of explaining people to each other.

We know that Jewett's magic does not work for everyone. Teaching her work, I find that some students make a connection to Jewett—while others are left cold. Those who respond, often respond deeply. In fact, I venture to speculate that the passion of the debate over interpreting Jewett has something to do with how intimate her address feels, when it works. It all becomes quite personal; to a reader who has been profoundly interpellated, another student's—or another critic's—distanced commentary may seem jarring, its disruption of communion disturbing and even disrespectful. I am enough under Jewett's spell myself to have experienced this as well as provoked it.

I use the language of the occult deliberately here. It is already present in the line referring to Mrs. Blackett's hospitality that Folsom uses for her title, "Tact is after all a kind of mind-reading" (414). The narrator also writes, in the sequence discussed above, of her greeting to Mrs. Todd, "I looked, and could see a tiny flutter in the doorway, but a quicker signal had made its way from the heart on shore to the heart on the sea" (405). As critics have noted, Mrs. Todd's herbal knowledge links her to witchcraft, and she is likened to a sibyl (381) as well. Patrick Gleason links her knowledge of mysteries, through the figure of Mrs. Tolland, to the practice of Quimbois in the Windward Islands of the Caribbean (36–7). In "Living for the Other World," which treats Jewett as a religious writer, Heller assembles evidence that demonstrates she is interested in these matters through the whole length of her career. Like Laurie Shannon in her insightful essay on Jewett's "intimism," Heller shows how Jewett links the cultivation of loving relationships with spiritual knowledge.

It is a demonstration of how persuasively Jewett integrates ordinary and extraordinary connections that when the supernatural appears more directly, it is unexpected. In the late, uncollected story "The Green Bowl" (it appeared in the *New York Herald* in 1901) the young protagonist Kate receives, as a gift from a countrywoman met by chance, one of two Chinese "sister" bowls. When owned by two "companions" who know the secret, each confers the gift of fortune-telling. The story calls on other aspects of the relation of country and city as well. The fact that Kate and her close friend explore remote rural regions provokes some concerned comment from the older ladies at the party where she is telling her story. The beauty of the green bowl leads to a discussion of china collecting—J. Samaine Lockwood has recently shown the significance of that practice for Jewett and her milieu, in *Archives of Desire: The Queer Historical Work of New England Regionalism*, and I will return to it briefly below. The hostess comments that she has gotten many fine pieces from such humble little houses, but now such people are "well educated in the real value of old plates and bowls, that they once gladly sold for a quarter of a dollar"—no explicit comment is made on this admission of exploitation, and report of growing sophistication in the countryside (*Uncollected*, 351). The focus is rather on Kate's bowl, freely given in expectation of true communion. At the end of the story, she does unambiguously and disturbingly see the future while looking into it—she knows that someone present is going to die. Kate is able—in Heller's words—to "join the mortal world with the spiritual world" (79). Thinking through what it means for Jewett to *stand between* means thinking about religion as well as region. In the next section I turn to that topic through a close reading of a story that brings the issues that concern me into focus.

Understanding "A Late Supper"

Jewett's story "A Late Supper" comes quite early in her career. It was initially published in 1878 (she was twenty-eight), in the first issue of a short-lived Massachusetts-based journal called *Sunday Afternoon*, then quickly reprinted in her first collection of stories, *Old Friends and New* (1879). The protagonist—as Jewett calls her, the "heroine" of the story—Miss Catherine Spring of Brookton, Massachusetts, is the last of a large family and lives alone in a country village on the edge of the mountains; she is a familiar local color character, a New England spinster who seems to live behind a fictive fence. Yet the opening of the story also presents her as quite thoroughly embedded in translocal relationships.

Miss Catherine's small income from investments has been dwindling. When a little girl looking for a place as a servant says to her "times are going to be dreadful hard, they say," contemporary readers would have recognized the allusion to the national depression that followed the Panic of 1873. Finance capitalists' manipulation and exploitation of railroad stocks was a particularly striking feature of this period, and Miss Spring is no longer able to make ends meet because of "the failure of a certain railway to pay its dividend." She has attempted to solve her difficulties by advertising for summer boarders in a Boston newspaper, but her notice has gone unanswered. Miss Spring is indeed a provincial person—at one point unable to provide information about a town between Brookton and the mountains—but she is also explicitly implicated in circuits of exchange. "A Late Supper" focuses intensely on face-to-face interactions, but it also addresses the impact of distant decisions and events on local life.

The story opens with Miss Spring doing domestic work and thinking over her difficulties. The girl's visit is its first event. Our protagonist lacks the funds to hire little Katie Dunning, but feeds her generously. Next, Miss Spring's nephew, his wife, and a friend arrive "from a town a dozen miles away" (89) for an unexpected visit. Miss Catherine asks them to spend the afternoon and have supper; they unknowingly convey to her that the solution to her financial problems she has reluctantly relied on, taking up residence with a niece in Lowell, is no longer possible—another relative has recently moved in there. Meanwhile, she has used all her cream for the little girl; she had planned to go without herself, but because of her guests decides to walk to a neighbor's to borrow some.

The railway now makes another appearance. The tracks run between Miss Spring's home and her neighbor's; on her return she finds her way blocked by a stopped train and climbs onto it to get by. The whole story pivots on the situation described in this passage:

> Miss Catherine waited in great anxiety; she could not afford to waste a minute. She would have to cross an impossible culvert in going around the train either way. She saw some passengers or brakemen walking about on the other side, and with great heroism mounted the high step of the platform with the full intention of going down the other side, when, to her horror, the train suddenly moved. She screamed, "Stop! stop!" but nobody saw her, and nobody heard her; and off she went, cream-pitcher and all, without a bit of a bonnet. It was simply awful. (94–5)

I will have something to say about the humor, and the point of view, here in a moment. But I want first to suggest that Jewett builds a story around this image, and it catches the reader's imagination, because of the historical resonance of the railroad. The locomotive is quite commonly used as a figure for the immense forces of modernity; in Frank Norris's *The Octopus* (1901) the railroad also has a double presence as an untrustworthy corporation and a dangerous machine cutting through the landscape of everyday life. It is comic, but not trivial, when Aunt Catherine rides off exclaiming, "I wish we never had sold our land for the track!" (95).

Jewett deploys a great deal of craft to manage our reaction to the story's humor, crucially qualifying the amusement provoked by the naive provincial. She moves us in and out of Catherine Spring's perspective, describing much but not everything from her point of view, using both dialogue and free indirect discourse to create the character—"without a bit of a bonnet," for example, is a phrase that comes from the narrator but is clearly in Miss Catherine's voice. Jewett varies what she calls her central character; she's most often "Miss Catherine," but sometimes "Miss Spring" and occasionally, when our sympathy is being enlisted, "Aunt Catherine." She uses this technique at the key moment when her protagonist embarks on her brief but consequential journey, for example. After the passage I have just quoted, Miss Catherine turns away from masculine domain of the smoking car, which is just behind her, and enters the Pullman—not only a quasi-domestic space but also one marked by class privilege. Here again the specific history of the railroad is relevant; the sleeping cars operated by George Pullman's company had been introduced in 1867, less than ten years before the story's publication. She's seen by a young lady who is in the passageway—"she looked over her shoulder, thinking Miss Spring was the conductor, to whom she wished to speak; and she smiled, for who could help it?" (95). The rhetorical question marks this text as participating in a realism that relies on reference to an assumed common knowledge of human nature, and the direct address to the reader appeals for intimacy. Looking over the lady's shoulder, assuming her position, provides readers with enough distance to relish the comedy of the speech that follows. " 'I'm carried off,' said poor Aunt Catherine hysterically" (95)—and in her distress she pours out what has happened to this stranger, jumbling together her wish that "we never had sold our land for the track" and her worry over the supper— "the biscuit ought to be eaten hot. Dear me!" (96). But the sympathetic adjective and familial positioning of "poor Aunt Catherine" work to moderate the tone of our amusement.

Jewett also shapes readers' reactions by specifying how her characters manage their own, embedding us in a drama of empathetic tact of the kind discussed in the previous section. The young lady, Alice West, is "quivering with laughter," but controls herself out of sympathy for Miss Catherine's feelings; she courteously tries to refrain from even a smile as they enter the compartment and she explains to her aunt what has happened (96). Aunt Catherine too can enter into others' sensations, however, and soon recognizes the situation is funny: " 'I know you want to laugh, dear,' said she. 'It's ridiculous, only I'm so afraid they'll be worried about me at home' " (97). The speech of her hostesses is more cultivated, closer to the language of the narrator than Miss Catherine's. But tact bridges the gap, and everyone laughs together; the isolation and humiliation that Miss Catherine fears if she had to go "into the car with all the people, and be stared at and made fun of" (101) are avoided. These empathetic Bostonians not only take Miss Spring into their compartment, but also loan her the fare for her return and a hood to cover her head, wrap her pitcher respectably in paper, even give her crackers and grapes so she will not be hungry as she journeys home. Eventually we learn that her guests have in fact been searching anxiously for her, fearing that she has been run over by the (persistently dangerous) train, or perhaps hanged herself in the garret (her nephew knows a bit about her money troubles). But they too rise to the occasion, and the excitement only improves the late supper Miss Catherine serves.

The mutual liking and recognition of worth established in this encounter lead the Boston ladies eventually to return and take the rooms Miss Catherine wished to rent—which allows her to continue to live in her own home, and also to give Katie Dunning a place. (That is, a job—but in effect, a home.) The enlarged household enriches Miss Spring economically and socially, and the boarders enrich the town in general. They increase its prosperity and they also bring "a great deal of pleasure and good-will to sober little Brookton, as two cultivated, thoughtful, helpful women may make any place pleasanter if they choose" (111). The connection is beneficial to Alice West and her aunt, as well; the house where they had planned to stay is alarmingly damp, and Miss Ashton is vulnerable because she has been ill. They are glad to find a happy, healthful place to stay, and they understand Miss Spring's and Brookton's true worth. In this story Jewett narrates the emergence of the kind of mutuality between the country and the city that she names, in the later preface to *Deephaven*, as her project. If Jewett's craft has worked, the reader—again directly addressed at the end—is also included in the chain of sympathy and well-wishing.

"A Late Supper" affirms an ethical imperative of generosity, and the providential ordering of events. The few critics who have written about this story have not pointed out that Miss Catherine's generosity to Katie Dunning sets the whole sequence in motion. If she had not extravagantly emptied her pitcher (87–8) because her "heart went out" (86) to the hungry little girl, she would not have needed to cross the track and would never have made these new friends. A similar relationship of surplus generosity exists between Miss Catherine and her neighbors; her nephew at first thinks she's simply been detained by one of them, for "they're always asking her advice about things" (102). Not only does Mrs. Hilton supply the requested cream, she says "with ready sympathy and interest... 'Now, what did you bring such a mite of a pitcher for? Do take this one of mine. I'd just as soon you'd have the cream as not'" (94). On the train Miss Catherine asks Alice West if her "aunty care[s] anything about cream," and "Miss Ashton's little tumbler was at once delightedly filled to the very brim" (100). I hesitate to make suggestions about the milk of human kindness, and the circulation of maternal fluids—but these exchanges clearly convey a vision of a benevolent social order based on nurturance and reciprocity.

In "A Late Supper," this is not only a spiritual but an explicitly religious vision. The narrator writes: "I am sure you will think, in reading all this, just what I have thought as I told it,—and what Miss Catherine herself felt,—that it was such a wonderfully linked-together chain. All the time she thought she was going wrong, that it was a series of mistakes. 'I never will be so miserable again,' said she. 'It was all ordered for the best; and may the Lord forgive me for doubting his care and goodness as I did that day!'" (112–13). The narrator, protagonist, and reader are syntactically entangled, and all ("I am sure") embrace a providential interpretation of the events of the story. Miss Catherine finds affirmation of her view in the next Sunday's sermon, and the narrator cites the title of a sermon in a book she "once happened to open" but "did not read": "Every Man's Life a Plan of God" (113). Both the firm Christian commitment and the intimate, even casual, tone towards its official forms are characteristic.

Jewett was brought up as a Congregationalist and confirmed as an Episcopalian. She was a convinced Christian throughout her life. In her biography, Paula Blanchard gives this topic its important place in Jewett's life; Terry Heller powerfully links Jewett's life to her work in the essay quoted above on her "religion of friendship." Of course she was sometimes critical of the actually existing church, particularly when embodied by men like Parson Dimmick with more book-learning than sympathy. And biographically she had moments of doubt, more apparently of herself than of God. Josephine Donovan's work on Swedenborg's influence on Jewett provides a helpful perspective; she writes that Jewett "was never doctrinaire, and like many women writers she strongly opposed the residual Calvinism that lingered in the New England mind-set long after the sect itself had declined. Part of the appeal of Swedenborgianism lay in the fact that it provided a more cheerful and optimistic alternative" ("Jewett and Swedenborg," 731–2). Mediated through her mentor Theophilus Parsons, Jr., who advocated "a literature of didactic moral purpose designed to influence people for the good" (734), this philosophy provided a warrant for her project and helped Jewett to see writing as a vocation that might legitimately structure her life. As we have seen, Plato is also—rather casually—enlisted as an authorizer. Like other distinguished New England writers, Jewett was flexible enough to see connections between Christianity and other belief systems. In an 1885 letter to Annie Fields, she wrote: "If we had better interpreters of Buddha's teaching we might reach heights of power and goodness that are now impossible" (Fields, *Letters*, 26).

In an early story like "A Late Supper," Jewett is more explicitly religious and didactic than she is later in her career. This has less to do with changes in her beliefs than with changes in the literary milieu of the late nineteenth century, in which the aesthetic increasingly is understood as incompatible with the didactic. The sacralization of literature supplants direct discussion of the sacred. In fact, in this early story she is already linking moral vision with serious literature. What succeeds the mention of the sermon and ends the story is a poem. Jewett closes with the passage that follows. "And here, for the last of the story, is a verse that Robert Browning wrote, that Miss Ashton said one morning, and Miss Catherine liked:—

> 'Grow old along with me!
> The best is yet to be,
> The last of life, for which the first was made:
> Our times are in His hand
> Who saith, "A whole I planned,"
> Youth shows but half; trust God: see all, nor be afraid!'" (114)

Clearly, although I am accepting much of Richard Brodhead's classic argument about nineteenth-century cultures of letters, I disagree with his assertion that Jewett's is "an almost wholly secular textual world" (*Cultures*, 160). It ignores not only her clearly stated views but her publication in a magazine like *Sunday Afternoon*, which its editor Washington Gladden characterized "at once wholesome and entertaining," including "stories of sound moral tendency" and discussing "questions of social life and national-well-being, but always in their relations to the Kingdom of God" (272–3). The push towards "the late nineteenth-century high-cultural presentation of literature as a sphere of its own of value in itself" (161) is real, however. Indeed, the secularism of university-based literary criticism is one of the legacies of that turn, and must be one reason why Jewett's belief has so often been occluded in interpretation. Another, I think, is the tact with which she integrates it into her narrative in later works.

This subtlety is already present in the unpretentiously allusive title of the story. This is not the Last, but a "Late," Supper. As Donovan writes in her article on Jewett and Swedenborg, the author created a symbolism "that established spiritual referents within this world so that she could then employ realistic, metonymic, details for metaphoric purposes: to figure forth revelations of the transcendent in the everyday" ("Jewett and Swedenborg," 748). My persistent association to this theme is perhaps idiosyncratic—it is with the religious paintings of Caravaggio, which were controversial in the sixteenth century because of their naturalism. Looking at his paintings of biblical figures as ordinary people imbued with extraordinarily vibrant life—for example, the glowing, sensual image of John the Baptist in *Youth with a Ram* in the Musei Capitolini in Rome—does make me see how the sacred and the everyday might be one. Jewett develops her own distinctive version of egalitarian religion, but it is a perspective that is also available elsewhere in her world. "A Late Supper" appearing in *Sunday Afternoon* means that it was edited by Washington Gladden, a leader of the movement we now call the Social Gospel, who later wrote that because "divine Fatherhood implies the human brotherhood," "the law of love covers all the relations of human life" (178), and "A man may be a Christian who is an aristocrat or a plebian, but the logic of Christianity is democracy" (185).

The elements of the story I have cited also offer material for a more hierarchical vision of the social order, however. The fact that in the characters' initial encounter Alice West and Miss Ashton are in a fenced-off space on the Pullman car is what enables them to protect our carried-off "heroine" from derision, and the crowd outside is not drawn into the circle of understanding. The narrator specifically mentions Miss Spring's enjoyment of their—presumably expensive, and indexing the emergence of new kinds of commodities—"hot-house" grapes (101). The story accomplishes understanding, without abolishing the difference, between the Boston ladies and their rural friend. How then—turning back to a broad view of Jewett's work, in the context of regionalism—are we to think about this simultaneously egalitarian and hierarchical project?

Double Vision

At the opening of "A Late Supper," Jewett describes Miss Catherine Spring's village. Brookton is "up in the country city people would say,—a town certainly not famous, but pleasant enough because it was on the outer edge of the mountain region, near some great hills. One never hears much about Brookton when one is away from it, but, for all that, life is as important and exciting there as it is anywhere; and it is like every other town, a miniature world, with its great people and small people, bad people and good people, its jealousy and rivalry, kindness and patient heroism" (80). This passage affirms the substantive being of the town. It is also relational in the sense in which I use the term in Chapter 1—it constitutes Brookton by contrasting, and thus linking, it with other places. It would be easy to say that it takes the perspective of the city, but that is not quite right. The narrator of this story often directly addresses the reader, as we have seen—but what we hear at this point is not "you in the city would say," but "city people would say." We stand outside both the country and the city, observing the difference in perspective. The next phrase, "One never hears much about Brookton when one is away from it," positions the narrator both in and away from the town, while using an impersonal pronoun that generalizes. The more one thinks about this locution, the odder and deeper it gets. It asks us to be in two places at once, and manages to be both intimate and distant. It is virtually imitative form—the sentence goes on to say not only that people's own lives are fascinating to themselves, but also that general significance inheres in that particularity. Here Jewett engages, in her distinctive way, the central puzzle of the nature of place that grounds my concept of the region.

As we have seen, by the end of the story it is clear that little Brookton is important enough to receive God's loving care—and in that too it is "like every other town." In "A Late Supper" Jewett voices her religious views didactically; in later fiction they are more often subtly integrated into the narrative. Throughout her career, however, she is trying to persuade the reader to value the everyday, and to believe—although we cannot always see—that the mundane and the sacred world simultaneously occupy the same space. Terry Heller's account of the role of transfiguration in Jewett's work is especially illuminating. In its context in a letter to Sara Norton, Jewett's often-quoted statement that there "is something transfiguring in the best of friendship" (Fields, *Letters*, 126) is followed by a discussion of a New Testament passage in which (quoting Heller's summary) "three disciples see Jesus transformed into a shining being, and a voice speaks out of a cloud identifying him as 'my son.' Then, suddenly, the vision is gone, and Jesus appears as merely a man (Matt. 17; Luke 22)" (Heller, 82). Any place, at any moment, is open to the transfiguring presence of God. Thus the center must be—in the sense that (following Lefebvre) I discussed in Chapter 1—movable.

Transfiguring friendship appears (as others have shown) throughout Jewett's work. In "The Green Bowl," as I have observed, a loving connection between two women literally gives access to the "other world." More often the spiritual remains implicit or is lightly touched, as in one of Jewett's most read and most loved stories, "Martha's Lady." It was first published in 1897, in *The Atlantic Monthly*, then in the 1899 *Queen's Twin* (the title story of the collection is another of Jewett's brilliant realizations of this theme). This narrative is fundamentally structured by sympathetic links; Martha and her lady meet only twice over many decades, but their connection seems to overcome time and space. When the charming Helena Vernon of Boston visits her aunt Harriet Pyne in the quiet village of Ashford, she is kind to the awkward, rustic servant Martha—who conceives a life-changing, lifelong devotion. It is not always noticed that she is not the only one to benefit from the visitor's lighthearted loving-kindness. She leaves behind two rejected suitors—but with their "pride unwounded," and "wider outlooks upon the world and a less narrow sympathy…Even Miss Harriet Pyne herself had lost some of the unnecessary provincialism and prejudice which had begun to harden a naturally good and open mind and affectionate heart" (878). Helena is an ambassador of cosmopolitanism at its best.

Helena goes forward into a privileged life sited elsewhere. Martha stays in place, but she has been awakened to love and to the potential of beauty in everyday life. Aesthetic and spiritual values blend in this story, as Martha is fulfilled by "the fine art of housekeeping" (885) and the joy of service. The social positions of the characters are woven inextricably into their interactions. It is while Martha is serving tea that she overhears Helena speak affectionately of her to Miss Pyne—because when she steps out of the room for a moment the "china-closet door was open a little way" (876). One of the eventual results of her transformation is the household's everyday use of "beautiful old china which Martha handled so lovingly that there was no good excuse for keeping it hidden on closet shelves" (885). Lockwood's work on antique collecting—the chapter is called "Out of the China Closet"—shows that such precious domestic objects are intimately woven into the practices through which a group of elite New England women, Jewett among them, constructed an intimate relationship with the past. She also notes that the insensitivity of rural and immigrant women was considered a danger to antique dishes—and one remembers that Julia Cochrane reportedly invented the automatic dishwasher less as a labor-saving device than to prevent her fine china from being chipped by servants. Martha also, however, gains a stake in the wider world, keeping a geography book in her room open to the map of Europe as she follows Helena—now Mrs. Dysart—through "the changes of a diplomatic life…For such a slow scholar Martha was not unlearned at last, since everything about life in these foreign towns was of interest to her faithful heart" (886). Far more than the other characters, Martha learns the cosmopolitan lesson that life is important and interesting in every town, and that they are all connected.

"Martha's Lady," like "Green Island" and "A Late Supper," is a drama of empathic tact. The central protagonists are Martha and Helena. There are secondary threads as well, in a story that deploys immensely subtle shifts in point of view. Miss Pyne fails utterly to understand Martha, although Martha does not realize it until the conclusion when Mrs. Dysart comes back to Ashford at last. More perceptive, the new cook Hannah sees the flowers in the hall and how the tea table is set, and realizes that the visitor "must be a very important person" (887). It seems at first that time has succeeded in dividing the protagonists, even though they share a common lot: "'Oh, my Miss Helena is an old woman like me!' and Martha gave a pitiful sob; she had never dreamed it would be like this; this was the one thing she could not bear" (888). But she is able to find the woman she loves in her unchanged smile and young eyes, and what matters most is that Martha's lady recognizes her love in the story's final, magical moment. "Helena called her back. She suddenly knew the whole story and could hardly speak. 'Oh, my dear Martha!' she cried, 'won't you kiss me good-night? Oh, Martha, have you remembered like this, all these long years!'" (888). The title "Martha's Lady" itself stands between, embodying Jewett's project of connection. Martha is at the center, but she is authorized by her lady's recognition. Both Christian belief and desire remain implicit, and class difference is explicit yet somehow does not matter.

I find this story moving. I also find it uncomfortable, because of its class politics. Transfiguring friendship makes Martha devout and elegant—she is "unconsciously beautiful like a saint" (884). It also makes her into someone who would never, ever, chip a piece of china—a contented and competent, indeed an inspired, domestic servant.

In "A Late Supper" and here, as elsewhere, Jewett does not see social distinctions as invidious—they are rooted in a benevolent social order. She criticizes the industrial system in a story like "The Gray Mills of Farley," she does not imagine that the privileged are more likely than the poor to be virtuous and intelligent, and she actively demonstrates that anyone in any rank may be deeply sensitive to God's presence in the world. Yet she does not disarticulate what it means to be cultivated from the cultural system through which she herself achieved refinement. It is precisely her interest in how groups of people develop their gifts that leads her to the attitudes about race voiced in, for example, *The Story of the Normans*. I have not written much about this topic, which is well covered by others (Zagarell, Foote, Schrag, Gleason). The evidence is so clear that I want to write that it is uncontroversial to notice that Jewett's attitudes on a range of issues are not considered progressive today. The controversy shows that I am wrong about that. I will say, instead, that I still find that distancing conclusion inescapable.

Of course, why should we expect to agree with the opinions of the authors we study and admire? It is not much to the point to rebuke Jewett for supporting England's rule over Ireland, 130 years after she expressed it in a letter to Annie Fields (22–3, quoting below from 23), more than one hundred years after her death and almost one hundred years after Irish independence. But in the context of this book it *is* very interesting that she justifies her view (in the midst of somewhat more complicated reflections on a still more complicated essay by Matthew Arnold) by writing that Ireland is—"backward." The weight and import of that word became clear in Chapter 1. It shapes time and space together, projecting both a normative modernity and the empire of civilization.

I deliberately implicated myself in that pattern, when (a few sentences ago) I used a word I ordinarily avoid: "progressive." Change is real, but it does not move steadily toward a bright future, or indeed carry us certainly in any fixed direction. It is exactly because racism is an utterly unsolved problem today that it is so fraught to write about Jewett's racialism and racism, to quote the words "darkeys" and "coolies" (Fields, *Letters*, 161 and 163) from her letters. (By "today" I mean: at the moment I write these words; on the date I foresee them appearing in print; and in the foreseeable future of their reading. We can hope for a moment in which these words are read and my statement is no longer true.) The challenge, in teaching and scholarship, is to historicize by acknowledging *both* that different periods are deeply different, and that we swim in the same historical stream. That is most worth doing, but still difficult, when a powerful writer is talking back to us. It is the way to turn the conversation away from attack and defense, and toward the accomplishments and complexities of her work. Then we can continue to work at the historical puzzle presented to Jewett—and to us—by our belonging in evolving solidarities that are unequal, yet aspire to democracy.

These questions about relations across time are entailed by the work of the literary scholar, and they also run recursively through Jewett's work. I suggested in Chapter 1 that regionalism as a form constitutively connects place and time. One of the beginning points of this book project was Jewett's affectionate description, in the first chapter of *The Country of the Pointed Firs*, of old, quaint Dunnet Landing's "childish certainty of being the centre of civilization" (377). The direct significance of the line is carried forward when (as already discussed) the limits of Johnny Bowden's knowledge are projected through his surprise that the narrator is ignorant of the meaning of the flag flying on Green Island. Blackett—not a child but an elderly man—is provincial in the same way. The view from the island's "great ledge" that he takes the narrator to see is beautiful, and cosmic: the ocean "circled this and a hundred other bits of island-ground, the mainland shore and all the far horizons. It gave a sudden sense of space, for nothing stopped the eye or hedged one in,—that sense of liberty in space and time which great prospects always give." Yet when William says, "There ain't no such view in the world, I expect," the narrator feels "as if an untraveled boy had spoken." That is so not because of William's appreciation of the view, but because he thinks it is unique. By implicitly disparaging other perspectives, he reveals his own limits. When the narrator adds, "and yet one loved to have him value his native heath" (413), Jewett confronts the paradox of place so fundamental to regionalism. For Rome or New York to consider itself the center is also childish. Although she leaves the category "civilization" unquestioned, her apparently simple phrase offers a complex corrective to the pretensions of the metropolis.

Jewett values the ontological certainty of the child in a good place. It was once a truism of criticism that children were scarce in the spinsterly world of the New England regionalists, but in fact her sense of affiliation with youth is visible throughout her work and especially in her letters. Most famously (and rather wonderfully), she wrote to Sara Norton in 1897: "This is my birthday and I am always nine years old" (Fields, *Letters*, 125). (She had just turned forty-eight.) It is not always good to be childish—for example, when Leonard Jaffrey—a middle-aged man speaking in the voice of a "whimpering boy," trying to justify his inappropriate love affair to his sister—says: "We are only as old as our hearts are" (282–3), it is cant. But Jewett is following a long literary tradition in her admiration of a childlike spirit, and she is participating in the intensified focus on childhood that characterized the late nineteenth and early twentieth centuries, in (at least) Britain and America. Carolyn Steedman has suggested that the figure of the child enables people to articulate a sense of their essential interior self. Angela Sorby's subsequent analysis of the pedagogical as a literary mode, and its link specifically to the cultural place of poetry in America, adds resonance to this dimension of Jewett's work and provides a link to my discussion of Eaton's quotations from poetry in Chapter 4. Jewett both imagines herself as a child and puts her deepest themes into her writing for actual children. (Figure 3.2 is Jewett at the age of eight.)

Both the framing and the events of Jewett's "Betty Leicester" stories for girls enact her religion of friendship. When they were collected she prefaced the volume with a direct address to the reader: "I wish to tell you how much pleasure it gives me to know that you like my stories, and especially that you are such a friend of

SARAH ORNE JEWETT
At the age of eight

FIGURE 3.2 *Sarah Orne Jewett at the age of eight. From Francis Otto Matthiessen, "Sarah Orne Jewett," published by Houghton Mifflin in 1929.*

Miss Betty Leicester! I must own that I took a great liking to her myself when I was writing her, and that she has always seemed to me to be a real person." In an 1897 letter to a thirteen-year-old girl, Jewett repeats her endorsement of Betty's reality, adding: "it is just the same way with Mrs. Todd" (Cary, *Letters*, 116)—linking what we think of as a minor and a major work in a somewhat unexpected way. Much of the story of Betty's summer with her aunts in Tideshead is about her efforts to improve herself, but from the first her presence benefits the village just as Alice West and Miss Ashton's does Brookton, and Helena Vernon's does Ashford. The residents have fallen into a dull routine; Betty's optimism and sociability awaken them to the possibilities of their own place. Jewett's idiosyncratic comment on Flaubert's *Madame Bovary*, in a letter to Annie Fields, was that "the very great pathos of the book to me, is not the sin of her, but the thought, all the time, if she *could* have had a little brightness and prettiness of taste in the dull doctor, if she could have taken what there was in that dull little village! She is such a lesson to dwellers in country towns, who drift out of relation to their surroundings" (Fields, *Letters*, 82). In the same spirit Betty adds to her nightly prayers, " 'Help me to have a good time doing every-day things, and to make my work my pleasure' " (136). This is more openly didactic than, but not different from, what Jewett affirms elsewhere.

I turn to Betty Leicester to knit Jewett's figure of the child into my argument about time, and also to emphasize the specifically Christian orientation of her vision. Bakhtin writes that the chronotope of the idyll is characterized by an "immanent unity" of time on the site of a home place (225). Regionalism, I have suggested, is a modern form that inhabits a more uneven landscape. In Jewett's fiction she asks us to believe that those two worlds coexist. She portrays social hierarchy as benevolent, but also as in some sense always flexible—because a radically different order simultaneously occupies the same space: one in which each person is equally, because infinitely, important. But I read her not just unexpectedly, but against the grain, when I see her project in Sartrean terms: as striving to create a universal through grounded action in the world, inhabiting the singularity of human life. (Their views of Flaubert certainly do not intersect.) It is more plausible to link Jewett to Alain Badiou, who writes that love "demonstrates how eternity can exist within the time span of life itself" (48). To work through these connections between her orientations and my own is not, however, to set aside Jewett's belief. In her work, religion is the necessary ground on which time and place collapse into transfiguration.

World-Making Words, by Edith Eaton and Sui Sin Far

Asian America (where's that?)

—KAREN TEI YAMASHITA, *I Hotel*

Edith Maude Eaton is a writer still emerging into visibility. Even what name we should use to refer to her is not settled. There are many scholarly discussions of her work, and most use the pseudonym "Sui Sin Far." I did so in articles that appeared in 2008 and 2011, and so does the Wikipedia article on her (at least as of this writing in 2017). A case can be made for that choice; Eaton made a large and successful investment in constructing the persona Sui Sin Far, and used it not only in publishing but also in correspondence.[1] But the historical person whose response to the possibilities of form, in her moment, I am studying was born and buried as Edith Eaton. She published under that name, and used not only Sui Sin Far and variant spellings of that name but also many other pen names. Both names are on the monument erected on the author's grave in the Mount Royal Cemetery in Montréal; carved in stone, it is an early and durable recognition of her public work and the complexity of her identity (see Figure 4.1).[2] Much of this chapter is concerned with the Chinatown-oriented author Sui Sin Far. But this life and work are best understood in the framework offered by the continuing recovery of "Edith Eaton," and I have now chosen to put that name first.

The project that has made this author visible, and legible, is the construction of an Asian-American literary history; that is the ground of possibility for my reading. Eaton's placement in that category is itself a profound and interesting problem, which weaves recursively into my topic in this chapter. She never set foot in Asia, did not grow up in (any) Chinatown or with an overseas Chinese community around her, presumably carried a British passport. My point is not that we should shuffle through the available labels to find the right one—"Chinese-Canadian" or "Eurasian-North American" might indeed be preferable—but I want rather to unsettle the categories themselves. Larissa Lai argues that the category of Asian Canadian literature, which is the formation that most appropriately hosts Eaton's work from a contemporary perspective, emerged in the 1980s and 1990s precisely

FIGURE 4.1 *Edith Eaton's grave, Mount Royal Cemetery, Montréal. Photograph by the author.*

as a "rupture," and is from the outset "profoundly relational" (1). This strategy, I will argue, follows the direction implicit in the publications signed Sui Sin Far—and is the only one that works for Edith Eaton.

A chapter on this author is a less predictable element of a book on American literary regionalism than one on Sarah Orne Jewett. Sui Sin Far's entry into the regionalist canon is relatively recent, and it is now clear that Edith Eaton wrote in a remarkable variety of forms. My opposition to seeing genre criticism as an exercise in classification does not emancipate me from answering the question, does it make sense to include this writer? Fortunately, it does mean that the issue is not, "is Sui Sin Far a local color writer?" or "does Edith Eaton belong in this box?"—but rather, "what happens when we put this author in relation to this category? Is it interesting, and productive?" Yes. Both Eaton's most successful access to national print culture, and the recovery of her work in recent scholarship, have been mediated through public interest in the particularities of race and place. Those of her stories that mobilize regional conventions, although they often seem straightforward at first, lead to some challenging conceptual problems about how those categories are mapped against each other and onto nationality. I will attend to what is distinctive about Eaton's writing, of course—but it is the perspectives she generates for considering the grounds and tendencies of regionalism that make this chapter necessary. I have thought these matters through *with* Eaton.

I begin by sketching Eaton's biography, and the history of her reception. Those accounts lead me to investigate the apparently simple statement that she often writes about Chinatown, and they raise questions about the *place* of literature in the contests of culture, which are carried forward into discussions of three short stories. Those interpretations in turn lead me to broad reflections on the categories of American and world (or, sometimes, global, or planetary) literature. Disciplinary divisions of labor have meant that regionalism rarely figures in discussions of the latter categories. Working with Eaton (among other influences) has shown me the importance of drawing these conversations together.

A (Possibly Surprising) Biographical Sketch

Edith Maude Eaton was born in 1865, the second child of a Chinese mother and a British father. I characterize her mother, Achuen Grace Amoy Eaton, as "Chinese" because of where she was born and her Han ethnicity—although she may have spent fewer years than her white husband in Asia, and although both lived in North America for decades. Mary Chapman has established that Eaton's mother was sold as a child into an acrobatic troupe that toured the United States, Europe, and Britain. While with them in London she was "rescued" by missionaries, and then educated in England. She returned (by way of Australia) to Shanghai to be a missionary herself.[3] There she met and married Edward Eaton, who came from a family active in the silk trade and was in the city on business.

The oldest child of their new family, a boy who was named Edward Charles, was born in China. Edith was the second, born after their return to Edward's home in Macclesfield in the northwest of England. A third child was born in Jersey City, after the Eatons had immigrated to the United States. Edward opened a wholesale drug and dye business there; when it failed the family returned to England for some years, then moved to Canada and was settled in Montréal by 1873. Edith's sister Winnifred—who also became a writer, often using the pseudonym Onoto Watanna—was born there in 1875, the eighth child of an eventual fourteen (of whom twelve survived). This story already begins to suggest the family's participation in colonial connections and what we now call globalization. Their national and ethnic affiliations were complex; at various moments, Eaton children presented themselves as white, Eurasian, English, Spanish, Mexican, Japanese, and Chinese-American. We take that last term for granted today, but Edith seems to have been the first to use it in print.[4]

The Eatons' class identity was also not simple. The English Eaton family was prosperous and respectable. At least one member of the North American branch claimed grand connections for which there is no evidence—Winnifred called her grandfather a "merchant prince" and represented herself as a descendant of Isaac Newton (Birchall, 6–7). The received story has been that Edward lost status by his business failures and by choosing the life of an artist, so that his children grew up poor—the family lived, frequently changing their lodgings, in Hochelaga, a mostly French working-class district of Montréal. Our view of Eaton's father is, however, considerably complicated by Mary Chapman's recent revelation that Edward was deeply involved in smuggling Chinese labor into the United States. This seems to have been true over a long period; he was arrested twice—once in 1896 (when it seems possible that Edith helped him escape from jail), and again twenty years later. (We could, of course, represent this business as resistance to the Exclusion Act, on which more follows.) I follow Chapman in suggesting that this surprising biographical information sharpens our appreciation of the importance of border-crossing in Edith's work, and underscores what we already knew: that the family was transnational. As she notes, Montréal was "a contact-zone where numerous cultures intermingled, including a Catholic francophone majority, a small ruling class of Protestant immigrants from Scotland and England, and a small but growing number of immigrants, including some from Asia" (*Becoming*, xxiv).

Winnifred's granddaughter and biographer Diana Birchall reconstructs a vivid image of the household Edith grew up in, representing it as "big, impoverished, noisy, artistic" and "Bohemian" (15). Both the boys and the girls in the family got some formal schooling, but mostly they were well educated in the English tradition—given the financial impossibility of boarding school—at home. Whatever sources of income came from Edward's activities, on their own testimony the Eaton children began to earn as soon as they could. As the eldest daughter, Edith worked especially hard, and she seems to have carried a heavy sense of responsibility to her family to the end of her life. She reports that she not only did domestic work and baby-minding at home, but also from the age of ten was sent to "tramp around" selling her father's paintings and her own lace—although she also sometimes represents her lacework as the consequence of her drive to create.[5] Her autobiographical writings report how much she suffered from the racial insults directed at her—and, much less prominently, that she was very sick with rheumatic fever as a child. Despite her ill health (which persisted), by the age of eighteen Edith was working as a compositor at Canada's largest newspaper, the *Montreal Star*, where she also taught herself shorthand. She was a writer from childhood and submitted for publication from her youth. The earliest stories that have been located are signed Edith Eaton, in *The Dominion Illustrated*—a short-lived "Canadian Pictorial Weekly" based in Montréal—beginning in 1888, when she was twenty-three. In the early 1890s she published journalism, visited her sister Grace and her new (British-born and literary) husband Walter Blackburn Harte in Boston, and lived away from home as a stenographer and reporter in Thunder Bay, Ontario.

By the time Edith turned thirty in 1895, she had a substantial record of publication and had opened an office in Montréal as a stenographer and typewriter, simultaneously working as freelance journalist. She had been writing articles on the Chinese in Montréal since 1890, and increasingly specialized in reporting on and advocating for the Chinese community. In a 1912 piece for the *Boston Globe*, "Sui Sin Far, the Half Chinese Writer, Tells of Her Career," the author says that the first suggestion that she and her mother should call on a recently arrived Chinese bride came from a clergyman. Both White-Parks and Ferens believe that Edith and Grace, active Presbyterians, would have become involved in mission work in Montréal's rapidly growing Chinatown. And demonstrably Eaton sought out similar connections for the rest of her life. The author told Boston readers that, "From that time I began to go among my mother's people, and it did me a world of good to discover how akin I was to them" (Ling and White-Parks, 292).

In 1896, Eaton first published using the pen name that would define her for a long time—spelling it, in those early years, "Sui Seen Far." The story appeared in her brother-in-law's little magazine *Fly Leaf*, which was "an intellectual revolt against the tyrannical, intolerant Smugocracy in letters" (quoted in MacLeod, 94). That story appeared in February, and others under the same by-line in June (in the better-known and longer-lived *Land of Sunshine*, based in California), in August and October (in *Lotus*, an undergraduate magazine that started in Kansas City and was then being edited by her sister and brother-in-law [Mott, vol. 4, 98]), and in November (*Land of Sunshine* again). Also during that eventful year, her father was arrested and somehow eluded confinement. In December, Edith went to Jamaica, taking over a position previously held by her sister Winnifred as a reporter for *Gall's Daily News Letter* in Kingston. Scholars have argued persuasively, and I agree, that the six months she spent there had an enormous impact on her understanding of race and nation. Her pseudonymous publications as "Fire Fly" suggest that, and "Sui Sin Far" also tells us much, in 1909 in an autobiographical essay titled "Leaves from the Mental Portfolio of an Eurasian" that she published in *The Independent*. In Jamaica her status was so low that no one questioned her whiteness, and she had the option "to set my heel upon the Ham people"—but she did not, because "I too am of the 'brown people' of the earth" (Ling and Parks, 225).

For the rest of her life Edith Eaton traveled and changed residences frequently, living in the United States—in San Francisco, Seattle, Los Angeles, and Boston—as well as periodically returning to Montréal. She combined journalism, fiction writing, and an as yet undetermined amount of office work to make a living and send money home. Mary Chapman's recovery work suggests that she was both more prosperous and more popular than scholars have thought. We also know that Eaton continued to spend time at Chinatown missions, and to write from her affiliation with "brown people." The 1882 Exclusion Act in the United States was initially authorized for ten years, was reauthorized in 1892, and made permanent in 1902. That was the historical terrain on which Eaton worked—and when we consider the time line of her recovery, we should remember that it was not repealed until 1943, almost three decades after her death. In Canada, the Head Tax did similar work—it was established in 1885, and renewed or raised in 1887, 1892, 1900, and 1904. Eaton consistently spoke for North American Chinese people—from her emergence into a continental print culture dominated by the United States, to the end of her life. Her most successful claim to broad attention was as Sui Sin Far, whose first story in a national magazine was "A Chinese Boy-Girl," in the April 1904 *Century*. Soon she was collecting checks from *Good Housekeeping*, and she published prolifically for the rest of her life. But she protested against being painted into a Chinatown corner, in "Leaves" mocking the "funny people" who thought that "to succeed in literature in America I should dress in Chinese costume, carry a fan in my hand, wear a pair of scarlet beaded slippers" (Ling and Parks, 230). And she maintained her affiliation with her sister Grace and the avant-garde, as Chapman's discovery of the surprising story "The Alaska Widow," which appeared under the name Edith Eaton in 1909 in *The Bohemian*, demonstrates.

"The Alaska Widow" is gradually getting the wide readership it deserves, as scholars parse its complexities. Although it has a happy ending that follows the "coupling convention," in other ways the story is unexpected. As Chapman has pointed out, it invokes the landscape of U.S. imperialism, connecting California, the Klondike, and the Philippines. The heroine Nora Leslie becomes vulnerable because of acts based on her sense of solidarity with a Native Alaskan woman who shows up at her wedding, with the groom's baby in her arms ("Cross-Cultural Affinities"). From the perspective of this study of regionalism, it matters that what this heroine does, when she is deserted and ailing, is to get a job as a country schoolteacher. Unsurprisingly for readers of this book, the village in which the story's next scenes take place (ironically named Wisdom) is not a pleasant refuge. The divorced Nora becomes the target of malicious gossip, and there is talk of a petition to the school board to have her removed (a sense of previous teachers' unhappy circumstances is quickly conveyed as well). There are other engaged and endangered teachers in Eaton's stories (most interestingly, Miss McLeod in "The Gift of Little Me") and Eaton's use of the topos underscores its availability and persistence. But the classroom is not one of the contact zones of central interest to her. What connects "The Alaska Widow" mostly closely to my reading of Eaton's work in this chapter is an unreferenced quotation in its first section. As the attention of the characters we know at this point only as "she" and "him" shifts from their work to their interest in each other, the narrator offers the observation that "[t]here are moments in one's life when 'Ambition's less than nothingness'" (164).

The quotation is not easy to identify because it is imprecise, but it is from Byron's 1814 "Ode to Napoleon."[6] Her line works as well or better than the exact one—"Ambition's less than littleness!"—for the story's opening situation, in which the protagonists' relationship develops in a law office as she prepares documents for him, and mutual attraction is a distraction from their work. The way both "The Alaska Widow" and the poem link the romantic and personal, and the transnational and political, is a potential thematic resonance (Byron makes conjectures about Marie Louise's reaction to Napoleon's abdication, for example). Also, the "Ode" ends by asserting that there is only one world-historical figure who does not deserve contempt: the "Cincinnatus of the West," George Washington. Byron was after all a revolutionary poet, involved in hopes for democracy sometimes represented by "America." He admired but was bitterly disappointed in Napoleon—just as many, at the turn into the twentieth century, were disappointed by the American venture into imperialism. Nora Leslie's lover becomes the Governor of Luzon, in the Philippines. This is just a beginning, in terms of thinking about Eaton and Byron—but whatever future research reveals, the connection between "The Alaska Widow" and the "Ode to Napoleon" confirms the centrality of poetry in Edith Eaton's mental portfolio.

At the same time that Eaton was gaining traction with a national audience of anglophone readers, she strove to connect with an audience that might be considered local or transnational—or both. The Eaton family spoke English at home, and in "Leaves" Edith wrote that "save for a few phrases, I am unacquainted with my mother tongue" (Ling and Parks, 227). So it is unsurprising that scholars' initial assumption was that "Sui Sin Far" did not speak Chinese. But "Leaves" is not wholly reliable, and in any case my quotation comes from a description of her move to the Far West in the late 1890s. Mary Chapman has shown that "by 1909 she was studying Chinese, interviewing people in Chinatown in Chinese, and publishing 'translations' of Chinese folktales," and had been "invited to submit a story to a San Francisco Chinese-language newspaper" ("Finding Edith Eaton," 265). As early as 2000, Xiao-huang Yin suggested that Eaton's work and the highly appropriate pen name she chose demonstrate that she had at least some grasp of the language: the syllables "Sui Sin Far" in Cantonese refer to the narcissus, which symbolizes "dignity, elegance, and love of homeland" (89). Eaton herself wrote about the flower and its resonance (see *Becoming*, xlvi). A horticulturalist who has studied the plant's history (who gives the pronounced phrase as "seui sin faa" without mentioning the author), describes how it was successfully imported from southeast China, how carefully it was cultivated, and how much it was loved (Todt). In English the *Narcissus tazetta* subsp. *chinensis* is often called the Chinese sacred lily or the joss flower; nongardeners might describe it as a small daffodil with clusters of flowers. Figure 4.2 is an image

FIGURE 4.2 *"The Chinese Sacred Lily, or Oriental Narcissus," from* The Geo. H. Mellen Co. Illustrated Catalogue of Bulbs, Roses and Plants, *Innisfallen Green Houses, Springfield, Ohio, 1899, p. 11.*

FIGURE 4.3 *The cover of the original edition of* Mrs. Spring Fragrance, *published by A. C. McClurg and Company of Chicago in 1912.*

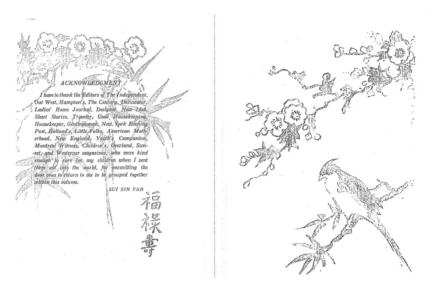

FIGURE 4.4 *Acknowledgements page, and facing blank page, from the original edition of* Mrs. Spring Fragrance, *showing its "Chinese" decorations.*

FIGURE 4.5 *The title page of Eaton's "The Son of Chung Wo," published in* Leslie's Illustrated Weekly *in 1910, demonstrating the use of a "chop suey" typeface.*

from an 1899 catalogue of bulbs. The plant can certainly thrive in the ground, but often, as shown here, it is grown inside during the winter in a bowl of pebbles and water. Its emergence from mud, fragile-seeming yet resilient stems, and deep associations with Chinese North American history and culture do indeed make "Sui Sin Far" an evocative and effective pseudonym.

The relation between Eaton's access to audiences and "authenticity" is vertiginously complex. In 1912, when a collection of her fiction titled *Mrs. Spring Fragrance* was published in Chicago by A. C. McClurg, the volume's binding and paper marketed her work by orientalizing it. The cover is red, stamped with gold and images of Chinese characters, the moon, dragonflies, and flowers that bear some resemblance to the narcissus. Inside the book, each recto page is decorated with flowers and characters, each verso with flowers and a bird. (See Figures 4.3 and 4.4.) This would, of course, have been nothing new to the writer Sui Sin Far—in most of her publications the design visually conveys a stereotypical Chineseness. Figure 4.5 is the title of her story "The Son of Chung Wo" as it appeared in *Leslie's Illustrated Weekly* in 1910. (Such fonts are often not legible to an OCR reader—one of the reasons her work has been difficult to locate, as noted in Chapman's "Finding Edith Eaton," 266.) The graphic designer and historian of design Peter Shaw says of the earliest typeface that imitated calligraphy, produced by the Cleveland Type Foundry in 1883, that "the strokes, forced onto the armature of Roman letters, are assembled in a manner that completely ignores a calligraphic emphasis on structural balance and harmony" (110). He goes on, however, to talk about what are called "chop suey" types in terms resembling my discussion of Chinatowns below—the involvement of ethnic entrepreneurs means that inauthenticity is too simple a category, whether we are talking about culinary or visual styles. Similarly: Sui Sin Far's claim to attention outside Chinatown was her ability to offer a connection to it, and the terms of her inclusion are profoundly subordinating. However, that does not necessarily mean that Eaton's developing connection with a Chinese-speaking audience was easier or more enabling than her experience with McClurg and other publishers. Language would not have been the only barrier to communication Eaton faced, as an educated mixed-race woman working in Chinatowns. The more we learn about her, the clearer it is that in every situation she was listening hard, and working even harder to be heard.

Edith Eaton died of her long-standing heart disease in 1914 in Montréal, at the age of forty-nine. She had written in the *Boston Globe*, just before the appearance of *Mrs. Spring Fragrance*, that she had "also written another book which will appear next year, if Providence is kind" (Ling and White-Parks, 288). That manuscript has not been found.

Eaton's work did not get any further attention in print for the next sixty years, as far as we know. Then, in 1975, she was mentioned in the now classic, still controversial anthology of Asian-American literature, *Aiiieeeee!* Scholars began to take notice, and Amy Ling included Sui Sin Far in the first edition of the *Heath Anthology of American Literature* (1989) and wrote about her in *Between Worlds: Women Writers of Chinese Ancestry* (1990). In 1995, Ling and Annette White-Parks edited a book that included most of *Mrs. Spring Fragrance* and some additional articles, and White-Parks published a biography. During the same period Fae Myenne Ng demonstrated that the author had become an influence on contemporary literature, by inventing the "Edith Eaton School" (14) as the workplace of the protagonist of her novel *Bone* set in San Francisco's Chinatown. The author is now the focus of considerable scholarly attention, and is an imaginative presence for Asian-American and Asian-Canadian writers. My epigraph comes from Karen Tei Yamashita's 2010 novel *I Hotel*, which refracts the story of social movements in San Francisco from 1968 through 1977, and includes in its first chapter a resonant passage that mentions both Eaton sisters: "We meet, then head out like a bunch of gangsters, rummaging around used book stores, looking for any discarded books by an Oriental. So far: Sui Sin Far and Onoto Watanna" (41).

Today Eaton's work is still becoming visible, in the most literal sense. In 1981 S. E. Solberg's list of her known publications numbered twenty-two; in 1995, when Annette White-Parks and Amy Ling brought out their edition of Sui Sin Far's writings, they knew of sixty-four. Research by Dominika Ferens, Mary Chapman, Martha Cutter, and others—I made a modest contribution myself with the discovery of "The Son of Chung Wo"—has now quadrupled that number. Chapman tells the story of this successful detective work in a 2012 article in *Legacy*, and in her introduction to her 2016 collection of Eaton's early work. We now know that this author published—in Chapman's words—"risqué sensation fiction signed 'Edith Eaton' for the Daily Story Company, a syndication service that supplied short fiction to regional newspapers across the United States; Chinatown fiction in *Out West*, the *Chautauquan*, and Seattle's *Westerner*; didactic fiction in conservative children's and women's magazines such as *Good Housekeeping*, the *Housekeeper*, *Children's Magazine*, *Gentlewoman*, and *American Motherhood*; more racialized (and racier) fiction in radical magazines such as the *Bohemian*; and middlebrow (white) women's fiction in *People's Magazine* and *New England Magazine*" ("Finding Edith Eaton," 265). I expect that new biographical information and works will continue to be discovered. I would write, not at the same pace—but hesitate because during late revisions to this book, in October 2017, I found "The Draught of Bewilderment," which appeared as a two-part serial in *Modern Priscilla* in 1908. It looks at this point like a significant story, in a magazine that was not yet on the list of Eaton's known publication venues. So: to be continued.

Coming to terms with this body of material is already producing a quite different writer than the one we have known. "Sui Sin Far" is only one aspect of Edith Eaton. I think, however, that there is also more to be understood about her most frequently read stories. It is her representations of Chinatown that made her available for consideration as a local color writer. They are my focus in what follows.

Where Is Chinatown?

Writers who portray ethnic districts in cities, such as Eaton and Abraham Cahan, often gained access to print as local colorists. In my courses on regionalism I juxtapose their work with stories located in other neighborhoods in the same city—in Cahan's case, often with Henry James's "The Jolly Corner" (1908). Each of these authors works within the capacious conventions of the varieties of realism, each is engaged with place; we might generate many comparisons between any given pair, pointing in many directions. When the interpretive pressure of genre is exerted, and we ask what we learn from considering these works in terms of regionalism, their relations to a center become the salient point. Like Eaton, Cahan works in multiple forms—I am bracketing most of his work; nor am I suggesting that he had any doubts, either in his massive body of publications in Yiddish or his relatively slender work in English, about the self-evident importance of his world. But when attention is claimed in terms of a particular place, the relational has arrived on the scene. A debate about the degree to which a writer like James simply *assumes* centrality might go on for a long time (a text like "The Jolly Corner," featuring a protagonist obsessively haunted by difference, would certainly be relevant). For my purpose here what matters is that it is less form than social positioning that makes James a realist, and Eaton and Cahan regionalists. In both common conversation and much literary scholarship, some neighborhoods are the world, and others are particular places.

Sui Sin Far, an authorial persona constructed by Edith Eaton, claims attention through her ability to represent an exotic place that exists within the American city, and—as Dominika Ferens demonstrates in her critical study of Edith and Winnifred Eaton together—through the ethnographic project of documenting difference. Her window of visibility opens at the cusp of place, and race. It widens as the categories of ethnic literature become available. At the same time, however, her writing works against classification. In an important essay on the autobiographical "Leaves from the Mental Portfolio of an Eurasian," published in the *Independent* in 1909, David Shih argues that "her installation as a foremother to current Asian-American writers, and to the field as a whole, requires her inter-pellation as a discrete *racial* and *national* subject—a Chinese-American—to the neglect of alternate subject positions developed in her autobiography, positions that deliberately work to destabilize race as a dangerous trope of difference" (49). One of his pieces of evidence is the photographic portrait that accompanied the article (see Figure 4.6), which, he suggests, "works in tandem with her words to promote an autonomous self free from racial or national determination" (49). I too have found, reading and rereading this author's work, that it generates a paradoxical place, simultaneously building a ground for her to stand on and un-doing its stability.

Interpreting such a writer is never an easy matter, and it is particularly difficult and urgent given the way regionalism and ethnicity intersect in Eaton's work. In *The Romance of Authenticity*, Jeff Karem suggests a powerful continuity between the ways in which readers and critics have judged regionalist and ethnic fiction. His account of the reception of writers from Faulkner to Silko shows they have been valued for conveying convincing accounts of particular—that is, remote—experience, conceived geographically, then (increasingly) racially. Karem shows

SUI SIN FAR.

Leaves from the Mental Portfolio of an Eurasian

BY SUI SIN FAR

FIGURE 4.6 *Portrait of Edith Eaton, published in the* Independent *in 1909.*

that a critical establishment warmly appreciative of Richard Wright's early work, which fit the frame of Southern authenticity, turned a cold shoulder when his scene shifted to Chicago and foregrounded conflict. Ironically, later Ernest Gaines's work was "received as outmoded pastoral because it dissented from the urban violence that had come to be expected of African American fiction, an expectation fostered in part by the ongoing legacy of Wright's *Native Son*" (14). Karem's careful and close examinations of instances both demonstrate the power of authenticity in literary history, and should inoculate us against believing in it. As Karem puts it, "Judgments of authenticity are always contingent; whether made by a cultural 'insider' or 'outsider,' they depend on the interpreter's own horizon of expectations regarding the culture in question" (7). The category is conceptually unstable, relying on the standard of an implicit center.

These proliferating instabilities point toward a question that is more complex and destabilizing than it seems at first: Where is "Chinatown"?

I have learned in teaching this work that although the location of the title story of *Mrs. Spring Fragrance* is clearly stated as Seattle, students do not always distinguish Seattle's from San Francisco's Chinatown. And in fact, Chinatowns all over the world signal their identity with similar architecture. They are located in particular places, but also imagined as global—connected to other Chinatowns all over the world, and to China. They connect to the past as well, in a virtually paradigmatic case of the invention of tradition. This is most strikingly visible in the *paifang*, the elaborate gate at the entrance to most Chinatowns; every aspect of its thick decoration is said to allude to an ancient Chinese tradition. When the new gate to Seattle's Chinatown (see Figure 4.7) was unveiled in 2008, the local newspaper reported that the "steel-and-ceramic structure features gold, yellow, green and blue—colors that emperors cherished" (Wong). The accuracy of such a statement matters very little; it asserts authenticity and constitutes locality by claiming translocal, transtemporal connections. In the twenty-first century most Chinatowns have such gates. Passing under them suggests that one is entering a distinctive, racialized space that is both here and elsewhere, and that links the present to the past.

The look of Chinatown originated as much in Chicago as in China, in fact—at the 1893 Columbian Exposition. China declined to participate in this World's Fair, as a protest against the exclusion laws. The "Chinese Village" was therefore sponsored and mounted by Chinese-American entrepreneurs. It was not in fact a village, but a free bazaar, an admission-charging replica of a temple, a teahouse, and a theatre. The goal of the Wah Mee Exposition Company was to simultaneously represent China and make money. Its multiple appeals are visible in the portion of their pamphlet I reproduce—Figure 4.8 shows the front and back covers, Figure 4.9 the first two interior pages—running the gamut from decorative stereotypes, through educational exposition, to the prices of light refreshments at the café. The visual vocabulary of the site was soon developed—again by entrepreneurs rather than by officials—at expositions in Atlanta in 1895, Omaha in 1898, and St. Louis

FIGURE 4.7 *Historic Chinatown Gate, Seattle, Washington, about two weeks before its formal unveiling, February 8, 2008. Photograph by Joe Mabel.*

in 1904 (when for the first time China also had a national exhibit). The message conveyed by the layout of these turn-of-the-century World's Fairs has become familiar in cultural history. As Mae Ngai writes, official participation denoted membership in the international community and civilized status, with "dignified displays of their respective histories, cultures, and contributions to industry, science, and the arts." The Chinese installations were located on the midways, where "[t]he primitive and the exotic...were not merely entertainment; they were also part of the didactic mission of the fairs, serving as foils for the demonstrations of the superiority of Western civilization presented on the main exposition grounds" (96). Figure 4.10 shows the Chicago Chinese Theatre in its context, on fairgoers' way to the Ferris Wheel. The humbler attractions of the village had many visitors, but the organizers' efforts to push beyond the limits of the Midway into prestigious cultural performance failed. Almost no visitors were equipped to appreciate Cantonese opera, as both the published comments and the fact that the company quickly went bankrupt indicate.

It was ironic (as Ngai writes) "that the task of representing China fell to Chinese-Americans who were themselves committed to assimilation, men who 'acted like [American] citizens' by investing in real estate, learning to speak English, and wearing Western-style clothes." But, she suggests, the "irony was characteristic of the ambivalent in-between status of immigrant culture brokers" (96–7). At these exhibitions, little was what it purported to be. Ngai comments that China's official

FIGURE 4.8 *Cover and back page of the "Guide Book to the Joss House" distributed by the Wah Mee Exposition Company at the Chicago World's Fair, 1893. Reproduced with permission from a pamphlet in the collection of the William L. Clements Library at the University of Michigan.*

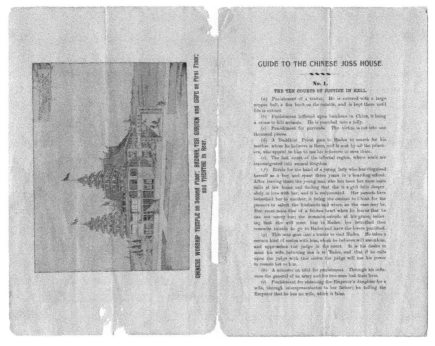

FIGURE 4.9 *Frontispiece and first page of the "Guide Book to the Joss House" distributed by the Wah Mee Exposition Company at the Chicago World's Fair, 1893. Reproduced with permission from a pamphlet in the collection of the William L. Clements Library at the University of Michigan.*

FIGURE 4.10 *The Ferris Wheel and Chinese Theatre (on the left) on the Midway Plaisance at the World's Columbian Exposition in Chicago. Photograph taken by E.R. Walker in 1893. Reproduced by courtesy of the University of Chicago Photographic Archive [apf3-00088], Special Collections Center, University of Chicago Library.*

pavilion at the Louisiana Purchase Exposition in St. Louis in 1904, because it was a miniature replica, was in effect "a parody of a Chinese palace. Its gateway and ornamentation were elaborate, to be sure, but it was so truncated that the defining element of Chinese imperial space—scale—was completely lost" (102). The Chinese people who were exhibited as ethnographic specimens on the Midway-equivalent Pike were, in fact, Chinese-Americans from San Francisco. (It is, incidentally, an index of the influence of the Chicago Exposition that the term "midway," which we take for granted for a group of carnival-like amusements, came from the name of the Chicago park where that part of the fair was situated; it was not used previously.) Not authenticity but syncretism—the creative amalgamation of different discourses—is the category we need here, as for thinking about Edith Eaton/Sui Sin Far and about "Chinatown."

In 1898, when Edith Eaton arrived in San Francisco for the first time, there was an approximately ten-block, densely populated area of the city called Chinatown. It was perceived as distinct, but it was not architecturally distinctive. In Arnold Genthe's famous pictures of the neighborhood, he did his best to make it seem as exotic and remote as he could. As John Kuo We Tchen has now shown, when Genthe exhibited and published photographs, he manipulated them in the darkroom to remove white people and English-language signs. That Chinatown was completely destroyed by the 1906 earthquake, fire, and looting.

In the issue of the *Overland Monthly* that immediately followed the disaster, it was actually suggested that the destruction of the district might have been providential: "Fire has reclaimed to civilization and cleanliness the Chinese ghetto and no Chinatown will be permitted in the borders of the city. Some other provision will be made for the caring of the Oriental. It seems as though a divine wisdom directed the range of the seismic horror and the range of the fire god" (Beringer, 398). In *The Lucky Ones*, Mae Ngai sketches the story of how the Chinese Village became Chinatown. There was indeed an effort, motivated by both racism and greed, to take over the valuable land occupied by the Chinese. The plan was to move them to an appropriately marginal space—the mayor of San Francisco proposed Hunter's Point at the extreme southern edge of the city. This plan ran into a number of barriers, however. One was the reluctance of the residents in any white area to accept the proposed new neighbors. Another was the city's urgent need for the large revenue that the Chinese community generated. A third, decisive factor was the determination of Chinese merchant leaders to reclaim their land; they started rebuilding immediately. Their vision was "to refashion Chinatown according to the architectural vision first seen in the Chinese Villages at the Chicago and St. Louis world's fairs—one meant to promote tourism and social reform in order to overcome Chinatown's reputation as overcrowded, diseased, and vice-ridden. Tourism in Chinatown was not new, but it had been associated with the Barbary Coast and middle-class slumming. Chinatown leaders now wanted a wholesome tourism for a broader audience, a climate in which restaurants and shops would thrive. Look Tin Eli wanted to create an 'Oriental city [of] veritable fairy palaces'" (Ngai, 127). A century later, adaptations of that vision can be found across the world.

The architecture of Chinatowns is certainly not "authentic." It is not even in any simple sense Chinese, although its relation to China has been constantly reinvented. According to newspaper coverage, Paul Wu, one of the architects who worked on the Seattle archway, traveled to Beijing, Xian, and southern China to study gates and incorporated what he learned in the design; some of its ceramic ornaments were imported from China. Tradition cannot really be separated from syncretism, the pressure of external definitions separated from self-construction. As Lisa Lowe writes in reference to Ng's *Bone*, "Chinatowns are at once the deviant space ghettoized by the dominant configurations of social space and the resistant locality that signifies the internalization of 'others' within the national space" (122). Complexities continue to accumulate and multiply. For example, there are now large centers of Chinese-American population outside the familiar Chinatowns: in New York, for example, in Flushing; in San Francisco, in the Richmond and Sunset districts. But Chinatowns are not just tourist attractions or sites for new immigrants—as Andrea Louie shows in her ethnographic study *Chineseness across Borders*. Many suburban Chinese-Americans in the Bay Area do not feel much affiliation with the downtown Chinatown, but community organizations make an effort to pull them in and maintain its status as a place that indexes identity. They not only sponsor programs about Chinese-American history and Chinese culture, but "roots tours" to China. Louie's book explores what those connections mean both to Chinese-Americans and to their Chinese hosts. This is the kind of *friction*—to use Anna Tsing's term, discussed in the first chapter—generated on sites where the local and the global are visibly constituting each other.

The category of authenticity was central to scholarly work on Edith and Winnifred Eaton during the early years after their rediscovery; discussion was dominated by what Dominika Ferens convincingly portrays as a "'good sister—bad sister' paradigm" (2). Certainly Eaton's career benefited when as a young journalist she was able to make the Chinese her "beat," and she profited by the market she was able to access as Sui Sin Far. But she was exploring her heritage, and became an advocate for Chinese-Americans. In contrast, much although by no means all of Winnifred's work appeared under the name Onoto Watanna. Between 1899 and 1912, she published ten novels, most of them like her bestseller *A Japanese Nightingale* romances about encounters between Japanese women and Western men. She provided false biographical information and talked in interviews about topics like her reaction to the Russo-Japanese war, posing for photographs in a kimono. When she wrote articles about cuisine with her sister Sara Eaton Bosse and they produced one of the first Asian cookbooks in America, its presentation as a *Chinese-Japanese Cookbook* implied collaboration between individuals of different ethnicities. Winnifred's entry into employment as a screenwriter also depended on those successful fictions, and her 1920s serial about the industry, *Movie Madness*, also carried the signature Onoto Watanna. The inauthenticity—indeed, fakery—would seem obvious.

Yet Ferens points out that both sisters grew up "surrounded by English Victorian culture in Canada, knew no people of Asian descent besides their mother, who had left China as a child, and their encounters with the Chinese and Japanese, whether firsthand or vicarious, were mediated by orientalist ethnography" (5). One can argue that Winnifred chose an easier path than Edith, given the contrast between public interest in what was considered Japan's advanced civilization and the pervasive disrespect for China itself, and given the immediate, intense racism directed against Chinese immigrants. But as Ferens shows, the difference between their writings is also linked to genre—they are drawing on two different discursive traditions: "ethnographic work on China was done most consistently by Protestant missionaries starting in the first half of the nineteenth century, whereas Japan was most energetically textualized by lay travellers in the last thirty years of the century" (4). A binary view of the sisters is further undercut by scholarship that demonstrates Winnifred's subtle antiracist interventions, and by Mary Chapman's discovery that Edith took advantage of the popularity of Japanese themes in several children's stories ("Finding Edith Eaton," 265). As in the Chinese villages, what we are talking about is racial performance, undertaken by Asian-Americans. It is creativity, exercised under severe constraints. The fact that the category "Asian-American" is anachronistic reminds us that these authors are constructing the categories through which we read them. Edith is recursively questioning them at the same time.

In the next section I offer the result of my intensive reading of three stories from *Mrs. Spring Fragrance*, building on previous interpretations and adding a focus on how they thematize practices of reading and writing. That examination will confirm the critical trend emphasizing that the author demonstrates her allegiance to Anglo-American culture, as well as criticizing it; both postures are indispensable as she claims her place as an "American" author. And it will provide further evidence for her close and critical engagement with Chinese literary culture. The scholarly conversation has not yet acknowledged how closely and originally Edith Eaton engages issues of literary interpretation and tradition; and how central she makes those issues to her portrait, and enactment, of Chinese-American syncretism.

What these stories have in common is that each of them locates "Chinatown" as a border region, through an episode of romance that is simultaneously about reading and writing in a multiracial and contested culture. They focus on the lives of Chinese-Americans—who only sometimes live in (a) Chinatown, but who like Eaton can never elude their connection to that particular place. A quoted passage of poetry plays a pivotal role in each story. To summarize rather tendentiously: in "Mrs. Spring Fragrance," a married couple is temporarily estranged by their differences on a point of literary interpretation. "The Americanizing of Pau Tsu" positions a husband's failure to grasp the significance of his wife's allusion as a turning point in the collapse of their relationship—a missed connection that continues in current readings of the story. " 'Its Wavering Image' " shows poetry mobilized to seduce, in a story that is explicitly concerned with the power of representation and publication. Through her accounts of literature, Eaton's stories demonstrate that Chinatown can be the center of the world.

I do not intend my interpretations to refute or replace others, such as Ferens's emphasis on the ethnographic elements of Eaton's writing or Chapman's exploration of her unorthodox feminism. Rather, I hope these analyses will prove complementary, as many scholars undertake to understand this challenging author. The depth of meaning found in canonical works is the result, I want to suggest, not only of their qualities but also of repeated interpretation. I do not mean to imply that such depth is unreal—that (say) Hawthorne is not complex. Rather, I want to point out that the same process of reading and rereading is at work creating value in the fiction of Mary Wilkins Freeman or Charles Chesnutt or—here—Edith Eaton.

National Language and Literary Education in "Mrs. Spring Fragrance" and "The Americanizing of Pau Tsu"

The opening lines of the title story of Sui Sin Far's collection are: "When Mrs. Spring Fragrance first arrived in Seattle, she was unacquainted with even one word of the

American language. Five years later her husband, speaking of her, said: 'There are no more American words for her learning'" (1). The title character is, in both stories in which she appears, exactly the sort of energetic and capable person this suggests. In the action of this story, she is worried about her friend Laura, the daughter of the family next door, who is about to enter into an arranged marriage although she loves another young man who is also a suitable husband, Kai Tzu. Mrs. Spring Fragrance goes to San Francisco, where she discovers that the man Laura is supposed to marry would also prefer a love match, and arranges for it all to work out. This plot is mostly offstage, however, because the story is centered in the point of view of Mr. Spring Fragrance. He overhears his wife's conversation with her friend Laura—including a passage of poetry—and from what he learns about the American attitude toward arranged marriages like his own, begins to fear that his very "Americanized" wife does not love him.

Readers may or may not react to the fact that Mrs. Spring Fragrance is not learning English but "the American language," underscored in the next sentence by "American words." But within a few paragraphs Eaton puts the question of national language and national literature so directly in our path that it would be difficult to ignore it. Mrs. Spring Fragrance comforts her friend by saying,

"Is there not a beautiful American poem written by a noble American named Tennyson, which says:

"'Tis better to have loved and lost,
Than never to have loved at all?'" (3)

Tennyson was indeed noble—he was a baron, the first Englishman to be raised to a peerage in recognition of his writing. What does it mean to call him American—twice in a single sentence?

Eaton's biographer Annette White-Parks tells us that the Eaton children's home-schooling was self-consciously English and class-conscious; they were educated as members of the Victorian elite, despite their pinched circumstances. Literature was emphasized; in fact, the children probably composed poetry every day as part of their curriculum. For British gentlemen and ladies, at home and across the empire, Tennyson epitomized literary refinement and the distinctive value of their civilization. He was the poet laureate from 1850 until his death in 1892—that is, from before Edith's birth, throughout her formative years, and into her early maturity. She would have been intimately familiar with him, and with the source of the quoted passage, *In Memoriam*. It was published the same year Tennyson was appointed laureate and was the most concentrated emblem of his status as the national poet. In other words, Eaton could not have chosen a more specifically British text.

Tennyson was equally admired in North America. As residents of Canada, of course, the Eatons were not only culturally English but also literally still subjects of the British monarch—although Edith's relation to the idea of national language and culture must surely have been complicated, not only by her mother's Chinese ancestry and Canada's place on the periphery of the empire, but also by living in French-speaking Montréal. In the United States, Tennyson stood at the very top of the hierarchy of cultural practices so effectively established in the second half of the nineteenth century. Ticknor and Fields's famous series of pocket-sized books with blue and gilt bindings—so familiar as a canon of literary excellence that the phrase "blue and gold" could appear without explanation—began in 1856 with two volumes of Tennyson's works. His prestige was enlisted to create, and then was constantly confirmed by, the institutions of cultural hierarchy (see Wadsworth). Mrs. Spring Fragrance not only quotes Tennyson but also specifically refers to her "American poetry books," which are material emblems of self-cultivation and social standing. In this sense, then, Tennyson *was* an American poet; like other English authors, he was a vital part of elite culture in the United States well into the twentieth century. Both the story's opening reference to the American language and its allusions to Tennyson display the complexity of the relation of language and literature to nation—they are both inescapably relevant, and never simple.

Eaton leaves open a comic reading of Mrs. Spring Fragrance's identification of Tennyson as American as a simple mistake. She is writing in the double-voiced mode of many resisting writers of the era; the story was first published in 1910 in *Hampton's*, a New York-based journal which had a muckraking, reforming tone at this time but whose audience was still, so far as we can tell, overwhelmingly white and predominantly racist. The reader who saw Charles Chesnutt's conjure stories as plantation folk tales, not very different from Joel Chandler Harris's Uncle Remus stories, could see Mrs. Spring Fragrance as an amusing, half-educated foreigner. But the narrative voice of the story does not collaborate with that reading; there is no condescension or irony directed against her. Rather, the reference is a metonym for a syncretic vision of culture. If Tennyson can be an American author, so can Mrs. Spring Fragrance; she sets out to write a book in the next story. So in fact can a biracial Chinese-Canadian who affirmed her complex identity when she signed both Edith Eaton *and* Sui Sin Far.

This concern with language and culture as shaping elements of social worlds characterizes not only the opening of "Mrs. Spring Fragrance," but also the entire story. Its characters are constantly reading and writing, and talking about reading and writing. At the moment when Mr. Spring Fragrance overhears his wife's quoting Tennyson to Laura, he is on the veranda "scanning the pages of the *Chinese World*"—presumably, the influential, long-lived California newspaper founded as *Mon Hing Bo*, a weekly, but by the time of the story's publication in 1910 retitled *Sai Gat Yat Po* (without changing its English name) and publishing daily. Eaton establishes the space from which Mr. Spring Fragrance listens by reference to an important institution of Chinese-language print culture—one which, not coincidentally, published a substantial amount of literary work (see Yin, 158, and H. M. Lai, 32). The discourses of the intimate sphere are also shown as divided—he hears only a fragment of their conversation because he walks away, not wanting to "hear more of the secret talk of women" (3). There are three embedded letters and a telegram; Mrs. Spring Fragrance reports on a lecture she attended; the young man who is their neighbor on the other side wants to be the only white man at Mr. Spring Fragrance's smoking party so he can write it up as a "scoop" (12). The text both refers to and embeds—one might almost say it is woven of—multiple competing discourses.

Tennyson is in fact not the first, and arguably not even the second but rather the third, English poet alluded to in the opening of "Mrs. Spring Fragrance." We have already learned that one of the accomplishments that attract Laura to Kai Tzu is his ability to sing "Drink to me only with thine eyes" to her piano accompaniment. The lyric of that love song is Ben Jonson's "To Celia." Mrs. Spring Fragrance's conversation with Laura begins with her poetic description of the walk she has just taken, mentioning the daffodils so strongly associated with Wordsworth. (They are also, of course, a variety of narcissus.) Laura bursts into tears. " 'That is the walk,' she sobbed, "Kai Tzu and I so love; but never, ah, never can we take it again' " (3). Their romance, in the time-honored pattern of Dante's Paolo and Francesca, depends on literary models, and her reaction depends directly on the assumption that the experience of love changes the inner self. She laments that she might have been able to accept the arranged marriage if she "had not gone to school with Kai Tzu, nor talked or walked with him, nor played the accompaniments to his songs" (5-6). Literary discourse both surrounds the characters and shapes their experience. It is pervasive and penetrating.

Eaton portrays her characters' Americanization as not only a matter of learning how to talk, but also of learning how to feel. Literature—in her implicit cultural analysis—is pedagogy for emotion. This is very much the role that Jürgen Habermas suggests the eighteenth-century English novel played in the emergence of the modern social organization. I have written elsewhere at greater length about his argument that the "relations between author, work, and public...became intimate mutual relationships between privatized individuals who were psychologically interested in what was 'human,' in self-knowledge, and in empathy. [The reader] from his experience of real familiarity...gave life to the fictional one; and in the latter he prepared himself for the former" (50-1). I borrow a phrase from Flaubert for this process: "sentimental education." Tennyson's *In Memoriam* expresses this paradox of public and private: it is a deeply personal expression of the poet's grief at the death of Arthur Hallam, and also a publication embraced by a wide audience and (then and now) viewed as an expression of its age. The attitude expressed in the lines "'Tis better to have loved and lost/Than never to have loved at all" is, precisely, an affirmation of the value of emotional experience. The self makes and knows itself through having such feelings—it is good to have the inner self deepened and expanded, even by pain. Mrs. Spring Fragrance's quotation is entirely apt.

Mr. Spring Fragrance is the one person in the story who dissents; he considers it "disobedient to reason" to court unhappiness in this way. He underscores the importance of the Tennyson quotation for the reader by repeating it to himself, and repeating it again to the son of the American family that lives next door, in order to ask for an interpretation—so that the lines appear three times within a few paragraphs. This young man is "a star student at the University of Washington, and had not the slightest doubt that he could explain the meaning of all things in the universe." But in fact he simply paraphrases and condescends, smiling "pensively and reminiscently. More than a dozen young maidens 'loved and lost' were passing before his mind's eye" (5). Annette White-Parks points out that in an early story Eaton gives the lines "'Tis better to have loved and lost/Than never to have loved at all" to a "masher" (65–6). Mr. Spring Fragrance's neighbor, despite his "air of profound wisdom" (5), is getting the poem quite wrong—a point relevant for the reading of regionalism proposed in previous chapters, because it is a critique both of book-learning and of the arrogance of the presumed center. The lines from *In Memoriam* do not refer to the kind of conquests implied here. Along with other phrases by Tennyson (notably "Nature red in tooth and claw" and "Theirs not to reason why"), the couplet entered American culture at large, and the youth's reading fits the way it is usually understood today—even though, as I have noted, the poem is not about heterosexual romance at all. Mr. Spring Fragrance assumes that his native-born, educated neighbor is a reliable guide to "American" poetry, but there is no such national ownership of culture, and interpretation is not so simple. Eaton accepts and dramatizes the dispersed institution of sentimental education—but shows its curriculum as contested.

Mr. Spring Fragrance is also misled when, later, he consults the same neighbor about American attitudes toward arranged marriage. "'Love,' said he, slowly and distinctly, 'comes before the wedding in this country, does it not?' 'Yes, certainly'" (13). He describes a hypothetical arranged marriage, and asks:

'Presuming that she marries you, knowing you not.—After she marries you and knows you, will that woman love you?'

'Emphatically, no,' answered the young man.

'That is the way it would be in America—that the woman who marries the man like that—would not love him?'

'Yes, that is the way it would be in America. Love, in this country, must be free, or it is not love at all.' (13–14)

Between what this implies about the feelings of his "Americanized" wife, and gossip that reaches him while she is away in San Francisco arranging a happy ending for Laura and Kai Tzu, Mr. Spring Fragrance worries himself into a sad state. He cryptically quotes the Tennyson lines again in a telegram to his wife; she happily thinks that he may have been "reading her American poetry books" (15). He has not, but soon enough he has "apostrophized" the cat because he thinks that it too misses her. In fact, lost in "the shadow which had been following Mr. Spring Fragrance ever since he heard his wife quote, ''Tis better to have loved,' etc.," he does not eat or sleep for four days (17–18)—suggesting that he is the most romantic person in the story. He is in the grip of a mistaken, ethnocentric sentimental education, facing—precisely—the prospect of losing what he loves.

Mrs. Spring Fragrance actually has a brilliantly syncretic solution to the tension between the values of American companionate marriage and her own history. When she thinks about the regrettable necessity of keeping her work on Laura's behalf secret from her husband, because he has old-fashioned ideas about such things and would not approve of circumventing an arranged marriage, she says to herself: "Strange that that should be so, since he had fallen in love with her picture before *ever* he had seen her, just as she had fallen in love with his! And when the marriage veil was lifted and each beheld the other for the first time in the flesh, there had been no disillusion—no lessening of the respect and affection, which those who had brought about the marriage had inspired in each young heart" (15–16). This device would work with any sort of portrait, but it seems fitting to think of the pictures as photographs, which were so important in constructing "Chinatown" (see A. Lee). It seems fitting as well that creative, technology-mediated adaptations of arranged marriage have become even more common in recent years.

Mr. and Mrs. Spring Fragrance are thoroughly reconciled at the end of the story. But Mr. Spring Fragrance does not ever learn how his wife narrates the story of their marriage, nor does he share his experience with her. Only the reader knows both. In fact, when Mrs. Spring Fragrance teases her husband about speaking openly of his love for her, and wonders if he has been reading her American poetry books, he rejects the idea vehemently. "'American poetry!' ejaculated Mr. Spring Fragrance almost fiercely. 'American poetry is detestable, *abhorrable!*'" (21). Again, a comic reading of "abhorrable" as a mistake is available—but the word can also be taken as an expressive neologism. Infusing the subjective vehemence of "I abhor" into the horrid object, it is evidence of Mr. Spring Fragrance's own creativity. The content and the form of his statement point in different directions—but both should be taken seriously. It would be wrong to say Mr. Spring Fragrance's sentimental education has Americanized him. Rather, just as his wife has reread arranged marriage, he has invented his own accommodation to the mixed culture in which he moves. At the end of the story, when he gives his wife the jade pendant he had purchased earlier for their wedding anniversary but withheld, his affirmation of their marital contentment is newly informed by a sense of its fragility. The same stone carries a new meaning.

Among the thematically related stories that begin *Mrs. Spring Fragrance*, the title story is most closely complemented by "The Americanizing of Pau Tsu." Some elements of the latter that might pass unnoticed become visible when they are juxtaposed—for example, the syncretic gestures that run through the story.[7] In describing the easy adaptation of Wan Lin Fo to American ways, despite his inner conviction of China's superiority, the narrator cites a motto hanging in his room: "when in Rome, do as the Romans do" (149). The biblical reference in the observation that his wife Pau Tsu patiently receives American visitors and bears their "curious smiles and stares…like a second Vashti—or rather, Esther" (151) may seem odd—it was Vashti's refusal to appear at a banquet that caused King Ahasuerus to set her aside and make Esther queen, so the first comparison is simply not right. Mentioning both women, however, foregrounds the multiculturalism of the society described in the Book of Esther. When Pau Tsu understands neither the language nor the topics of her husband's conversations with his friend Adah Raymond, it is "all Greek, or rather, all American" to her (152). Taken separately, each stock phrase or allusion seems to refer to something obvious. Taken together, they undermine each other—evoking a welter of mutually defining and incommensurate categories, and reminding us that the relations of nation, culture, and language are highly labile.

There are also several references to literature in "The Americanizing of Pau Tsu," although it is less central than in "Mrs. Spring Fragrance." Wan Lin Fo attends the Chinese Literary Club (largely social, but partly cultural), and the story ends with Adah Raymond quoting Shakespeare. I want to focus on just one important moment. Pau Tsu is miserable in her forced Americanization, jealous of Adah Raymond, and unwell. She sings a song "said to have been written on a fan which was presented to an ancient Chinese emperor by one of his wives."

> Of fresh new silk,
> All snowy white,
> And round as a harvest moon,
> A pledge of purity and love,
> A small but welcome boon.
> While summer lasts,
> When borne in hand,
> Or folded on thy breast,
> 'Twill gently soothe thy burning brow,
> And charm thee to thy rest.
> But, oh, when Autumn winds blow chill,
> And days are bleak and cold,
> No longer sought, no longer loved,
> 'Twill lie in dust and mould.
> This silken fan then deign accept,
> Sad emblem of my lot,
> Caressed and cherished for an hour,
> Then speedily forgot.   (155–6)

Through this lyric Pau Tsu clearly expresses her own sadness and sense of vulnerability. Wan Lin Fo hears the song and is worried, but does not recognize that—like the emperor's wife—she feels she is losing her husband.

In fact, a good Chinese literary education would have enabled him to recognize his wife's song. Eaton's narrative gives accurate information about its source, although it omits the name of the author: Pan Chieh-Yü, or the Lady P'an. This is the best known of the very few poems of hers that survive from the first century BCE. The biographical tradition emphasizes Lady P'an's virtue, talent, and her struggles with other occupants of the imperial harem; in Chinese poetry, the poem and its image of the autumn fan immediately evoke the deserted wife or courtesan. As I noted earlier, even before the biographical evidence of Eaton's familiarity with the language emerged, Xiao-huang Yin saw internal evidence that "she was not only familiar with Chinese culture but also knew how to use it appropriately in regard to the personality of her characters," demonstrating an "extraordinary familiarity with Chinese literature, culture, history, and customs" (92). "The Americanizing of Pau Tsu" is an example of this sophistication. Pau Tsu's specifically Chinese refinement is expressed through her choice of a song that conveys her situation. Wan Lin Fo has spent the past several years working as a merchant in the United States, and his time at the Literary Club has been spent discussing "other things"; he misses the allusion.

As Patricia Chu has pointed out, the lyrics themselves are complexly effective within the story. For example, they combine the Chinese association of whiteness and death with the Western association of whiteness and purity and thus link purity and death. Chinese imagery is presented in the style of English poetry—as she notes, the poem "is strikingly Victorian in prosody, diction, and sentiment" (118). These qualities lead Chu to suggest that Sui Sin Far wrote the poem herself, but in fact they derive from the translation she is using, by W. A. P. Martin. This eminent American Presbyterian missionary and author actively promoted Western culture in China, and Chinese culture in the West, and it is not surprising that Eaton knew his work. She could have seen both the Chinese original and Martin's translation in his widely read volume of essays *Hanlin Papers, or Essays on the Intellectual Life of the Chinese* (1880), titled "Lines Inscribed on a Fan," with the gloss "Written by Pan Tsieh Yu, a Lady of the Court, and presented to the Emperor Chêng Ti of the Han dynasty, 18 B.C." (388–9). Or she might have taken it from Martin's small volume *Chinese Legends and Other Poems* (1894), where he reprints only the translation and adds to the gloss the suggestion that the verses might be sung: "This plaintive little song has been set to music by Mrs. A. E. Pirkis, and the music published in London and New York" (18). Martin, a colonialist who also knew and appreciated Chinese culture, is an appropriately cosmopolitan and ambivalent figure for Eaton to reference here. A century later, we may enrich our own context for the poem by noting that it has had a subsequent life in English as well; both Amy Lowell and Kenneth Rexroth included it among their translations from the Chinese.

In her conversation with her husband after she sings Lady P'an's poem, Pau Tsu anticipates her own death. This aspect of the story has been interpreted in terms of her previous illness, in which her modesty has been outraged by her husband's insistence that she be examined by Adah Raymond's male physician, and her general melancholy over the conditions of her life in America. What seems to have been missed are the clear indications that she is pregnant. That is the source of her sense of vulnerability; a century ago it was less easy to forget the fact that child-birth entails the risk of death. When she says in the note in which she announces that she is leaving her husband that she "lacks the courage to face the ordeal before her" (156), what she cannot bear is the idea of being attended in labor by a man. Wan Lin Fo's later statement that if he finds Pau Tsu, he will "take her for a trip to China, so that our son may be born in the country that Heaven loves" (159), con-firms that pregnancy is the precipitating occasion for her action.

The resolution of the story is enabled by a reversal of the couple's positions. Pau Tsu does "Americanize," as the title indicates—enough to step substantially out of bounds and ask her husband to divorce her, "as is the custom in America" (156). And when Adah Raymond confronts Wan Lin Fo about how he has been treating his wife, he wonders, "how he could ever have wished his gentle Pau Tsu to be like this angry woman" (159). He also tells Adah that if he can find his wife he "will not care if she never speaks an American word" (159) and expresses his willingness to travel to China with her. The story affirms a connection to the homeland in the context of the birth of a child—a gesture we might juxtapose with the deaths of Mrs. Spring Fragrance's babies (7), and the tragic story of "The Wisdom of the New" (in which a mother poisons her son rather than lose him to American schooling). Eaton resists any simple correlation of China with tradition and the past, or America with the future, just as she unsettles any simple and stable repre-sentations of race and nation.

The final paragraph of the story returns us to the literary. When Wan Lin Fo awkwardly asks Adah Raymond not to visit his wife just then, she too realizes the situation and adds a condemnation of her own blindness to her criticism of him, "soliloquiz[ing]": "Lord, what fools we mortals be!" (161). Again the source is not specified, but Adah is of course quoting Shakespeare (another English author who was often considered American). Eaton invokes the notion of the soliloquy in a very precise way (as she did the apostrophe, in "Mrs. Spring Fragrance"). Within the story Adah is speaking only to herself, but she is also speaking to the reader. In the same way, Lady P'an's poem functions more richly for the reader than for the characters. Pau Tsu knows its origins, although her husband does not (Adah is entirely absent from the scene), but the author and nature of the translation are irrelevant for her—she would have been singing in Chinese. The full resonance of the poem as we have seen it is available only when the story is considered as a communication between English-, or rather American-, speaking author and reader.

The conversations among the Chinese characters in the previous story require the same horizon. Clearly Mrs. Spring Fragrance would have said "'Tis better to have loved and lost" in exactly those words. We can imagine that her whole conver-sation with Laura might be in English, and her husband's with their American neighbor certainly would be. But what language would the couple speak together? We know that the narrator must be silently translating Pau Tsu and Wan Lin Fo's conversation, because her lack of English is a central theme of the story; and it seems likely that the intimate talk of the other couple would also be in their native language. Yet how then are we to think about the word "abhorrable"? The stories do not invite us to ask such questions. Rather, they take for granted a common ground that the narrator, characters, and readers occupy together. They project, in public— a space of discourse that comes into being through discourse, so long as people consent to inhabit it. Arguably Eaton's message is still arriving. As we read and reread these stories, her address to readers constitutes (in Michael Warner's phrase) poetic world-making.

Racialized "Sentimental Education" and Comparative Literature in "Its Wavering Image"

"Its Wavering Image" focuses explicitly on San Francisco's Chinatown, taking the division between racialized worlds as its topic. Its treatment of mixed-race identity and journalism make it, as Annette White-Parks comments in her biography, "the most self-referential piece of writing in Sui Sin Far's mature fiction" (228). So far, no magazine publication has been located. That could change at any point, of course. Or it could mean that Eaton was not able to place the story, or that she took the opportunity of putting together a book to write an especially challenging story. Rachel Lee shows that she "uses this narrative to tackle the issue of how to write about Asians without exposing them to a critical white gaze" (268), and other critics have also written acutely about the story. I will argue, however, that consequential elements have remained unrecognized.

In "Its Wavering Image," a Eurasian girl named Pan who has been raised by her father exclusively within the Chinese community forms a sudden close companionship with a white journalist, Mark Carson. Through her, he gains an insider's access to the district, and ultimately he betrays her by publishing a newspaper story revealing Chinatown secrets.

In the story's key moment, Pan and Carson are upstairs in her home, gazing up at a crescent moon in the night sky, and down into the "lantern-lighted, motley-thronged street." He contrasts the two scenes—"How beautiful above! How unbeautiful below!"—and tells Pan that she does not belong in Chinatown, that she is white. When she protests that these are her people, he replies, "Your real self is alien to them. What interest have they in the books you read—the thoughts you think?" (89). A little later, he sings to her. The verses provide the title of the story:

> And forever, and forever,
> As long as the river flows,
> As long as the heart has passions,
> As long as life has woes,

> The moon and its broken reflection,
> And its shadows shall appear,
> As the symbol of love in heaven,
> And its wavering image here. (90)

Pan is moved to tears, and Carson tells her, "Those tears prove that you are white" (91). Simply telling the story demonstrates that Carson is invoking something like the notion of sentimental education.

The racializing of sympathy that was implicit in Sarah Orne Jewett's work is explicit here. Carson asserts that Pan's deep interiority, developed by books, and her responsiveness to natural beauty and poetry, index her race. In this familiar developmental model, "civilization" is mapped onto both time and space; allegedly primitive peoples and the lower classes are cast as less finely organized than the elite. Pan does not belong with the Chinese, who are being left behind by progress. Thus Carson later justifies betraying Pan's confidences by telling her his revelations do not matter—"It is mere superstition anyway. These things have got to be exposed and done away with" (94). According to Carson's map of the world, Pan and Carson's placement above the Chinatown throng in this central scene manifests their place in the social hierarchy.

Eaton's work often, as the condition of its appearance, comes to an accommodation with orientalism. But in "Its Wavering Image" we have a text that explicitly evokes and rebukes stereotypes of the Chinese and the developmental model of civilization. Mark Carson, the spokesman of those attitudes, is an untrustworthy and repugnant character, who "in the reporter's room...was spoken of as 'a man who would sell his soul for a story'" (86). The conversation I have quoted is followed by their first kiss, and on my reading the possibility that there is considerably more sexual activity is left open. Once Mark Carson has accomplished this final penetration of the secrets of Chinatown, as embodied in Pan, he is finished. The narrative is breathtakingly brief.

> Listening to that irresistible voice singing her heart away, the girl broke down and wept. She was so young and so happy.
> "Look up at me," bade Mark Carson. "Oh, Pan! Pan! Those tears prove that you are white."
> Pan lifted her wet face.
> "Kiss me, Pan," said he. It was the first time.
> Next morning Mark Carson began work on the special-feature article which he had been promising his paper for some weeks. (90–1)

The description of Pan's reaction to this betrayal is much longer. It explicitly equates the violation of Pan's, and the Chinese community's, trust with the violation of her body. She "would rather that her own naked body and soul had been exposed, than that things, sacred and secret to those who loved her, should be cruelly unveiled and ruthlessly spread before the ridiculing and uncomprehending foreigner" (92). And she thinks her lover knew that. The story is unambiguous in indicating what we should think of Mark Carson, and the values he represents.

Carson leaves town immediately after the story is published, and Pan becomes deathly ill during his absence of two months. A tragic ending is within the possibilities of the narrative. But Pan refuses the Western plot of seduction and betrayal. The narrator refuses it so firmly that events are told out of sequence, ensuring that the reader knows that Pan survives and scorns Carson before the scene in which she comes close to death. As her fever rages (not impossibly, a consequence of infection after an early miscarriage) a mother with a toddler visits, comforting her with the vision of the child she will some day bear. Here, as in "Pau Tsu," to choose China is to choose family and survival. Tracking back from the *sujet* to the *fabula*, and the last moment of the narrated events: when Carson returns he finds Pan in Chinese dress and utterly rejecting any description of her as white. "I would not be a white woman for all the world. *You* are a white man." The result of Pan's supposed sentimental education is her affirmation, "I am a Chinese woman" (94–5). This is a strategic essentialism, as previous critics have shown. It does not arrest the fluidity of race in Eaton's work. It does declare Pan's defiance of Mark Carson's values, Sui Sin Far's advocacy for the residents of Chinatown, and Edith Eaton's independence.

Carson uses poetry to seduce, but his verses function in the story with a complexity that exceeds his limited perspective. Rachel Lee points out that he admires the moon and implicitly disparages the "wavering image": "Carson's song refers to the moon and its watery reflection in the river. It also alludes to the Platonic and aesthetic division between ideal, 'beautiful' forms, and worldly, 'unbeautiful' appearances. Chinatown's street-life, like the 'broken reflection' below, corresponds to this lesser world of ugly appearances" (268). The narrator has already undermined Carson's interpretation, however. Immediately before he sings, the narrator writes that he and Pan contemplate "the silver stream and the crescent moon…It was a very beautiful evening" (90). The phrase "symbol of love in heaven" has two meanings—not only the moon in the heavens, but also divine love in heaven. In a Christian frame of reference, the point that both the moon and the reflection are symbols becomes central, and it will not do to see only the former as beautiful, for daily life holds the prospect of the infinite and ordinary people have immortal souls. To incarnate the river as the throng underscores that point. The refractive epistemology conveyed here is quite intricate.

Carson's song is the last two stanzas of Henry Wadsworth Longfellow's poem "The Bridge." This source was not identified in criticism of "Its Wavering Image" until an essay I published in 2008, but it is important to the story and to the reading of Eaton that I am proposing. Again she mobilizes a thoroughly canonical poet, one as axiomatically American as Tennyson is English. At the same time she has chosen lines that include images of moving water, pervasive in Chinese literature and art, so that—as in Martin's translation of Lady P'an's poem—the national cultures mingle. And again the person who might seem the inheritor of that tradition—in

"Mrs. Spring Fragrance" the star university student, in "The Americanization of Pau Tsu" the educated Chinese man, here the white writer—does not know how to read it.

"The Bridge" was published in Longfellow's *Belfry of Bruges*, in 1845. It says something about what has happened to Longfellow's reputation that a passage from one of the important poems in a very successful book could go unrecognized for so long. In his day Longfellow was the preeminent national poet; in fact, in the biography that began the current revival, Charles Calhoun calls him the "American answer to Tennyson" (2). Longfellow too embodied literary excellence, although—fittingly for an American poet—in a more accessible and popular mode than the British laureate. When he visited England and met Queen Victoria, she told him that all her servants read him; he was apparently never sure if that was simply an observation about his fame, or a slight—Calhoun suggests it could even have been praise for his broad, uplifting influence. In America, Longfellow was the second author to be published in Ticknor and Fields's "blue and gold" series. And in the 1880s, when Houghton Mifflin succeeded Ticknor and Fields as the leading marketer of distinguished literature to American buyers, Longfellow was the first to receive a de luxe edition (Brodhead, *School*, 59). Longfellow had always had scathing critics (most famously, Edgar Allan Poe and Margaret Fuller). It is commonly observed that his critical reputation began to decline in the late nineteenth century, but he was still inevitably among the chosen when, in 1900, "America's great living men" selected the "national immortals" to be installed in New York University's Hall of Fame (Brodhead, *School*, 52).

In fact, by 1900—Angela Sorby tells us—Longfellow was "not merely popular but compulsory." His poetry was "taught in almost every school in America. Catholic as well as public school textbooks reprinted him; African-American teachers streamed out of normal schools such as Hampton armed with Longfellow lesson plans; and school ceremonies drew on his work to add solemnity and authority to the occasion" (3). Edith Eaton would have learned Longfellow's poems at home, but Sui Sin Far is relying on his integration into the social, and penetration into the interior, lives of her readers. In her analysis of Longfellow as a "schoolroom poet," Sorby attributes his extraordinary power to the way he invites readers into the American center. On her interpretation he was especially "appealing" to "marginally professionalized" (27) schoolteachers; she shows his work playing a role similar to that of the schoolteachers in local color stories discussed in Chapter 2. The poems she focuses on—not the very personal and implicitly sexual "The Bridge," but others like *Hiawatha* and "Paul Revere's Ride" whose names (at least) remain familiar today—enable mediation in the classroom. As Sorby puts it, they ask "students to negotiate (rather than simply to learn and repeat) national narratives that included them as active reading subjects" (2). She shows for example that Mary Antin found Longfellow—or rather, his books and his image—a valuable ally (xxxiv). The successful assault, led by George Santayana and Van Wyck Brooks, that reduced Longfellow's status so immensely did not begin until early in the second decade of the twentieth century, just about the time that *Mrs. Spring Fragrance* was published.

I would argue, then, that the difficulty of recognizing that "Its Wavering Image" includes an encounter with a canonical poet is something of a historical accident. The quoted passage from "The Bridge" was never so proverbial as "'Tis better to have loved and lost," but in 1912 it was not nearly so obscure as it has become. Eaton must have expected some, or even most, readers to recognize it. Clearly the status of the poet is less central thematically than it is in "Mrs. Spring Fragrance"— she does not mention Longfellow's name. But she is equally interested in her characters' responses to the poem, and she is even more complexly engaged with the meaning of the quoted lines.

Carson has strong cultural authority for considering Pan's tears an index of her responsiveness to literature. It helps here to recognize the quoted poem, and read the story through its full text. "The Bridge" fits precisely into the sentimental tradition in which represented tears—"A flood of thoughts came o'er me/That filled my eyes with tears" (lines 23–4)—are answered by the reader's. The poem is very much about sympathy; the speaker, gazing at the water below and the sky above, thinks of his own past emotions and the many others who have crossed the bridge with similar feelings:

> I see the long procession,
> Still passing to and fro,
> The young heart hot and restless,
> And the old subdued and slow!   (lines 49–52)

Carson's view that Pan's tears "prove that [she is] white" invokes the general correlation of literary taste and racialized cultivation. But it also has something to do with the fact that, at the moment he says so, she is responding to the words of Longfellow, a poet powerfully identified with New England, America, and the Yankee as normatively American.

The story itself powerfully refutes Carson's claim that Pan's tears are somehow white. Scholars' interpretations of the story demonstrate that one need not identify the source of Carson's song to recognize that he is wrong, and Pan is right, about her and about Chinatown. But reading "Its Wavering Image" with "The Bridge" in its entirety confirms and enlarges that view, letting us see as well that Mark Carson is misreading the poem. The religious undercurrent emerges more clearly, as for example when we read the first stanza's description of the moon rising "Behind the dark church-tower" (line 4). And the biographical context of the poem—which was well known at the time—underscores how profoundly he has perverted the poem by using it to seduce. "The Bridge" emerged out of Longfellow's long and difficult courtship of his second wife; he crossed the Charles River many times, visiting her and returning to his home. (The bridge described in the poem was on the site now occupied by what is called the Longfellow Bridge.) Unlike *In Memoriam*, this is indeed a poem about heterosexual love. But it is about enduring devotion, in the context of spiritual values, and it culminates in a sense of compassion for all humankind. Carson, quite lacking in sympathy for the people passing below on the street, and willing to manipulate and exploit an innocent girl, gets Longfellow completely wrong. Pan is a better interpreter. When she is disoriented by her intense distress over the newspaper story, the poem guides her: "she stumbled up the dark stairs which led to the high room open to the stars and tried to think it out. Someone had hurt her. Who was it? She raised her eyes. There shone: 'Its Wavering Image.' It helped her to lucidity" (92). Pan understands that the moon itself is an imperfect symbol of a high principle, and its light helps her overcome the temptation to find excuses for her lover and instead to face his betrayal directly.

What we engage here is not only Pan's understanding of the fragment Carson sang to her, but also Eaton's reading of Longfellow's poem. As in the two previous stories, none of the characters has access to all the meanings that the quoted lines of poetry take on in the course of the narration. For example, Pan's passionate feelings and her dangerous fever surely allude to the "hot and restless heart" of the young. And her final statement, "I am a Chinese woman," may be read as completing Eaton's audacious interpretation of "The Bridge." She enlarges Longfellow's geography, and presses his themes of fluidity still further. In "The Bridge," fresh and salt waters mingle in a complex series—Charles River and Atlantic Ocean waters mix, and the speaker's "flood of thoughts" and his tears are shared with his readers. Sui Sin Far—Eaton—asks her readers to consider the Pacific, as well. And the "procession" crossing the bridge is identified with the river itself. It probably alludes to Dante, and thus links forward to the crowd on London Bridge in T. S. Eliot's "Waste Land." (Temporarily disregarding temporality, I ally myself with Longfellow's evocation of kairos in the midst of chronos—as Sorby implicitly does in her readings of him, as well.) The throng flowing through the streets of China is specifically not white, extending Longfellow's democratic and spiritual vision to include anti-racism. And they carry lanterns that offer another wavering image of the moon. When Pan asserts that she "is a Chinese woman," she chooses to immerse herself in her community and to affirm that "silver stream" as both beautiful and numinous. This is a sophisticated and plausible reading. Eaton affirms the full humanity of the throngs of Chinatown (including the women), and stakes her own claim to full participation in literary culture.

Eaton underscores the key role of literature in the story by staging another small scene near its end, just as, in "Mrs. Spring Fragrance," she emphasizes the issue of literary nationalism by reiterating the characterization of Tennyson as American. When Mark Carson comes to see Pan again he is apprehensive; he falters, enters Portsmouth Square (conventionally, the heart of Chinatown), and sits "on one of the benches facing the fountain erected in memory of Robert Louis Stevenson." The monument honoring Stevenson, in the square where he spent time during a brief residence in San Francisco, is a historical fact (dating to 1897, and still there) (see Figure 4.11). Its presence enables Eaton to draw another famous author into her network of associations. On this site, Carson asks himself

FIGURE 4.11 *The Robert Louis Stevenson monument in Portsmouth Square, San Francisco. Reproduced from the 1907 book* Stevensoniana: An Anecdotal Life and Appreciation of Robert Louis Stevenson, *ed. Sir John Hammerton (facing p. 308).*

why Pan would ignore the note he wrote her. Once again he is both aggressive and cowardly, reassuring himself that Pan is a white woman and he has done no wrong. Her behavior—like Chinatown—is enigmatic, but her "true self was above it all...Would Robert Louis Stevenson have known why? Yes—and so did Mark Carson. But though Robert Louis Stevenson would have boldly answered himself the question, Mark Carson thrust it aside" (93). Again a literary figure is invoked as a character confronts a difficult truth. Pan, helped by the moon's "wavering image," achieves honesty, but the outcome in Carson's parallel scene is different. He ignores the monument in front of him, and its opening to planetary connections. Stevenson was a Scottish contributor to English-language literature, and thus himself a colonial; he spent time in the Pacific Islands, and tried to be an advocate for indigenous people and cultures. Eaton adopts him as an ally, as she has adopted Longfellow.

Eaton's vision of writing is not utopian. It includes sententious quotations from canonized, trivialized poetry, and the shallow exoticism of the newspaper feature story. But it hopefully contests racialized, masculinist visions of sentimental education and national literature—and imagines something else. Recognizing the depth and the breadth of her engagements requires both intensive reading and a willingness to think broadly, in terms of world literature. Her unrecognized link to Longfellow is especially resonant given his ongoing revival as a prescient environmentalist and multiculturalist and a risk-taking cosmopolitan (see Willis, Irmscher and Arbour, Vogelius). Longfellow was (we can now remember) famously polyglot, an active translator and promoter of studies across national and linguistic boundaries, a founder of comparative literary studies in America. His understanding of literature was capacious enough that the Longfellow Institute at Harvard, whose mission is to "support the study of non-English writings in what is now the United States and to reexamine the English-language tradition in the context of American multilingualism," is named after him. He fits well into the literary history that Edith Eaton/Sui Sin Far is constructing for herself. I am suggesting the opposite of an Eliot-like vision of ideal tradition—this is a hermeneutic operating in history. In the next section I engage broad-ranging scholarly conversations about the nature of literary history, and its connection to the nation, carrying Eaton's implicit challenge forward. I am engaging in synthesis, not proposing my own original views—but the result changes the grounds on which we think about regionalism.

National Words and Literary Worlds

Literary history is impossible. We just do it anyway.

David Perkins had already reached that conclusion in 1993. In his brief classic *Is Literary History Possible?* Perkins shows with devastating clarity that the enterprise is neither truly literary nor rigorously historical, and that the categories it depends on—authors, periods, genres—are muddled and ultimately indefensible. Since then the evidence has only piled up, both in theoretical discussions and in the growing difficulty of bounding American literature.

Most simply and empirically, the terms of inclusion that make Londoners Henry James and David Plante, and London-born Jhumpa Lahiri, "American" authors—and leave out New York residents Salman Rushdie, Zadie Smith, and Colum McCann—are, not so much wrong, as obviously questionable. Scholars have asked, as well: why is the most widely read fiction of an era not considered part of the national tradition? Jay Fliegelman posed this question about Dickens, for the nineteenth century. Caroline Levander points to Gabriel García Márquez and Isabel Allende, for the twentieth. Edith Eaton, of course, is opening up these topics in the opening lines of "Mrs. Spring Fragrance." Let us question the boundaries of what we consider "literature" as well. Stephen King is a Maine author, in the context of this book—is he part of American literary history? How about E. L. James, the Chilean-Scottish-English author of *Fifty Shades of Grey* who is wildly popular in the United States?

Cutting more deeply into the question of comprehensibility, the Longfellow Institute directs our attention to the large body of work published in languages other than English, and often ignored in American literary history. It was once more recognized than it is now. The volumes of the *Cambridge History of American Literature* published from 1917 through 1921 include three chapters on the topic of non-English literature, as well as a chapter on "The English Language in America."[8] The stiffened border between the English and other languages of the literatures of the United States matters immensely for the late nineteenth- and early twentieth-century moment when local color was prominent in literary culture. It was of course a period of massive immigration, characterized by an extensive and vibrant multilingual print culture. My exclusive focus on English-language fiction is— I frankly acknowledge—a limit of this book. It is still useful to contemplate the defamiliarizing force of a term like the Longfellow Institute's shorthand "LOWINUS": Languages Of What Is Now the United States. It reminds us that the coordination of temporal, geographical, and linguistic horizons that produces "American English" is not a natural fact but an historical product.

The instability of the category "nation" itself subtends this challenge. As long ago as 1882, in his famous Sorbonne lecture "Qu'est-ce qu'une nation?" ("What Is a Nation?"), Ernest Renan demonstrated that none of the obvious candidates— geography, language, race, common interests, and customs—actually provides a unifying principle. Rather, as so many fine works of scholarship in the past quarter-century have discussed, a nation is imagined into being. It is—certainly not only, but crucially—constituted by a story of the past and the future, as much by what people choose to forget as by what they choose to remember. (The long history of American multilingualism is an example of that forgetting.) The nation's existence is, as Renan put it, "un plébiscite de tous les jours"—"a daily plebiscite" (27, 53). Literary history has always been national, because it emerges in this project, part of the poesis of the nation.

One cannot (of course) understand nation-making, in general or in any instance, without a materialist analysis—saying that it is necessary to reckon with imagination does not mean that is *all* that is necessary. For several centuries now the circulation of print, which as Anderson demonstrates shapes the imagination, has been recursively foundational to every other kind of movement. For the United States, Trish Loughran has influentially argued that "there was no 'nationalized' print public sphere in the years just before and just after the Revolution, but rather a proliferating variety of local and regional reading publics scattered across a vast and diverse geographical space" (xix). Interestingly, she suggests that it was this fragmentation that enabled U.S. nationalism to emerge, as localities imagined themselves through the fiction of the nation. On her account, the national print culture that came into being by 1850 heightened sectional tensions—*Uncle Tom's Cabin* is an especially persuasive example.

We are then precipitated into the period of the Civil War—when, for example, Richard Malcolm Johnston's "The Goosepond School" (discussed in Chapter 2) failed to circulate very far. For the postbellum period, scholars have long debated, and continue to discuss, both what Nina Silber called *The Romance of Reunion* and the persistence of hostilities between the combatant regions. Silber recently reviewed the large body of current scholarship on reunion and reconciliation in the *Journal of American History* (2016), concluding that *many* kinds of narrative gained traction in the period. "Reconciliation may have been pervasive, but so were Lost Cause tributes, celebrations of the Union triumph over treason, and black efforts to tell stories about slavery, emancipation, and the ongoing struggle for racial justice" (69). An emphasis on the distinctiveness of the South is a common thread running through these narratives, addressed clearly in Natalie Ring's *The Problem South*—a recent work that is particularly relevant for thinking about regionalism. Ring anatomizes in detail the constantly voiced view of the former Confederacy as in need of uplift, reform, modernization, as (in a word that appears as frequently in her book as it has in this one) "backward."

Ring goes on to suggest connections during her broad period, from 1880 to 1930, between the discourse of reunion and reconciliation, and the emergence of U.S. imperialism—as the South's economy was represented as colonial, the poor education and uncompliant nature of its labor force was deplored, the extension of democracy implied threats to civilization, and so on (9–13). Much in this argument remains to be worked out in future studies, but for my purpose the suggestion is enough. The discourse of progress links retrograde regions in the United States with primitive places abroad—let us say, both are "the boondocks." As discussed in Chapter 1, a Tagalog word becomes part of American English.

Silber inserts an evocative image into the conversation, a tableau staged by a St. Louis photographer in 1898 that connects reconciliation to the Spanish-American War (see Figure 4.12). I read against the grain when I see it as a reminder that state power in the form of armies was deployed, again and again, in North America—in the Indian Wars, and the Mexican-American War, as well as the Civil War—to create the conditions for sending military forces to Cuba and the Philippines. (And so on.) Indeed, its role in the battle for hearts and minds at home presumably depended on what seems most peculiar about the image today: that white people represent both the Blue and the Gray, and Cuba. There is no trace of the issue of emancipation and the participation of African-Americans in the Civil War. The little blonde girl who personifies Cuba not only seems to imply that (contrary to the historical record) the island waited, chained, for rescue, but also erases *mestizaje*. In the context of this chapter, it is relevant that there is a Chinese component in the Cuban mix. The first Chinese contract laborers arrived in 1847; between 1850 and 1875, 11 percent of emigrants from China left for Cuba. (For comparison: 17 percent went to the immensely larger combined region of Hawai'i, the United States, and Canada.) These men and their multiracial descendants did fight in the Spanish-American War, and in other struggles for Cuban independence. Havana's monument to their participation dates to the nineteenth century, although the prominent *paifang* at the entrance to *el Barrio Chino* was apparently funded by the People's Republic of China in the late 1990s (Westad, 27 and 228).

FIGURE 4.12 Cuba Libre, c.1898. Attributed to F. W. Guerin, St. Louis. From the Library of Congress, https://www.loc.gov/item/2005688946.

I have already mentioned places in Edith Eaton's work we can turn to for direct engagement with the Caribbean or with imperialism—to the journalism she published during her sojourn in Jamaica, to "The Alaska Widow." But Eaton also challenges the boundaries of national cultures in the three Chinatown stories I have interpreted. Since she wrote, national borders have become even more entrenched in the institutions of knowledge-making—in disciplines and departments, in library classifications and everyday assumptions. Critics' and readers' failure to recognize Eaton's allusions is only partially explained by the contingent fact of Longfellow's declining reputation; it also results from, is overdetermined by, the division of labor in literary history. Scholars who know Pan Chieh-Yü do not know Eaton, and those who read "Its Wavering Image" rarely read Longfellow. Of course, the national model of literary history has also been critiqued, as I have begun to delineate. The challenge is to approach American literature as itself requiring a comparative perspective, and as a part of world literature; many scholars are engaged in that endeavor. My long immersion in Eaton's fiction prepared me for Wai Chee Dimock's planetary view, and Paul Giles's "deterritorialization" of American literature. Caroline Levander asks *Where Is American Literature?*, and shows that it has always been a "messy global stew" (39). Those perspectives, recursively, make Eaton's work more legible.

For those engaged in the impossible enterprise of literary history, rising to the challenge of global connections means telling a story that is not, despite all temptation, progressive—that does not assume that Western modernity constitutes the center of the world, and is not teleological. This imperative connects directly to my effort to do justice to both the substantive and the relational aspects of regionalism, and the theoretical discussions of the first chapter show why it is so much easier said than done. In Eric Hayot's concise phrase, "putting progress at the center of historicity is one of the things that makes us moderns" (1). Throughout the history of literary history, the assumption that genres are discrete entities leads us, when we do comparative work, to think in terms of literary forms originating somewhere and their influence radiating out from that point. Thus it constantly turns out—again in Hayot's words—that "modern Western art develops new techniques and the rest of the world copies them." This notion of diffusion can be found not just in accounts of realism, modernism, postmodernism but also (as he says) "across the entire aesthetic history of the modern period from the sixteenth century forward" (3–4). Current powerful reimaginings of world literature, most prominently by Franco Moretti and Pascale Casanova, do not escape this problem. Their valuable work in showing literature as a global system still fails to decenter Europe, let alone the West. Moretti has—in his individual work and especially in his collaborative projects—truly challenged business-as-usual national literary history, and broadened the ambitions of comparative literature. Yet his relative disinterest in the local, and the absence of another paradigm, leave current conceptual arrangements intact. While Casanova brilliantly analyzes how value is negotiated in global spaces, her rivalrous world in the end reinforces the centrality of Paris.

Christopher Hill offers a strong alternative in his 2009 article "The Travels of Naturalism and the Challenges of a World Literary History." He offers a detailed specific account that reckons with the immense impact of Zola without dispensing with heterogeneity. Rather than radiating from a point of origin in France, he shows that the form is shaped by unexpected alliances with other kinds of writing and flourishes in unexpected places—from Argentina and Brazil to Japan, China, and Korea—to produce a narrative full of overlapping and unevenness. Shifting from origin, reception, and diffusion to *travel* reveals the way the former categories occupy that familiar slanted terrain; they cannot help but imply that teleological geography of world civilization I discussed in the first chapter.

In *On Literary Worlds* Eric Hayot proposes a still more ambitious program, arguing that literary history should shift to a focus on the world-creating force of aesthetic objects. The book is more successful as critique than as alternative, I think. We need to begin with an analysis of the very category "world," like the one Debjani Ganguly undertakes in her recent *This Thing Called the World: The*

Contemporary Novel as Global Form. I have used the term somewhat impression-istically. Yet in considering regionalism across different periods and settings I have striven for something like this de-centered view. I would argue that both the con-cept of regionalism I have developed, and Edith Eaton's work, point that way. I have suggested that her engagement with literary history makes a place for her as an author precisely through world-making. Other theoretical frameworks can also help make this aspect of Eaton's work legible, of course. I think of "border gnosis," Walter Mignolo's term in *Local Histories/Global Designs* for the knowledge-making that becomes possible at the edge of an empire; in a broad temporal framework Eaton is arguably located between not two but three empires, the British, the American, and the Chinese. Dalia Kandiyoti's rethinking of national literature as diaspora literature in *Migrant Sites* meshes in multiple ways with this study, as it emphasizes spatiality and translocality and links turn-of-the-twentieth-century works with recent fiction.

This is the merest glimpse of the scholarly conversations over—to use the term with the longest pedigree—world literature. It is a large but not, I think, excessive horizon for Eaton's deployment of "American words" and dramas of literary interpretation. It is a necessary one in Chapter 5, in which I continue into the twentieth century and on to the twenty-first.

Regionalisms Now

Still is still moving to me.

—WILLIE NELSON

Place and time are inevitable, in life and in fiction. *Region* is not.

In this chapter, I bring the concept of region and the analysis of regionalism I have developed to bear on literature and culture of the later twentieth century and beyond. It will prove helpful to think about the portability of "the center of the world," and the tension between local knowledge and book-learning (Chapter 2), to think from the perspectives of religious belief (Chapter 3), and the global history of colonialism and imperialism (Chapter 4). The perspectives of previous chapters all come into play as I return to the literary-historical mode of the second chapter, linking multiple texts rather than interpreting a single author's body of work. (I still read closely.) My goal is not a continuous narrative, although I will follow the travels of the form through the middle of the twentieth century as well as dive down into study of recent works. What I most want is to understand the frequently observed flourishing of regionalism in the age of globalization, and to continue to refine the concept I have developed and make it useful for today. Crucially, moving to this period will require me to consider multiple media. It seems to me that this is so even in order to understand prose fiction—which exists today as part of an expanded media system differing profoundly from nineteenth-century arrangements.

I begin with an instance from 2014 that links network television and literary fiction, and continue with reflections on the role of regionalism in mass culture. Then I offer a rapid account of the literary histories that provide, in my view, the most helpful frameworks for approaching the question of place in contemporary fiction. Finally, I turn to accounts of authors who—in varied ways—align themselves with the tradition of regionalism, and are productively read in the terms I have established in this study.

Somewhere in...

In April 2014, an episode of the CBS drama *Criminal Minds* titled "Blood Relations" was broadcast—set, according to the onscreen legend at the opening, "somewhere in West Virginia." The show was at that point in its ninth season (as of this writing it is still running). It features an ensemble cast of Federal Bureau of Investigation "profilers" who analyze serial murders and, through their understanding of "criminal minds," identify and capture the "unsub"—that is, unknown subject—responsible for the horrors depicted. The series generally traffics in the familiar, but even by its standards this particular episode qualifies as a clichéfest. Appalachian stereotypes abound—there are trailers, trucks, firelight, hunting, whiskered men and plaintive women, incest that produces a defective serial killer, and—of course—a feud. Moonshine and revenooers are not mentioned, but one agent remarks, "They're going to be reluctant to talk to federal agents. It's not like we're popular in this neck of the woods."

The episode's opening sequence is set in 1965. It is shown in black and white and is thus explicitly archaic, although the image of a frightened woman fleeing through the woods is one that the show constantly repeats. The tracing of the causes of violence into the past, and the fact that members of the team are placed at risk, are also conventional elements of the show. What is unusual is that the "Killer Woodsman," as he is called on the fan-produced *Criminal Minds* wiki, escapes. Because the team believes he has drowned, the pursuit is not even continued into another episode. But the audience sees a final sequence in which he is about to kill a young couple "somewhere in Kentucky."

The Killer Woodsman—born of incest, raised in isolation in the backwoods—enacts a nightmare version of the deprived provincial. He remains at large in Appalachia, as the profilers take off in their jet; the team's ability to protect people (themselves, the couple in Kentucky, and everyone watching) is put into question. The FBI agents are well-versed in every aspect of forensic investigation and the book-learning of criminal psychology. But misunderstandings throughout, as well as the outcome, show them as hindered by the way they drop in from the sky with their federal badges. Doubts about how much purchase official knowledge and power actually have on the ground, out in the world, are frequent in *Criminal Minds*, and rarely stronger than in this episode. The disturbing question—are the locals, and the metropolitan enforcers of the law, on the same side?—links it closely to the topic of this study. The link between particular places and *time* is also explicitly thematized. Every episode of *Criminal Minds* is bookended by quotations, voiced by one of the cast, and sometimes (as here) appearing as text on the screen. In this case: we see Faulkner's "The past is never dead. It's not even past."

These lines have been quoted frequently (not always exactly) in recent years. They are originally from *Requiem for a Nun* (1950), spoken by Gavin Stevens in the portion of the work formatted as a play. The passage has been cited before in public discourse—its current prominence derives from its paraphrase in an important speech during the 2008 campaign for the Democratic presidential nomination, by then-Senator Barack Obama. Soon after, in 2011, the lines were used in Woody Allen's film *Midnight in Paris*—and received further publicity when Sony Pictures was sued by the Faulkner estate, because although the author was cited no permission fee had been paid. The judge dismissed the suit, finding the film's usage of the passage both minimal and transmogrifying, qualifying it as "fair use." Here we are on the cusp between mass and elite (therefore, niche) cultural practices. The sentiment is circulating, and available. Yet it is not—at least, not yet—common sense. The *Criminal Minds* script tracks back to the specific words Faulkner used, and his prestige in the literary domain is invoked. This labile movement between cultural domains is characteristic of regionalism as a cultural form, though certainly not unique to it.

Attention to place is pervasive in television, not only—inevitably—in its content but also in its institutional structure. Media policy in many countries prescribes a certain amount of local content, although in the neoliberal era those regulations have mostly been repealed in the United States. In terms of television's address to readers, Victoria Johnson in *Heartland TV* analyzes the profoundly paradoxical role of the Midwest in network shows from the 1950s through the 1990s; it is both imagined as, and distinguished from, the nation. Later, with the expansion enabled by cable, reality TV brought very local representations to our screens. One might argue over the degree to which *An American Family* (1973) was located in Santa Barbara, or was—or was represented as—somehow typical or symbolic. And how much does it matter which city hosts MTV's *The Real World*, in any given year from 1992 to 2015 (and beyond)? (*Road Rules* of course was by definition peripatetic, linked to place in a different way.) Recently the *Real Housewives* franchise defines shows around the distinctive inhabitants of a specific city, yet also treats them as interchangeable by expanding indefinitely. It began in Orange County, added New York and Atlanta (the most popular show), then New Jersey, D.C., Beverly Hills, and Miami—and is now international, with Athens, Vancouver, Melbourne, and Cheshire, as well as a show about French residents of Beverly Hills. MTV's *Jersey Shore* is more resolutely, idiosyncratically local—but also has international spinoffs such as *Geordie Shore*. We could read *North Woods Law* (about game wardens in Maine) with *Law and Order*, with Hemingway's "Big Two-Hearted River," or with the endless numbers of New England-set mysteries. Readings of these shows vary widely, depending upon the affiliations and attitudes of the critic or viewer. Is *Here Comes Honey Boo Boo* exploitive, or authentic and even courageous? I find it unwatchable—but the same question might be asked about another Southern show that I loved, about a wedding chapel in New Orleans: *Big Easy Brides*.

A crucial, although not fully explicit, aspect of all these shows is that they offer access to local language. I imagine that everyone who teaches local color has puzzled over the fact that dialect fiction was so popular in the late nineteenth century, yet is so difficult—even distasteful—to student readers today. I speculated in the first chapter of this book that the easy availability of recorded sound has made the difference. To *listen* to non-standard speech (sometimes with subtitles available) is one thing—once we have that option, imagining it based on misspelled words is quite another. Intuitively, we feel that distinctive speech offers a connection to local life. As I suggested, the justifiably admired HBO drama *The Wire* powerfully mobilized the apparent authenticity of many varieties of Baltimore speech, lending plausibility to its account of urban experience. In 2014, a series with the evocative English title *The Hinterland*, set in Aberystwyth, Wales, received considerable media attention, in part because of its double identity as the Welsh series *Y Gwyll*— all the speaking scenes were filmed twice, in English and then in Welsh. The coverage makes it clear that global interest in "TV noir" about particular places—specifically, the print and then multi-media Scandinavian mysteries *Girl with the Dragon Tattoo* and *Wallender*—has made this production possible. (*Hinterland*'s bilingual version was sold for broadcast in Denmark before filming began.) The *Guardian* review says exactly what is so often said about regional fiction: the landscape "becomes a character in its own right."

I am not suggesting that the examples I have cited from television "are" regionalism in any strict sense. Rather, they draw from a storehouse of images and phrases about place and time that has been shaped by regionalism, and remain available for it, but circulate far more broadly through and across cultural forms. Thus, for example, watching the first episode of Neil DeGrasse Tyson's revival of Carl Sagan's series *Cosmos* in March 2014, I was struck by how closely the images that represented the earth's location in space and time corresponded to the analysis I had already written for the first chapter of this book. (The institutional does matter; it is impossible not to wonder what might have been different if the show had been produced by PBS, rather than Fox.) Standing in his "ship of the imagination," the astronomer says, "In the dimension of time, the past lies beneath us. Here's what earth looked like 250 million years ago"—and a window opens up in the floor to show Pangea rotating below. "If you want to see the future, look up"—another window looking onto a globe opens above—"and this is how it could appear 250 million years from now." Tyson and his scriptwriters (most visibly Ann Druyan) argue at length and passionately that science teaches us that we must realize we are not the center of the universe—as that recognition happens to us individually, it has happened to "our civilization." Yet the progressive view I analyzed in the first chapter subtends the narrative. *Cosmos* locates the "cosmic address" of our moment on earth at that midpoint between up and down, past and future, and thus centers the world. Again, my point is not that this is (or is not) regionalism. It is that thinking in terms of region helps us to understand the workings of place-time.

Similarly, I have long been intrigued by Janet Dailey's Americana series—a collection of fifty short novels published between 1976 and 1982, one set in each state—but have found that its deployment of place is significantly different from most of the other works I am studying. Although she does not have the mainstream name recognition of Stephen King or J. K. Rowling, Dailey's sales are roughly in the same vicinity—in 2013 her *New York Times* obituary offered the statistic that she had sold 300 million books. That is, however, the same number that appeared in Pamela St. Regis's *Natural History of the Romance Novel* in 2007 and the total is presumably larger now. Dailey is always called a "pioneer" because she was the first American author to publish with Harlequin, and played a powerful role in shaping what St. Regis calls the romance boom. She later crossed over into the general fiction market, but the Americana series was crucial to her success and remains a constant reference point in both fan and scholarly discussions of her career. The series has been reprinted several times and the novels are all currently available, including as e-books, and are still being rated and marked as "to-reads" on Goodreads. But it is less the novels' recognition of place, than the sheer accomplishment of writing a book for each of the fifty states, that is recognized—the fact that the series was included in *The Guinness Book of World Records* is frequently mentioned. These are what I call in the first chapter "denoted" regions, which exist primarily through official classifications. Dailey acknowledged in an interview that although she believed that settings should never be arbitrary, she had a difficult time with some states: "Trying to find that marriage of story idea and a setting in Delaware just drove me up a wall" (Massie and Greenberg, 196). In fact, in *The Matchmakers* virtually the only local material is a description of getting hot pretzels on the boardwalk at Rehoboth Beach (146–8). Delaware's tourism website proclaims that "Rehoboth has a quaint small town feel—a real walking downtown and all the fun, relaxation or excitement you could ask for." The word "quaint," of course, connects us to structures of feeling and thought that characterize regionalism.

Other novels in the series engage more closely and sometimes critically with the topoi of place. *Summer Mahogany* (1978), set in Maine, is particularly notable for its engagement with dialect and the tension between the locals and others who, the book tells us, are always said to be "from away" (6). The heroine Gina Gaynes, herself a "Maine-iac" (22), at times translates for her romantic interest and his friends (22–3, 98–9). The title of the novel comes from the group he belongs to, "the yachting set. It was a descriptive and picturesque term, considering the sun-browned appearance of the boating crowd that descended on Maine in the summer. It separated them from the regular 'summer complaints,' an affectionate term for tourists who visited the coastal resorts of Maine" (6). What it might imply about race is never explored, but the ambiguity of the relation between locals and tourists is central, and does marry the setting to the story. Dailey gives Gina a critical attitude towards stereotypes of her region. She contradicts the assertion that her community's speech reflects its isolation—in effect its backwardness: "'It may seem as if we're isolated, but it's far from the truth. Look at all the seasonal visitors we get from all parts of the country and the world,' Gina had argued. 'And Mainers have always been known for their association with the sea, whether it was fishing commercially or shipping. The history of the people is very cosmopolitan. The old idioms linger because they indicate an individuality. Also'—a bright twinkle had entered her eyes—'it makes us remembered. People come from away, hear the way we talk, and go back to tell all their friends what quaint things we said. Everyone knows word of mouth is the best advertisement. What better way to encourage more tourists to come to our resorts?'" (24–5). Evidently Gina shares a viewpoint with Sarah Jewett's Captain Littlepage. And Dailey's account of the relation between authenticity and commerce is concise but complex.

It seems clear that one of the pleasures readers find in the Americana series is learning about places. Dailey's career famously began as she and her husband toured the United States with a trailer, and her HarperCollins author website said that they "travel extensively to scout story locations, and have visited all 50 states." Dailey did research, as well—the same website reports that she "reads voraciously about every aspect of any subject she writes about" and she believes, "Accuracy is important in genre fiction; you have to get it right, zero in on the real details." Janice Radway argued as long ago as 1984, in her classic *Reading the Romance*, that readers value not only the entertainment—the *"escape"*—but also the *information* these novels offer. We do not have an equivalent empirical study, but I speculate that accuracy about particular places is also important for readers of regional mysteries. Those works, like Dailey's, rely a great deal on the pleasure of the serial. But the Americana series looks to what I called in the first chapter "denoted" regions, invoking the abstraction of the fifty states, and to authorial research (that is, book-learning). Regional mysteries inhabit specific sites, book after book. However many volumes there are in the series, the foregrounded appeal is to local knowledge. The progression of *this* book has demonstrated, I hope, that those categories are best understood not as opposites but as mutually constitutive. That productive antagonism inheres diffusely in the notions about place and particular places that are constantly, massively circulating; I select for discussion textual moments when the concerns I have identified as regionalist emerge systematically to view.

Regional mysteries are immensely popular. The sociologist Wendy Griswold wrote in 2008 that mysteries are about a quarter of all fiction published, and contended that they "probably account for a much higher proportion of what is actually read." For American and British titles, about half of those "have characteristics that mark them as regional" (29). Indeed, based on my experience in San Francisco and Ann Arbor, walking through the main public library of a city, or any branch, will demonstrate that we are talking about a *lot* of books. There are many authors, and each usually writes many books. A May 2012 article in *Publishers Weekly* chose six prominent authors to profile (Hahn). The amount of updating required at the moment when I write, in 2017, says much about their continuing success. In 2012, Archer Mayor was about to publish the twenty-third novel about his Vermont detective Joe Gunther—in 2017, he is about to publish his twenty-eighth. Margaret Maron was about to add the eighteenth to her Deborah Knott series, set in the fictional North Carolina county of Colleton; that count now stands at twenty (it is not her only series). Dana Stabenow had published twenty mysteries in her Kate Shugak series set in Alaska; she has continued to be prolific but seemed to have moved on to other series until she added another in 2017. Steven Havill has two series set in the fictional Posadas County, New Mexico, with three of the twenty-one appearing in the past five years. Joan Hess has two series set in Arkansas—the one discussed in the article remains at sixteen, but the other has expanded from eighteen to twenty. P. L. Gaus, discussed below, is a relative outlier—in 2012 he had published seven novels about the Ohio Amish, and has added two since. Writing multiple novels about the same place is of course is key to the writers' ability to narrate a community, and to create the sense of a world.

I have read (or sometimes sampled) many of these works. I think they demonstrate not only that regional stereotypes are active in current publications, but also that many of the topoi associated with regionalism are circulating together. Many of them foreground a native who has returned (Hess's Arley Hanks is a striking example, as is Bell Elkins in Julia Keller's recent novels about West Virginia). Tensions between locals and tourists or other outsiders, and between local and metropolitan or abstract knowledge, often appear (they are a complex element of Stabenow's novels about Aleut investigator Kate Shugak; I think too of Joseph Heywood's "Wood Cop" series set in Michigan's Upper Peninsula). So does distinctive local language (Heywood again, or the best-documented example is British—the Northeastern British dialect in Sheila Quigley's *Bad Moon Rising*, analyzed in an article by Susan Mandala on "Crime Fiction as Regional Fiction"). So does attention to the powerful presence of the past and to the regional landscape (I could cite the Southerner Maron for the former, the western novels of Havill for the latter—but both are pervasive).

These thousands of novels of course have widely varied ambitions, and are written with widely (even wildly) varied levels of craft. The mystery itself is a genre that needs to be reckoned with—Gramsci was interested in the detective novel, and Carlo Ginzberg has proposed that clues index an epistemological model that emerged in the late nineteenth century. Chester Himes and, later, Walter Moseley narrated African-American experience through mysteries whose literary achievement has been recognized. Narrower—although not more precise—formal and marketing categories are intersecting here as well. Regional mysteries are often classified as "cozies," constructing narratives of community in rural, traditional places. Yet Mayor's strongly regional Vermont novels are admired as police procedurals, and the classic noir novels of the British-American Raymond Chandler are strongly located in Los Angeles. Daniel Woodrell, whose literary fiction about the Ozarks is much praised, began his career by writing crime novels set in New Orleans; he coined the term "country noir" and then came to feel it had gotten "wrapped around his throat." Sara Paretsky's novels about V. I. Warshawski, credited with transforming the place of women in the crime novel, are also novels of Chicago—yet are too urban to usually be considered regional.

An examination of the first two novels of P. L. Gaus's "Ohio Amish" series shows how the issues I have been considering resonate in regional mysteries. I do not want to claim either that this author is typical, or that he is uniquely interesting. Gaus's work *is* very interesting, but my point is rather that close reading demonstrates that these issues not only *persist*, but persist *as a group*.

These "Amish" novels are not located within that community, but rather are
focalized through three "English" (that is, non-Amish) residents of the non-fictional
Holmes County. In *Blood of the Prodigal* and *Broken English*, published in 1999
and 2000 respectively, the central position—both in the narrative and on a spectrum
from insider to outsider—is occupied by Michael Brandon, a history professor who
was born in the region and now teaches at a college there. His perspective is crucially
complemented by two men who have been his close friends since boyhood; the chief
of police is less sympathetic to the Amish than Brandon, and an idiosyncratic farmer
and pastor is closer to them. In the first novel, the dead body of a young man who
grew up Amish but has left the community sets off the mystery. It turns upon
themes that continue those of my second chapter, because the first sign of Jonah's
disaffection was his curiosity in school, his enjoyment of reading books even
beyond those assigned. His former teacher explains the problem to Brandon's
wife this way:

> "There are two Amish proverbs. First: 'The Peasant Believes Only the Father.'
> Second: 'je gelehrter, desto verkehrter.'"
> Caroline waited for a translation.
> "The more learned, the more confused." (44)

Throughout, the novel is concerned with how different kinds of knowledge conflict or work together. It should be said that Gaus is not glamorizing Jonah's path
(he becomes a self-destructive drinker), any more than he does the cooperative values
and close-knit social fabric of the Amish. As he portrays it, both have strengths
and dangers. But the scholar-teacher Brandon does embrace the classroom as the
site of translation and connection between different kinds of knowledge. During
the first book he is considering leaving the region to accept an endowed professorship elsewhere. In its conclusion he decides to stay, and the retention package he
gets from his college is a pool of ten tuition scholarships for young people who
grew up Amish and are leaving the community.

Gaus follows a familiar common sense in the way he locates the "traditional"
Amish way of life in place-time—it is down, and back. In *Broken English*, for
example, the narrator writes: "the road takes a straight course south for about
seven miles before it drops into a deep pocket where Fredericksburg sits at the
intersection of small country roads. Those travelers who drop down into that little
burg and spend enough quiet time soon realized that they've found the old world"
(38). But he is also critical of regional stereotypes. This passage, focalized through
an Amish woman, demonstrates that sometimes the person in the buggy, rather
than the person in the Cadillac, has the cognitive advantage. Like Dailey's Gina,
she links language difference to profit and shifts the meaning of the novel's title.
This is a subtle implicit analysis, and I quote at some length.

> "Oh, listen, darlin," one woman said to the other as they stood in front of Abigail's
> little roadside stand. "They gather the reeds themselves, off the land. It's the way
> they do everything, isn't that right, dear? Off the land."

Their husbands sat in the long Cadillac, dozing after an early lunch at the Harvestfest Authentic Amish Restaurant on Route 250 south of Kidron. The lady friend stood over Abigail's folding table and peeled off bills to pay for five baskets.

"Well, I know they make everything at home. That much I do know," the first chirped confidently. "I've been coming down here for four years now. But, do you, my dear?" she asked Abigail. "You know. Gather your own reeds off the land?" Both ladies waited eagerly for an answer.

Abigail had been selling baskets there beside the road for ten years. In those years, she had learned to listen to the prattlings of the English tourists without an opinion or a thought showing on her face. And she knew that a little broken English would help sales more than anything.

Abigail counted back change and said a few words in Low German. Then, haltingly, she said, "We gather, yes."

In an audible whisper, the veteran of four day-trips to Holmes County explained to her neophyte friend, "They don't speak that much English."

Abigail looked up and, in Low German, said the equivalent of, "We gather the reeds by post. They come in crates from an art supply wholesaler out of New York City."

The ladies smiled at the German, understanding nothing whatsoever of it, and then gathered up their baskets, roused their husbands, and drove off with the satisfying knowledge that they had garnered another secret of the mysterious Amish ways. Certain that they had unearthed another of the authentic mysteries of Holmes County, Ohio. (111–12)

In local color writing, as we have seen, the perspective of the Standard English narrator is often but not always privileged; here the local knows more than the tourist. My argument is that it is the tussle, not the outcome, that draws us into the orbit of the genre.

The reader is now the one who possesses a secret about Amish ways. Of course, it is hard to stop doubting authenticity once the question has been raised. It is not necessarily part of the norms of mystery-reading to go on to wonder if we too are being sold a bill of goods—misleading, whether cynical or well-intentioned. We must trust the narrator, so it is not surprising that the paratextual material for regional mysteries goes to considerable lengths to support the credibility of the writer. Author pages cite local roots, relevant professional experience, and rigorous research. Gaus's website tells us that he was born in Athens, Ohio and has lived in Ohio most of his life and in Wooster for thirty-eight years, that his "extensive knowledge of the culture and lifestyle of the Ohio Amish comes from over thirty-five years of travel throughout Holmes and surrounding counties in Ohio, where the world's largest Amish and Mennonite population sprawls out over the countryside near Millersburg, Wooster, and Sugarcreek." The specificity itself is a claim to knowledge, and we learn further that he "lectures widely about Amish culture at libraries, bookstores, literary societies, and the like."

The fact that Gaus had the "advice and encouragement" of Tony Hillerman is a less direct but important credential. Hillerman was one of the authors who established the regional mystery form (the first of his eighteen Navajo Tribal Police novels was published in 1970) and his works were consistent bestsellers. His priority and popularity no doubt contribute to his position, but he also embodies a kind of gold standard of authenticity. Hillerman himself freely acknowledged that there were occasional criticisms—but the response of the Navajo Nation to his work, and his relationship with the tribe, were both positive and well-publicized. He proudly and frequently cited the award he received in 1987 as a Special Friend of the Diné. His obituary in *Indian Country Today* reported, for example, that "his books are taught in schools across the Navajo Nation." Let me acknowledge, however: whatever the authors' credentials we are all (outsiders and insiders, in-betweeners and wannabes) required to make a judgment. These circulating forms mediate, and there is no final answer about authenticity.

Gaus's academic affiliation is also cited (he was a chemistry—not history—professor at Wooster College, now retired), but the books probably gain more credibility from the fact that the first seven novels were published by Ohio University Press. Their sales are attested by the fact that the eighth and ninth appeared with Plume (a Penguin imprint that focuses on "voices previously neglected by mainstream publishing"), and the others not only reprinted but turned into e-books, audiobooks, and large-print editions. Ohio University Press publishes another regional mystery series, one set in Columbus (and including a novel involving Buckeye football), as well as other Ohio and regional titles. Most university presses do. Such publications are not only seen as a public service, but have the potential to sell better than most academic books. Not only regional fiction but also memoirs, local histories, travel guides, field guides, and many other topics appear on such lists. For example, the University of Michigan Press website (as of August 30, 2017) lists 197 volumes under "Michigan and Great Lakes" subject category. (I can attest that the mushroom-hunting books are locally famous.) Cookbooks in particular are money-makers, to judge by how frequently they appear. And of course—whether they are published by university presses, commercial publishers, or self-published—talking about such books takes us immediately back into endlessly debatable questions about regions. In spring of 2014, National Public Radio ran a story about an Amazon website helping interested readers sort through "zillions of cookbooks coming out every year," by "curating" its vast collection and offering a guide to five hundred of the best regional cookbooks. The comments section immediately turned into a debate over whether the article neglected the Midwest or not, and the quality of food in the Midwest (as well as over the impact of Amazon.com).

I began with *Criminal Minds*—a hard-edged mystery series, what is called a police procedural. Another very popular broadcast television series was cozier. The retired schoolteacher Jessica Fletcher, played by Angela Lansbury, lives in the fictional Maine Village of Cabot Cove; she is both the author of detective novels and an amateur sleuth (to use a well-worn phrase). The show constantly, recursively refers back to print mysteries, as well as engaging cultural productions of many kinds throughout its twelve seasons. The run of *Murder, She Wrote* was from 1984 to 1996, but it continued in TV movies and as recently as 2014 there was talk of a "reboot" (reportedly killed off by Lansbury's disapproval [McMillan]). The series is still in syndication and often appears on broadcast television, to say nothing of its availability through streaming services and (this is how I mostly watched it) on DVDs in local libraries. Cabot Cove is central to the identity of the show, but most episodes take place elsewhere—the first season for example ranges from New York to Wyoming and San Francisco to a Mediterranean island. Even the episodes set in Maine include only perfunctory gestures to regional specificity, and the town is played throughout the show's run by Mendocino, California. Region, it seems, can exert a powerful appeal even when it has become reduced to a few conventions. The emptiness of the pattern is especially apparent in how bad actors' Maine accents are, on the rare occasions when they make an attempt—Tom Bosley's Sheriff Amos Tupper is usually singled out as the worst offender. (*Murder, She Wrote* also includes an episode that has justifiably been called "one of the single worst shows involving Amish characters" [Igou].) My consideration of television is certainly insufficient; yet it would be even less satisfactory to omit the topic, which is important in itself and thoroughly intertwined with "literature." *Murder, She Wrote* books are still appearing, often listed on Amazon as co-authored: "Jessica Fletcher is a bestselling mystery writer who has a knack for stumbling upon real-life mysteries in her various travels. Donald Bain, Jessica Fletcher's long-time collaborator, is the writer of over eighty books, many of them bestsellers." There is *Murder, She Wrote* fan fiction as well. It is a tiny part of an immense body of work that continues to remake the boundaries that once seemed to exist between reading, watching, and creating, and between print and electronic media.

Media are always interconnected. Let us remember that almost forty years ago Amy Kaplan was analyzing how—one hundred years previously—the realism of William Dean Howells was responding to the competition of the mass media. One no longer needs to be prescient to observe that the topic is indispensable; the impact of the media system on its parts is, in the twenty-first century, difficult to miss. The archive of possible examples is immense—I stop here, but invite readers to continue whatever thought experiments they have begun.

We have seen not only that ideas about regions are scattered all through contemporary culture, but that they are sometimes bundled in patterns that can be understood in terms of the concept of region I have developed. They may even, as in the Faulkner passage quoted on *Criminal Minds*, be explicitly linked with regional literature. We see too that self-reflective perspectives appear in popular forms—as formulas appear in literary fiction. No genre, no "brow," is necessarily critical or uncritical. The rewards offered by different media and different genres are different in kind, and I have not been concerned here to explain these works on their own terms, but rather to understand their connection to the continuing presence of regionalism in literary history. I turn now to the question of just what that presence is, beginning with the views of other scholars.

Surveying the Literature, Revisited

Literary historians of the United States agree about this, at least: regionalism is a persisting, but variable, element of the genre system. I will try to avoid the metaphors of waxing and waning, ebbing and flowing, that are commonly used. Such figures imply that the form is an entity, substantial and at least somewhat cohesive; I see it rather as a recurring pattern. Of course, if we look for *place* in expressive culture we will always find it; stories inevitably project spaces and temporalities. Meanwhile, common-sense notions and expert testimony about regions are constantly circulating. Not only in everyday speech, but also in much scholarship, anything—from fiction to food—that manifests an affiliation with a particular place is likely to be referred to as "local color." I am not objecting to that usage. But deploying a stronger sense of "region" does, I have found, offer an analytic advantage in studying twentieth- and twenty-first-century fiction.

Gordon Hutner's authoritative survey of "better fiction" in the central decades of the twentieth century—examining not ambitiously literary or avant-garde works, or mass culture, but the novels that were widely read and admired by the middle-brow middle class—demonstrates that regionalism was important and popular in the 1920s and throughout the next decade. Most of the Pulitzer Prize-winning novels of the 1930s, he points out, focused on particular places: T. S. Stribling's *The Store* (1933) on Alabama, Caroline Miller's *Lamb in His Bosom* (1934) on Georgia, Josephine Winslow Johnson's *Now in November* (1935) on Missouri, H. L. Davis's *Honey in the Horn* (1936) on Oregon. Only Margaret Mitchell's *Gone with the Wind* (1937, set in Georgia and frequently standing in for "the South") and Marjorie Kinnan Rawling's *The Yearling* (1939, Florida) are still frequently read and referenced today. In those two cases, a successful movie adaptation extended the work's audience; so did being enlisted (despite blatant racism) into the romance and young adult categories, respectively. Hutner considers the form in decline in the 1940s, and it barely figures in his discussion of the 1950s. Yet in his study of U.S. literary regionalism since the Depression, Jason Arthur begins with authors associated with those decades: James Agee and Jack Kerouac. Clearly regionalism became influential again in the 1980s—in mysteries, as I have noted, and in fiction in general. In later chapters Arthur turns to Maxine Hong Kingston, Russell Banks, and Jonathan Franzen, and he notes that many of the novels that won Pulitzer Prizes in the first decade of the twenty-first century were, once again, focused on small towns. Such accounts depend (of course, tautologically) upon how one understands the genre.

In some cases it is clear that the writers of the novels are claiming a relationship to regionalism. Mary Ellen Chase, author of *Wind-Swept* (a 1941 bestseller) and other novels of Maine, has a strong and specific connection to Sarah Orne Jewett. We could know this from the work itself—most clearly perhaps when she writes of her character Mrs. Haskell that her employer thinks she is "one of the ageless among the enforced dwellers on this earth. Her stout percale and gingham skirts might have swept the asphodel and thyme of Grecian hillsides, the lilies of Judean fields" (223)—the reference of course is to Mrs. Todd. There is additional evidence. Chase edited *Country of the Pointed Firs*, and in her introduction to it (published 1968) recounts the story of being taken by her father to meet Jewett, in 1900 when she was thirteen; he knew her and loved her work, and Chase was already "her faithful disciple" (Norton, xxiv). When the author asked her what she wanted to do when she grew up, she answered, "I want to write books as you do"—to which Jewett replied that she was sure she would—"And good ones, too—all about Maine." Chase goes on to say that her books "*have* been about Maine, according to her prophecy, perhaps indeed, *because* of it. And about the coast of Maine, which she knew and understood as no other writer has done before or since that day…Her care and vision unite in revealing its incomparable loveliness and its distinctive contribution not only to the state but to the country at large" (xxv). Such biographical evidence is interesting for interpreting a particular author (in this case it seems to me that the story itself manifests how much more ambition and reach Jewett had), but it is not necessary for tracing the travels of a genre. The aesthetic ideology of regionalism as an expression of the distinctiveness of place, and the capabilities of the form, are available in any case. It is a satisfying connection that Chase prominently cites Captain Littlepage's comments on the cosmopolitan consequences of shipping, and Maine dialect. But I find it equally important that *Wind-Swept* includes some attention to a one-room schoolhouse, and a teacher who boards with the locals and is very successful at making connections between social classes, and between kinds of knowledge (248–50).

Even beyond my particular interest in schoolteachers, some of the important factors shaping regional writing were not legible to writers in their own moments. A striking example is the persuasive case that Jeff Karem makes in *The Romance of Authenticity* for a connection between late nineteenth-century local color, and mid- and latter twentieth-century ethnic literatures. "In each of these periods American publishers, editors, and readers exhibited a romantic interest in authenticity, a fascination with and desire for texts they believed distilled the exotic essences of the nation's cultural margins" (1). Karem mobilizes an enormous amount of information about the composition, publication, and reception of William Faulkner, Richard Wright, Ernest Gaines, Rolando Hinojosa, and Leslie Silko; he shows how these authors are constantly working with and often against the "horizon of expectations" (23) about the particular places and people they represent. He demonstrates (citing Brodhead's work in an earlier period, on Chesnutt) that "Write what you know!" (11) enabled access, but commodified difference and also produced constraints. For example, Wright shifted the expectation that African-American literature would be Southern and pastoral to a focus on urban conflict—and Gaines subsequently faced a resistant market for his rural fiction. As evidenced in my first chapter, Karem's skepticism about authenticity is widely shared by critics today, but his meticulous analysis of how the paradigm works on the ground makes this an especially powerful and consequential argument.

Karem notes that by the end of Faulkner's career, readers had come to see him as "America's folk genius" (52). His stories of the South were understood to offer "a wellspring of authenticity that was not merely regional but national" (60). Indeed, in handbooks for literary study, when local color is subordinated to regionalism, the implicit reference is Faulkner's universality. Certain residents of the backwoods, it seems, have uncanny knowledge of the center. But in discussions of Faulkner, universality is almost always conscripted as nationality. Indeed, reading across the criticism, what strikes me is how often (across all periods) the pattern Johnson identifies in *Heartland TV*—in which the Midwest sometimes represents and sometimes is distinguished from the nation—recurs. New England, the South, the west can all represent America *or* provide an alternative. Jennifer Greeson explicitly suggests this for an earlier era, writing that "[w]ith remarkable fluidity, 'our South' aligns with and diverges from 'the United States' writ large, creating a symbolic *ideological juxtaposition* in which each term is defined by reference to the other" (1, emphasis in original). In *The Nation's Region* Leigh Anne Duck demonstrates that the South plays a similar role in the twentieth century—providing "both alternatives and supplements to national models of affiliation" (11). The labile and charged relation of region to solidarities at every level, and particularly the nation— both in the literature and in the criticism—constitutes a recurring and important pattern. Chase is acknowledging it as well in her comments on Jewett and the Maine coast, although these recent accounts are more sophisticated and self-reflective.

Duck is also a fine analyst of temporal difference in representations of the South. She avails herself of Bakhtin's concept of the chronotope, and establishes a critical distance from the conventional notions that Southern literature is obsessed with the past, and that the South somehow exists in the past. That formation invokes—as I discussed in the first chapter—a profound politics of time. Duck shows that different writers imagine regional and national time differently, from those who "recorded and responded to the paradoxically frenetic production of southern backwardness, which they placed in dialogue with equally assertive accounts of national progressiveness" (9), to those who "depict individuals in the process of delineating their own temporal boundaries—situating themselves in idiosyncratic relationships to modernization, folklore, or antebellum history" (12). What these writers, on her account, have in common is the way social organization, and in particular the racial regime, is mapped by the coordination of time and place. This too is a pattern that links the literature of different periods.

I also see a new pattern emerging in contemporary criticism: a foregrounded effort to articulate a perspective that is both local *and* translocal. Already in 1997 Anthony Appiah was affirming his father's belief in "a rooted cosmopolitanism, or, if you like, a cosmopolitan patriotism. Like Gertrude Stein, he thought there was no point in roots if you couldn't take them with you. 'America is my country and Paris is my hometown,' Stein said. My father would have understood her" (618). Recent critics of regionalism repeat this "both/and" gesture. Tom Lutz writes about regionalism, and literature in general, as cosmopolitan. Philip Joseph argues for discriminating between nostalgic versions of regionalism and those that can contribute to a modern dialogue about globalization. More recently, Paul Giles has written about "metaregionalism," and Jason Arthur about "regional cosmopolitanism." It is already clear, I am sure, that—whatever my detailed disagreements with these literary scholars' arguments—I too embrace this meshing of antinomies. The goal of my analysis throughout has been to deepen our sense of what it implies.[1]

If these formulations are paradoxical, it is a paradox inherent in how we think about place. As I have argued from the beginning: the most powerful concept of "region" is both substantive and relational. I have suggested as well that this dynamic tension plays out in quite regularly patterned ways, and that many authors, particularly Jewett and Eaton, offer similar insights. The view I've arrived at meshes most closely with the work of Douglas Reichert Powell and Dalia Kandiyoti, who—from very different vantage points—ask us to revise accepted accounts of American literary history. Powell writes about "critical regionalism" (2007), acknowledging the term's relation to architecture (which I noted in Chapter 1) and showing how regional works are always connected elsewhere, but also articulating a substantive view by constantly linking back to a specific place (Johnson City, Tennessee). He is also one of the few professors who explicitly grounds his argument in the classroom.[2] In *Migrant Sites* (2009) Kandiyoti argues that a sense of place is crucial in narratives of immigrant experience, both through a relation to homelands which take many forms and through a relation to the localities they inhabit. The clear lines around ghettos, the limits on opportunity imposed by racism, the imbrication of languages and dialects with Standard English—all these elements help us to understand why an apparently so-different writer like Abraham Cahan was so easily read as part of the local color tradition. Rather than identifying regionalism with enclosure and the rural, diaspora with movement and the city, she shows how these forms intertwine and argues that national literature *is* diaspora literature. Like Karem (although without citing his work), she demonstrates the strong connection between regional writing and contemporary ethnic literature, and places her work in the context of comparative literature as well.

The opposition between locals and outsiders that has characterized so much discussion of local color writing is necessarily shifted by a perspective that brings regionalism in relation to cosmopolitanism. Mediating figures like the returned native and the schoolteacher become particularly interesting. Research by the sociologist Wendy Griswold supports this turn with empirical information about the current readership of regional fiction. She and her collaborators have found that people who move somewhere "usually know as much about the literature of the region they currently live in as do the people who have always lived there. In other words, newcomers turn into regionalists just like the old-timers" (92). She suggests two possible reasons and offers support for both. One, supported by considerable evidence, is that movers tend to be cosmopolitans who simply know more about culture in general. The other is that they "are cowbirds, people who come in and absorb the cultural characteristics of their new homes, just as cowbirds infiltrate and thrive in the nests made by other birds" (92). Griswold's conclusion parallels what linguists say about language variation; against the widespread notion that differences are vanishing, her book argues that regional culture continues to be reproduced and recreated and is in fact thriving.

One of the attractive features of Griswold's analysis is that she acknowledges differences within the motives and practices of regionalism—that for example it is produced both internally, by people with deep roots in the place and through their influence on others, and also externally as the relatively small and privileged "reading class" registers the value placed elsewhere on regional literature and culture. As Griswold puts it, "Being a knowledgeable local is not at the opposite pole from being a cosmopolitan, as the old dichotomy had it. Instead, attaining local cultural knowledge is one of the ways people enact and demonstrate their cosmopolitanism" (100). Lisa Gitelman makes a similar but even broader point in her comparative study of the emergence of recorded sound and digital networks, at the turn into the twentieth and twenty-first centuries respectively: "global media help to create a world in which people are local not only because of where they are or are from but also because of their relationships to media representations of localism and its fate" (17). This is the horizon we need in order to understand regionalism as a form.

What, however, are we to do with the notion of the cowbird? Surely the tension between locals and others reasserts itself in this figure. In explaining her metaphor, Griswold uses the words "parasitic" and "invade" but does not seem to register their force. The way cowbirds "make themselves at home" (90) in other birds' nests is to find a time when they are unattended and lay eggs in them, sometimes tossing out or eating the eggs that were already there. Their chicks often hatch earlier and are larger than those of the other species, giving them an advantage for survival. There is debate about how much impact the Brown-headed cowbird has on songbird populations in North America—but the image of "movers" killing off the locals' young and replacing them with their own is deeply inconsistent with Griswold's affirmative depiction of their creative collaboration with "stayers." Indeed, the cowbird could be developed into a parable about the need for deep, not movable, roots and the dangers of global development. Cowbirds are parasites exactly because they are nomadic. They do not make their own nests because they followed the bison; now they associate instead with humans' livestock, and thus have a grotesquely expanded range—and endanger more species of songbird. I do not mean to suggest that Griswold's work is invalidated by her choice of metaphor—it is not. Yet in writing about regionalism we need to pay attention to the particulars of landscapes and their creatures, human and otherwise. The cowbird functions here as a reminder that the politics of place can be painful, and violent. It should not be easy to think local and global, rooted and cosmopolitan, together.

I open my study of contemporary literary fiction with Wendell Berry—a committed regionalist who believes in deep roots, and certainly cares about particularities like the behavior of cowbirds.

Let me acknowledge the tendentiousness of my intervention in literary history, in the pages that follow. Drawing on the terms developed in the first chapter: I focus my attention not on (what Raymond Williams would call) "encapsulated" novels but on works that allow me to see (following Henri Lefebvre) "the center of the world" as movable. I go on, as well, to suggest that "rooted cosmopolitanism" is increasingly explicit and available in contemporary anglophone fiction. But by beginning with Berry, I set myself a challenge. He affirms the substantive and is wary of the relational. Despite his wide circulation in print, he is skeptical about book-learning. He explicitly rejects the kind of inquiry I am engaged in—I am, in his terms, an "explainer" (I explain what that means, below). Yet Berry's work— like that of the other authors I go on to discuss—has helped me to understand "region" as a field of force.

Mr. Wendell Berry of Kentucky

I pay sustained attention to Wendell Berry for several reasons. He is strongly identified with the form—widely read, and unequivocally addressing his audience from a particular place. He reflects systematically on the nature of regionalism. And, as I have just said, his work connects with my concerns at many points, but there is a lot of friction between our perspectives. Certainly his work supports my case against seeing regionalism as literary tourism, but it also challenges the notion of rooted cosmopolitanism. Berry makes me think hard. If it is to hold, my concept of region and my account of literary history must be adequate to his body of work. I often find it uncomfortable, and I greatly admire it.

Berry is an eloquent advocate of the local, speaking for the *here* against the elsewhere and the everywhere. In his non-fiction essays he is explicitly and resolutely agrarian and anti-modern. Berry portrays urban-dwellers, let alone cosmopolitan "frequent flyers," as victims of a disease of our era: the restless desire to have something one doesn't have, to be somewhere else. He dislikes paved roads both for their destructive impact on the environment, and for what they represent. This passage from his short novel *Remembering* is characteristic, although it is not in his own voice but focalized through the protagonist Andy Catlett as he heads home on the interstate highway. "The city is behind him now, except for the road itself that is the city's hardened effluent, passing through its long gouge without respect for what was there before it or what is now alongside it. The road reminds him, as it always has before, of the power of words far removed from what they mean. For the road is a word, conceived elsewhere and laid across the country in the wound prepared for it: a word made concrete and thrust among us" (215). This antipathy is shared by many of Berry's admirable characters and, we know from evidence outside his fiction, by the author. In an often-reprinted 1972 essay, Berry wrote that our nomadic society is "moving about on the face of this continent with a mindless destructiveness . . . that makes Sherman's March to the Sea look like a prank" (976). The reference specifies Southern history, but its implications are global.

Berry's literary reputation began with his poetry, and he is probably now best known as an activist and essayist. His writing across different forms is strikingly cohesive. Like the essay I have just quoted, "Imagination in Place," his work is always indispensably rooted in a particular place and always simultaneously, powerfully, concisely articulates a unified vision of the world as a whole. Berry's short stories and novels focus on the fictional town of Port William, Kentucky, which is based on Berry's home town of Port Royal; the nearby, somewhat larger Hargrave derives from Carrollton, located about 15 miles away at the site where the Kentucky and Ohio Rivers join (and in fact once called Port William). His fiction is above all a narrative of community. As the back cover of the 2001 edition of *A Place on Earth* says—in familiar terms—the "central character is not a person but a place." His fiction constructs an intensely imagined world in which a group of human beings is united, across generations, through their relationships and their connection to the landscape; Berry calls this the Port William "membership." As Berry's wayward saint Burley Coulter explains in "The Wild Birds," "The way we are, we are members of each other. All of us. Everything. The difference ain't in who is a member and who is not, but in who knows it and who don't" (356). This fellowship is individually chosen and located in place-time, yet also infinite and eternal. I will engage the complexities of Berry's ideas—he is both conservative and radical, an anti-capitalist pacifist environmentalist Christian. My central concern, however, is not to explicate his intellectual commitments, but to consider the extended body of his fiction in terms of the long travels of regionalism.

The ur-narrative of Port William is Berry's *A Place on Earth*. In his Author's Note, Berry comments that the novel has "an editorial history sufficiently humbling to its author"—he began it in 1960, recognized after its publication in 1967 that the book was "not satisfactory" (xi) and revised it (mostly through cutting) for new editions in 1983 and 2001. The novel is set during the Second World War, weaving that worldwide conflict's impact on the region together with other sequences like the consequences of a small flash flood, and always including local memories of earlier times. Narratives of community are inevitably difficult to plot, and *A Place on Earth* can seem structurally diffuse. It is a challenge for the reader to keep track of its many characters—a knowledge of the later works helps, as do the map and the genealogical chart (printed over an image of the map) provided in Berry's recent publications. (See Figures 5.1 and 5.2.)

Fundamentally, all of Berry's fiction is one long story. The best key to that body of work may be *That Distant Land*, which collects the stories published before 2004, labeling each with the year when its main action takes place and presenting them in chronological order and noting where each of the novels belongs in that series. His characters are constantly engaged in narration; many of the short pieces read as heightened transcriptions of the stories they tell each other. And Berry's

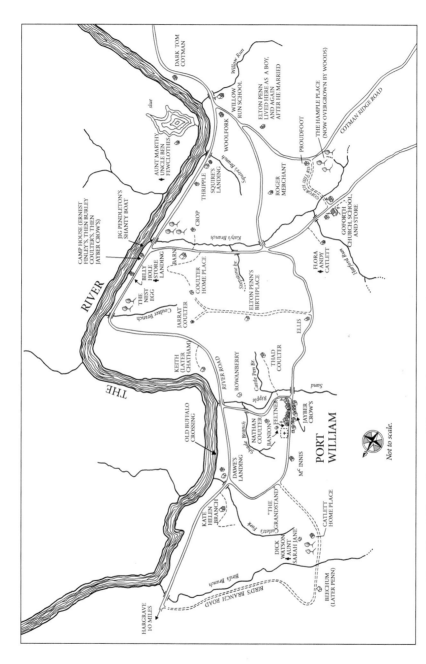

FIGURE 5.1 *Map of Port William, from Wendell Berry's* That Distant Land. *Drawn by Molly O'Halloran and reprinted by permission of Counterpoint Press.*

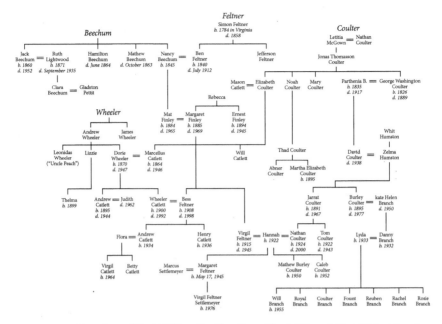

FIGURE 5.2 *Genealogy of Port William families, from Wendell Berry's* That Distant Land. *Drawn by Molly O'Halloran and reprinted by permission of Counterpoint Press.*

central, recurring characters are constantly visited by thoughts of the past—not only of their own experiences, but also of earlier days they know through stories they have been told and embrace as part of their membership. Many of the longer pieces are structured as what we might call memoirs. Their significance inheres less in the outcome of events than in their telling of time, the way they imagine past, present, and future embodied in a *here and now*. Memory is in the landscape, very much in the way Keith Basso shows it is for the Western Apache, in *Wisdom Sits in Places*. Art Rowanberry "had a compound mind, as a daisy has a compound flower, and his mind had something of the unwary comeliness of a daisy. Something that happened would remind him of something he remembered, which would remind him of something that his grandfather remembered. It was not that he 'lived in his mind.' He lived in the place, but the place was where the memories were, and he walked among them, tracing them out over the living ground" (*That Distant Land*, "Are You All Right?", 368). My references will range across this body of work, and conclude with *Remembering*, which is an interesting outlier—it is still engaged with Port William, but its action is set mainly in San Francisco.

Berry articulated his view of the tradition in "The Regional Motive," an essay published in 1972, and often reprinted since. He wrote, "as a writer whose work—and whose life—have been largely formed in relation to a specific place, I am often in the neighborhood of the word *regional*. And almost as often as I come within its neighborhood I find that the term very quickly becomes either an embarrassment or an obstruction. For I do not know any word that is more sloppily defined in its usage, or more casually understood" ("The Regional Motive," 972). He disclaims both regionalism based on pride, which (he notes) "behaves like nationalism," and the falsity of the "quaint and the eccentric and the picturesque" (972)—he is particularly specific and critical about notions of the South. He refuses any narrowed perspective in which "a man is unable to bring to bear on the life of his place as much as he is able to know" (974)—on that view for example "Faulkner would have had to disavow that part of his mind that knew the "Ode on a Grecian Urn" (975). Thus, on his deathbed Mat Feltner—one of the practical and spiritual pillars of the Port William membership—quotes Milton to his grandson Andy Catlett. But he learned the lines he recites from his mother, and does not know their author (nor does Berry cite it, any more than Edith Eaton does in the stories discussed in Chapter 4). What matters is their substance and quality; as Mat says to Andy, "wasn't he a fine one!" (*That Distant Land,* 313). Berry consistently and completely rejects *distinction*, in Pierre Bourdieu's sense. Port William's barber, Jayber Crow, is not only a reflective man but also took classes at a university for a time, and is a constant reader—but he keeps his books upstairs in his room over the shop, where others do not see them. Burley writes to his nephew, "I've known Jayber mighty well for a long time, and I never knew he read books…When he seen I was interested, Jayber told me that books has meant a lot to him, and there's some of them he puts a good deal of stock in" (*A Place on Earth*, 108). But he pays at least equally close and careful attention to his neighbors.

As Berry puts it: "The regionalism that I adhere to could be defined simply as *local life aware of itself*…The motive of such regionalism is the awareness that local life is intricately dependent, for its quality but also for its continuance, upon local knowledge" ("The Regional Motive," 975). Berry appreciates book-learning, but in his view the balance between different kinds of knowledge has become grotesquely distorted—so he defends the local and particular. He values, in fact, precisely the kind of classroom that was my focus in the second chapter. In "A Consent," set in 1908, he gives an affectionate portrait of Miss Minnie Quinch, who is from Port William and has trained at a teacher's college and returned home to teach grades one through eight—not using the "cunning methods" (26) she learned elsewhere but succeeding as a teacher because of her love of children and books, and her relationships with local families. Berry's stories about Miss Minnie and the man she marries, Tol Proudfoot, are comic. But their themes are serious, often revolving around knowledge and generally demonstrating the power of Tol's grounded understanding. For example, in "The Lost Bet" in which he gets the better of a Louisville storekeeper who is mocking him for being a country bumpkin, Miss Minnie, ever the generous mediator, comments that she knows "he was half sorry just as soon as he did it" (144). In his novel/memoir Jayber Crow laments the closing of the school, in 1964, as a "never-healing wound" to the community (279). For local life to know itself, attention must be paid. What Berry wants is for schools to value the local, to be local, and indeed for education as a whole to be redefined. In *Remembering*, Andy Catlett thinks of his grandfather riding, as a child, with

Jack Beechum on a mule-drawn plow, and talking all afternoon—and he thinks, "*Was that a school? It was a school*" (79, emphasis in original). In contrast, Andy's own modern schooling was oriented to the city and devalued the country; "his teachers all advised and he believed" that he "needed an education, and the purpose of an education was to take him away" (71).

My motive here is partly to establish that the topos of the one-room schoolhouse, and the mapping of kinds of knowledge I focused on in the second chapter, *do* give us a purchase on Berry's work. Also, I want to consider his relation to literary tradition; there are many moments in his fiction that invite us to make connections to other writers, often to American regionalists. An early passage in *Jayber Crow* is clearly a tribute to Mark Twain. One sentence reads: "It was wonderful the way the river and the banks and the whole valley would be quiet, preoccupied with the lights and shadows and the regular business of a summer morning, and then you would hear that whistle, and all of a sudden there would be this commotion: the sound of a big engine, a bell ringing, shouts, blocks creaking as the plank was lowered, cattle bawling, pigs squealing, men cursing, the roustabouts chanting as they passed bags or boxes from hand to hand" (18). In case one doubts that this echoes the famous description of the dawn in Chapter 19 of *Huckleberry Finn*, the narrator goes on discuss "the age of steamboating" (19). Of course, in making this connection I must defy the author's posted "Notice," as the multitudes who have written about *Huck Finn* have. Twain wrote that "persons attempting to find a motive in this narrative will be prosecuted; persons attempting to find a moral in it will be banished; persons attempting to find a plot in it will be shot." Berry forbids any effort to "explain, interpret, explicate, analyze, deconstruct, or otherwise 'understand'" the book, but his proposed penalty is milder—we are to be "exiled to a desert island in the company only of other explainers" (n.p.). It is perhaps safer to note Berry's compliment to Wallace Stegner in *Remembering*. Andy's seat companion on his plane home is reading *Beyond the Hundredth Meridian*, "a book that Andy knows, by a writer he loves" (100). Stegner was Berry's teacher in the creative writing program at Stanford; like Milton, and Twain, he is not named.

Deep patterns like attention to schooling are more debatable, but—for my analysis of the genre—even more interesting. They rely not on allusion, but on participation in the forms that make narration possible. It would I think be distasteful to Wendell Berry to suggest that he belongs to a membership that includes romance-novel readers or streaming viewers of *Criminal Minds*. Brother Tom Murphy (of the Order of Carmelites) runs a website about him, but prominently notes: "This site is not owned, operated or sanctioned by Mr. Berry, whose disapproval of computer technology is well-documented. 'I hear that I have a website, but I didn't do those things. My instrument is a pencil.'" Nevertheless Berry's work inevitably circulates and connects. Turning back to the past—his story "Making It Home," recounting Art Rowanberry's return from his military service during the Second World War, has much in common with Hamlin Garland's "Return of a Private." Or, the relationship between Gideon

Crop and Roger Merchant (the names are of course significant) in *A Place on Earth* might productively be compared with the drama enacted between tenant and landlord in Garland's populist classic "Under the Lion's Paw."

These juxtapositions suggest questions. Berry renews our attention to the role of the Haskins' neighbors, the Councils (again, the name is meaningful). Garland's frank economism invites us, across time, to reconsider Mat Feltner's role on the board of the local bank. An important element of the story of Port William starts with the moment when Jayber Crow buys its empty barbershop. Burley Coulter recognizes him—a drifter, although born nearby—as a potential contributor to the membership; he imagines and negotiates the deal. Mat considers and consents to their notion, and as a member of the local bank's board he writes out the contract. Does positioning a lending institution as the "Independent Farmers Bank" (100) negate its inherent loyalty to the abstraction of money? Perhaps. Mat embodies the perfect combination of justice and generosity, and Jayber notes that he and Burley did not just "get me started and then leave me to fare the best I could" (*Jayber Crow*, 103)—like the Councils, they disregard economic logic and *help* their neighbors, thereby enriching the membership. So this is not a question that arises within the narrative. But continuing the conversation in this way is very much in the spirit of the early Garland, and of Berry throughout his career. Both refuse any separation of literature, ethics, and economics.

Berry never alludes to Sarah Jewett's stories, and perhaps it is surprising that I see a strong connection between the two writers. After all, Port William is very much a man's world. It is relatively rare for Berry to focalize a story through a woman, and an effort like *Hannah Coulter* is (in my opinion) among his weaker works. Their Christianity is a link, but of course many other writers I discuss are convinced believers (Edward Eggleston for example). The affinity is less religious than spiritual or perhaps philosophical. As Jewett affirms the transfiguring moment, Berry endows the beloved place with the ability to represent the eternal and infinite. On two occasions in the stories in *That Distant Land*, Burley Coulter expresses his ontological certainty by humorously rejecting the notion that he could be lost in the woods:

> '*I* know where we are.'
>   And they all turn to him.
>   'Where?'
>   'Where?'
>   'Right here.' ("The Wild Birds," 347, emphasis in original; see also "Watch with Me," 111)

Burley gives the same answer as he is dying, when he wakes up after his son Danny has moved him from the hospital to Stepstone Hollow and asks if he knows where he is—although in this case he does literally know, as well. He is "Right here" ("Fidelity," 392), solid and correct in the center of the world (in the sense I have given that phrase). My many readings of Jewett and Berry have given me the title of this book.

We can also read Berry through the category of "empathetic style" that Marcia McClintock Folsom developed in her analysis of *Country of the Pointed Firs*. As she showed, the texture and pleasure of the work comes from fact that Jewett does not so much describe the communication that binds her characters together as demonstrate or perhaps enact it, enabling the reader to participate in their cognitive processes. So when in "Fidelity" Danny decides that he cannot allow the comatose Burley to remain plugged in to machines, he does not tell anyone. But the rest of the membership reads the signals and, because they understand the situation and each other, take action to protect him. They do not talk with each other either—to do so, after all, would be to conspire in a crime. But Danny's cousin Nathan Coulter is able to guess where he has gone and move his truck out of sight; because the description of the man who took Burley from the hospital includes a blue shirt, he provides a change of clothes. When Danny has completed his vigil and buried his father, he returns to the road.

> The absence of his truck startled Danny when he got back to where he had left it, but he stood still only for a moment before he imagined what had happened. If the wrong people had found the truck, they would have come on up the branch and found him and Burley. The right person could only have been Nathan, who would have known where the key was hidden and who would have taken the truck to the nearest unlikely place where he could put it out of sight.   (419)

They both know the landscape intimately; Danny walks to an old barn nearby—"he smiled when he stepped through the door of the old barn and saw his truck. He laid his tools in with the other fencing tools in the back, and then, opening the passenger door to toss in his bundle, he saw Nathan's green shirt lying on the seat. He smiled again and took off the blue shirt he was wearing and put the green one on" (419). When he enters the room where his family and neighbors—including the lawyers Wheeler and Henry Catlett—are assembled, with the detective Kyle Bode, the frustrated man shouts, "Where *have* you been?...He's dead, isn't he, and you have buried him somewhere in these end-of-nowhere, godforsaken hills and hollows?" (427). But there is no evidence against Danny. He even manages to avoid lying, although only the membership knows what his economic metaphor means: "I had an account to settle with one of my creditors" (427).

Like Jewett's, Berry's work manifests the way these inclusions also entail exclusions. I have already discussed the racial politics of Jewett's work. Berry similarly implicitly accepts the attitudes of his characters when for example Nettie and Joe Banion, African-Americans who work for the Feltners, eat separately after the family (*A Place on Earth*, 14). The explicit content of this and other novels indicates that the relations of several generations of Banions and Feltners are respectful and affectionate. Yet their segregated dining marks this as "the Jim Crow world of masters and servants" (Berrey, 48), in which white belief in interracial amity sustains the system of racial inequality, and is sustained—as here—by the absence of inquiry into what Black people actually think. There is no effort to capture the Banions' perspective. There is, as well, a note of primitivism in the treatment of Joe's mother Fanny and her "ominous knowledge" (252). The Banion and Fewclothes places appear on the map of Port William, but the families do not appear on the genealogical chart—Berry does not comment explicitly, but it seems taken for granted that these nonwhite characters are excluded from the membership. Literally and metaphorically, they do not sit at the same table as Berry's central characters. Throughout his work, Berry refrains from introducing a critical perspective on the racism endemic to his world. For example, the way communities are constituted through such racialized attitudes and institutions is expressed in many common turns of speech—when Uncle Stanley expresses his appreciation of the fairness of a proposal that Jayber Crow has made to him: "that proposition you just made, now, by grab, that was mighty kind. It was *white*, by grab" (78).

In reporting a moment when the membership is acting powerfully, in "Fidelity," and by noting its roots in a settled system of racial inequality, I run the risk of making it seem that Berry shows the Port William membership as something powerful and settled. It is not. Berry shows it as always difficult to achieve, and by the latter twentieth century almost lost. Kyle Bode—sad, stubborn agent of the state—even calls the place "godforsaken"; for him that is a cant expression, but it implies a real danger. Berry's short novel *Remembering*, set in 1976, tells the story of a crisis in the life of one of the younger generation of the membership, interwoven with his memories and his memories of others' memories (like Art Rowanberry, he has a compound mind). Andy Catlett is a returned native. After college he became a journalist, working in San Francisco and then in Chicago for a magazine called *Scientific Farming*. An encounter with an Amish farmer changes his thinking and his direction, and he returns to Port William to farm traditionally. Andy Catlett is clearly the most autobiographical character in Berry's work, although that is not particularly consequential for my interpretation of the book.

At the moment when the action of the book begins, Andy is estranged from the membership and indeed from himself. He has lost his right hand in an accident with a corn-picking machine, and it seems to him that it "had been the one with which he reached out to the world and attached himself to it. When he lost his hand he lost his hold. It was as though his hand still clutched all that was dear to him—and was gone" (28). He remains deeply critical of industrial agriculture. Indeed, in the description of his accident the picker becomes an incarnation of the cruel apparatus of modernity: "He heard the long persistence of the noise of the machine that did not know the difference between a cornstalk and a man's arm. He felt its relentless effort to pull him into itself, while the bloodied rollers wore against flesh and crushed bone, and the oblivious metal rattled and shook" (14). His mutilation—and his reaction to it—separates him from the wholeness of the world and pushes him into anger and abstraction. At the conference he attends in the opening pages, he must take notes with his left hand and so in awkward code, even more cryptic and removed from located meaning than the words being mouthed by the speakers. He denounces their notion of progress and their reductions—but cannot recover his connection to the living world. He travels next to a speaking engagement in San Francisco, but when addressed by the person meeting him he denies that he is Andrew Catlett. The novel opens in the darkness of an anonymous room in San Francisco.

Andy's situation is a reworking of the story of Ernest Finley in *A Place on Earth*. Ernest too was damaged by the destructive nature of modern life—he was seriously wounded in the First World War, and must use crutches. After his return he lives with his sister Margaret and her husband Mat Feltner. Despite his limitations he has become a very capable carpenter; the townspeople were at first surprised that he can "lift and carry and climb and, more alone than not, frame and wall up and roof a sizable building" (36). But he considers himself damaged, defeated, although he never complains. He is silent, closed away from the membership. When Ernest spends time repairing buildings on the Crop farm while Gideon is away after the flash flood, he falls in love with Ida—and commits suicide.

Ernest's stirring toward a woman awakens him to his despair. Ida is unavailable, a self-destructive choice. Yet there is no clear reason why Ernest could not marry and support a family, which in Berry's world is the way one fully joins the community. The membership implicitly reaches out to Ernest; when he says he is "half contraption" (35) Mat does not consent, and like Andy's neighbors he is matter-of-fact and kind in dealing with disability. At the same time, his rejection is overdetermined. What Berry values in all his work is an organic wholeness that is highly embodied and highly normative. In this context, its simplest name is "ableism." This structure of inclusion also implies exclusion. Berry does not consent to the cruelty of the townspeople renaming Ernest "Shamble" (36)—but he does not oppose the prescriptive implications of the category of mutilation. Indeed, because his poesis links physical injury and cognitive, spiritual desolation, he endorses it—just as people do in everyday speech, when they express disrespect by calling something "lame." Andy too fears being part contraption. He hates his prosthetic hand, which does not work very well, and represents the intrusion of the unthinking machine world into his most intimate self.

Andy remains in dialogue with the membership, through his memories. Unlike Ernest, he finds his way back, during a long walk he takes in San Francisco. This walk occupies the third chapter of this short novel, and it shares its title with the book. It becomes clear in this context that the usual sense of *Remembering* simultaneously means re-membering: the healing of the individual through the reassembled membership. The themes of the chapter are embodied "on the living ground," as Berry put it in "Are You All Right?" The best way to read the chapter is to literally take the walk, and I have done that. Let us retrace Andy's steps here, and consider the significance for contemporary regionalism of Berry's engagement with a place that is very different from Kentucky.

Andy is staying downtown; we do not know exactly where, but his walk begins before dawn somewhere in the vicinity of Union Square—the area, in 1976 as now, has many hotels. From there, he walks up Nob Hill. As I followed his path with the book in hand, I had a fresh perception of just how steep the hill is—a recognition that can only be conveyed here in a limited way. At the top, the large buildings he mentions are the Fairmont Hotel and the Pacific Union Club. These were the only structures in the area that survived the earthquake of 1906, and they are important to the history of San Francisco. Reading about them on my smartphone brought the city's past alive around me—Berry's disapproval of such technology is well known, but that thickening of meaning is precisely the vantage point he is suggesting. Descending the hill, the views from the street corners are as Berry describes them; yes, there is a humming under the street as the cables for the cars run. At the place where he hears a baby cry and a light goes on in a window, there is a row of several-storied residences where the passer-by could easily observe such a moment.

Andy continues to a brief intersection with a topic central to this book. "He walks again, crossing on Jackson to Powell, and turning again northward. The names on windows and awnings are in Chinese now. The street reeks with the smell of yesterday's fish" (46). Coming from this direction, Chinatown starts in more or less the same place; in the years since, it has expanded at the other end. And in 1976, as the fictional Andy walks by, a few blocks away the struggle over the International Hotel referenced in the previous chapter is going on—the last residents were evicted in 1977. He misses it entirely. Indeed, "reeks" expresses an embodied aversion, and marks another exclusion. The word is especially resonant here, of course—the Exclusion Act, in force from 1882 to 1943, shaped Chinese-American history. It seems to me that Andy's distaste consents to the treatment of the residents of the district as foreigners, who do not belong organically to his America. I dissent and walk on.

Washington Square is, as the narrative says, an island of green. On the day I took this walk someone had, as usual, placed a bottle in the outstretched hand of one of the figures in the monument to the city's firemen that is mentioned. I have taught this novel many times, and one of the questions I wanted to answer on my walk was: is there really a quotation from Dante on the façade of the church of Peter and Paul in Washington Square? Yes, there is. The inscription reads: LA GLORIA DI COLUI CHE TUTTO MUOVE PER L'UNIVERSO PENETRA E RISPLENDE. (See Figure 5.3; the page in *Remembering* is 48.) As usual Berry does not mention the source in the text. He disregards the Italian-American presence in North Beach, and the multi-ethnic character of the neighborhood in general, but exactly observes a more literal fidelity to the place. I had thought that the detail of the Good Earth Realty, at least, was too good to be true, but there it was, at 785 Columbus Avenue—selected, not invented, for its thematic resonance. Nor is the beauty of the scene when one emerges at the foot of Hyde Street and the Bay opens up before you with the Golden Gate Bridge in view, exaggerated. Throughout, Andy has brief interactions with people, imagines a life in the city, remembers the past, observes keenly and poetically ("as the buses move and stop, the people sway in unison in their seats, unresisting as underwater weeds" [47]). He keeps walking, to the "outermost

FIGURE 5.3 *Saints Peter and Paul Church in the North Beach neighborhood of San Francisco. Photograph by the author.*

arc of the pier. There, with the whole continent at his back" (50) he stands looking west into the wind.

The narrative works to bring all these impressions into focus to inform the moment when Andy—having come thousands of miles from his home, and reached a limit, changes direction and chooses his life again. He thinks of a moment when his grandmother Dorie Catlett—a presence throughout the book—said to him, "Oh, my boy, how far away will you be sometime, remembering this?," and his emotion corrects his damaged vision: "The wind blows his tears back like the earpieces of a pair of spectacles. The bridge has begun to shine. He turns and sees that the sun has risen and is making a path toward him across the water" (57). Quoting Berry's descriptions out of context is unlikely to convey their power. I confess that I was not there at dawn—but the whole is a staging of redemption compelling even for me as a non-communicant. It ends with an English version (again, unmarked) of the passage from Dante's *Paradiso*: "the whole bay is shining now, the islands, the city on its hills, the wooden houses and the towers, the green treetops, the flashing waves and wings, the glory that moves all things resplendent everywhere" (59).

Berry's Christianity is eclectic—a great deal has been written about how it connects with and differs from various churches and doctrines. Like Jewett, he is a believer whose clergymen are rarely the most reliable guides to spiritual matters. The preacher who visits to comfort Mat and Margaret Feltner after Virgil is declared missing, in *A Place on Earth*, misses the mark just as badly as Reverend

Fosdick does in his visits to Joanna Todd's island, in *Country of the Pointed Firs*. The metaphor of vision is relevant here as well—as Brother Preston talks, "the lenses of his glasses reflect the window. In his rapt intent face the opaque discs of light look exultant and blind" (99). Mat turns away from his too-easy assurances of heaven, accepting his fear for his son as he embraces the world, looking through the window to notice that the maple buds are swelling and spring is approaching. In the same spirit, Andy accepts his life and its limits. They are one and the same: "He will be partial, and he will die; he will live out the truth of that. Though he does not hold, he is held. He is grieving, and he is full of joy. What is that Egypt but his Promised Land?" (167). He radically rereads the places of the Bible to affirm that its pledge of redemption is not fulfilled in the future, or elsewhere. It is always right here.

Andy heads immediately for Port William, although this is the turning point, not the end, of the book. Much of its pattern is woven during his "five-and-a-half-hour, two-thousand-mile journey" (118) home. He observes the lost souls of modern life, and continues to remember. He thinks of his wife Flora—one of Berry's persistent themes is the sacredness of marriage. (Always independent, he has outraged many of his conservative readers by his public support of same-sex marriage.) We follow Andy even after he arrives back at his farm, falls asleep under an oak, and is guided to a vision of a perfected, eternal Port William in which his right hand is restored—but again chooses to return to the located, partial place. Still, the whole is in the parable he thinks of at the pier. Mat Feltner tells him a story of Mat's own childhood, of taking breaks to go to a nearby swimming hole in the creek while working hard in a cornfield on a hot day.

> It was a good hole, deep and shady, with the sound of the riffles above and below, and a kingfisher flying in and seeing them and flying away. All that afternoon when they got too hot, they went there.
> "Well sir," Mat says, "it made that hard day good. I thought of all the times I'd worked in that field, hurrying to get through, to get to a better place, and it had been there all the time. I can't say I've always lived by what I learned that day—I wish I had—but I've never forgot."
> "What?" Andy says.
> "That it was there all the time."
> "What?"
> "Redemption," Mat says, and laughs. "A little flowing stream." (58–9)

Saying Fort William, instead of Port William, is a not-uncommon slip when people reference Berry's work—in *Remembering*, the conference organizer introducing Andy makes that mistake. The role that water plays here demonstrates the crucial difference between a name that evokes the military, and one that evokes moving water.

The concept of region as both substantive and relational holds, in reading Berry's work. I certainly have not unsettled the view that he is committed to the local. But his work is not—in Raymond Williams's term—"encapsulated." We have already seen that in "The Regional Motive" Berry explicitly disclaims both the prideful celebration of one place over another, and the complacent refusal of knowledge created elsewhere. His treatment of San Francisco reminds us that what he calls for is *attention* to place. He does not want us to move to Kentucky—rather, each of us needs to know and care for our *own* place, and understand it in the broadest possible perspective. He does appeal to us to slow down.

Ernie Hebert and the Darby Chronicles: *Never Back Down*

Ernest Hebert's fiction creates an intensely imagined, thoroughly described world that is inextricably connected to an actually existing place. In this, he is (despite their ample differences) like Wendell Berry: he asks readers to pay attention to the substantive, uncompromisingly particular nature of his region, and does not necessarily present an easy case for relational analysis. Yet I hope to show that Hebert's work also opens up when read in the terms I have developed, and more—that he purposefully prises open the category "New England" and challenges the terms of "regionalism." Hebert has zero interest in the cosmic-Christian horizon that links Jewett's Maine to Berry's Kentucky. But he does engage questions of ethnic, racial, and national identity—although Asian-America has been peripheral to his work so far, a character from one of Eaton's stories could easily join the action and further complicate things in Darby. Hebert extends the reach of regional writing, in an immensely inventive and increasingly multi-generic body of work.

In his online "Guide to the Darby Chronicles," Hebert demonstrates how fully this place is imagined (see Figures 5.4 and 5.5), and explains in detail how the specific landscape of southern New Hampshire is transformed into Darby and its environs. Upper-class Upper Darby is based on sections of Dublin and Jaffrey, he imagines Avalon Hillary's farm (in *Whisper My Name*) along River Road in Westmoreland, and so on. Of his personal stake in the particular place he writes, "My physical body has resided in places I loved—Westmoreland, NH, Nelson, NH, and New Orleans—and places that made me feel like a stranger, but in my mind I live in fictional Darby." He has set seven novels there, and all his other works also link to that landscape. Hebert says explicitly what I have said of Berry's fiction: "I don't actually see my books as individual entities; in my mind they're part of a long, single work that I am writing and that will only end when I die or go dotty" (interview in the Reading Group Guide to *Spoonwood*, 304). The historical novel *The Old American* begins in Keene, in 1746, and invents the Conissadawaga Indians, who reappear in the announced-as-final Darby novel, the 2014 *Howard Elman's Farewell*. Jack Landry, the protagonist of Hebert's autobiographical non-Darby novel *Never Back Down*, is mentioned as well. Even the alternate worlds of *Mad Boys* and *I Love U* take place on versions of the same terrain, and contribute characters to that last Darby novel.

From the outset of his career, Hebert has explicitly and critically engaged notions of region. *The Dogs of March*, published in 1979, is built around a conflict between insiders and outsiders that originates in the circulation of conventional images of

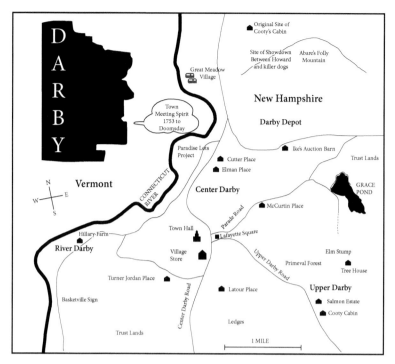

FIGURE 5.4 *Map of the Darby region, reproduced courtesy of Ernest Hebert.*

FIGURE 5.5 *"Cooty's Cabin," reproduced courtesy of Ernest Hebert.*

New England. The protagonist is Howard Elman—who is central to Hebert's series about Darby, although he is not the focus of every novel. His antagonist is Zoe Cutter, who at the beginning of the novel has recently purchased the Swett farm, the property adjoining Howard's. As a girl in Kansas City, Zoe (then Gladys) saw a picture in a *National Geographic* magazine: "forested hills, fields that rode the lower slopes, a tidy stone wall bordering a country lane, white birches in the foreground like two angels, white church steeple just showing behind maples in the background." She has held that image in her mind all her life, and after marrying her fortune in New York (she continues to manage it after her husband's death) has come to Darby to inhabit that New England. More accurately, she is creating it on the actually existing New Hampshire ground, so she can possess it: "it was the picture in the mind, beautiful and perfect, that fired her anger now as she surveyed the real fields and woods through her binoculars" (59). Her stone wall is crooked and messy; she will have it straightened and tidied. The trees need pruning and thinning. But the most necessary improvement is to get rid of the eyesore that is Howard Elman's land, with its junked cars and bullet-riddled old appliances—a vivid example of a landscape that is inhabited and constantly changing, messily and humanly alive.

Given the literary history of regionalism, it is a telling detail that the photograph Zoe remembers appears in a national magazine. *National Geographic* is an excellent candidate for carrying forward what Richard Brodhead calls local color's "appetite for under-development" (138) into the twentieth century (see also Lutz and Collins). The struggle between Zoe and Howard is in some sense over whose aesthetic will regulate the landscape—in addition to pressing him to sell, she proposes a town ordinance requiring property owners to screen unregistered vehicles from the road. The ideal of pristine nature with no visible traces of the industrial is powerful but not so dominant that it has suppressed alternatives.[3] I was surprised to find, teaching the novel to undergraduates at the University of Michigan, that many of them—especially those from rural areas—would not have voted for the ordinance; I do not think it would have passed in my class. It does not in Darby, although for a reason that expresses Hebert's affectionate skepticism about the direct democracy of the town meeting: a crank who also opposes all federal funding asks why they need something they haven't had before. After that, "Only the new people voted for it" (194). Howard does sell his land, but triumphs over Zoe by keeping enough land for a "garden spot" (251)—where he places a trailer and eventually recreates his vision of the living land. In *Spoonwood*, a more ambivalent antagonist, Persephone Salmon, reconciles with the Elmans and begins to see his place through his eyes: "From this vantage point the barn and the junked cars looked like sculpture, a diorama of country life in the twilight of the century" (271).

Whether we foreground property or aesthetics, the conflict between Howard Elman and Zoe Cutter is fundamentally about social class. Kent Ryden, one of the most thoughtful analysts of New England regionalism, groups Hebert with Carolyn Chute and David Budbill as writers who offer gritty counter-narratives to the received images of New England (*Sum of the Parts*). He calls them neo-realists; I might have said naturalists.[4] Hebert does certainly resist the dominant (and never backs down), but I think Ryden underestimates the degree to which Hebert also incorporates opposing terms into his narrative and offers multiple narratives. Throughout the Darby novels, Hebert weaves in extraordinary small analyses of the kinds of people who inhabit Darby and its environs, and gives room to many characters who spout social theories. Thus, leading into the scene of the town meeting, the narrator offers a single—but very long—paragraph about each of the four kinds of people in attendance (one hundred of the four hundred registered voters).

Farmers are "plain, frugal, independent, literate, deep, and as narrow as the furrow made by a plow" (181); they mistrust all government and attend habitually. "They worked to be free from work, when in fact they were defined by it. They invented ways of relieving work, and then they invented ways of creating work. They were crazy—and productive in their craziness. In short, they were American" (182). *Commuters* reside in Darby but they work and play in the city and their "family roots might be anywhere" (183). They are made uneasy by their divided lives, constantly adjusting their clothing and their thoughts, and few attend—they are "used to being governed" (184). *Shack people* derive from "the rough, complex order of the forest floor...spiritual sustenance and messy habits"; they are "rarely sad or nervous, but often angry and out of control" (184). If they come to the town meeting they make jokes. *New people* are full of ideas, and they attend "to participate in self-government" (185). They think they are pioneers, but they are the privileged children of commuters from New York, New Jersey, and Connecticut—most will return there, but those who remain "carry on, in a way as yet unfathomed even by themselves, the tradition of town meeting" (185). Alternatively, in *Spoonwood* Persephone explains the social landscape to her—and Howard's—grandson Birch in terms of five social classes: "Old Money, New Money, Funny Money, Hunger Money, and No Money" (182). In *Howard Elman's Farewell* Howard explains people to Birch by comparing them to trees—commuters to pine trees ("ugly and numerous," 12); New Hampshire farmers to red oaks; delta and plains farmers to white and southern oaks; Upper Darby people to sugar maples; and so on.

Hebert's social analysis is—as I hope can be seen here—vigorous and complex. His loyalty is also vigorous, but simple: it is to laborers and the poor. He comments in his dedication to *Never Back Down*: "*casual slander against working people is so common it's hardly noticed. I've heard people who would never use sexist or racist language refer to people who work at McDonald's as 'losers' and working people as 'trailer trash,' 'white trash,' and worse*" (n.p.; emphasis in original). This dedication is an essay in itself, addressing "*You who park the cars, cook and serve the burgers, mop the floors, pick up the trash*"—and so on—mentioning specific working men like his father and working women like those who cared for his parents in nursing homes in their final years, and ending with "*my book is dedicated to you, the unsung heroes of America.*" In his online dedication to the Darby series as a whole, he expands that horizon: "I dedicate the Darby Chronicles to you who hauled the stone to build the pyramids, you who fell off the scaffolds in constructing the great cathedrals, you who fabricated my smart phone, you who served my Buffalo wings, all of you, Working People, the unsung heroes of human civilization." Hebert's work is dedicated, in every sense, to correcting the balance of contemporary attention, telling the story and celebrating the value of the working class.

In the first chapter of the first Darby novel, *The Dogs of March*, the little finger of Howard Elman's left hand is chopped off while he is fixing a loom at the textile mill where he works. This is only one of the many such instances of damage in the series—it is arguably not even the first, since the accident results partly from Howard's hearing loss (he has worked in the noisy mill for many years). Less directly: he woke up that morning with the words *"Teeth, straight teeth"* in his mind—they are in fact the first words of the novel. Howard's wife Elenore's and his daughter's buck teeth are an index of the way class is written and visible on the body—and his college-student son Freddy is demanding that his youngest sister get braces. Soon we see how Elenore's addiction to store-bought sweets and TV evangelism manifest the abuse she suffered in the foster care system and how the circumstances of her life deprive her of better sustenance and are manifested in her ill health. I will return to the implications of Freddy's ambivalent efforts to rise in the system, but he also cannot escape the way class is written onto him. In a later novel, when he and Persephone's daughter (they will be Birch's parents) are challenged entering the town hall,

> Frederick assumed the pose of the offended workman—stooped, sullen, no eye contact.
> Lilith, like Frederick, assumed the pose of her own class, body carriage erect, head and shoulders straight to the front, commanding with her eyes as well as her voice. (*Live Free or Die*, 111)

Hebert's commitment to class as an analytic inheres not only in his plots, and his commentary, but also in his rendering of each character. He values, admires, the work his characters do, and they often enjoy their labor; nevertheless the injuries of class are permanent and unforgivable.

Howard's loss is a metonym for his other losses, and it thematizes a distorted, unjust social system, as do the mutilations in Wendell Berry's work (Ernest Finley's war injuries, Andy Catlett's loss of his hand to agricultural machinery). It does not, however, mark the loss of an organic or integrated world. There is no parallel to Andy's reaction to his prosthesis, or his sense that the highway is a wound. In the last novel of the series, the narrator observes, "Even at his advanced age Howard Elman drove too fast. He liked motion. He liked power at his fingertips. He liked objects in service to his desires, his robots. A car, a toaster, an electric drill, a penile implant (which Howard was contemplating, if only he could find an accomplice to use it with)" (11). The characters in *Howard Elman's Farewell* that seem to be cyborgs are not repulsive, and the erosion of the boundary between human and machine seems far less threatening than the machinations of global capital. The cause of dye foreman Filbin's suicide in *Dogs of March* is not fully explored, but it happens after the mill is bought by a Florida corporation and then closed, and he is unable to find another job. There are spiritual ills in Hebert's world—but there is no doubt that the appropriate response to the injuries we see would be in the realm of the Occupational Safety and Health Administration, or a union if the workers had one, rather than any church.

The conflict between Howard Elman and Zoe Cutter is not only over land and landscape, but over the future—of Darby, but also embodied in Howard's children Freddy and Heather. Its outcome is ambiguous; for example, Zoe takes Heather away from the Elmans, but at the end of the last novel of the series Howard may have rescued Heather's runaway daughter Tahoma. (*May*: the ambiguities are many.) By the end of his chronicles Hebert is thinking the future not only of the region, but also of the planet, through Darby. He is dealing with issues of technology, economy, environment, culture that could not have been anticipated in *Dogs of March* in 1979, and few of them are resolved. Indeed, I would not take for granted that the Darby series is actually closed—this is the third time Hebert has said the latest novel is the last. There is a valedictory tone to *Howard Elman's Farewell*, and Hebert does bring many characters' stories to closure, but he is as vital and imaginative as ever and one may hope for another continuation.

Arguably, Howard and Zoe's struggle is no more central to *The Dogs of March* than the growing conflict between Howard and Freddy that is centrally defined and developed through the tension between book-learning and local knowledge. When Freddy argues that Heather needs braces, he literally pulls a book from his pocket and reads to his father about social class and teeth; Howard knocks the book from his hand. The reader sees this scene through the protagonist's memory, as Howard is fixing the loom and about to make the mistake that costs him a finger. He wonders why Freddy cannot understand that it is not the issue of Heather's teeth, but "the reading, the slap in the face at his ignorance" that sets him off. He understands that Freddy at some level is not defying but trying to teach him, and that his wife and youngest daughter (even "at age eleven") empathize, recognize his limits, in a way his son cannot. "The boy had his own special brand of ignorance" (15). That headstrong focus, amounting to blindness, is gendered, and as Howard muses may be inherited from his father—but it is also what book-learning entails.

This drama is not merely a conflict between father and son, but an element of the difficult circumstances of Howard's life. His illiteracy is both a practical problem, and a source of shame, for him. Confronted, in the conversation with his boss where he learns that the mill has been sold, by the words "Pensacola" and "conglomerate," his disability produces inchoate anger. "The talk of the educated, the talk in books, confused him, as if on purpose, as if education itself were a conspiracy to make certain that the knowledge of the world was unavailable to him. And yet he believed in his own intelligence, took pride in the way his thoughts came together like the cocking of a revolver" (12). Howard is of course not wrong—either about how schools work, or about how powerful the applied knowledge of the subordinated can be. There could hardly be a more eloquent statement of the acute version of this problem. More immediately, as readers progress through the novel, we understand that Howard is both proud that Freddy is attending college, and frightened both of the alien powers with which his son is consorting, and of losing him.

His time in Durham has already given Freddy new horizons. He does indeed want to get Heather away from their family—to "save her from getting pregnant in high school and marrying some garage mechanic. He wanted his little sister to grow up to be beautiful and sensitive and cultured, and share the company of the thoughtful. Such persons, he noted, did not have buck teeth" (41). Hebert invites us both to sympathize with Freddy and to be amused at his naivety. (The narration continues with an ironic note: "It wasn't that he disliked his family. Not really. It was just that as a sophomore in college he believed he had outgrown them" [41].) Our positionality in terms of dialect is invoked, as well, when Freddy meets Zoe and hears how she says the town's name—"'*Dar*-bee' instead of 'Dah-bee,' the way the locals said it"—he feels he is hearing the word pronounced "correctly for the first time" (53). Freddy does became able to separate cultivation from social class—or perhaps more accurately, to recognize that they are separable and complexly related—and to reclaim his respect for the kind of knowledge possessed by, say, a garage mechanic. By the middle novels of the series, he (now Frederick) recognizes that he does not want upward mobility but, rather, to be free of the whole system—of modernity itself, as he lives a kind of hand-made life with his small son on "Forgot Farm."

At that point Frederick's views of education converge with his father's. "*I hate progress and people, but I love general knowledge, and I wished to give my son the best education possible. Accordingly, I felt it best to keep him far away from school*" (*Spoonwood*, 157). This is not his final view—he is a character who undergoes enormous transformations in the course of the series, changing his name to LaTour (his father's birth name) and marrying a professor of social geology. But this is another demonstration of how deeply regionalism is structured by attention to the locations and kinds of knowledge. The narrator's description, in *The Dogs of March*, of commuters' attitudes to education converges with Wendell Berry's views: restlessness and discontented themselves, they want to make "their children more capable of great rather than small dissatisfactions" and achieve this by sending "their children to a succession of schools, each farther and farther from home, until, when the children graduated from the last school, they were totally separated from the place of their upbringing and must themselves go questing" (184). Indeed, it would not be out of place in Eric Zencey's critique of "The Rootless Professors" (see Chapter 2).

At the end of that first novel, far from rejecting book-learning, Howard conquers his illiteracy; that development brightens the conclusion. He relishes learning new words and takes great pleasure in reading *Time* magazine—but he does not change his class allegiance or relinquish his intellectual independence, in this last chapter or in the later books. The last in the series begins with a phrase Howard uses, throughout the series, to convey many things—"sarcasm, exasperation, frustration, criticism, irony, cosmic outrage, even affection" (*Dogs of March*, 38): "*Ain't you smaht!*" (*Howard Elman's Farewell*, 1). It is not always printed as I have quoted it here, with eye-spelling foregrounding dialect and the challenge of the local to more privileged perspectives. But what it always does is to relativize, to throw the right answer and the direction of future into question. This refrain—and Hebert's work as a whole—democratizes by insisting that every knowledge can and should be challenged by another, differently positioned knowledge.

My reading of Hebert's Darby series has foregrounded his engagement with images of "New England" and with the politics of knowledge, issues that link his work to my own reading of regionalism. I should note, however, how much that leaves out. Among other things it makes Hebert's account of the place seem as if it focused only on people, when in fact the natural landscape is important as well. At the moment when Hebert first wrote about "social geology" it may have been a playful invention, but it is now seriously, and convincingly, proposed as an interdisciplinary field—although it is less interested in New England rock walls than in the dangers posed by floods and volcanoes. In fact one of its central concerns is the tension between privileged, do-gooding, book-based planning, and local knowledge and experience: "Solutions proposed by outside experts rarely work for the people they are trying to serve" (Gross). Rocks play a role, as limestone does in Berry's work, but Hebert's books have much more—an enormous amount—to say about trees. He has written in his own voice about the way being in the woods orients him in the universe, and he shows that experience through his characters as well as anatomizing the species of the Northeastern North American forest. Or, one of the most eloquent sections of *Live Free or Die* fully integrates an account of fish kinds—brook trout, hornpout, black bass, smallmouth bass—and gendered humanity. For example, he describes the moment when the Upper Darby—that is, moneyed—fly fisherman realizes, "like the stocked brookies of Grace Pond, he doesn't belong in Darby. Yet he was born there, he's a native. Home is nowhere. At that moment of realization, he understands why he fishes: to reach through a surface and come away with something alive" (209–10). Too many kinds of knowledge are compressed in those lines to classify it in terms of any discipline (which is perhaps simply to say that it is what we call literature).

Throughout the Darby novels Hebert, in effect, embeds essays in his fiction. He simply disregards the dictum "show don't tell" that shapes so much contemporary American fiction, in what Mark McGurl calls "the Program Era." Hebert was, like Ernest Gaines and Wendell Berry, a student in the Stanford creative writing MFA program; he initially worked with Donald Davies but also gained entry to Wallace Stegner's class. That workshop, according to Hebert's blog, "did its job, which was to tell me I was a fiction writer all right but not one cut out for grad school" ("Origins of the Darby Series"). It is ironic that Wendell Berry is able to farm (perhaps, like Robert Frost, aided by the income from his publications), while Hebert earns a living teaching creative writing at Dartmouth and thus has left the working class. He laments that "as a college professor I've lost touch with those folks who had given me material" ("An Interview with Ernest Hebert," in *The Old American*, 298). Yet he reaches out through his website, which has an aesthetic more akin to fan fiction than to most literary and academic authors' solemn online self-presentations. He told me I should use my own judgment and call him "Ernie" rather than "Ernest" when I wished (as I do in the heading of this section). That is what most people call him, as he says online in a characteristically revealing and expansive essay on names in the Darby series and his own name.

When I asked Ernie about the embedded essays in *Live Free or Die* and his other novels, in a conversation in 2013, he smiled and said that he worked as a journalist and wrote plenty of "op-eds," so such writing comes easily to him. The novel, he thinks, can contain many different kinds of prose in its attempt to hold life—he suggested as a comparison the way Charles Ives sends a marching band through a symphony. *Howard Elman's Farewell* is partly structured as a mystery (who cut down the ancient elm?), and as I have noted includes science-fictional elements. Hebert's relation to the boundaries between kinds of writing is always mischievous, as when he defends Darby's "town gossip" as a kind of journalist ("Mrs. McCurtin" in his online Guide to the Darby Chronicles). I suspect that his freewheeling embrace of what Fredric Jameson calls, and I have called, generic discontinuity poses a problem in the marketplace; his works are at once hedged in by the category regional, and finally unclassifiable. His commitment to representing working people is surely another issue. However, the previous Darby novels are all now back in print, republished in a uniform edition by the University Press of New England at the same time *Farewell* appeared.

The Old American, one of Hebert's best-received books, operates within the generic framework of the historical novel—although it remains regional and creates a characteristically original voice. Building from his childhood fascination with a historical plaque in Keene, about a settler captured by Indians, Hebert spent a year researching the intertwined worlds of the multiple European and Native American peoples who inhabited Québec and New Hampshire in the mid-eighteenth century. He tells the story from the perspective of the old Indian king—a former slave, a translator, and a philosopher—Caucus-Meteor. The novel begins with an extended exercise in empathy, as this Native American narrator observes Nathan Blake, the Englishman he will capture—throughout, the reader participates in his efforts to understand people from different cultures (repeatedly concluding, "I admire him very much" (12, 54, 92, 125, 257)). The Conissadawaga village north of Quebec City that Hebert and, within the narrative, Caucus-Meteor invent is syncretic—composed of people of different origins, pulled together from tribes devastated by the disease and war that result from the European occupation, inhabiting a small place and trying to create a good human life. "We are, therefore, the first American tribe" (33). At the same time, Hebert shows the term "American" being appropriated by European settlers—they are, in Philip Deloria's phrase, "playing Indian" to distinguish themselves from the powers across the Atlantic. Throughout, the novel asks readers to take in knowledge rarely encountered outside Native American history and cultural studies, projecting a map of the region that looks less like the current standard than like the ones Lisa Brooks shows us in *The Common Pot: The Recovery of Native Space in the Northeast* (see Figure 5.6).

After the raid, Caucus-Meteor invites Nathan Blake to empathize with the Squakheag members of the group that has captured him, through their common situation on the contested landscape of North America. Nathan says that no one challenged his claim to the property where he built his cabin, but Caucus-Meteor knows a previous generation was driven out by the Mohawks: "Just as you have never stepped foot in Old England, these brothers had never stepped foot in their ancestral lands until the day they burned your town" (28). By the end of the novel, its title belongs not to Caucus-Meteor but to Blake—because he "was a strong supporter of the revolution in 1776 and reflects the values of the new nation, they also call him the Old American" (284). Asked about "the challenges of creating a character from another culture" Hebert replied:

> Though Caucus-Meteor is Native American by blood and heritage, he was torn from his people by war at the age of nine and raised as a slave by another culture; he's really a mixture of cultures with all the flexibility and confusing that mixture brings. I too am a mix—Yankee, Yuppie, and Franco-American...You have to be

FIGURE 5.6 The Indigeneous northeast: a network of waterways. From Lisa Brooks, *The Common Pot: The Recovery of Native Space in the Northeast*, p. xvii (copyright University of Minnesota Press, 2008), p. xvii. Reprinted by permission.

a bit of a horse's ass to write any fiction at all, because so much of it is about crossing lines into territory where you don't belong. Am I concerned about how readers might respond to the idea of a white man writing from the point of view of a Native American? Yah, I'm concerned, but at this point, now that the book is finished, it's not up to me any more.   (296–7)

As I said, the novel has been well received, although Native American readers and critics have not (yet) weighed in on how convincing they find it. From my perspective, *The Old American* and Ernie Hebert's body of work make it clear that regionalism continues to propose formidable alternative accounts of knowledge—and that in our moment it is less and less separable from other genres.

Contemporary Fiction and the Global Village

Today, the literary fiction that is widely read in the United States and beyond often claims, and somewhat less often gains, attention by paying attention to a particular place.

That may or may not mean that it enlists readers from that place; it may or may not mean that people elsewhere notice or care. For a long time, critical exchanges over local color writing in the late nineteenth and early twentieth centuries have cast its regional and national orientations as antagonists. The latter is winning the debate, at least in the sense that it prevails among scholars. I have tried to even things up by restoring the local (the *local* local) to the landscape. I also dig down to a deeper conceptual level where the opposition itself becomes the object of analysis. And I have argued that writing we call regional is not necessarily (what Raymond Williams calls) "encapsulated," demonstrating that point through close readings. I want now to acknowledge and analyze the way, increasingly, the project of representing a particular place invokes a planetary perspective.

In considering literature at the present moment, I see that there are now—as in the past—authors who represent places as both substantive and relationally constituted, and who thematize both space and time. Shifting from theory and interpretation to a more empirical perspective, I find that holding both sides of a binary, or even both sides of two binaries, in mind may not be enough. Wendy Griswold reports in *Regionalism and the Reading Class* that some authors whose focus is a particular place circulate mostly there, while others have a broader audience and a few (for example, Faulkner) are read nationally and internationally. I agree, but am drawn to a less vertically organized account of the evidence. Readerships—more abstractly publics, or solidarities—exist on many scales, and shift unpredictably.

Local authors are usually prominently displayed in local bookstores, and often assigned in schools or chosen by book clubs in their region. Ernest Hebert told me that he accepts every invitation he can from a book club or library, and values those readers. He (implicitly) mentioned the people Griswold calls "cowbirds":

when someone moves to New Hampshire, he said, someone gives them a copy of *Dogs of March*. He also said that he worries that his audience is more and more confined to New England.

On the other hand, when I was on sabbatical in an apartment near the Pacific Ocean in the fall of 2013, writing about regionalism and wanting to read the recently published *The Burgess Boys*—a new novel by the New England author Elizabeth Strout—I found myself number seven on the waiting list for one of the seventy-seven copies San Francisco Public Library had acquired. This was *before* the HBO mini-series based on her *Olive Kitteridge* aired in 2014, and before it won eight Emmys in 2015. By the standards of *Criminal Minds*, any arrangement of these audiences produces small numbers—but they indicate Strout's national readership.

Not many months later, Marilynne Robinson published *Lila* (2014), which was widely reviewed and sent me back to read an important contemporary region-alist I had missed. I don't quite know why—general busyness?, resistance to the word *Housekeeping*?, my secular orientation? The reason was not, I think, geo-graphical. Robinson is something of an outlier in my grouping because she does not write about one particular place, varying her scene between the Midwest and the west. But starting with Iowa and adding Kansas (the addition is questionable, given how far removed it is from the history invoked in *Gilead*)—including not Idaho but the rural sections of other states in the Far West (the location of Fingerbone is ambiguous)—we are still light years away from enough book-buyers to explain the status Robinson has achieved. Perhaps it captures her position best to say that she is the most regionally oriented member of the current faculty at the celebrated Iowa Writer's Workshop.

I want to keep the local in view, while retaining a keen awareness of the role of the national, and the dependence of the literary on the national, and simultane-ously increasing attention to the global. To put it another way: analysis goes wrong whenever the separation of the substantive and relational is more than heuristic. In the literary history of the United States, the national *is* indispensable in thinking about local color. Let us remember that (as discussed in Chapter 2) Bret Harte's "Luck of Roaring Camp" offered what many in California considered a rude and unacceptable portrait of the region, and his success resulted from enthusiasm for the story in the east. We know this. Reception on any given scale is mediated by what happens on other scales. Wendell Berry would be my candidate for a contem-porary writer whose alarming views get him in less trouble at home because of his fame elsewhere.

It is uncontroversial to position the contemporary authors I have devoted most attention to—Ernest Gaines, Wendell Berry, and Ernest Hebert—as regional writ-ers. Each has each written a series of novels located in very specific fictional towns and recognized regions. So has Strout. So has Robinson, with the difference I have noted. Deploying categories I have used throughout, such as the narrative of com-munity, and the juxtaposition of local knowledge and book-learning, is produc-tive for their work. To do so reveals not only similarities but also differences, of course.

A commonality: in the work of each writer, narratives focalized through multiple perspectives show the depths of thought and emotion people experience in everyday, apparently simple, activities. Strout expresses that perception directly in a moment in *The Burgess Boys* that also evokes Walt Whitman's "Crossing Brooklyn Ferry." One of her characters looks around as he is "pressed against others as the train rumbled beneath the streets of Manhattan and then beneath the East River. Everyone on the train seemed innocent and dear to him, their eyes unfocused with morning reveries that were theirs alone, perhaps words spoken to them earlier, or words they dreamed of speaking; some read newspapers, many listened through earbuds to their own soundtrack, but most stared absently as Bob did—and he was moved by the singularity and mystery of each person he saw" (295). A comparison that includes commonality and difference: in Strout's New England people work more often than play—her gritty landscape has much in common with Hebert's. Yet her everyday is often exalted in a way that makes her more like Berry than Hebert.

A set of differences: each writer motivates action and composes coherence differently (and differently in different fictions). Berry and Robinson have each written several novels from the point of view of one member of their particular town—yet made that individual's efforts to empathize with others in the community central to those narratives. Berry, unlike the others, often uses the short story form. Robinson and Gaines (in *Gilead* and *Miss Jane Pittman*) position autobiographical narration in an explicitly historical situation. Strout's *Olive Kitteridge* is distinctive because of how its separate, interwoven short stories balance between the perspectives of the title character and the other residents of Crosby, Maine. We have a complex view of a complex woman, live the interior drama of her life with her yet also see her—often unfavorably—through others' eyes. It seems to me that its power derives from the way this "novel in stories" manages to be a narrative of community with a movable center.

It is in the nature of genre criticism to generate such *combinatoires*. I could go on. Kent Haruf's *Plainsong* (1999), for example, creates Holt, Colorado, in sections focalized through the history teacher Tom Guthrie, his sons Ike and Bobby, the pregnant teenager Victoria Roubideaux, the bachelor farmers McPheron brothers, and Maggie Jones, to build up a "chorus" of voices—as the metaphor of his title invites one to say, and the citation for the National Book Award quoted on the back cover does. But is it, as the citation also says, about "the whole community"? The last section is titled "Holt" but in effect it composes the focal characters into a kind of family. Maggie Jones is central because she is the solution to other people's problems; other characters are seen only from the outside, even as enemies. Ella Guthrie, who has left her family, is excluded. Like Olive Kitteridge she is a wife and mother struggling with the conditions of her existence, but she is precisely the opposite of a central character. Or we might consider Charles Baxter's linked stories of Minneapolis in the 2015 *There's Something I Want You to Do*; in each, the consequences of actions ricochet through characters' lives on the common ground of the city. They are bound together by cause and effect, but it is impossible to locate anything that could be called community. Cohesion inheres, rather, in themes and structural repetition—Baxter's exploration of the virtues and vices that title the stories ("Bravery," "Loyalty," "Lust," and so on), and the way each is built around a request or demand (the device that gives the volume its title).

These comparisons generate useful frameworks for interpretation and thinking about form, but they turn us away from equally important topics. The conditions in which these authors address readers are shaped both by the rise of the academic creative writing program during the second half of the twentieth century, and the growing influence of prizes in literature and the arts in allocating prestige and attention, effectively delineated by James English. Of course, they have that in common with multitudes of other writers.[5] All of them can be usefully considered— indeed, in order to understand them in any capacious way, must be considered—in terms other than regionalism. We see in Wendell Berry's work that the environmental movement gives a new kind of purchase to place-based writing. A comprehensive discussion of regionalism in contemporary fiction—even a comparison of the writers I have mentioned so far in this section—would require us to address fault lines of gendered narration I have implied but not unpacked. Gaines should be read in terms of African-American literature—not "of course," but in relation to Kenneth Warren's provocative argument for periodizing that category in *What Was African American Literature?*

Most crucially for the project of this book, the role that the category "American literature" plays in our thinking about these writers has been left implicit in my discussion so far. It too may be periodized and put in the past tense. There is, as I suggested in Chapter 4, historical evidence for Paul Giles's argument that the identification of American identity with its current geographical boundaries emerged in 1865, or let us say in the period following the Civil War. He may in the long run prove to be right in his less well supported claim that the national period ends in 1981 (despite my discomfort with such abrupt punctuation). Nevertheless, not only academic canons but also the publishing, distributing, and reviewing practices that institutionalize national literature churn on. Pervasively and persistently, professional and lay readers are interested in what is "American" about a particular text—and they (we) often imagine literature representing the nation through its parts. Regionalists are perhaps especially likely to be enlisted in this project, but any writer who references particular places may be. In July 2015 the "Summer Reading" section of *Time* was titled "A Nation of Books"—*Time* is of course very much a national magazine, although as it happens I bought my copy in Canada, or rather in Québec. The reviewer recommended fiction and also histories and a memoir. They range from Ann Beattie's short-story collection *The State We're In* representing Maine, and Stephanie Clifford's "Manhattan-set class satire" *Everybody Rise*, to weather-forecaster Al Roker's *Storm of the Century* about the 1900 Galveston hurricane, and William Finnegan's life story *Barbarian Days:*

A Surfing Life representing Hawaii [*sic*]. The subhead evokes both the substantive and the relational, both denoted regions and an imagined community: "transport yourself across the country with yarns from seven states."[6]

In this section I range even more widely, in terms of both genre and geography. I am bracketing questions that deserve attention on their own terms. For example, I have merely alluded to the "program era" and the prize economy. I have used the terms "present" and "contemporary" commonsensically, and will continue to do so.[7] I hope, however, that the category "world" has already accrued some complexity from the previous chapter. The kind of attention exerted there brings apparently inert elements of "A Nation of Books" alive. New York is a world city, in which class satire has expansive implications. The history that incorporated Hawai'i as the fiftieth of the United States is strange and tragic. These last pages try to simultaneously remain loyal to the local, attend to the national, and reckon with the global.

I admire the work of Giles and Ganguly, and think they (and others) are right to suggest that new narrative capabilities have appeared. On my view, of course, the relational has been acknowledged in regionalism from the first moment it announced itself. I also observe that we are seeing more and more explicit references to the global in literature, and the development of formal devices that aspire to figure particular places in relation to the whole round world. What follows is a quite partial analysis of that movement, exploring its links to regionalism, but to consider writing about particular places in the contemporary moment entails addressing this topic. Reciprocally, the concept of regionalism, the literary history I have traced, can help us to resist facile cosmopolitanism, and to think well about the new chronotope that may be emerging.

Elizabeth Strout, for example, shifts sharply towards addressing global connections in *The Burgess Boys*. The book is about the family referenced in the title—its members originating and some still residing in Shirley Falls, Maine, with some in New York City—but also about the Somali immigrants who have arrived in Shirley Falls. The plot is driven by their "otherness" and a local's hostile reaction. Zach, one of the younger generation of Burgesses, harasses them and gets caught, requiring his now-urban lawyer uncles to return to the region. Strout makes strenuous efforts to include the Somali perspective (she has talked about her extensive research in interviews). Whether one finds the sections of the novel focalized through Abdikarim successful or not (I do not), there is a striking difference between this novel and the references to Muslims in *Olive Kitteridge*. Then, Zach's problems are solved, and his attitudes adjusted, by spending time in Sweden. Strout's previous novels were not encapsulated, in the sense I have used the term; Olive is a teacher, and people certainly come and go. But *The Burgess Boys* shows America as an explicitly international place.

Gish Jen's *World and Town* (2010), also set in New England, is even more fully focused on an encounter between recent immigrants and villagers—the title itself concisely makes the point that the local and global are encountering each other, on the ground in America. (It takes for granted that the encounter takes place in English, although both novels make reference to difficulties of translation.) The community of Riverlake, Vermont struggles to incorporate a family of Cambodian refugees, who come trailing their own complex histories and are also profoundly affected by the beliefs and values they encounter in this new locality. It matters a great deal that the narrator is Hattie Kong, herself a biracial Chinese-American. She is a retired teacher (a resonant occupation for my concerns) who is thinking through questions of her own racial and national identity. We are reminded that these are not new topics when a different character comments, "it's always been a question, hasn't it...Whom America can be America for. And who keeps America, America" (353). The reference to Langston Hughes's poem "Let America Be America Again"—with its several versions of the refrain "America never was America to me"—links Jen's novel to a self-conscious literary history that simultaneously constructs, collaborates with, and critiques U.S. national-ism. Yet the novel ends, on my reading, with more thoroughgoing exposure of American exceptionalism. It works through the characters' reactions to the events of September 11, 2001 and suggests we understand it not as an utterly unprecedented event, but as continuous with a world history in which America is not the protagonist but a participant.

Jhumpa Lahiri's *Lowland* (2013) is a transnational novel that has vivid portraits of particular places, including a neighborhood in Calcutta (later Kolkata) and the Rhode Island shoreline, and offers vivid renderings of particular historical moments. It tells the story of two brothers in terms that parallel Hamlin Garland's "Up the Coulee" (although I am not suggesting a direct influence). Subhash Mitra, like Howard McLane, is able to leave his home place—he goes to the United States for higher education, becomes absorbed in his life there, and fails to pay attention to the family he has left behind until it is too late. When he returns he finds himself an outsider. Udayan, certainly not less talented, stays in India; he is radicalized by his circumstances and joins the Naxalite movement. Let me say clearly: the scales and stakes of the two narratives are very different. Grant becomes a populist and his anger threatens class rebellion, especially given its juxtaposition with "Under the Lion's Paw"—but neither brother's story moves from threat to action. In contrast, Udayan commits real political violence. Hunted by the police in its aftermath, he is captured—as his mother and pregnant wife watch—on the flooded plain that gives the book its title, and deliberately shot by the police. The differences between Garland's and Lahiri's stories are particularly marked in the roles of women in the two narratives. Mrs. McLane is a pathetic figure, and Grant's wife Laura has only a moment to express her aspirations and disappointments to Howard. In contrast, portions of *Lowland* are focalized through Bijoli (briefly) and Gauri (at length). Subhash marries his brother's widow to rescue her. The failure of that connection is arguably the novel's central action, but the marriage takes Gauri to the United States—in India, a widow's life would be over, but instead she becomes a protagonist and we are able to recognize her as a political actor. *Lowland* offers multiple points of view: Bela, Gauri's daughter with Udayan (biologically) and Subhash (who raised her), gains her own voice late in the novel as well. The narrative shifts frequently between different moments in the characters' lives, as it links places to histories. The somewhat erratic relation of *fabula* and *sujet* is the novel's weakest aspect, making it difficult for non-Bengalis to grasp the story's historical significance (and Bengalis are clearly not the book's primary audience). Most relevant for my comparison of "Up the Coulee" and *Lowland*: each fiction asserts that brothers in very different places are equals, thus challenging the slanted landscape of power. At the same time, each is focalized mostly through cosmopolitan characters. The reader is asked to attend to the lowland, but implicitly located above.

As these novels remind us, immigration is the very stuff of the continent's history and literature. "Immigration" and "emigration" each imply at least two places, entail scenes of arrival and departure, departure and arrival, and they often direct our attention to a complex circulation. Both economic migrants and refugees cross many borders to many destinations, often many times. It is a curiosity of how this history is taught in the United States—so much in terms of arrivals embracing the American dream—that few high-school graduates know how many emigrants from Europe and Asia returned home or went on to another place. This is surely an example of the amnesia that, as long ago as 1882, Renan identified as fundamental in nation-making. "Americans" are defined by what they (in my case, we) choose to remember, but even more by what they (or we) choose to forget. And surely, for it to be so neglected, official education must obscure recognition of the fact that borders too move. In 1848, after the Treaty of Guadalupe Hidalgo, a great many people arrived in the United States without stirring a step. (See Kandiyoti for an account of how this shapes the spatialization of Chicano/a literature.)

The structures of feeling I am evoking are certainly not only American, although they are woven into the fabric of North American literature. Membership and mutuality matter, of course. That means one writer reading another, and writers reading the same writers, or reading writers who are reading each other: the complex set of rereadings that we call a tradition. To some degree they follow from fundamentals like time and space, and much more from common historical circumstances such as (to use the rough and ready, familiar terms) modernity and postcoloniality. A vivid example: V. S. Naipaul's *A Bend in the River*. If the Caribbean is part of the Americas, then we should consider Naipaul an American writer, but that is a considerable reduction. He is a Trinidadian of South Asian heritage who went to Oxford at eighteen and stayed in Britain. His work is part of English literature, just as Joseph Conrad's is, and part of world literature.

The title of *A Bend in the River* announces that the narrative's perspective is from a particular place. The narrator, Salim, describes his origins exactly: "Africa was my home, had been the home of my family for centuries. But we came from the east coast, and that made the difference. The coast was not truly African. It was an Arab-Indian-Persian-Portuguese place, and we who lived there were really people of the Indian Ocean. True Africa was at our back" (10). His family is

Muslim, but in "customs and attitudes we were closer to the Hindus of northwestern India, from which we had originally come" (11). His relatives take their lives for granted, but Salim from childhood understands that he does not live at the center of the world, that their ways are "antiquated" (15)—a perception he attributes to seeing postage stamps issued by the British administration of the region. They depict "local scenes and local things," such as the Arab dhow—but he understands that they show what about his home strikes an outside observer. "Whenever I saw them [the dhows] tied up at the waterfront I thought of them as something peculiar to our region, quaint, something the foreigner would remark on, something not quite modern" (15). The metonym is striking; trade and travel, the novel shows in many ways, are ancient and universal. But Naipaul invokes the historical specificity of the postal system—its temporal regularities and the visual aesthetic it incorporates—as well.

The action of the story begins when Salim leaves home and embarks on a business venture that requires him to go, implicitly, backwards—he penetrates far into the interior of Africa to arrive at the town at the bend in the river, in an unnamed, newly independent nation. I am dealing of course only very partially with the novel, which is deeply engaged with the complexities of African and twentieth-century global history. It says something, however, about the power of the topoi I have been pressing into visibility that "at our back" can so easily be interpreted in terms of my discussion in Chapter 1, and that we can productively read the novel in terms of the tension between local knowledge and book-learning. Raymond, the white historian (and former teacher) who figures importantly in the second half of the book, is writing about the settlements of freed slaves established by well-intentioned white activists in the nineteenth century. When Salim reads the article he comments, "Raymond gave the names of all the liberty villages that had been established. Then, quoting and quoting from letters and reports in the archives, he tried to fix the date of the disappearance of each. He gave no reasons and looked for none...He didn't seem to have gone to any of the places he wrote about; he hadn't tried to talk to anybody. Yet five minutes talk with someone like Metty [Salim's servant]...would have told Raymond that the whole pious scheme was cruel and very ignorant, that to set a few unprotected people down in strange territory was to expose them to attack and kidnap and worse. But Raymond didn't seem to know" (181–2). His disregard of local knowledge—his arrogant failure even to realize that there are things he doesn't know about the place where he lives—is disabling, although less destructive than the ignorance of the historical figures he studies.

Reading place-focused novels from across the world, I have been tempted to postulate a genre I would call the parable of the global village. These works are more concentrated than *A Bend in the River*, and even less tethered to a specific location. Naipaul does not name the country or city where the novel is set, but it is clearly in east or central Africa. Coetzee's *Waiting for the Barbarians* (1980) is set in an unnamed village, on the edge of any empire. The magistrate shows us how cruel, abstract decisions made far away in the name of "civilization" are enacted by functionaries upon living people. As the tale unfolds its world is described closely, but it is not located on any particular continent. So too Dino Buzzati's less widely read *The Tartar Steppe* (originally 1945, in Italian). Or Olga Tokarcyzk's *Primeval and Other Times* (1997, in Polish), which tells the brutal history of the European twentieth century from the point of view of a repeatedly devastated village. In both novels the backwards place is the opposite of static and unchanging. Rather, unfortunately for residents, their "here" is a crossroads of change. The details are vivid and circumstantial, but the evocative name of the town that provides *Primeval*'s title—like the Cavafy poem "Waiting for the Barbarians" from which Coetzee's novel takes its title—sets a fantastic, even mythic, tone. The novel begins (in English translation): "Primeval is the place at the centre of the universe" (9). We have become familiar with this gesture, cognate with the chronotope of regionalism.

John Berger's trilogy *Into Their Labors* is another such highly particular parable. In the acknowledgments to the last volume Berger tells us that he worked on these remarkable fictions for fifteen years (*Lilac and Flag*, 172). They are based on his life in Haute-Savoie in France, but also claim much more—in effect, to be the true story of the world, from the perspective of the peasant. *Pig Earth* (1979) attempts to recreate the world of an Alpine village; *Once in Europa* (1987) shows the impact of the modern on the inhabitants of the village; in *Lilac and Flag* (1990) the scene changes to the world city where their descendants live. This is, certainly, a Western history, and there are dislocated traces of its origin in Europe—in the "Mond Bank," or a T-shirt referring to Alexanderplatz. But the world city is, evocatively and ominously, called Troy. Berger writes in the last chapter: "It is possible you have been to Troy without recognizing the city. The road from the airport is like many others in the world. It has a superhighway and is often blocked. You leave the airport buildings which are like space vessels never finished, you pass the packed carparks, the international hotels, a mile or two of barbed wire, broken fields, the last stray cattle, billboards that advertise cars and Coca-cola, storage tanks, a cement plant, the first shanty town, several giant depots for big stores, ring-road flyovers, working-class flats, a part of an ancient city wall, the old boroughs with trees, crammed shopping streets, new golden office-blocks, a number of ancient domes and spires, and finally you arrive at the acropolis of wealth" (209). This passage aspires to be nothing less than a description of the planet under the aspect of modernity. But it leads to Berger's eloquent, although hypothetical, recognition of Zsuzsa—a character whose progression from beauty and hope, to damage, we have seen in the course of the novel. Despite the assaults she has suffered, the narrator believes that "in order to play this world she will still believe, and make others believe, that she's its centre, its prize and its capital, and she is probably right" (210). Berger's bet, not yet decided, is that all stories *can* be about this miraculous, ordinary person.

Probably the best-known global village in world literature is Macondo, created in Gabriel García Márquez's *One Hundred Years of Solitude*. In his appreciation on the occasion of Márquez's death, Salman Rushdie wrote about his work as embodying general truths about places with colonial histories: "When I first read

García Márquez I had never been to any Central or South American country. Yet in his pages I found a reality I knew well from my own experience in India and Pakistan." Rushdie makes a distinction between Márquez's "village sensibility" and his own more urban-oriented fictions, but also makes even broader claims. "We live in an age of invented, alternate worlds. Tolkien's Middle-earth, Rowling's Hogwarts, the dystopic universe of 'The Hunger Games' "—he is skeptical about fantasy, but confident that "in the finest of literature's fictional microcosms there is more truth than fantasy. In William Faulkner's Yoknapatawpha, R. K. Narayan's Malgudi and, yes, the Macondo of Gabriel García Márquez, imagination is used to enrich reality, not to escape from it." I would add Berry's Port William, Hebert's Darby, Margaret Laurence's Manawaka—and so on. We see here that more than 150 years after it was first explicitly deployed in reference to painting, "reality" can still be valorized in aesthetic ideology. Our assessments of what is and is not believable matter a great deal in interpretation. But, as I have argued before, we will not understand the capabilities and historicity of forms by assigning one genre to the column "truth" and another to "escapism." What links Rushdie's comments to my topic in this chapter is, rather, his focus on worldness, and the erosion of distinctions implied by his referencing these various authors together.

I might also postulate the emergence of a new kind of composite novel (my long-standing interest in thinking about literary parts and wholes makes this particularly tempting). Many contemporary novels use the formal strategy of alternating chapters that are focalized through different characters, or told by different narrators, which can be very effective at conveying the convergence of global connections on a particular site. Let me cite two examples. Colum McCann's prizewinning *Let the Great World Spin* (2009) is a prominent example, with no fewer than eleven protagonists. They are linked through interwoven events on a single day, most visibly Philippe Petit's famous 1974 walk on a tightrope between the two towers of the World Trade Center. McCann calls that image of a "man a quarter of a mile in the sky" a "catalyst" but, as he comments in an interview, "the further the novel goes along, the less important the tightrope walk becomes, until it disappears from sight altogether, and the thing that holds the novel together is the very low tightrope of human intention that we all negotiate."[8] The novel is a simultaneously intimate and expansive portrait of New York as, precisely, a world city. The image of Petit's walk inevitably invokes the headline events of 9/11/2001, but that relation is left implicit. On the other hand, the temporal complexity enabled by narrative juxtaposition moves front and center in Dinaw Mengestu's *All Our Names* (2014). It shifts between the first-person perspectives of an African exchange student arriving in a Midwestern college town, and his assigned social worker. As Helen tells the story of their developing romance, we learn the events of Isaac's past in alternating chapters. (Of two Isaacs, in fact; we deduce gradually that the speaker has renamed himself after a friend who played a central role in his life in Africa.) The asynchronous counterpoint creates thematic links between stories that might seem separate, making them mutually illuminating.

This is not, of course, a new genre (any more than the parable is). An investigation of its genealogy would have to ponder the alternating perspectives of the epistolary novel. Scanning backward and forward rapidly—for the nineteenth century we might think of "Esther's Narrative" in Dickens's *Bleak House,* or the intertwined strands of *Moby Dick.* Such works are both at the heart of the simultaneity Benedict Anderson famously identified as fundamental to the novel as a national form, and pushing its limits. In the twentieth century, Ursula Le Guin's *Dispossessed* (1974) deploys the formal strategy of alternating narratives to powerful effect, coordinating time and place complexly. The novel opens with a scene of departure and arrival, in a chapter headed by images of the twin planets Annares and Urras; those that follow alternate between a series of events unfolding on each planet. They prove, however, to have a single protagonist, at different points in his life—so that the final chapter brings one of the narratives back to the first scene, which launched the second sequence. Or most recently, in N. K. Jemison's *Fifth Season* (2015), although the three alternating speakers have different names they are the same person at different points in her life (which this reader, at least, realized only late in the novel and found very surprising—apologies for the spoiler). The much-discussed author David Mitchell uses alternating narrators throughout his body of work, structuring their connections with great (and, novel by novel, increasing) complexity. Most famously, in *Cloud Atlas* (2004) he nests six stories that range widely in genre as well as place and time, all linked to the Pacific and by the protagonists' encountering each others' stories in sequence.

Related strategies are being used in other media, from the movie *Crash* (2004), which interweaves the perspectives of disparate residents of Los Angeles over a two-day period, and Ry Cooder's concept album *Chávez Ravine* (2005), which offers a sonic history of one site in that region, to the Netflix television series *Sense8* (2015), which was explicitly announced as being about empathy on a global scale, and filmed on location in eight countries.

To focus very briefly on cinema: there are of course many films—in fact, multiple traditions of film-making—that consider place deeply and do not use the device of juxtaposed separate narrations. Let Tornatore's *Cinema Paradiso* (1988) stand in for the relevance of the chronotope of regionalism to film; the intense locality of its portrait of post-Second World War Sicily is balanced by the fascinating, illuminated beckoning of Rome and Hollywood. The power of the village world is so great that Alfredo tells Salvatore that once he is able to leave, he must never come back—although (like Howard McLane and Subhash Mitra) he does so, belatedly.

The Australian film *The Dish* (2000) offers an apparently conventional narrative that effectively conveys a planetary perspective. The role that the Parkes radio telescope played in the broadcast of the first moon landing in 1969 is an historical fact, and the opening of the movie puts it in world-historical perspective. In the framing of the film, a central character revisits the site and reflects on its significance, with footage of John Kennedy's speech committing the United

States to reaching the moon and of rocket launches—then the movie cuts back in time to a local schoolroom in New South Wales, where every child's "show and tell" is about the Apollo 11 mission. The fact that the instrument is in a sheep paddock—it still functions, and it still is—puts the binary of backwater and glossy modernity into play (see Figure 5.7). This contrast was replayed in the media during the New Horizon spacecraft's highly publicized flyby of Pluto in July 2015, which relied on the Canberra Deep Space Communication Complex similarly located in Tidbinbilla among sheep-dotted hills. *The Dish* humorously pushes back, showing the importance of local knowledge that the dominant may disregard. The title's allusion to gendered domesticity is subtle. But the invisibility of the kitchen is surely relevant when we consider the attitudes of the NASA team arriving in Parkes. They are dismayed to find that "every coordinate in this book has been changed"—but soon acknowledge that the transposition is necessary in the Southern hemisphere. The unthinking assumption of men in the global North that their knowledge is universal runs up against the undeniable actuality of the planetary. Seeing the Earth from space—as the "blue marble"—can remind us that the center is movable.

It is clear, I hope, that my purpose is *not* to enlist all these varied works into the category of regionalism. I want rather (as I wrote earlier in this chapter) to show

FIGURE 5.7 *Publicity poster for* The Dish, *2000. Reproduced by permission of Working Dog Productions PTY LTD.*

that *patterns* in representing the coordination of time and place persist, and to demonstrate that the conceptual framework I have developed provides analytic purchase in the present.

Much has changed, of course. "Regionalisms now" is a moving target. I believe Lisa Gitelman is right in her claim that "global media help to create a world in which people are local not only because of where they are or are from but also because of their relationships to media representations of localism and its fate" (17). If we think of media as including literature, this is consistent with my claims throughout. The question of how scales connect remains difficult, however. Whether we turn to Eaton, Giles, or *Time* magazine, it is clear that the framework of the national still matters—and also clear that it is in question. Let us take the position of Colum McCann as a metonym of this challenge, an indicator of the flexible thinking about citizenship it requires. McCann is an "Irish author," born in Dublin. He lives in New York City and was there on 9/11; *Let the Great World Spin* is "United-States-set" (on the model of Emily Satterwhite's "Appalachian-set"). The novel's title is in fact a quotation from Tennyson—linking this Irish and American author, like the Chinese and Canadian Edith Eaton, with British literature. Like Longfellow, Tennyson tries to reach beyond the national project in which he is implicated and beyond the limits of the anglophone. In discussing his title McCann explicitly cites Tennyson's interest in the Mu'allaqāt, an important group of early Arabic poems; an English translation is said to have inspired "Locksley Hall," the poem in which the quoted line appears. We might also consider Mohsin Hamid, who has written eloquently about what it means to have lived his life in Lahore, and California, and New York, and London—he cites another "Lahore-born nomad" as the originator of their identification as water lilies, who drift and also have roots. He writes about how the events of 9/11 changed his situation as the carrier of a Pakistani passport, putting "great strain on the hyphen bridging that identity called Muslim-American" (*Discontent*, 43–4). (He has since become a dual citizen of the U.K.) His 2017 novel *Exit West* attends equally to the particularity of place, and the inevitability of the global—and its formal innovations open our horizons, inviting us to consider what might come next.

I conclude with two twentieth-century works. I have read and taught each of them in the context of regionalism, although that is not the canon in which either usually appears, and they have shaped my thinking. As a literary historian I resist, yet am always tempted by, the literary-critical habit of relying on texts to carry an argument. These fictions carry the analysis—where or when?—not forward—let me say rather that they complement and frame my thinking, the first example apparently close to the ground and the second taking us to space. They should not be understood as vertically arranged, however (I echo my disclaimer of the concentric in Chapter 1), and emphatically they do not correspond to past and future. When I write about Alexander Posey, Gertrude Bonnin, and D'Arcy McNickle there is a jar between the categories of American and Native American literature that opens to an alternative way of thinking about place and nation. As Scott Lyons writes in his introduction to the essay collection *The World, the Text, and the Indian*, "this literature has been globalized from its inception" (1). Science fiction is more familiarly planetary, but I will read it terms of the local. In writing about it I imagine that I glimpse changes under way in the genre system. (Fellow fans might think of Kim Stanley Robinson's *Mars* trilogy, or China Miéville's *Embassytown* and *The City & the City*, as well as Ursula Le Guin.) Let us think of these works as brackets—ones that can be turned inside out, that connect rather than separate literary regionalism from other forms.

In D'Arcy McNickle's *Wind from an Enemy Sky* (1978) we immediately encounter the opposition of local knowledge and book-learning. The opening is focalized through Antoine, a boy who has recently returned to his tribe from captivity in a government boarding school. The context provided in Chapter 2 helps here, although it only begins to elucidate the exchanges described in the nine pages of the novel's first chapter. Antoine has read about the dam that is being built in the local newspaper, and tells his grandfather—who responds: "Am I talking to you or to a piece of paper?" (1). The novel is in English, but constantly comments on the treacheries of translation—words "never pass from one language to another without some loss of flavor and ultimate meaning" (2), as for example in the inadequate rendering of the grandfather's name as "Bull." To translate "from one man's life to another's" is still more difficult (26). *Wind from an Enemy Sky* plays out multiple dramas of insiders and outsiders; it is fundamentally about failed transcultural connections, and invokes impassible differences between Indian and white views of identity (individual or communal) and the land. Yet it also enacts the persistent hope that misunderstanding can be overcome. Louis Owens comments in his Afterword to the book, "Ironically, it is communication that fails repeatedly and inevitably in D'Arcy McNickle's novels, and it is communication that McNickle devoted his life to realizing" (264).

The consequential miscommunications of the novel are precisely sited in a meticulously described, also historically defined, landscape. When Bull climbs the mountain to see how the river has been stopped, he observes every detail but also looks down and sees "the open valley far below, a white man's world. A world he sometimes passed through, but never visited" (2). Ironically, the passage relies on our apprehending McNickle's subtle distinction in English between passing through and visiting. *Wind from an Enemy Sky* includes characters who cross between worlds, or try to. When the industrialist Adam Pell visits, later in the novel, there is a moment when he glimpses the Indian perspective. He is repelled by the imposition of an abstract grid on the living land (and also recognizes that the model of agriculture imposed on the tribe is a trap). "From the vantage point of the hilltop it was possible to see a large expanse of the valley, all of it cut into squares and rectangles by fence lines. Only the irrigation canals had a way of their own and followed contour lines without regard for geometrical symmetry." Pell comments, "Settlement of the Great Plains was responsible for the monstrous custom of applying straight lines and right angles to the earth—but I guess it was the only thing to do when you set up your transit and aimed it at an infinity of grass. It simply doesn't lend itself to a pleasant mountain valley like this one…Let's get out of here, it makes me sick" (229). Figure 5.8 illustrates and complements this perspective, through wonderfully analytical aerial photography.

Pell, deeply interested in Indians and considering himself their friend, has other such moments. Yet he utterly fails to understand what it means to Bull's band that the sacred Feather Boy bundle they hope to retrieve has been destroyed, through carelessness at Pell's museum. His notion of making up for the loss by giving them a gold figurine of a naked woman, a possibly Inca artifact from South America, is as ignorant as the establishment of the Liberty Villages. It depends fundamentally on the capitalist understanding of values as commensurable (see Tsing, *Mushroom*); the novel shows us on every page how impossibly wrong that view is, in Indian Country. Bull is right: "Maybe he is a good man—I watched him, and that is what I think—and yet he will destroy us" (187). None of the protagonists is alive at the end of the novel, and it seems entirely possible that those who live have been too damaged to survive in any but the most technical sense. "*No meadowlarks sang, and the world fell apart*" (256, emphasis in original).

As the last line suggests, the disaster portrayed in this novel is far-reaching. Nowhere is the question of particular versus generalizable meaning more fraught than in conversations about Native American literature. I invoke that category, but also acknowledge tribal specificity when I mention authors. That tension is defining

FIGURE 5.8 *"Wheat Strips on Plateau," from* Taking Measures across the American Landscape *by James Corner (author) and Alex S. MacLean (photographer) (Yale University Press, 1996), p. 128. Reprinted by permission.*

for *Wind from an Enemy Sky*, which is—very unusually for this author and this tradition—not located on a single site or about a specific people. McNickle's mother was Métis-Cree and his father was Irish, but he was born on the Flathead Reservation in Montana, and was an enrolled member of the Salish and Kootenai tribes. The landscape of the novel clearly evokes that place, and its events are based on the building of the Kerr dam. The story of the Feather Boy bundle, however, seems to be drawn from the Gros Ventre tribe's reclaiming of a sacred artifact in 1938 (McNickle participated in the negotiations; see 260). McNickle is able to give details about the Feather Boy bundle precisely because it is fictional. In a book published as part of the Flathead Reservation's Tribal History Project, compiled by David Rockwell, it is noted that "many of the ways in which the Salish, Pend d'Oreille, and Kootenai traditionally use the river are not discussed in this book. The tribes prefer not to describe specific spiritual traditions and beliefs in a public document" (3). In *Wind from an Enemy Sky* McNickle—enabled by his particular and privileged perspective—chose to tell a pan-tribal story including the sacred. Yet he was apparently never satisfied with the way any version (after the one submitted and rejected in 1944) scaled up from incident to history. He labored on the manuscript intermittently for three decades, and it was eventually published after his death. That is hardly surprising when, to quote the novel itself, Pell's "fatal mistake of generalizing about Indians [is] perhaps the most common error in the history of Indian-white relations" (263).

The author I enlist to provide my second bracket, Ursula Le Guin, has published many, many books and invented at least two universes. *Four Ways to Forgiveness*, a collection of four connected novellas published in 1995, is part of what is sometimes called her "Hainish cycle" (although the author herself finds the term too systematic). In its eight volumes and many short stories there are more than eighty planets with human societies, all of them—including Terra, that is, Earth—resulting from colonies established by the now-peaceful world of Hain. This is an influential series: for example, the notion of the ansible (a device based on entangled particles that allows instantaneous communication once it has been physically moved across interstellar space) is routinely adopted by other writers. The effect of worldness can be projected by the parable of the global village, but also by multiple narratives. It is invoked at the opening of *Four Ways to Forgiveness*, when the protagonist of "Betrayals" (the first story) is reading about Gethen, the setting of Le Guin's very widely read Hainish novel *The Left Hand of Darkness* (1969). The novellas are all set on the twin planets of Yeowe and Werel, and tell, through a series of unlikely heterosexual romances, the story of the system's struggles over slavery and freedom.

Like all Le Guin's work, these stories constantly portray how human perception and behavior are shaped by culture, and are profoundly and surprisingly variable. The second story, "Forgiveness Day," is focalized both through a cosmopolitan woman and a conservative, provincial man, revealing both their perspectives as limited. The third story, "A Man of the People," opens with a child sitting beside his father at an irrigation tank—we might say his uncle, but the narrator writes, a few paragraphs later, "Granite was Havzhiva's mother's brother, of course; that is what a father was" (94). This story is one of only a few Le Guin has set on Hain itself. Because of its immensely long history the planet is covered by ruins, which are (as always) richly evocative of the relation of time and place. They also become an opportunity to disrupt our automatic thinking not only about kinship but also about time and transportation: "Ruins of an enormous bridge are visible on the landward side, and another half-sunk fragment of ruin is the basis of the town's boat pier and breakwater. Vast works of other ages encumber all Hain, and are no more and no less venerable or interesting to the Hainish than the rest of the landscape. A child standing on the pier to watch his mother sail off to the mainland might wonder why people had bothered to build a bridge when there were boats and flyers to ride. They must have liked to walk, he thought" (95).

This child is the protagonist Havzhiva (to use one of several versions of his name); he is growing up in Stse, and the fact that he is of a particular lineage prescribes who he can pair with, what profession he can practice, and much else. Le Guin gives a vivid portrait of the contrast between the pueblo and life elsewhere, through a relative who has chosen to leave and become a historian, who comes back for a visit. She explains, "There, I'm not a Buried Cable woman. I'm a woman. I can have sex with any person I choose. I can take up any profession I choose. Lineage...has no meaning and no use, anywhere else in the universe...There are two kinds of knowledge, local and universal. There are two kinds of time, local and historical" (103). When Havzhiva leaves Stse and comes to understand that everything he learned there can be labeled "*typical pueblo culture of north-western South Continent*," he accuses the scholars of withholding knowledge from the pueblos, or the pueblos of withholding knowledge from their people. No, he is told, everything is accessible although the pueblos choose not to have many books, preferring living knowledge. "'You were taught that certain things were true, or necessary; and those things are true and necessary. They are the local knowledge of Stse. They are childish, irrational beliefs!' he said. They looked at him, and he knew he had said something childish and irrational" (109). I am not suggesting a direct influence—but Havzhiva's recognition evokes the recursive paradox embodied in Jewett's "childish certainty of being the centre of civilization" (371). As his teachers tell him, "Local knowledge is not partial knowledge" (109).

This is both an evocative, and a textbook, portrait of the traditional and modern. It unfolds throughout the volume but is also challenged and complicated. *Four Ways to Forgiveness* does not relax into a facile relativism. It engages the question of how to think about the gods and the sacred, on this view of knowledge. And its fundamental topic—how profoundly everyone and everything in a slave society is twisted by the effects of bondage, and how change might be achieved—does not lend itself to easy answers. In the fourth novella, "A Woman's Liberation," Rakam, who becomes Havzhiva's committed companion, tells the story of her life. We encounter again the cruelty of the good intentions of the powerful (seen in the scheme of the Liberty Villages, and in Adam Pell's effort to be a friend of the Indian). Her abolitionist owner (and father), when his father dies and he inherits, hands freedom papers to all the family's "assets" and flies off to the capital. So he leaves them to be killed, or raped and re-enslaved by the owners of other plantations. Rakam describes horrors; telling the story of a girl who dies while being brutally used sexually, she asks—"All knowledge is local, my friend has said. Is it true, where is it true, that that child had to die in that way? Is it true, where is it true, that she did not have to die in that way?" (166).

Like *Wind from an Enemy Sky*, this narrative calls on a specific history, but aspires to the general. It engages complexly with the history of slavery on Earth; for me the reference to the United States is strongest in the Sorrow Song from Werel's plantations—"O, O, Ye-o-we,/Nobody never comes back" (202)—that runs through the volume, printed with musical notes and evoking Du Bois's *Souls of Black Folk*. It is broadly concerned with the oppression of women in post-emancipation societies. We may dismiss the "coupling convention," or we may hear even broader references to feminist thought—and/or, even more anachronistically, Badiou's theory of love—when, at the end of the book, Rakam defends the narrative form she has chosen. "I have closed…as so many stories close, with a joining of two people. What is one man's and one woman's love and desire, against the history of two worlds, the great revolutions of our lifetimes, the hope, the unending cruelty of our species? A little thing. But a key is a little thing, next to the door it opens. If you lose the key, the door may never be unlocked. It is in our bodies that we lose or begin our freedom, in our bodies that we accept or end our slavery. So I wrote this book for my friend, with whom I have lived and will die free" (208). It matters too that she becomes a teacher, a writer, a historian. When Havzhiva's superior (the protagonist of the second story) asks him if they are aiding a revolution, he replies, "It is education, ma'am" (130).

Rakam's appeal to her friend, her partner Havzhiva, could be taken as positioning this claim as local knowledge. But these are not in fact the last words of the volume—turning the page, we find detailed "Notes on Werel and Yeowe," provided in support of the worldness of Le Guin's Hainish fictions. This recursion opens the door that interests me most. Can book-learning remain true to local knowledge? Similarly, when Havzhiva is hailed as "the Envoy from the Future" he thinks of the fact that he "grew up in a pueblo" (120). The slanted landscape of power is all we have to walk on. But we can go—not forward, or back—somewhere.

Sometimes, literature categorized as science fiction points out that the planet is a region.

In the Place of a Conclusion

*It is time to turn attention to the nonscalable, not only as objects for description
but also as incitements to theory.*

—ANNA LOWENHAUPT TSING, *The Mushroom at the End of the World*

In choosing to write this book, and in all its claims, I make a case for taking regional writing seriously. Story-telling about particular places has been a way of attending to the nearby, the distant, and the horizon, and to the entanglement of place and time. It is not always that; it can be encapsulated and quaint. But it continues to be a vital resource for contemporary creators. My enterprise has been to follow this writing into its most ambitious reaches, to read it with other efforts to understand the puzzles of place-time and generally how the world works—and to articulate what I see, as accessibly as I can.

I have learned a lot, writing this book. That has not made it easier to sum up. If anything, I am warier than I was of words out of context. And—in the circumstances of publishing today—I am no longer sure that a conclusion addresses readers who have stayed with me, rather than someone dropping in for a look. In any case, I have put recapitulations of my arguments about genre and literary history, showing that regionalism matters, into the Preface. I have ended the last chapter with the most capacious interpretations I can achieve. What remains for me to do here is to reflect on the stakes of my project. Why have I cared so much about understanding regionalism?

The juxtaposed epigraphs of Chapter 1 look in different directions. Taken together, they imply both the problem of audience, and the difference it makes to think about region both substantively and relationally. In *Whitefoot*, a children's book about a mouse, Wendell Berry affirms life as local: "That one lives at the center of the world is the world's profoundest thought" (11). His specificity could be read as individualism, yet his address is potentially infinite. Read in the framework of my inquiry, his choice of humble protagonist and impersonal syntax suggest that Berry is embracing a broad community of fate that includes both the human and the non-human. Doreen Massey makes a less sweeping but also consequential claim, speaking to geographers and feminists across the disciplines: "what defines the uniqueness of any place is by no means all included within that place itself" (5).

Her work addresses and explicitly challenges the academy, proposing that we see places as complex, connected, and always changing. I admire the balance each writer has struck between modesty and reach. The distance between them establishes an ample horizon, and leads me to the challenge Anna Tsing poses in the epigraph above (39). I am trying to think of places on their own terms without either isolating them, or arranging them in concentric circles and ranked orders. It is no easy matter to pay sustained attention to the divergent and incommensurable; to detach from gated grids and time zones and the pervasive, "driving beat" of progress; to "look around rather than ahead" (Tsing 21–2).

Writing this book has led me to notice metaphors of place everywhere. Whether or not the reader finds that sentence's imitative form mildly funny (I do), it makes the point. A moment's reflection will multiply examples, from "peak experience" to "slippery slope" and "down the rabbit hole." More specifically, any given book or broadcast, any conversation that goes on for a while, is likely to include a phrase that maps time and value onto physical location.

I offer one of many instances I thought about during my last weeks of writing, in the late fall of 2017. One day as I drove from home to campus to teach, I listened to an episode of the National Public Radio show *1A* about "Statehouses and Sexual Harassment." My attention sharpened when the conversation turned to the point that state capitals are frequently in small cities; Jefferson City, Missouri, for example, is not even on the interstate highway. A participating journalist commented: "It's a backwater." It is not necessary to take any position on the causes of the problem under consideration to see the absurdity of this explanatory move. The topic was in the news precisely because of scandals over the behavior of men living in the limelight of Hollywood and Capitol Hill. Its illogic is obscured by mental, or more properly discursive, habits that derive from and support a teleological understanding of modernity. A "backwater" is a place out of the main current—it is stagnant, being left behind. The implication is that the speakers on the show, addressing the nation from a radio station based at a university campus in Washington, D.C., are (in contrast) part of a lively stream headed in the right direction: the future. Listeners are assumed to be "progressive," and it requires an effort to paddle the other way and not condescend to the remote. I invite readers to recognize, instead, the ubiquity of correlations of space, time, and power—from every reference to civilization and savagery, to a casual expression like "dumbing down."

The contrast between country and city is very old, and takes many forms. There is nothing inevitable or even predictable about how it maps onto politics. During the emergence of local color in the United States, in the late nineteenth century, radicalism was widespread in agricultural districts. Katherine Cramer examines the new configuration of the twenty-first century in her study of "rural consciousness" in Wisconsin, *The Politics of Resentment*. She did her research from 2007 through 2012, beginning before the polarizing rise of Scott Walker, and finishing before the divisive national election of 2016. Whatever has just happened or happens next, working on region has called me to reckon with her rural informants' conviction that decision-makers in government ignore them, tax them, redistribute their earnings elsewhere—and with their sense that the state university where she works is very, very far away. Her point is not that they are correct, but that it is important to understand how their views make sense of experience on a particular ground. As Craig Calhoun writes in an essay on cosmopolitanism I quoted in the first chapter: "Democracy must grow out of the life-world; it must empower people not in the abstract but in the actual conditions of their lives. This means to empower them within communities and traditions, not in spite of them" ("Class Consciousness," 875). It is no help, of course, to reverse the polarity and shift from "backwater" to imagining the countryside as another kind of still water, a reservoir of hard-working citizenship. (As Cramer shows, in her state that claim enables racism.) Pulling on either end of the rope in this tug of war, accepting the form of the opposition between center and province, prevents us from looking *around*, in Tsing's sense. Refusing the entailed correlations, declining to "scale up," gives us a better chance of understanding the particularity of places—which always includes their connections.

The title of this book uses "writing" as a placeholder to claim such everyday metaphors as part of my topic, and to keep the relation of kinds of knowledge unsettled. I too am a writer. I hope I am in dialogue with the writers I read—not looking down to critique, but also not deferring to great authors. The term "writing" does not really stretch far enough, since I have included television, cinema, and now radio, but it is more accessible than "expressive culture" or "inscription." Most of the works I examine *are* what is conventionally called "literature." I have read all my varied sources closely, intensively, and also extensively in terms of their place and horizons.

My specialist study of the multiple orientations of regional writing connects energetically with the broad stakes of my inquiry. People wrote from many places, and their words were set in type and sent back to many places. In Chapter 1 I argued for increased attention to the local publication and reception of local color stories. Chapter 2 is about the relationship of local knowledge and book-learning; there (beginning with how residents of his home town of Vevay, Indiana responded to Edward Eggleston's *Hoosier School-Master*) and in subsequent chapters, I attend both to broad patterns and to particular readings. In the same way, it is not enough to position NPR as central because it is national, and public, and operates on a broadcast model—or to point out all the speakers on that *1A* episode were based in the capital city of the United States. The show is syndicated, and I was listening in Michigan, and wondering how listeners in Missouri were reacting. (I investigated; stations based in Cape Girardeau, Farmington, Rolla, and St. Louis, Missouri would have been playing it.) The show's host is from West Palm Beach, Florida, and the speaker who used the term "backwater" is a native of Seattle. All this is to say: discourse *circulates*.

On the horizon of the academy and (inter)disciplinarity, one consequence of these connections is that I think literary history and media studies should have a closer connection. In the moment and location of my writing, as a citizen of the world, I am most concerned with what is happening to local news. Readers, consult any source you wish (we depend on unevenly attentive accounts, and hope for reliable aggregation). The *Columbia Journalism Review* published an alarming issue on the topic in Spring 2017, and an update in November which began "Since 2000, nearly half of newsroom jobs—more than 20,000 of them—have disappeared." My own local newspaper in Ann Arbor, which had published under various names since 1835, was closed by the immense media company Advance Publications in 2009. I am not looking back to a golden age of journalism. Edith Eaton's efforts to get stories of Chinese North Americans into print, recounted in Chapter 4, may serve us as a reminder that many communities, in the country and the city alike, have been systematically underrepresented. But studying regionalism has led me to feel more and more urgency about understanding the media transformation we are living through; it had led me to hear oppositions of time and place, locality and book-learning, when Charles Sennott laments that "We live in a world of 24/7 reporting, of people who comment from cubicles, people who give their opinion from a university or from a think tank. What we don't have, and what we need, is to get those journalists on the ground." He is the founder of the GroundTruth Project, whose name itself connects their work to the balancing of perspectives—the horizon—that has concerned me: "The origin of the term comes from NASA, and refers to part of the calibration process used in satellite imagery. When NASA measures something with a satellite, an employee on the ground takes the same measurement. That human measurement is known as 'ground truth.'"

I have already written, in Chapter 2, about the urgency of such balancing in my own workplace: the school. I love book-learning, and embrace the longest perspectives and broadest landscapes I can find. I also believe, with Paolo Freire, that one cannot "reconcile adherence to an ideal of democracy and of overcoming prejudice with a proud or arrogant posture in which one feels full of oneself. How can I listen to the other, how can I hold a dialogue, if I can only listen to myself, if I can only see myself [?] ... Humility helps me avoid being entrenched in the circuit of my own truth" (72). My studies lead me to suggest that the center is anywhere and everywhere—which entails imagining a world full of classrooms in which local knowledge and dialects are respected, with their windows open to everywhere else. That would be accessibility, in its strongest sense. The fight for social justice seems to me continuous with the fight for education as a public good.

There are many sites of learning that are not called schools, of course. As I stop writing, I am still thinking about how many topics and perspectives I have not included. I have connected writing about particular places with the remarkable (scientific, historical, cultural) human accomplishment of seeing the world as round. My work implies accepting the responsibility of seeing the planet in our hands. It also implies paying attention to the incommensurable, and trying to work free of habits like assuming that north is up and the future is forward. We have much more to imagine.

{ ENDNOTES }

Chapter 2

1. Jonathan Zimmerman's *Small Wonder: The Little Red Schoolhouse in History and Memory* chronicles and reflects on the significance of this fascination.

2. See Totten. Writers of color may sometimes be incorporated into discussions of regionalism simply to make them more inclusive, as he suggests. I think, however, that my reading demonstrates the distinctively indigenous perspective from which Zitkala-Sa engages the form. We should also not allow that specificity to obscure her aspirations to broad significance. It is of course unnecessary, on my view of genre, for me to argue that her work "is" regionalist.

3. Throughout, I use the names Zitkala-Sa, and Gertrude Simmons or Bonnin, purposefully. The biographical person Gertrude Simmons adopted the pseudonym Zitkala-Sa in 1897; it did also become a persona she sometimes adopted and even used to sign letters. It is not an "authentic" Indian name—as Kiara Vigil notes, "Although it is Sioux in origin (Lakota), it is not from her native dialect (Nakota)" (165). She married Raymond Bonnin in 1902 and subsequently used her married name. I explore the complexity of the relation between name and pseudonym further in Chapter 4, on Edith Eaton and Sui Sin Far.

4. The story is included in *The Best-Loved Short Stories of Jesse Stuart*, and also easily available online in multiple versions. Searching the title of the story will quickly demonstrate its continued popularity—I include citations to the online "Classic Short Stories" site, and a few of the many examples showing its use in the classroom—usually in the United States, but also by the Israeli Ministry of Education.

5. I rely here on Satterwhite's account (136–49). On the novel's return to the bestseller list, see 289 n. 19.

6. I quote the characterization of Kennedy's work as absurdist from his obituary in the *New York Times* ("Raymond Kennedy, Novelist, Dies at 73").

7. "The Literacy Myth refers to the belief...that the acquisition of literacy is a necessary precursor and invariably results in economic development, democratic practice, cognitive enhancement, and upward social mobility" (Graff, 35). My point here is partly to say that schools cannot do everything—we tend to turn to them for more solutions than they can provide (which is not to say we should not try to do better in them).

Chapter 3

1. As my formulation here indicates, what I regret about my widely cited 1996 article on Jewett is that I did not do more to make it clear that I was writing as *both* a feminist and a historicist. I regret the binary division itself, in fact; but as Jennifer Fleissner makes clear in her fine essay "Is Feminism a Historicism?", those were very much the terms of the discussion when I was writing. I was, in other words, a creature of my moment—just as Jewett was, just

as (I believe) we all are. Where Fleissner and I seem to diverge is that I believe that a thoroughgoing historicism *entails* an analytic attitude towards one's own position—the kind of one-up attitude towards the writers of the past that she critiques seems to me in fact a failure of historicism. (Fredric Jameson's "Marxism and Historicism," which Fleissner and I have both cited, carries this question forward in complex and powerful ways.)

Sometimes I have wanted to tell those who took issue with my work on Jewett that they have misunderstood it. I have relegated this material to a note in recognition of the fact whether or not this is true, it is not important. But for the record, in my Introduction to *New Essays on Country of the Pointed Firs* I was not apologizing that the book is not a timeless masterpiece, but rejecting that category. Based on conversations over the years I suspect Tom Lutz (87) was not the only person who carried away the wrong impression. In the end, however, I am grateful for the interest that book and my subsequent article generated. The only element of the response that troubles me is that the framework of the 1996 essay has been taken up so much more often than my reading of "A Late Supper"—I hope to give that a second life by including a revised version in the text of this chapter.

2. I think Jewett critics (myself included) do tend to focus on her optimistic stories; I appreciate Gavin Jones's attention, in *Failure and the American Writer*, to a sad story like "Marsh Rosemary" and agree with his analysis of her weak plots as resistance to "grand narratives of rise and fall" (131). However, not only our different understandings of regionalism but also my emphasis on the importance of religion in Jewett's work mean that our readings differ sharply—the spiritual strength of the spinster protagonists of both "Marsh Rosemary" and "A Village Shop" makes me unwilling to read them as primarily stories of failure.

Chapter 4

1. The complexity of the issue is indicated by the immediate need for a clarifying note. Annette White-Parks has suggested (2003) that "Sui Sin Far" may have been a family pet name, because of the appearance of the address "Miss Sui" in the autobiographical essay "Leaves from the Mental Portfolio of an Eurasian." However, "Miss Far" also appears, and the improbability of a name that (like "Mark Twain") is a single phrase being broken into a personal and a family name must be multiplied by the fact that the speaker is someone who does not know she is Chinese. I return to a similar crossing between languages at the conclusion of my reading of "The Americanizing of Pau Tsu," below.

For a detailed analysis of a situation in which the author used both names, see Cutter on her correspondence with Charles Lummis (272). For an example from primary sources, see two brief pieces in the same issue of *The Westerner*, one titled "Word from Miss Eaton" and the other "A Word from 'Sui Sin Far.'"

The unreliability of Eaton's self-representations is entailed by her situation, but makes her testimony less than dispositive on this and other points—as will appear throughout.

2. What the monument actually says is "Sui Sun Far"—the letters are clear not only in the photograph I supply, but also in the one in the Birchall biography. I suspect it is an indication of how solid the persona "Sui Sin Far" became in the late twentieth century that as far as I know there has been no comment on this—people do not seem to see it.

3. I quote "rescued" from Joseph Salter's 1873 book, *The Asiatic in England* (169). In this sketch I am informed by the biographical studies of the Eaton sisters by Parks, Birchall, and

Ferens, which remain important. However, my main sources are Mary Chapman's recent edition *Becoming Edith Eaton: Early Fiction, Journalism, and Travel Writing by Edith Maude Eaton* (2016) and her *Dictionary of Literary Biography* entry for Eaton. I am grateful to the Nineteenth-Century American Women Writers Study Group for inviting me to participate in their session on the Eaton sisters in Washington, D.C. in April 2010; I learned a great deal and my subsequent work on Eaton has been shaped by that conversation. I am especially grateful to Mary Chapman for sharing the results of her ongoing research with me. She directed me to the Salter book, for example, and discovered Eaton's sojourn in northern Ontario (*Becoming*, xvi).

4. It appears in "Chinese Workmen in America," in the *Independent* 75 (July 3, 1913): 56–8. The article is reprinted in the Ling and White-Parks collection of Sui Sin Far's work (231–2).

5. "Tramp around" is the phrase Eaton uses in "Leaves from the Mental Portfolio of an Eurasian," and I also refer to the account of her lacemaking in the *Boston Globe* article, in the Ling and Parks edition of *Mrs. Spring Fragrance*, 222 and 290–1 respectively.

6. The same substitution of "nothingness" for "littleness" appears in a brief article in the London-based miscellany *The Mirror of Literature, Amusement, and Instruction*, in 1830. That seems an unlikely source for Eaton, however—I speculate that she knew her Byron, and misquoted from memory.

7. Another link between the stories, not directly related to my argument here, is that Adah Raymond is said to mediate the awakening of love in an arranged marriage, as portraits did in "Mrs. Spring Fragrance." This is an interesting moment, as Wan Lin Fo and Adah's conversation is staged in a way that provokes a frisson over the prospect of interracial romance. This is an example of something that is true, and I hope apparent, throughout: I am focusing on particular aspects of these stories, and there is much more that could be said.

8. My account is most directly from Joshua Miller's *Accented America* (11) and is also influenced by the work of Werner Sollers (one of the founders of the Longfellow Institute).

Chapter 5

1. I discuss the relationship of regionalism and cosmopolitanism in terms of a specific fictional work in "Here/There, Now/Then, Both/And: Regionalism and Cosmopolitanism in Edith Wharton's *Old New York*."

2. I discuss the significance of this gesture in Chapter 2.

3. William Cronon's "The Trouble with Wilderness" was published sixteen years after *Dogs of March*, more than twenty years ago—it remains a useful reference point here.

4. See my essay "Sand in Your Mouth" on this point.

5. My references are to Mark McGurl's *The Program Era: Postwar Fiction and the Rise of Creative Writing* and James English's *The Economy of Prestige: Prizes, Awards and the Circulation of Cultural Value*.

6. Daniel D'Addario, "A Nation of Books," 102.

7. See Hungerford and Hutner in *American Literary History*.

8. I quote McCann's interview with Bret Anthony Johnston, posted on the National Book Award website.

{ BIBLIOGRAPHY }

Book, Films, and Articles

Adams, David Wallace. *Education for Extinction: American Indians and the Boarding School Experience, 1875–1928*. Lawrence: University Press of Kansas, 1995.

Adams, Michael. *Slang: The People's Poetry*. New York: Oxford University Press, 2009.

Allen, James Lane. "Local Color." *The Critic* 8 (1886): 13–14.

Ammons, Elizabeth. *Conflicting Stories: American Women Writers at the Turn into the Twentieth Century*. New York: Oxford University Press, 1992.

Appiah, Kwame Anthony. "Cosmopolitan Patriots." *Critical Inquiry* 23, no. 3 (Spring 1997): 617–39.

Arthur, Jason. *Violet America: Regional Cosmopolitanism in U.S. Fiction since the Great Depression*. Iowa City: University of Iowa Press, 2013.

Augé, Marc. *Non-Places*. London: Verso, 2008.

Aull, Laura Louise. *Forgotten Genres: The Editorial Apparatus of American Anthologies and Composition Textbooks*. PhD diss., University of Michigan, 2011.

Ayscough, Florence Wheelock, and Amy Lowell. *Fir-Flower Tablets: Poems Translated from the Chinese*. Boston: Houghton Mifflin, 1921.

Badiou, Alain, and Nicolas Truong. *In Praise of Love*, trans. Peter Bush. New York: New Press, 2012.

Bain, Donald [and "Jessica Fletcher," pseud.]. *Murder, She Wrote: Murder on the QE2*. New York: Berkley, 1997.

Bakhtin, M. M. *The Dialogic Imagination: Four Essays*, edited by Michael Holquist, trans. Caryl Emerson and Michael Holquist. Austin: University of Texas Press, 1981.

Bal, Mieke. *Travelling Concepts in the Humanities: A Rough Guide*. Toronto: University of Toronto Press, 2002.

Basso, Keith H. *Wisdom Sits in Places: Landscape and Language among the Western Apache*. Albuquerque: University of New Mexico Press, 1996.

Baxter, Charles. *There's Something I Want You to Do: Stories*. New York: Pantheon Books, 2014.

Beavers, Herman. *Wrestling Angels into Song: The Fictions of Ernest J. Gaines and James Alan McPherson*. Philadelphia: University of Pennsylvania Press, 1995.

Berger, John. *Pig Earth*. New York: Pantheon Books, 1979.

Berger, John. *Once in Europa*. New York: Pantheon Books, 1987.

Berger, John. *Lilac and Flag: An Old Wives' Tale of a City*. New York: Pantheon Books, 1990.

Beringer, Pierre. "The Destruction of San Francisco." *Overland Monthly* 47 (1906): 391–440.

Berman, Russell A. "Presidential Address 2012—Teaching as Vocation." *PMLA* 127, no. 3 (May 2012): 451–9.

Berrey, Stephen A. *The Jim Crow Routine: Everyday Performances of Race, Civil Rights, and Segregation in Mississippi*. Chapel Hill: The University of North Carolina Press, 2015.

Berry, Wendell. "The Regional Motive." *The Southern Review* 6 (1972): 972–7.

Berry, Wendell. *Remembering*. San Francisco: North Point Press, 1988.

Berry, Wendell. *Jayber Crow: The Life Story of Jayber Crow, Barber, of the Port William Membership, as Written by Himself: A Novel*. New York: Counterpoint, 2000.

Berry, Wendell. *A Place on Earth (Revision)*. Berkeley: Counterpoint, 2001.

Berry, Wendell. *Hannah Coulter: A Novel*. Washington, D.C.: Shoemaker & Hoard, 2004.

Berry, Wendell. *That Distant Land: The Collected Stories*. Berkeley: Counterpoint, 2004.

Berry, Wendell. *Whitefoot: A Story from the Center of the World*. Illustrated by Davis Te Selle. Berkeley: Counterpoint, 2008.

Bial, Raymond. *One-Room School*. Boston: Houghton Mifflin, 1999.

Birchall, Diana. *Onoto Watanna: The Story of Winnifred Eaton*. Urbana: University of Illinois Press, 2001.

Black, Daniel. *They Tell Me of a Home*. New York: St. Martin's Press, 2005.

Blanchard, Paula. *Sarah Orne Jewett: Her World and Her Work*. Reading, MA: Addison-Wesley Pub. Co., 1994.

[Bonnin, Gertrude Simmons.] Zitkala-Sa. *American Indian Stories*. Washington: Hayworth Publishing House, 1921.

Borges, Jorge Luis. "On Exactitude and Science." In *The Aleph (Including the Prose Fictions from the Maker)*, translated by Andrew Hurley, 181. New York: Penguin Books, 2004.

Bowden, Brett. *The Empire of Civilization: The Evolution of an Imperial Idea*. Chicago: University of Chicago Press, 2009.

Boym, Svetlana. *The Future of Nostalgia*. New York: Basic Books, 2001.

Bramen, Carrie Tirado. *The Uses of Variety: Modern Americanism and the Quest for National Distinctiveness*. Cambridge, MA: Harvard University Press, 2000.

Brinkley, Alan. *The Publisher: Henry Luce and His American Century*. New York: Alfred A. Knopf, 2010.

Brodhead, Richard H. *The School of Hawthorne*. New York: Oxford University Press, 1986.

Brodhead, Richard H. *Cultures of Letters: Scenes of Reading and Writing in Nineteenth-Century America*. Chicago: University of Chicago Press, 1993.

Brooks, Lisa Tanya. *The Common Pot: The Recovery of Native Space in the Northeast*. Minneapolis: University of Minnesota Press, 2008.

Byron, George Gordon. "Ode to Napoleon Buonaparte." In *The Works of Lord Byron*, edited by Ernest Hartley Coleridge. London: John Murray, 1904.

Buzzati, Dino. *The Tartar Steppe*. Translated by Stuart Hood. Boston: D. R. Godine, 2005.

Caldwell, Charlotte, and Linda Grosskopf. *Visions and Voices: Montana's One-Room Schoolhouses*, Clyde Park, MT: Barn Board Press, 2012.

Calhoun, Charles C. *Longfellow: A Rediscovered Life*. Boston: Beacon Press, 2005.

Calhoun, Craig. *Critical Social Theory: Culture, History, and the Challenge of Difference*. Cambridge: Blackwell, 2003.

Calhoun, Craig J. "The Class Consciousness of Frequent Travelers: Toward a Critique of Actually Existing Cosmopolitanism." *The South Atlantic Quarterly* 101, no. 4 (2002): 869–97.

Calhoun, Craig. "Cosmopolitanism in the Modern Social Imaginary." *Daedalus* 137, no. 3 (2008): 105–14.

Carpenter, Cari M. "Detecting Indianness: Gertrude Bonnin's Investigation of Native American Identity." *Wicazo Sa Review* 20, no. 1 (2005): 139–59.

Carpenter, Cari M. *Seeing Red: Anger, Sentimentality, and American Indians.* Columbus: Ohio State University Press, 2008.

Chapman, Mary. "Finding Edith Eaton." *Legacy: A Journal of American Women Writers* 29, no. 2 (2012): 263–9.

Chapman, Mary. "Cross-Cultural Affinities between Native American and White Women in 'The Alaska Widow' by Edith Eaton (Sui Sin Far)." *MELUS: Multi-Ethnic Literature of the U.S.* 38, no. 1 (2013): 155–63.

Chapman, Mary. *Making Noise, Making News: U.S. Suffrage Print Culture and Literary Modernism.* New York: Oxford University Press, 2014.

Chase, Mary Ellen. *Windswept.* New York: Macmillan Co., 1941.

Chesnutt, Charles W. "The Bouquet." *Atlantic Monthly* 84 (1899): 648–54.

Chesnutt, Charles W. The March of Progress." *The Century* 61, no. 3 (Jan. 1901): 422–7.

Chesnutt, Charles W. *The Conjure Woman.* Ann Arbor: University of Michigan Press, 1969.

Chesnutt, Charles W. *Mandy Oxendine: A Novel,* edited by Charles Hackenberry. Urbana: University of Illinois Press, 1997.

Chin, Frank, ed. *Aiiieeeee! An Anthology of Asian-American Writers.* Washington, D.C.: Howard University Press, 1974.

Chu, Patricia P. *Assimilating Asians: Gendered Strategies of Authorship in Asian America.* Durham: Duke University Press, 2000.

Cinema Paradiso. Directed by Giuseppe Tornatore. 1988. Miramax Films.

Coetzee, J. M. *Waiting for the Barbarians.* New York: Penguin Books, 1982.

Conforti, Joseph A. *Imagining New England: Explorations of Regional Identity from the Pilgrims to the Mid-Twentieth Century.* Chapel Hill: University of North Carolina Press, 2001.

Conolly-Smith, Peter. "Prose Pictures of *Kleindeutschland*: German-Language Local-Color Serials of the Late Nineteenth Century." In *Transnationalism and American Serial Fiction,* edited by Patricia Okker, 84–110. London: Routledge, 2012.

Conrads, Margaret C. *Winslow Homer and the Critics: Forging a National Art in the 1870s.* Princeton: Princeton University Press in association with the Nelson-Atkins Museum of Art, 2001.

Cosgrove, Denis E. *Apollo's Eye: A Cartographic Genealogy of the Earth in the Western Imagination.* Baltimore: Johns Hopkins University Press, 2001.

Cramer, Katherine J. *The Politics of Resentment: Rural Consciousness and the Rise of Scott Walker.* Chicago: University of Chicago Press, 2016.

Crash. Directed by Paul Haggis. 2004. Lions Gate Films.

Cronon, William. "The Trouble with Wilderness." In *Uncommon Ground: Rethinking the Human Place in Nature,* edited by William Cronon, 69–90. New York: Norton, 1995.

Curzan, Anne. "Teaching the Politics of Standard English." *Journal of English Linguistics* 30, no. 4 (December 1, 2002): 339–52.

Cutter, Martha J. "Sui Sin Far's Letters to Charles Lummis: Contextualizing Publication Practices for the Asian American Subject at the Turn of the Century." *American Literary Realism* 38, no. 3 (2006): 259–75.

D'Addario, Daniel. "A Nation of Books." *Time* 186, no. 1/2 (July 6, 2015): 102.

Dailey, Janet. *Summer Mahogany.* New York: Harlequin, 1987.

Dailey, Janet. *The Matchmakers.* New York: Harlequin, 1988.

"De Quincy's 'Life of Raphael.'" *The North American Review* 46, no. 98 (1838): 106–26.

Deleuze, Gilles, and Felix Guattari. *Kafka: Toward a Minor Literature.* 9th edition. Minneapolis: University of Minnesota Press, 1986.

Deloria, Philip J. *Playing Indian.* New Haven: Yale University Press, 1999.

Deloria, Philip J. "From Nation to Neighborhood: Land, Policy, Culture, Colonialism, and Empire in U.S.-Indian Relations." In *The Cultural Turn in U.S. History: Past, Present, and Future,* edited by James W. Cook, Lawrence B. Glickman, and Michael O'Malley, 343–82. Chicago: University of Chicago Press, 2009.

Delpit, Lisa D. *"Multiplication is for White People": Raising Expectations for Other People's Children.* New York: New Press, 2012.

Dewey, John. *Democracy and Education: An Introduction to the Philosophy of Education.* New York: The Macmillan Company, 1916.

Dimock, Wai-chee, and Lawrence Buell. *Shades of the Planet: American Literature as World Literature.* Princeton: Princeton University Press, 2007.

The Dish. Directed by Rob Sitch. 2000. Warner Brothers.

Donovan, Josephine. "The Unpublished Love Poems of Sarah Orne Jewett." *Frontiers: A Journal of Women Studies* 4, no. 3 (1979): 26–31.

Donovan, Josephine. *New England Local Color Literature: A Women's Tradition.* New York: F. Ungar Pub. Co., 1983.

Donovan, Josephine. "Jewett and Swedenborg." *American Literature* 65, no. 4 (1993): 731–50.

Donovan, Josephine. "Jewett on Race, Class, Ethnicity, and Imperialism: A Reply to Her Critics." *Colby Quarterly* 38, no. 4 (December 2002): 403–16.

Donovan, Josephine. *European Local-Color Literature: National Tales, Dorfgeschichten, Romans Champêtres.* New York: Continuum, 2010.

Doyle, James. *The Fin de Siècle Spirit: Walter Blackburn Harte and the American-Canadian Literary Milieu of the 1890s.* Toronto: ECW Press, 1995.

Doyle, Laura, and Regenia Gagnier. "The Global Circulation Project's Forum on Global Modernisms." *Literature Compass* 9, no. 9 (September 2012): 589–92.

Du Bois, W. E. Burghardt. "A Negro Schoolmaster in the New South." *Atlantic Monthly* 83, no. 1 (January 1899): 99–104.

Du Bois, W. E. B. *The Souls of Black Folk.* 1903. New York: Oxford University Press, 2007.

DuCille, Ann. *The Coupling Convention: Sex, Text, and Tradition in Black Women's Fiction.* New York: Oxford University Press, 1993.

Duck, Leigh Anne. *The Nation's Region: Southern Modernism, Segregation, and U.S. Nationalism.* Athens: University of Georgia Press, 2006.

[Eaton, Edith Maude.] Sui Sin Far. "A Draught of Bewilderment: A Tale of Modern China [first part]." *The Modern Priscilla* 22, no. 4 (June 1908): 5–6, 31–2.

[Eaton, Edith Maude.] Sui Sin Far. "A Draught of Bewilderment: A Tale of Modern China [second part]." *The Modern Priscilla* 22, no. 5 (July 1908): 21–2.

[Eaton, Edith Maude.] Sui Sin Far. "Leaves from the Mental Portfolio of an Eurasian." *Independent* 21 (1909): 125–32.

[Eaton, Edith Maude.] Sui Sin Far. "Word from Miss Eaton." *The Westerner: The Truth about the West* 11, no. 5 (November 1909). n.p.

[Eaton, Edith Maude.] Sui Sin Far. "A Word from 'Sui Sin Far.'" *The Westerner: The Truth about the West* 11, no. 5 (November 1909): 34–5.

[Eaton, Edith Maude.] Sui Sin Far. *Mrs. Spring Fragrance.* Chicago: A.C. McClurg & Co., 1912.

[Eaton, Edith Maude.] Sui Sin Far. *Mrs. Spring Fragrance and Other Writings*, edited by Amy Ling and Annette White-Parks. Urbana: University of Illinois Press, 1995.

[Eaton, Edith Maude.] Sui Sin Far. *Mrs. Spring Fragrance*, edited by Hsuan L. Hsu. Peterborough: Broadview Press, 2011.

Eaton, Edith Maude. "The Alaska Widow." *MELUS: Multi-Ethnic Literature of the U.S.* 38, no. 1 (Spring 2013): 164–70.

Eaton, Edith Maude. *Becoming Sui Sin Far: Early Fiction, Journalism, and Travel Writing.* Edited by Mary Chapman. Montreal: McGill-Queen's University Press, 2016.

Eggleston, Edward. *The Hoosier School-Master: A Novel.* New York: Orange Judd, 1871.

Eggleston, Edward. "Preface to the Library Edition: Being the History of a Story." In *The Hoosier Schoolmaster: A Story of Backwoods Life in Indiana, Revised with an Introduction and Notes on the District by the Author* [1892]. New York: Grosset & Dunlap, 1913.

Elliott, Michael A. *The Culture Concept: Writing and Difference in the Age of Realism.* Minneapolis: University of Minnesota Press, 2002.

Evans, Brad. *Before Cultures: The Ethnographic Imagination in American Literature, 1865–1920.* Chicago: University of Chicago Press, 2005.

Faulkner, William. *Requiem for a Nun.* New York: Random House, 1959.

Ferens, Dominika. *Edith and Winnifred Eaton: Chinatown Missions and Japanese Romances.* Urbana: University of Illinois Press, 2002.

Fetterley, Judith, and Marjorie Pryse. *Writing out of Place: Regionalism, Women, and American Literary Culture.* Urbana: University of Illinois Press, 2003.

Fields, Annie, ed. *Life and Letters of Harriet Beecher Stowe.* Boston: Houghton Mifflin Co., 1897.

Folsom, Marcia. "'Tact Is a Kind of Mind Reading': Empathic Style in Sarah Orne Jewett's The Country of Pointed Firs." *Colby Quarterly* 18, no. 1 (March 1982): 66–78.

Foote, Stephanie. *Regional Fictions: Culture and Identity in Nineteenth-Century American Literature.* Madison: University of Wisconsin Press, 2001.

Foster, Ruel E. *Jesse Stuart.* New York: Twayne Publishers, 1968.

Freeman, Mary Eleanor Wilkins. *A New England Nun and Other Stories*, edited by Sandra A. Zagarell. London: Penguin, 2000.

Freire, Paulo, et al. *Teachers as Cultural Workers: Letters to Those Who Dare Teach.* Boulder: Westview, 2005.

Frow, John. *Genre.* London: Routledge, 2006.

Frow, John. "'Reproducibles, Rubrics, and Everything You Need': Genre Theory Today." *PMLA* 122, no. 5 (2007): 1626–34.

Fuller, Wayne Edison. *One-Room Schools of the Middle West: An Illustrated History.* Lawrence: University Press of Kansas, 1994.

Gage, Cully [Charles Van Riper]. *The Northwoods Reader.* AuTrain: Avery Color Studios, 1983.

Gaines, Ernest J. *The Autobiography of Miss Jane Pittman.* New York: Dial Press, 1971.

Gaines, Ernest J. *A Lesson before Dying.* New York: Knopf, 1993.

Gaines, Ernest J. *Conversations with Ernest Gaines*, edited by John Lowe. Jackson: University Press of Mississippi, 1995.

Ganguly, Debjani. *This Thing Called the World: The Contemporary Novel as Global Form.* Durham: Duke University Press, 2016.

Garland, Hamlin. *Crumbling Idols: Twelve Essays on Art, Dealing Chiefly with Literature, Painting and the Drama* [1894], ed. Jane Johnson. Cambridge, MA: The Belknap Press of Harvard University Press, 1960.

Garland, Hamlin. *Main-Travelled Roads* [1891]. Lincoln: University of Nebraska Press, 1995.

Gaul, Theresa Strouth, and Sharon M. Harris, eds. *Letters and Cultural Transformations in the United States, 1760–1860*. London: Routledge, 2009.

Gaus, Paul L. *Blood of the Prodigal: An Ohio Amish Mystery*. Athens: Ohio State University Press, 1999.

Gaus, Paul L. *Broken English: An Ohio Amish Mystery*. Athens: Ohio State University Press, 2000.

Genthe, Arnold, and John Kuo Wei Tchen. *Genthe's Photographs of San Francisco's Old Chinatown*. New York: Dover Publications, 1984.

Giles, Paul. *The Global Remapping of American Literature*. Princeton: Princeton University Press, 2011.

Gitelman, Lisa. *Always Already New: Media, History, and the Data of Culture*. Cambridge: MIT Press, 2006.

Gladden, Washington. *Tools and the Man: Property and Industry under the Christian Law*. Boston: Houghton Mifflin, 1893.

Glazener, Nancy. *Reading for Realism: The History of a U.S. Literary Institution, 1850–1910*. Durham: Duke University Press, 1997.

Gleason, Patrick. "Sarah Orne Jewett's 'The Foreigner' and the Transamerican Routes of New England Regionalism." *Legacy* 28, no. 1 (2011): 24–46.

Goodrich, Samuel Griswold. "The Politician of Podunk." In *The Token and Atlantic Souvenir: A Christmas and New Year's Present*, 109–11. Boston: Otis, Broaders & Co., 1840.

Graff, Harvey J. *Literacy Myths, Legacies, & Lessons: New Studies on Literacy*. New Brunswick: Transaction Publishers, 2011.

Greene, Sarah Pratt McLean. *Cape Cod Folks*. Boston: De Wolfe, Fiske & Co., 1881.

Greeson, Jennifer Rae. *Our South: Geographic Fantasy and the Rise of National Literature*. Cambridge, MA: Harvard University Press, 2010.

Griswold, Wendy. *Regionalism and the Reading Class*. Chicago: University of Chicago Press, 2008.

Gulliford, Andrew. *America's Country Schools*. Washington, D.C.: Preservation Press, 1984.

Gura, Philip F. "The Real History of Men and Women: Edward Eggleston's *The Transit of Civilization*." *Reviews in American History* 17, no. 4 (1989): 639–47.

Habermas, Jürgen. *The Structural Transformation of the Public Sphere: An Inquiry into a Category of Bourgeois Society*. Cambridge, MA: MIT Press, 1989.

Hall, David D. *Worlds of Wonder, Days of Judgment: Popular Religious Belief in Early New England*. New York: Knopf/Random House, 1989.

Hamid, Mohsin. *Discontent and Its Civilizations: Dispatches from Lahore, New York, and London*. New York: Riverhead Books, 2015.

Hamid, Mohsin. *Exit West: A Novel*. New York: Riverhead Books, 2017.

Hancox, Dan. *The Village against the World*. London: Verso, 2013.

Harmon, Katharine. *You Are Here: Personal Geographies and Other Maps of the Imagination*. New York: Princeton Architectural Press, 2003.

Harmon, Katharine, and Gayle Clemans. *The Map as Art: Contemporary Artists Explore Cartography*. New York: Princeton Architectural Press, 2010.

Harte, Bret. *The Luck of Roaring Camp: And Other Sketches*. Boston: Fields, Osgood, & Co., 1870.

Harte, Bret. "The Rise of the 'Short Story.'" *Cornhill Magazine* 7, no. 37 (July 1899): 1–9.

Haruf, Kent. *Plainsong*. New York: Knopf/Random House, 1999.

Harzinski, Kris. *From Here to There: A Curious Collection from the Hand Drawn Map Association*. New York: Princeton Architectural Press, 2013.

Hayot, Eric. *On Literary Worlds*. New York: Oxford University Press, 2012.

Hebert, Ernest. *The Dogs of March*. New York: Viking Press, 1979.

Hebert, Ernest. *Whisper My Name*. New York: Viking, 1984.

Hebert, Ernest. *Live Free or Die*. New York: Viking, 1990.

Hebert, Ernest. *Never Back Down*. Boston: D. R. Godine, 2012.

Hebert, Ernest. *The Old American: A Novel*. Hanover: University Press of New England, 2012.

Hebert, Ernest. *Howard Elman's Farewell*. Hanover: University Press of New England, 2014.

Hebert, Ernest. *Spoonwood*. Hanover: University Press of New England, 2014.

Heise, Ursula K. *Sense of Place and Sense of Planet: The Environmental Imagination of the Global*. New York: Oxford University Press, 2008.

Hell, Julia and Andreas Schönle, eds. *Ruins of Modernity*. Durham: Duke University Press, 2008.

Heller, Terry. "Living for the Other World: Sarah Orne Jewett as a Religious Writer." In *Spectral America: Phantoms and the National Imagination*, edited by Jeffrey Andrew Weinstock, 78–100. Madison: University of Wisconsin Press/Popular Press, 2004.

Heller, Terry. "Eunice and the Jade Gods: Jewett's Religious Rhetoric in A Country Doctor." *Legacy* 22, no. 2 (2005): 158–75.

Hill, Christopher L. "The Travels of Naturalism and the Challenges of a World Literary History." *Literature Compass* 6, no. 6 (November 2009): 1198–210.

Hitchcock, Bert. *Richard Malcolm Johnston*. Boston: Twayne Publishers, 1978.

Hobsbawm, E. J, and T. O. Ranger, eds. *The Invention of Tradition*. New York: Cambridge University Press, 1983.

Holbo, Christine. "Hamlin Garland's 'Modernism.'" *ELH* 80, no. 4 (2013): 1205–36.

Homestead, Melissa J., and Terry Heller. "'The Other One': An Unpublished Chapter of Sarah Orne Jewett's *The Country of the Pointed Firs*." *J19: The Journal of Nineteenth-Century Americanists* 2, no. 2 (2014): 331–65.

Hönnighausen, Lothar, and Marc Frey, James Peacock, and Niklaus Steiner, eds. *Regionalism in the Age of Globalism: Concepts of Regionalism*. Madison: Center for the Study of Upper Midwestern Cultures, University of Wisconsin-Madison Press, 2005.

Howard, June. *New Essays on The Country of the Pointed Firs*. New York: Cambridge University Press, 1994.

Howard, June. *Publishing the Family*. Durham: Duke University Press, 2001.

Howard, June. "Sand in Your Mouth: Naturalism and Other Genres." In *Oxford Handbook of American Literary Naturalism*, edited by Keith Newlin, 92–103. New York: Oxford University Press, 2011.

Howard, June. "Here/There, Now/Then, Both/And: Regionalism and Cosmopolitanism in Edith Wharton's *Old New York*." In *Edith Wharton and Cosmopolitanism*, edited by Meredith L. Goldsmith and Emily J. Orlando, 166–83. Gainesville: University Press of Florida, 2016.

Howells, William Dean. *Literary Friends and Acquaintance: A Personal Retrospect of American Authorship*. New York: Harper & Brothers, 1900.

Hsu, Hsuan L. *Geography and the Production of Space in Nineteenth-Century American Literature*. New York: Cambridge University Press, 2010.

Hutcheon, Linda, and Mario J. Valdés. *Rethinking Literary History: A Dialogue on Theory*. New York: Oxford University Press, 2002.

Hutner, Gordon. *What America Read: Taste, Class, and the Novel, 1920–1960*. Chapel Hill: University of North Carolina Press, 2009.

Irmscher, Christoph, and Robert Arbour, eds. *Reconsidering Longfellow*. Madison: Fairleigh Dickinson University Press, 2014.

Irmscher, Christoph. "Longfellow Redux." *Raritan* 21 (2002): 100–29.

Jackson, Korey B. *Literatures of Language: A Literary History of Linguistics in Nineteenth-Century America*. PhD diss., University of Michigan, 2011.

James, Henry. "The Jolly Corner." *The English Review*, December 1, 1908.

James, Henry. *The Tragic Muse*. New York: Charles Scribner's Sons, 1908.

Jameson, Fredric. *The Antinomies of Realism*. London: Verso, 2013.

Jen, Gish. *World and Town: A Novel*. New York: Knopf/Random House, 2010.

Jewett, Sarah Orne. *Old Friends and New*. Boston: Houghton, Osgood, 1879.

Jewett, Sarah Orne. *The King of Folly Island, and Other People*. Boston: Houghton Mifflin, 1888.

Jewett, Sarah Orne. *Betty Leicester: A Story for Girls*. Boston: Houghton Mifflin, 1889.

Jewett, Sarah Orne. *Tales of New England*. Boston: Houghton Mifflin, 1890.

Jewett, Sarah Orne. *Deephaven*. Boston: Houghton Mifflin, 1893.

Jewett, Sarah Orne. "The Old Town of Berwick." *New England Magazine* 16 [new series 10] (July 1894): 585–609.

Jewett, Sarah Orne. *The Country of the Pointed Firs*. Boston: Houghton Mifflin, 1896.

Jewett, Sarah Orne. *The Queen's Twin*. Boston: Houghton Mifflin, 1899.

Jewett, Sarah Orne. *Letters of Sarah Orne Jewett*, edited by Annie Fields. Boston: Houghton Mifflin, 1911.

Jewett, Sarah Orne. *Sarah Orne Jewett Letters*, enlarged and revised, ed. Richard Cary. Waterville: Colby College Press, 1967.

Jewett, Sarah Orne. *The Country of the Pointed Firs, and Other Stories*, ed. and introd. Mary Ellen Chase. New York: W. W. Norton, 1968.

Jewett, Sarah Orne. *The Uncollected Short Stories of Sarah Orne Jewett*, edited by Richard Cary. Waterville: Colby College Press, 1971.

Jewett, Sarah Orne. *Sarah Orne Jewett: Novels and Stories*, ed. Michael Davitt Bell. New York: Library of America, 1994.

Jewett, Sarah Orne. *The Irish Stories of Sarah Orne Jewett*, edited by Jack Morgan and Louis A. Renza. Carbondale: Southern Illinois University Press, 1996.

Johanningsmeier, Charles. *Fiction and the American Literary Marketplace: The Role of Newspaper Syndicates, 1860–1900*. New York: Cambridge University Press, 1997.

Johanningsmeier, Charles. "Sarah Orne Jewett and Mary E. Wilkins (Freeman): Two Shrewd Businesswomen in Search of New Markets." *The New England Quarterly* 70, no. 1 (1997): 57–82.

Johanningsmeier, Charles. "Welcome Guests or Representatives of the 'Mal-Odorous Class'? Periodicals and Their Readers in American Public Libraries, 1876–1914." *Libraries & Culture* 39, no. 3 (2004): 260–92.

Johanningsmeier, Charles. "Realism, Naturalism, and American Public Libraries, 1880–1914." *American Literary Realism* 48, no. 1 (2015): 1–24.

Johnson, Victoria E. *Heartland TV: Prime Time Television and the Struggle for U.S. Identity*. New York: New York University Press, 2008.

Johnston, Richard Malcolm. *Dukesborough Tales; the Chronicles of Mr. Bill Williams* [1871, 1892]. Ridgewood: Gregg Press, 1968.

Jones, Gavin. *Strange Talk: The Politics of Dialect Literature in Gilded Age America*. Berkeley: University of California Press, 1999.

Jones, Gavin. *Failure and the American Writer: A Literary History*. New York: Cambridge University Press, 2014.

Joseph, Philip. *American Literary Regionalism in a Global Age*. Baton Rouge: Louisiana State University Press, 2007.

Kaestle, Carl F., Helen Damon Moore, Lawrence Stedman, Katherine Tinsley. *Literacy in the United States: Readers and Reading since 1880*. New Haven: Yale University Press, 1991.

Kalman, Bobbie. *A One-Room School*. New York: Crabtree, 1994.

Kandiyoti, Dalia. *Migrant Sites: America, Place, and Diaspora Literatures*. Hanover: University Press of New England, 2009.

Kaplan, Amy. "Nation, Region, and Empire." In *Columbia History of the American Novel*, edited by Emory Elliott, 240–66. New York: Columbia University Press, 1991.

Kaplan, Amy. *The Social Construction of American Realism*. Chicago: University of Chicago Press, 1988.

Karem, Jeff. *The Romance of Authenticity: The Cultural Politics of Regional and Ethnic Literatures*. Charlottesville: University of Virginia Press, 2004.

Keithan, Mary. *Michigan One-Room Schoolhouses*. Ann Arbor: University of Michigan Press, 2008.

Keller, Julia. *Bitter River*. New York: Minotaur Books, 2013.

Kennedy, Raymond. *The Romance of Eleanor Gray: A Novel*. Hanover: University Press of New England, 2003.

Kilcup, Karen L., and Thomas S. Edwards, eds. *Jewett and Her Contemporaries: Reshaping the Canon*. Gainesville: University Press of Florida, 1999.

Lahiri, Jhumpa. *The Lowland: A Novel*. New York: Knopf/Random House, 2013.

Lai, H[im] M[ark]. "The Chinese-American Press." In *The Ethnic Press in the United States: A Historical Analysis and Handbook*, edited by Sally M. Miller, 27–43. New York: Greenwood Press, 1987.

Lai, Larissa. *Slanting I, Imagining We: Asian Canadian Literary Production in the 1980s and 1990s*. Waterloo, Ontario: Wilfrid Laurier University Press, 2014.

Lauck, Jon K. *From Warm Center to Ragged Edge: The Erosion of Midwestern Literary and Historical Regionalism, 1920–1965*. Iowa City: University of Iowa Press, 2017.

Laurence, Margaret. *A Jest of God*. New York: Knopf, 1966.

Lauter, Paul, and J. Bruce-Novoa, eds. *The Heath Anthology of American Literature*. Lexington: D.C. Heath, 1990.

Lazier, Benjamin. "Earthrise; or, The Globalization of the World Picture." *The American Historical Review* 116, no. 3 (June 1, 2011): 602–30.

Lear, Bernadette A. "Libraries and Reading Culture at the Carlisle Indian Industrial School, 1879–1918." *Book History* 18, no. 1 (2015): 166–96.

Le Guin, Ursula K. *The Left Hand of Darkness*. New York: Harper & Row, 1969.

Le Guin, Ursula K. *Four Ways to Forgiveness*. New York: HarperPrism, 1995.

Lee, Anthony W. *Picturing Chinatown: Art and Orientalism in San Francisco*. Berkeley: University of California Press, 2001.

Lee, Rachel C. "Journalistic Representations of Asian Americans and Literary Responses, 1910–1920." In *An Interethnic Companion to Asian American Literature*, edited by King-Kok Cheung, 249–73. New York: Cambridge University Press, 1997.

Lefebvre, Henri. *The Production of Space*, translated by Donald Nicholson-Smith. Hoboken: Wiley Blackwell, 1991.

Levander, Caroline Field. *Where Is American Literature?* Hoboken: Wiley Blackwell, 2013.

Levin, Janna. *How the Universe Got Its Spots: Diary of a Finite Time in a Finite Space.* Princeton: Princeton University Press, 2002.

Levine, Lawrence W. *Highbrow/Lowbrow: The Emergence of Cultural Hierarchy in America.* Cambridge, MA: Harvard University Press, 1988.

Lewis, David L. *W.E.B. Du Bois.* New York: H. Holt, 1993.

Lewis, G. Malcolm, ed. *Cartographic Encounters: Perspectives on Native American Mapmaking and Map Use.* Chicago: University of Chicago Press, 1998.

Ling, Amy. *Between Worlds: Women Writers of Chinese Ancestry.* New York: Pergamon Press, 1990.

Lockwood, J. Samaine. *Archives of Desire: The Queer Historical Work of New England Regionalism.* Chapel Hill: University of North Carolina Press, 2015.

Lomawaima, K. Tsianina, and T. L. McCarty. *To Remain an Indian: Lessons in Democracy from a Century of Native American Education.* New York: Teachers College Press, 2006.

Longfellow, Henry Wadsworth. *The Belfry of Bruges and Other Poems.* Boston: J. Owen, 1846.

Loughran, Trish. *The Republic in Print: Print Culture in the Age of U.S. Nation Building, 1770–1870.* New York: Columbia University Press, 2007.

Louie, Andrea. *Chineseness across Borders: Renegotiating Chinese Identities in China and the United States.* Durham: Duke University Press, 2004.

Lowe, Lisa. *Immigrant Acts: On Asian American Cultural Politics.* Durham: Duke University Press, 1996.

Lutz, Catherine A. and Jane L. Collins. *Reading National Geographic.* Chicago: University of Chicago Press, 1993.

Lutz, Tom. *Cosmopolitan Vistas: American Regionalism and Literary Value.* Ithaca: Cornell University Press, 2004.

Lyons, Scott Richard, ed. *The World, the Text, and the Indian: Global Dimensions of Native American Literature.* Albany: State University of New York Press, 2017.

MacLeod, Kirsten. *American Little Magazines of the Fin de Siècle: Art, Protest, and Social Transformation.* Toronto: University of Toronto Press, 2018.

Mandala, Susan. "Crime Fiction as Regional Fiction: An Analysis of Dialect and Point of View in Sheila Quigley's *Bad Moon Rising.*" *Style* 46, no. 2 (2012): 177–200.

Marshall, Catherine. *Christy.* New York: McGraw-Hill, 1967.

Martin, Jay. *Harvests of Change: American Literature, 1865–1914.* Englewood Cliffs: Prentice-Hall, 1967.

Martin, William Alexander Parsons. *Hanlin Papers, or Essays on the Intellectual Life of the Chinese.* London: Trübner & Company, 1880.

Martin, William Alexander Parsons. *Chinese Legends and Other Poems.* Shanghai: Kelley & Walsh, 1894.

Massey, Doreen B. *Space, Place, and Gender.* Minneapolis: University of Minnesota Press, 1994.

Massie, Sonja, and Martin Harry Greenberg, eds. *The Janet Dailey Companion: A Comprehensive Guide to Her Life and Her Novels.* New York: Harpercollins, 1996.

Matthiessen, F. O. *Sarah Orne Jewett.* Boston and New York: Houghton Mifflin, 1929.

McCann, Colum. *Let the Great World Spin: A Novel.* New York: Random House, 2009.

McCourt, Frank. *Angela's Ashes: A Memoir*. New York: Scribner, 1996.

McCourt, Frank. *'Tis: A Memoir*. New York: Scribner, 1999.

McCourt, Frank. *Teacher Man: A Memoir*. New York: Scribner, 2005.

McCracken, Elizabeth. *The Women of America*. New York: Macmillan, 1905.

McCullough, Kate. *Regions of Identity: The Construction of America in Women's Fiction, 1885–1914*. Stanford: Stanford University Press, 1999.

McGurl, Mark. *The Program Era: Postwar Fiction and the Rise of Creative Writing*. Cambridge, MA: Harvard University Press, 2011.

McHenry, Elizabeth. *Forgotten Readers: Recovering the Lost History of African American Literary Societies*. Durham: Duke University Press, 2002.

McNickle, D'Arcy. *Wind from an Enemy Sky* [1978]. Afterword by Louis Owens. Albuquerque: University of New Mexico Press, 1988.

Mengestu, Dinaw. *All Our Names*. New York: Alfred A. Knopf, 2014.

Mignolo, Walter D. *Local Histories/Global Designs: Coloniality, Subaltern Knowledges, and Border Thinking*. Princeton: Princeton University Press, 2012.

Miller, Joshua L. *Accented America: The Cultural Politics of Multilingual Modernism*. New York: Oxford University Press, 2011.

Montgomery, Michael. "Myth 9: In the Appalachians They Speak Like Shakespeare." In *Language Myths*, edited by Laurie Bauer and Peter Trudgill, 66–76. New York: Penguin, 1999.

Mott, Frank Luther. *A History of American Magazines*. 5 vols. Cambridge, MA: Harvard University Press, 1938.

Nabokov, Peter. "Orientations from Their Side: Dimensions of Native American Cartographic Discourse (Chapter 11)." In *Cartographic Encounters: Perspectives on Native American Mapmaking and Map Use*, 241–69. Chicago: University of Chicago Press, 1998.

Naipaul, V. S. *A Bend in the River*. New York: Knopf /Random House, 1979.

Ng, Fae Myenne. *Bone*. New York: Hyperion, 1993.

Ngai, Mae M. *The Lucky Ones: One Family and the Extraordinary Invention of Chinese America*. Boston: Houghton Mifflin Harcourt, 2010.

Nurhussein, Nadia. *Rhetorics of Literacy: The Cultivation of American Dialect Poetry*. Columbus: Ohio State University Press, 2013.

Okker, Patricia, ed. *Transnationalism and American Serial Fiction*. New York: Routledge, 2012.

Oliviere, Lucia Newell. *Old Houses*. New York: Press of O.A. Randel, Inc., 1928.

Ostergren, Robert. "Concepts of Region: A Geographical Perspective." In *Regionalism in the Age of Globalism: Concepts of Regionalism*, edited by Lothar Hönnighausen et al., 1–14. Madison: Center for the Study of Upper Midwestern Cultures, University of Wisconsin-Madison Press, 2005.

Partridge, Jeffrey F. L. *Beyond Literary Chinatown*. Seattle: University of Washington Press, 2007.

Pawley, Christine. *Reading on the Middle Border: The Culture of Print in Late Nineteenth-Century Osage, Iowa*. Amherst: University of Massachusetts Press, 2001.

Perkins, David. *Is Literary History Possible?* Baltimore: Johns Hopkins University Press, 1992.

Perry, Theresa, et al. *Quality Education as a Constitutional Right: Creating a Grassroots Movement to Transform Public Schools*. Boston: Beacon Press, 2010.

Posey, Alexander Lawrence. *The Fus Fixico Letters*, ed. Daniel F. Littlefield and Carol A. Petty Hunter. Lincoln: University of Nebraska Press, 1993.

Proust, Marcel, trans. Lydia Davis, ed. Christopher Prendergast. *Swann's Way*. New York: Viking, 2003.

Radway, Janice A. *Reading the Romance: Women, Patriarchy and Popular Literature*. Chapel Hill: University of North Carolina Press, 1984.

Rains, James W., Jr. *Today Speaks in Yesterday's Voice: Writing American Indians into History in the Fiction of D'Arcy McNickle*. PhD diss., University of Michigan, 2004.

Randel, William Peirce. *Edward Eggleston, Author of The Hoosier School-Master*. New York: King's Crown Press, 1946.

Reck, Gregory, and Una Mae. "Living Is More Important than Schooling: Schools and Self-Concept in Appalachia." *Appalachian Journal* 8, no. 1 (1980): 19–25.

Regis, Pamela. *A Natural History of the Romance Novel*. Philadelphia: University of Pennsylvania Press, 2003.

Reichert Powell, Douglas. *Critical Regionalism: Connecting Politics and Culture in the American Landscape*. Chapel Hill: University of North Carolina Press, 2007.

Renan, Ernest. *Qu'est-ce qu'une nation? Conference faite en Sorbonne, le 11 Mars 1882*, 2nd ed. Paris: Michel Lévy Frères, 1882.

Renan, Ernest. "What Is a Nation?" trans. Martin Thom. In *Becoming National: A Reader*, edited by Geoff Eley and Ronald Grigor Suny, 42–55. New York: Oxford University Press, 1996.

Rexroth, Kenneth. *Love and the Turning Year: One Hundred More Poems from the Chinese*. New York: New Directions, 1970.

Ring, Natalie J. *The Problem South: Region, Empire, and the New Liberal State, 1880–1930*. Athens: University of Georgia Press, 2012.

Rioux, Anne Boyd. *Constance Fenimore Woolson: Portrait of a Lady Novelist*. 1st edition. New York: W. W. Norton & Company, 2016.

Robinson, Kim Stanley. *Red Mars*. New York: Bantam Books, 1993.

Robinson, Marilynne. *Housekeeping*. New York: Farrar Straus Giroux, 1980.

Robinson, Marilynne. *Gilead: A Novel*. New York: Farrar Straus Giroux, 2004.

Robinson, Marilynne. *Lila*. New York: Farrar Straus Giroux, 2014.

Rocheleau, Paul. *The One-Room Schoolhouse*. New York: Universe, 2003.

Rockwell, David B; revisions by Bill Swaney. *Člq̓étkʷ ntx̣ʷ étkʷs 'a·kinmituk: The Lower Flathead River, Flathead Indian Reservation, Montana: A Cultural, Historical and Scientific Resource*. Pablo: Salish Kootenai College Press, 2008.

Rose, Mike. *Why School? Reclaiming Education for All of Us*. New York: New Press, 2009.

Rosen, Jeremy. "An Insatiable Market for Minor Characters: Genre in the Contemporary Literary Marketplace." *New Literary History* 46, no. 1 (2015): 143–63.

Ryden, Kent C. *Landscape with Figures: Nature and Culture in New England*. Iowa City: University of Iowa Press, 2001.

Ryden, Kent C. *Sum of the Parts: The Mathematics and Politics of Region, Place, and Writing*. Iowa City: University of Iowa Press, 2011.

Santos, Boaventura de Sousa. *Another Knowledge Is Possible: Beyond Northern Epistemologies*. London: Verso, 2007.

Satterwhite, Emily. *Dear Appalachia: Readers, Identity, and Popular Fiction since 1878*. Lexington: University Press of Kentucky, 2011.

Sausssure, Ferdinand de. *Course in General Linguistics.* New York: McGraw-Hill Book Co., 1966.

Schrag, Mitzi. "'Whiteness' as Loss in Sarah Orne Jewett's 'The Foreigner.'" In *Jewett and Her Contemporaries: Reshaping the Canon,* edited by Karen L. Kilcup and Thomas S. Edwards, 185–206. Gainesville: University Press of Florida, 1999.

Schroeder, Jonathan David Shelly. "The Painting of Modern Light: Local Color before Regionalism." *American Literature* 86, no. 3 (September 1, 2014): 551–81.

Shannon, Laurie. "'The Country of Our Friendship': Jewett's Intimist Art." *American Literature* 71, no. 2 (1999): 227–62.

Shaw, Paul. "Stereotypes." *Print* (August 2008): 109–10.

Sherman, Sarah Way. *Sarah Orne Jewett: An American Persephone.* Hanover: University Press of New England, 1989.

Shih, David. "The Seduction of Origins: Sui Sin Far and the Race for Tradition." In *Form and Transformation in Asian American Literature,* edited by Zhou Xiaojing and Samina Najmi, 48–76. Seattle: University of Washington Press, 2005.

Silber, Nina. *The Romance of Reunion: Northerners and the South, 1865–1900.* Chapel Hill: University of North Carolina Press, 1993.

Silber, Nina. "Reunion and Reconciliation, Reviewed and Reconsidered." *Journal of American History* 103, no. 1 (June 1, 2016): 59–83.

Smith, Jon, and Deborah Cohn, eds. *Look Away! The U.S. South in New World Studies.* Durham: Duke University Press, 2004.

Sollors, Werner, ed. *Multilingual America: Transnationalism, Ethnicity, and the Languages of American Literature.* New York: New York University Press, 1998.

Sorby, Angela. *Schoolroom Poets: Childhood and the Place of American Poetry, 1865–1917.* Hanover: University of New Hampshire Press, 2005.

Steedman, Carolyn. *Strange Dislocations: Childhood and the Idea of Human Interiority, 1780–1930.* London: Virago Press, 1995.

Stegner, Wallace. *Crossing to Safety.* New York: Random House, 1987.

Still, James. *The Hills Remember: The Complete Short Stories of James Still,* edited by Ted Olson and Teresa Perry Reynolds. Lexington: University Press of Kentucky, 2012.

Stowe, Harriet Beecher. "Uncle Lot." In *The Mayflower, and Miscellaneous Writings,* 9–42. Boston: Phillips, Sampson, and Company, 1855.

Stowe, Harriet Beecher. *The Pearl of Orr's Island: A Story of the Coast of Maine.* Ridgewood: Gregg Press, 1967.

Strout, Elizabeth. *Olive Kitteridge.* New York: Random House, 2008.

Strout, Elizabeth. *The Burgess Boys: A Novel.* New York: Random House, 2013.

Strychacz, Thomas. "The Kitchen Economics of Sarah Orne Jewett's *The Country of the Pointed Firs.*" *Legacy* 32, no. 1 (2015): 53–74.

Stuart, Jesse. *The Thread That Runs So True* [1949]. New York: Scribner, 1958.

Stuart, Jesse. *The Best-Loved Short Stories of Jesse Stuart,* edited by H. Edward Richardson. New York: McGraw-Hill, 1982.

Stuart, Jesse. *Jesse Stuart on Education,* edited by J. R. LeMaster. Lexington: University Press of Kentucky, 1992.

Tocqueville, Alexis de. *Democracy in America,* trans. Harvey C. Mansfield and Delba Winthrop. Chicago: University of Chicago Press, 2000.

Todt, Donn L. "Relict Gold: The Long Journey of the Chinese Narcissus." *Pacific Horticulture* 73, no. 1 (2012): 42–5.

Tokarczuk, Olga. *Primeval and Other Times*, trans. Antonia Lloyd-Jones. Prague: Twisted Spoon Press, 2010.

Totten, Gary. "Zitkala-Sa and the Problem of Regionalism: Nations, Narratives, and Critical Traditions." *The American Indian Quarterly* 29, no. 1 (2005): 84–123.

Truettner, William H., and Roger B Stein, eds. *Picturing Old New England: Image and Memory*. New Haven and Washington, D.C.: Yale University Press and the Smithsonian, 1999.

Tsing, Anna Lowenhaupt. *Friction: An Ethnography of Global Connection*. Princeton: Princeton University Press, 2005.

Tsing, Anna Lowenhaupt. *The Mushroom at the End of the World: On the Possibility of Life in Capitalist Ruins*. Princeton: Princeton University Press, 2015.

Tuan, Yi-Fu. *Space and Place: The Perspective of Experience*. Minneapolis: University of Minnesota Press, 1977.

Twain, Mark. *Collected Tales, Sketches, Speeches & Essays: 1852–1890*, edited by Louis J. Budd. New York: The Library of America, 1992.

Vigil, Kiara M. *Indigenous Intellectuals: Sovereignty, Citizenship, and the American Imagination, 1880–1930*. New York: Cambridge University Press, 2015.

Vogelius, Christa Holm. "'Kéramos' in Harper's: The Contexts of Global Collection." *American Periodicals: A Journal of History & Criticism* 23, no. 2 (2013): 142–55.

Wadsworth, Sarah. *In the Company of Books: Literature and its "Classes" in Nineteenth-Century America*. Amherst: University of Massachusetts Press, 2006.

Warner, Michael. *Publics and Counterpublics*. New York: Zone Books, 2005.

Warren, Kenneth W. *What Was African American Literature?* Cambridge, MA: Harvard University Press, 2011.

Watts, Edward. *An American Colony: Regionalism and the Roots of Midwestern Culture*. Athens: Ohio University Press, 2001.

Webb, Dorothy Ann. *Particular Places: Local Color Writing in the United States 1870–1910*. PhD diss., University of Michigan, 1997.

Weber, Clara Carter, and Carl Jefferson Weber. *A Bibliography of the Published Writings of Sarah Orne Jewett*. Waterville: Colby College Press, 1949.

Weber, Eugen. *Peasants into Frenchmen: The Modernization of Rural France, 1870–1914*. Stanford: Stanford University Press, 1976.

Westad, Odd Arne. *Restless Empire: China and the World since 1750*. New York: Basic Books, 2012.

Westbrook, Perry D. *Acres of Flint: Writers of Rural New England, 1870–1900*. Washington, D.C.: Scarecrow Press, 1951.

White-Parks, Annette. *Sui Sin Far/Edith Maude Eaton: A Literary Biography*. Urbana: University of Illinois Press, 1995.

White-Parks, Annette. "Edith and Winnifred Eaton: Chinatown Missions and Japanese Romances (Review)." *Legacy* 20, no. 1 (Nov. 2003): 197–8.

Williams, Raymond. *Border Country: A Novel*. New York: Horizon Press, 1962.

Williams, Raymond. *The Country and the City*. New York: Oxford University Press, 1973.

Williams, Raymond. *Writing in Society*. London: Verso, 1983.

Willis, Lloyd. "Henry Wadsworth Longfellow, United States National Literature, and the Canonical Erasure of Material Nature." *American Transcendental Quarterly* 20 (2006): 629–46.

Willis, Lloyd. *Environmental Evasion: The Literary, Critical, and Cultural Politics of "Nature's Nation."* Albany: State University of New York Press, 2011.

Winter, Kate H. *The Woman in the Mountain: Reconstructions of Self and Land by Adirondack Women Writers.* Albany: State University of New York Press, 1989.

Witgen, Michael J. *An Infinity of Nations: How the Native New World Shaped Early North America.* Philadelphia: University of Pennsylvania Press, 2012.

Wong, Sau-ling Cynthia. *Reading Asian American Literature: From Necessity to Extravagance.* Princeton: Princeton University Press, 1993.

Wood, Denis. *Rethinking the Power of Maps.* New York: Guilford Press, 2010.

Wood, Denis. *Everything Sings: Maps for a Narrative Atlas.* 2nd revised edition. Los Angeles: Siglio, 2013.

Wood, Joseph Sutherland, and Michael Steinitz. *The New England Village.* Baltimore: Johns Hopkins University Press, 1997.

Woolson, Constance Fenimore. *For the Major and Selected Short Stories*, ed. Rayburn S. Moore. New Haven: College & University Press, 1967.

Yamashita, Karen Tei. *I Hotel: A Novel.* Minneapolis: Coffee House Press, 2010.

Yin, Xiao-huang. *Chinese American Literature since the 1850s.* Urbana: University of Illinois Press, 2000.

Yoshihara, Mari. "Putting on the Voice of the Orient: Gender and Sexuality in Amy Lowell's 'Asian' Poetry." In *Amy Lowell, American Modern*, edited by Adrienne Munch and Melissa Bradshaw, 120–35. New Brunswick: Rutgers University Press, 2004.

Yourcenar, Marguerite. *Memoirs of Hadrian*, translated by Grace Frick. New York: Farrar, Straus and Young, 1954.

Zagarell, Sandra A. "Narrative of Community: The Identification of a Genre." *Signs* 13, no. 3 (1988): 498–527.

Zagarell, Sandra A. "Crosscurrents: Registers of Nordicism, Community, and Culture in Jewett's *Country of the Pointed Firs.*" *The Yale Journal of Criticism* 10, no. 2 (1997): 355–70.

Zencey, Eric. *Virgin Forest: Meditations on History, Ecology, and Culture.* Athens: University of Georgia Press, 2000.

Zhou, Xiaojing, and Samina Najmi. *Form and Transformation in Asian American Literature.* Seattle: University of Washington Press, 2005.

Zimmerman, Jonathan. *Small Wonder: The Little Red Schoolhouse in History and Memory.* New Haven: Yale University Press, 2009.

Web-Based Sources

"2009 National Book Award Winner Fiction—Interview with Colum McCann—National Book Foundation." Accessed October 1, 2016. http://www.nationalbook.org/nba2009_f_mccann_interv.html#.V-86FT_klGA.

Ali, Christopher and Damian Radcliffe. "8 Strategies for Saving Local Newsrooms." November 6, 2017. Accessed December 14, 2017. *Columbia Journalism Review*, https://www.cjr.org/tow_center/8-strategies-saving-local-newsrooms.php.

"Amazon Book List Reveals What's Hot in American Regional Cuisine." *NPR.org.* Accessed September 23, 2016. http://www.npr.org/sections/thesalt/2014/04/29/307770050/a-cookbook-map-reveals-whats-hot-in-american-regional-cuisine.

"Amish-Country Mysteries." *P.L. Gaus.* Accessed August 31, 2017. http://plgaus.com/.

"Anticipation Guide for 'Split Cherry Tree' by Jesse Stuart." *Teachers Pay Teachers*. Accessed August 13, 2016. http://www.teacherspayteachers.com/Product/Anticipation-Guide-for-Split-Cherry-Tree-by-Jesse-Stuart.

Association of European Border Regions. Accessed August 27, 2017. http://www.aebr.eu/en/members/border_regions.php.

"Brown-Headed Cowbird." *Audubon*. Accessed November 13, 2014. http://www.audubon.org/field-guide/bird/brown-headed-cowbird.

Carkonen, Shawn. Amazon.com review, *Teacher Man*, by Frank McCourt. Accessed August 16, 2017. https://www.amazon.com/Teacher-Man-Memoir-Frank-McCourt/dp/0743294173.

"Catherine Marshall." The Christy Awards. Accessed September 13, 2016. http://www.christyawards.com/ca_new/index.php?option=com_content&view=article&id=74:catherine-marshall&catid=40:about&Itemid=57.

"Collegiality." *Wikipedia*, August 24, 2017. Accessed December 15, 2017. https://en.wikipedia.org/w/index.php?title=Collegiality&oldid=796992234.

Committee of Regions. "Mission Statement." European Union, April 21, 2009. http://cor.europa.eu/en/about/Pages/mission-statement.aspx

Gross, Essa L. "Getting a Master's in Social Geology." *Earth: The Science behind the Headlines*, September 24, 2009. http://www.earthmagazine.org/article/getting-masters-social-geology.

"Guide to the Darby Chronicles | Ernest Hebert Guide to the Darby Chronicles." Accessed September 21, 2014. http://erniehebert.com/category/guide-to-the-darby-chronicles/.

Hahn, Bob. "Country Crime: Six Regional Mystery Authors." *PublishersWeekly.Com*, May 2012. https://www.publishersweekly.com/pw/by-topic/new-titles/adult-announcements/article/51821-country-crime-six-regional-mystery-authors.html.

Igou, Brad. "Amish on TV," Amish Country News. Accessed December 3, 2017. http://www.amishnews.com/amisharticles/amishinmedia.htm#Part 4: AMISH ON TV.

Ireland, Corydon. "The Many Lives of Henry Wadsworth Longfellow." *Harvard Gazette*. Accessed September 23, 2016. http://news.harvard.edu/gazette/story/2007/02/the-many-lives-of-henry-wadsworth-longfellow/.

"Janet Dailey." *HarperCollins US*. Accessed September 23, 2016. http://www.harpercollins.com/cr-103861/janet-dailey.

Lewin, Tamar. "Many States Adopt National Standards for Their Schools." *The New York Times*, July 21, 2010. http://www.nytimes.com/2010/07/21/education/21standards.html.

"Longfellow Institute Home Page." Accessed September 23, 2016. http://www.fas.harvard.edu/~lowinus/.

"Lucia Newell Oliviere." *Grems-Doolittle Library Collections Blog*, March 8, 2012. http://gremsdoolittlelibrary.blogspot.com/2012/03/lucia-newell-oliviere.html.

McMillan, Graeme. "Don't Call It a Reboot: The Strange Case of Murder, She Wrote." *Time*. http://entertainment.time.com/2014/01/22.

Monmaney, Terence. "No Place Like Home." *Smithsonian*. Accessed September 23, 2016. http://www.smithsonianmag.com/science-nature/no-place-like-home-1-73426396/.

Moss, Stephen. "Hinterland—the TV Noir So Good They Made It Twice." *The Guardian*, July 30, 2013, sec. Television & radio. https://www.theguardian.com/tv-and-radio/2013/jul/30/hinterland-tv-noir-wales.

"Mr. Wendell Berry of Kentucky." *Mr. Wendell Berry of Kentucky*. Accessed September 23, 2016. http://brtom.typepad.com/wberry/.

"Nasa's First Close-up Images of Pluto to Come to Canberra Tracking Station | Science | The Guardian." Accessed October 2, 2016. https://www.theguardian.com/science/2015/jul/14/nasas-first-close-up-images-of-pluto-to-come-to-canberra-tracking-station.

Okamoto, Lisa. "Five Reasons Why People Code-Switch." *NPR.org*. Accessed September 23, 2016. http://www.npr.org/sections/codeswitch/2013/04/13/177126294/five-reasons-why-people-code-switch.

"Oldest Dated Rocks—Wikipedia, the Free Encyclopedia." Accessed September 23, 2016. https://en.wikipedia.org/wiki/Oldest_dated_rocks#Oldest_terrestrial_material.

"Our Mission," GroundTruth Project. Accessed December 13, 2017. http://thegroundtruth-project.org/about/.

"Raymond Kennedy, Novelist, Dies at 73." *The New York Times*, February 23, 2008. https://www.nytimes.com/2008/02/23/books/23kennedy.html.

Rehoboth Beach-Dewey Beach Chamber of Commerce. Accessed October 22, 2017. http://www.visitdelaware.com/listings/rehoboth-beach-dewey-beach-chamber-of-commerce/1521/.

Rushdie, Salman. "Gabriel García Márquez's Work Was Rooted in the Real." *The New York Times*, April 21, 2014. http://www.nytimes.com/2014/04/21/books/review/gabriel-garcia-marquezs-work-was-rooted-in-the-real.html.

"Sarah Orne Jewett Text Project." Accessed January 28, 2016. http://public.coe.edu/~theller/soj/contents.htm.

"The Schuman Declaration—9 May 1950." *European Union Website, the Official EU Website—European Commission*. Accessed June 16, 2016. https://europa.eu/european-union/about-eu/symbols/europe-day/schuman-declaration_en.

Sister Mary Murderous [pseud.], "Cabot Cove: Murder Capital of the World." *Read Me Deadly*. Accessed November 9, 2012. http://www.readmedeadly.com.

"Snopes.com: BFE." Accessed December 14, 2015. http://msgboard.snopes.com/cgi-bin/ultimatebb.cgi?ubb=get_topic;f=95;t=000830;p=0.

"Sony Pictures Wins 'Midnight in Paris' Lawsuit over Faulkner Quote (Exclusive)." *The Hollywood Reporter*. Accessed September 23, 2016. http://www.hollywoodreporter.com/thr-esq/sony-pictures-wins-midnight-paris-588515.

"Split Cherry Tree by Jesse Stuart," Thinking Through Literature and Culture. Ministry of Education English Inspectorate (Israel). Accessed August 13, 2016. http://tlc.cet.ac.il/ShowItem.aspx?ItemID=263e47e4-8191-4f14-bae5-2400e3dbe57a&lang=EN

"Statehouses and Sexual Harassment." *1A* from National Public Radio, November 29, 2017. https://www.npr.org/podcasts/510316/1a.

Stuart, Jesse. "Split Cherry Tree." Classic Short Stories. Accessed August 13, 2016. http://www.classicshorts.com/stories/cherry.html.

"Sui Sin Far." *Wikipedia, the Free Encyclopedia*. Accessed December 3, 2017. https://en.wikipedia.org/wiki/Sui_Sin_Far.

Thompson, Matt. "Five Reasons Why People Code-Switch." Accessed May 11, 2018. https://www.npr.org/sections/codeswitch/2013/04/13/177126294/five-reasons-why-people-code-switch.

"Tony Hillerman, 83; Penned Navajo Series." *Indian Country Today Media Network.com*, October 28, 2008. http://indiancountrytodaymedianetwork.com/2008/10/28/102808-tony-hillerman-83-penned-navajo-series-75233.

Ulukau: Hawaiian Electronic Dictionary. Accessed October 26, 2017. wehewehe.org.

Vanderstaay, Steven. "In the Right Direction." *The Chronicle of Higher Education*, June 10, 2005. http://www.chronicle.com/article/In-the-Right-Direction/14811/.

Vitello, Paul. "Janet Dailey, 69, Dies; Romance Author Who Sold in Hundreds of Millions." *The New York Times*, December 17, 2013. http://www.nytimes.com/2013/12/18/books/janet-dailey-romance-author-dies-at-69.html.

"Where to Hear Us," 1A. Accessed December 10, 2017. https://the1a.org/stations.

Wong, Brad, and P.-I. Reporter. "Historic Gate Provides Another Link to Chinatown's Roots." *Seattlepi.com*. Accessed September 16, 2016. http://www.seattlepi.com/local/article/Historic-gate-provides-another-link-to-1260821.php.

{ INDEX }

Notes
1. Page numbers in bold italic indicate illustrations
2. Square brackets around authors' names indicate that, while these authors are not mentioned in the text, one or more of their publications are referenced.

accessibility xi, 25, 34, 35, 151, 216, 218, 220, 221
Adams, David Wallace 73–4; *Education for Extinction* 73, 227
Adams, Michael 38, 227
Africa 70, 206, 207, 209
African-American(s) 19, 66, 67, 70, 71, 72, 75, 94, 151, 157, 184; literature 77, 86, 167, 173, 203
Agee, James 172
Aiiieeeee! 130, 229
Alaska 6, 126, 166
Algebra Project 94
Algonquian 36
Allen, James Lane: "Local Colour" 18, 227
Allende, Isabel 155
American English 34, 36, 156, 157
American Family, An 163
American Historical Association 61
American Indians 7, 33, 72, 73, 74, 75, 76, 93, 190, 198, 213, 214, 215, 217, 223
American Library Association 27
American literature viii, 14, 16, 34, 40, 49, 155, 158, 159, 203, 206, 212; *see also* African-American literature; Native American literature
Americanization 142, 145
Amish 167–9, 171, 185; novels 168–9
Anderson, Benedict 14, 156, 210
Angel of History (Benjamin) 36
Anishinaabewaki 15
Ann Arbor xiii, 15, 166, 221
Antin, Mary 151
Apollo-11 211
Apollo-17 8, **9**
Appalachia 29, 33, 38, 42, 78, 79, 82, 83, 85, 93, 95, 162
Appalachian-set fiction 29–30, 33, 77, 212
Appiah, Anthony 95, 174, 227
Arab-Americans 15
Arabic culture 38, 207, 212
Arbour, Robert 155, 234
Arena 29
Argentina 159
Arkansas 77, 167

Arnold, Matthew 117
Arnow, Harriette 29
Arthur, Jason: *Violet America* 21
Asian-American literature and identity 121, 130, 132, 138
Asian-Canadian literature 121, 130
Association of European Border Regions (AEBR) xiv, 4–5, **5**, 242
Atlantic Monthly, The 17, 25, 28, 68, 72, 74, 75, 100, 104, 116
Atlantic Ocean 18, 153, 199
Augé, Marc 3, 227
Aull, Laura xiii, 48, 227
Austin, Mary 20
Australia(n) 38, 40, 121, 210
authenticity viii, 21, 23, 30, 31, 76, 80, 81, 129, 133, 136, 137, 138, 163, 164, 166, 169, 170, 173, 174, 223
autobiography 66, 68, 72, 76, 79, 124, 125, 132, 185, 190, 202, 224

backwoods 53, 57, 83, 162, 174
Badiou, Alain 106, 120, 217, 227
Bakhtin, Mikhail ix, 31, 35, 39, 40, 120, 174, 227
Bal, Mieke 1–2, 97; *Travelling Concepts in the Humanities* 1–2, 227
Baltimore 34, 64, 164
Banks, Russell 172
Baron Munchausen 55, 58
Basel 4–5
Basso, Keith: *Wisdom Sits in Places* 180, 227
Baxter, Charles: *There's Something I Want You to Do* 202–3, 227
Beard, Frank 53, 56; Bull (in *The Hoosier School-Master*) **56**; First Acquaintance with Flat Creek (in Eggleston, *The Hoosier School-Master*) **52**; Hank Banta's Improved Plunge-Bath (in Eggleston, *The Hoosier School-Master*) **54**; Old Jack Means (in Eggleston, *The Hoosier School-Master*) **54**; Jeems Phillips (in Eggleston, *The Hoosier School-Master*) **60**

Beattie, Ann: *The State We're In* 203
Beavers, Herman 90, 227
Beijing 7, 137
Bell, Michael Davitt 100
Benjamin, Lazier 36, 235
Berger, John x, 1; *Into Their Labors*
    trilogy 208; *Lilac and Flag* 208, 227; *Once
    in Europa* 208, 227; *Pig Earth* 208, 227
Beringer, Pierre 137, 227
Berman, Russell 96; "Teaching as
    Vocation" 92–3, 227
Berry, Wendell x, 39, 44, 47, 93, 176, 177–90, 194,
    196, 197, 198, 201, 202, 203, 209, 218; "Are
    You All Right?" 180, 186; "A Consent" 181;
    Hannah Coulter 183, 228; "Imagination in
    Place" 178l *Jayber Crow* 181, 182–3, 185, 228;
    "The Lost Bet" 181; "Making It Home" 182;
    A Place on Earth 178, 181, 183, 184, 186, 188;
    Port William 178, *179*, 180, *180*, 181, 183, 185,
    189, 209; "The Regional Motive" 180, 181,
    189; *Remembering* 172, 177, 180, 181, 182,
    185–9, 228; *That Distant Land* 178, *179*, 180,
    180, 181, 183, 228; "Watch with Me" 183;
    Whitefoot 1, 218, 228; "The Wild
    Birds" 178, 183
Bible 75, 83, 84, 189; Book of Esther 145
"Big Blue Marble, The" 8
biography 25, 41, 61, 62, 63, 66, 67, 68, 72, 74, 76,
    78, 79, 81, 98, 101, 103, 107, 113, 122, 124, 125,
    130, 131, 132, 138, 140, 146, 148, 151, 152, 173,
    185, 190, 202, 224
Birchall, Diana 123, 124, 224, 228
Bixby, Tams 31
Black, Daniel: *They Tell Me of a Home* 77, 228
Black English Vernacular 32
Blanc-Bentzon, Madame 108
Blanchard, Paula 113, 228
Blue Marbles Project 8–10, *10*, *11*
Bohemian, The 126, 130
Bonnin, Gertrude Simmons xiii, 72–4, 76, 77,
    80, 212, 223, 228; "An Indian Teacher among
    Indians" 73–5; *Old Indian Legends* 73
book-learning 58, 104, 105, 106, 143, 162, 166, 177,
    181, 195, 196, 221; and local knowledge
    48–96, 98, 161, 201, 207, 213, 217, 220, 221
border gnosis 160
Borges, Jorge Luis: "On Rigor in
    Science" 16, 228
Boston 17, 18, 29, 57, 63, 98, 100, 110, 111, 112, 114,
    116, 124, 125
Boston Globe 26, 27, 124, 130, 225
Bourdieu, Pierre 181
Bowden, Brett: *The Empire of
    Civilization* 41, 42, 228
Boylan Heights, North Carolina 7
Boym, Svetlana: *Future of Nostalgia* 40, 228

Bramen, Carrie Tirado 22–5: "The Uneven
    Development of American Regionalism" 24;
    The Uses of Variety 22, 228
Brazil 159
Brexit 4
Brickhouse, Anna 101
Brinkley, Alan 41, 228
Britain *see* United Kingdom
Brodhead, Richard 24, 53, 99, 173, 192; *Cultures
    of Letters* 21, 25, 26, 61, 62, 114, 228;
    The School of Hawthorne 151, 228
Brooklyn 38, 59
Brooks, Lisa: *The Common Pot* 199, 228
Brooks, Van Wyck 151
Brower, David 10
Browning, Robert 113
Brussels 4
Budbill, David 192
Buddha 113
Burgess, Anthony: *A Clockwork Orange* 34
Burke, Kenneth 91
Buzzati, Dino: *The Tartar Steppe* 208, 228
Byron, George Gordon, Lord 126, 225; "Ode to
    Napoleon" 126, 228

Cable, George Washington 19
Cahan, Abraham 131, 175
Calcutta (later Kolkata) 205
Calhoun, Charles 151, 228
Calhoun, Craig: "The Class Consciousness of
    Frequent Travelers," 12–13, 95, 220, 228;
    "Cosmopolitanism in the Modern Social
    Imaginary" 13, 228; *Critical Social
    Theory* 40, 228
California 17, 24, 125, 126, 141, 171, 201, 212
Calvinism 113
Canada 5, 40, 77, 123, 124, 125, 138, 140, 141,
    157, 203, 212
Canberra Deep Space Communication
    Complex 211
capitalism 39, 40, 42, 109, 178, 214
Caravaggio, Michelangelo Merisi da 114
Caribbean 6, 98, 108, 158, 206
Carkonen, Shawn 80, 242
Carlisle Industrial Indian School 73, 75
Carpenter, Cari: "Detecting Indianness"
    76, 228
Carr, Jesse xiii
Cary, Alice and Phoebe 20; *Clovernook* 20
Cary, Richard 120, 234
Casanova, Pascale 159
Cason, Zelma 61
Catalonia 16
Catherwood, Mary Hartwell 28
Catholicism 28, 75, 124, 151
Cavafy, C. P.: "Waiting for the Barbarians" 208

center of the world viii, 1, 43, 44, 57, 139, 159, 161, 177, 183, 207, 218
Central America 209
Century 25, 71, 125
Chandler, Raymond 167
Chapman, Mary xiii, 123, 124, 125, 126, 130, 138, 139; *Becoming Edith Eaton* 124, 225; *Dictionary of Literary Biography* entry for Edith Eaton 225; "Finding Edith Eaton" 127, 129, 229
Charles River 152, 153
Chase, Mary Ellen 173, 174; *Wind-Swept* 172, 229
Chaucer, Geoffrey 22
Chesnutt, Charles 24, 66–7, 70–2, 76, 139, 141, 173; "The Bouquet" 70, 229; *The Conjure Woman* 33, 229; "The Grey Wolf's Ha'nt" 33; *Mandy Oxendine* 66–7; "The March of Progress" 70–1, 229
Chicago 59, 129, 133, 134, 136, *136*, 137, 185
Child, Brenda J. 74
China x, 2, 7, 56, 57, 123, 127, 133, 134, 137, 138, 146, 147, 150, 153, 157, 159; *see also* People's Republic of China
Chinatown x, 121, 122, 124, 125, 127, 129, 130, 131–9, 140, 148, 149, 150, 152, 153, 154, 158, 187
Chinatown Gate, Seattle *134*
Chinese 57, 109, 121, 123–5, 127, *128*, 128, 130, 133, 134, 136–51, 153, 157, 160, 187, 212, 224
Chinese Exclusion Act, 1882 (US) 124, 125, 187
Chinese-Americans 132, 134, 136, 138, 139, 187, 205, 221
Chinese-Canadians 121, 141, 212
Christianity x, 19, 39, 57, 58, 75, 81, 113, 114, 117, 120, 150, 178, 183, 188, 190
chronotope ix, 35, 39, 42, 47, 52, 79, 98, 120, 174, 204, 208
Chu, Patricia 146, 229
Chute, Carolyn 192
Cincinnati 20
city and country *see* country and city
Civil Rights (US) 86, 94
civilization 16, 41, 42, 44, 55, 57, 67, 74, 75, 76, 94, 95, 117, 118, 134, 137, 138, 140, 149, 157, 164, 194, 207, 216, 219
class 23, 24, 28, 29, 33, 67, 68, 90, 101, 111, 117, 123, 124, 172, 176, 190, 192–8, 204, 205, 208
consciousness 12, 14, 140, 220
Cleveland Type Foundry 129
Clifford, Stephanie: *Everybody Rise* 203
Coetzee, J. M.: *Waiting for the Barbarians* 207–8, 229
Columbian Exposition 1893 133, *136*
comedy 47, 71, 110, 111, 141, 144, 181
comparative literature 148, 159, 175
Conolly-Smith, Peter 34, 229

Conrad, Joseph 206
contemporary fiction 161–217; and global village 200–17
Cooder, Ry: *Chávez Ravine* 210
Corner, James: *Taking Measures across the American Landscape* **214**
Cosgrove, Denis: *Apollo's Eye* 8, 229
cosmopolitanism ix, 11–14, 23, 29, 33, 41, 42, 47, 48, 55, 93, 95, 98, 103, 104, 116, 146, 155, 165, 173–6, 204, 206, 215, 220, 225; critical 14; rooted 95, 174, 176, 177
country and city 19, 23, 24, 39, 47, 59, 98, 102–3, 107, 109, 112, 115, 219, 221
country noir 167
Craddock, Charles Egbert *see* Murfree, Mary Noailles
Cramer, Katherine 219–20; *The Politics of Resentment* 219, 229
Creek Nation 30
Criminal Minds (CBS) 161, 162, 163, 170, 171, 182, 201
Cronon, William: "The Trouble with Wilderness" 225, 229
Cuba 157
Curzan, Anne 32, 229
Cutter, Martha 130, 224, 229

D'Addario, Daniel: "A Nation of Books" 225, 229
Dailey, Janet 164–6, 168; Americana series 164; *The Matchmakers* 165, 229; *Summer Mahogany* 165, 229
Dante (Dante Alghieri) 142, 153, 187; *Paradiso* 188
Davies, Donald 197
Davis, H. L.: *Honey in the Horn* 172
Dawes Commission 31
De Quincey, Thomas: *Life of Raphael* 18
de Tocqueville, Alexis 16, 19, 28
Delaware 165
Deloria, Philip 199; "From Nation to Neighborhood" 31, 230
Delpit, Lisa: *Other People's Children* 94
Deming, Philander 20
Denmark/Danish xiv, 37, 52, 164
Derrida, Jacques: "The Law of Genre" 45
Detroit 15, 27
Dewey, John: *Democracy and Education* 96, 230
Dickens, Charles 18, 62, 155; *Bleak House* 210
Dickey, James: *Deliverance* 83
Dimock, Wai Chee 159, 230
Dish, The 210, 211, **211**, 230
Donovan, Josephine 18, 21, 100; "Jewett and Swedenborg" 113, 114, 230; "Jewett on Race" 30, 104, 230; *New England Local Color Literature* 21, 230
Dorfgeschichte (village tales) 18

Druyan, Ann 164
Du Bois, W. E. B. 47, 67–72, 76; "A Negro
    Schoolmaster in the New South" 67–8, 230;
    "Of the Meaning of Progress"
    71–2; *The Souls of Black Folk* 68–70, 217, 230
DuCille, Ann 106, 230
Duck, Leigh Anne: *The Nation's Region* 174, 230

Earlham College, Indiana 74
Earth 9, **9**, 16, 211, 215, 217
Eaton, Achuen Grace Amoy 123
Eaton, Edith (aka "Fire Fly" and "Sui Sin
    Far") ix, x, 47, 97, 100, 119, 121–60, **122**, **132**,
    175, 181, 190, 212, 221, 223, 224, 225; "The
    Alaska Widow" 126, 158, 229; "The
    Americanizing of Pau Tsu" 139, 144–7, 224;
    Becoming Sui Sin Far 127, 231; *Bone* 130;
    "A Chinese Boy-Girl" 125; *Chinese-Japanese
    Cookbook* 138; "Cross-Cultural
    Affinities" 126, 229; "A Draught of
    Bewilderment" 131, 230; "The Gift of
    Little Me" 126; " 'Its Wavering Image' "
    139, 148–52, 153, 158; *A Japanese
    Nightingale* 138; "Leaves from the Mental
    Portfolio of an Eurasian" 125, 132, **132**, 224,
    225, 230; *Mrs. Spring Fragrance* **128**, 129, 130,
    133, 139, 144, 152, 225, 230, 231; "Mrs. Spring
    Fragrance" 139–45, 147, 151, 152, 153, 155, 225;
    "The Son of Chung Wo," 129, **129**, 130; "Sui
    Sin Far, the Half Chinese Writer, Tells of
    Her Career" 124; "The Wisdom of the
    New" 147; "Word from Miss Eaton" 224,
    230; "A Word from 'Sui Sin Far' " 224
Eaton, Edward 123
Eaton, Grace 124, 126
Eaton, Winnifred (aka Onoto Watanna) 123,
    124, 125, 131, 138; *Movie Madness* 138
Eaton Bosse, Sara 138
education 50, 53, 56, 58, 63–5, 67, 69, 70, 72–5,
    77–9, 84, 86–90, 92, 93–5, 133, 145, 157, 181,
    182, 195, 196, 206, 217, 221; childhood 96;
    and conquest 72–7; higher 50, 67, 79, 92,
    93, 96, 205; Native 75, 76; sentimental
    142–4, 149, 150, 154–5
Eggleston, Edward 25, 28, 30, 32, 51–63, 65,
    66, 68, 78, 80, 81, 183, 220; *The Hoosier
    School-Master* 32, 51–61, **52**, **54**, **56**, **60**, 64,
    66, 69, 75, 78, 81, 220, 231; "Our Saturday
    Feuilleton" 59; "The Struggle in the
    Dark" 61–2; *The Transit of Civilization* 63;
    "Up the Coolly" 59
Egypt 38, 189
Einstein, Albert 35
Eli, Look Tin 137
Eliot, T. S. 155; "The Waste Land" 153

Elkins, Bell 42, 167
Elliott, Emory 21; *Columbia History of the
    American Novel* 21
Elliott, Michael 21; *The Culture Concept* 21, 231
Ellul, Jacques 10
emigration 206
empathetic style 184
encapsulation 24, 99
England 17, 39, 52, 63, 117, 123, 124, 151
English, James 203; *The Economy of Prestige* 225
Eufaula 30, 31
Eurasians 121, 123, 148
Europe 5, 15, 19, 98, 116, 123, 159, 206, 208
European Coal and Steel Community 4
European Committee on Regions 7
European Union 4, 14
Evans, Brad 101; *Before Cultures* 21

Faulkner, William xi, 132, 162, 163, 171, 173, 174,
    181, 200; Yoknapatawpha 209
Ferens, Dominika 124, 130, 131, 138, 139, 225, 231
Fetterley, Judith 20; *Writing Out of Place* 107, 231
Fields, Annie 19, 100; *Letters* 106, 108, 113, 115,
    117, 118, 119, 120, 231
Finnegan, William: *Barbarian Days* 203–4
"Fire Fly" *see* Eaton, Edith
First World War 186
Flathead Reservation, Montana 215
Flaubert, Gustave 98, 142; *Madame Bovary* 120
Fleissner, Jennifer: "Is Feminism a
    Historicism?" 223
Fliegelman, Jay 155
Florida 172, 195, 220
folk tale 68, 141
Folsom, Marcia McClintock 107, 108, 184;
    " 'Tact is a Kind of Mind-Reading' " 107, 231
Foote, Mary Hallock 28
Foote, Stephanie 21, 117; *Regional Fictions* 21, 231
Foster, Frances Smith x
Foster, Ruel 78, 231
France 4, 94, 159, 208
Franzen, Jonathan 172
Freeman, Mary Wilkins 27, 139;
    The Jamesons 46
Freire, Paulo 79, 94, 96, 221
Frost, Robert 198
Frow, John: " 'Reproducibles' " 46, 231
Fuller, Margaret 151
Fus Fixico, *see* Posey, Alexander

Gage, Cully *see* Van Riper, Charles
Gaines, Ernest 86–91, 173, 197, 201, 202, 203;
    The Autobiography of Miss Jane Pittman 86,
    202, 231; *Conversations* 90; *A Lesson before
    Dying* 77, 86, 87–91, 231

Ganguly, Debjani 159, 204; *This Thing Called the World* 160, 231

García Márquez, Gabriel 155; Macondo 209; *One Hundred Years of Solitude* 208-9

Garland, Hamlin 22-3, 24, 29, 183; *Crumbling Idols* 22, 231; *Main-Travelled Roads* 22, 232; "Return of a Private" 182; "Under the Lion's Paw" 183; "Up the Coulee" 22

Gaul, Therese Strouth 100, 232

Gaus, P. L. 167-9; *Blood of the Prodigal* 168-9, 232; *Broken English* 168, **232**; Ohio Amish series 167

Geddes, Patrick 10

gender 3, 17, 23, 29, 68, 79, 95, 99, 195, 197, 203, 211

genre ix, x, 1, 20, 23, 24, 25, 26, 28, 30, 45-7, 61, 66, 80, 81, 97, 103, 131, 138, 155, 159, 166, 167, 169, 171, 172, 173, 182, 200, 204, 207, 209, 210, 213, 218, 223; criticism ix, 45, 46, 91, 122, 202; regionalism as 16, 31, 34, 98

Genthe, Arnold 136

geography 14, 21, 64, 65, 68, 85, 116, 153, 156, 159, 204

Georgia 26, 64, 70, 172

Germany 4, 18

Giles, Paul 159, 175, 203, 204, 212

Ginzberg, Carlo 167

Gitelman, Lisa 176, 212

Gladden, Washington 114

Glazener, Nancy 28

Gleason, Patrick 98, 101, 108, 117

Global South 6, 13

global village 208; and contemporary fiction 200-17

globalization 8, 42, 123, 161, 175

"golden age" 39, 221

Goodreads 165

Goodrich, Samuel Griswold (aka Peter Parley) 37

Google Earth 9

Graff, Harvey 95, 223

Gramsci, Antonio 167

Great Lakes 2, 5, 15, 170

Greenberg, Martin Harry 165, 236

Greenwich Mean Time 20

Greeson, Jennifer 19; *Our South* 16, 21, 174, 232

Griswold, Wendy 166, 175, 176; *Regionalism and the Reading Class* 200, 232

GroundTruth Project 221

"Guide Book to the Joss House" **135**

Gulliford, Andrew 52

Gura, Philip 63

Habermas, Jürgen 142

Hadrian 44

Hahn, Bob 166

Hall, David 63

Hallam, Arthur 142

Hamid, Mohsin: *Discontent* 212, 232; *Exit West* 212, 232

Hampton Institute (later University) 75, 151

Hardy, Thomas 23, 84; *Return of the Native* 23

Harmon, Katherine: *The Map as Art* 7, 232; *You Are Here* 7, 232

Harris, Sharon M. 100

Harris, Joel Chandler 19; "Brer Rabbit" 19; *Uncle Remus* 19, 141

Harte, Bret 17-19, 25, 28, 51, 66; "The Idyl of Red Gulch" 51; "Mliss" 51; *Overland Monthly* 17; *The Luck of Roaring Camp* 51, 201, 232; "The Rise of the 'Short Story'" 18, 232

Harte, Walter Blackburn 124

Haruf, Kent: *Plainsong* 202, 232

Harvey, William 102

Harzinski, Kris 7

Havana 38, 157

Havill, Steven: Posadas County series 166-7

Hawaii 6, 36, 157, 204

Hawthorne, Nathaniel 139; *The House of Seven Gables* 105

Hayot, Eric 159; *On Literary Worlds* 159, 233

Hecataeus of Miletus 43; world map, 500 BCE **43**

Hebert, Ernest x, xiii, 190-200, 201, 202, 209; "Cooty's Cabin" **191**; Darby 190-200, **191**, 209; *The Dogs of March* 190-2, 194-7, 201, 225, 233; "Guide to the Darby Chronicles" 190, 198, 242; *Howard Elman's Farewell* 190-3, 194, 195, 197, 198, 233; *I Love U* 190; "An Interview with Ernest Hebert" 198; *Live Free or Die* 194, 197, 198, 233; *Mad Boys* 190; map of Darby region **191**; *Never Back Down* 190, 193, 233; *The Old American* 190, 198-200, 233; "Origins of the Darby Series" 198; *Spoonwood* 190, 192, 193, 196, 233; *Whisper My Name* 190, 233

Heise, Ursula 8, 11; *Sense of Place and Sense of Planet* 8, 233

Heller, Terry 101, 106, 109, 113, 115; "Living for the Other World" 108, 233

Hemingway, Ernest: "Big Two-Hearted River" 163

Herodotus 82

Hesiod 39

Hess, Joan 167

Heywood, Joseph: Wood Cop series 167

Hill, Christopher 159; "The Travels of Naturalism" 159, 233

Hillerman, Tony 169–70; Navajo Tribal Police novels 170
Himes, Chester 167
Hinojosa, Rolando 173
Hitchcock, Bert 64
Hobo-Dyer Equal Area Projection *12*
Hobsbawm, E. J.: *The Invention of Tradition* 41, 233
Holbo, Christine 23
Hollywood 210, 219
Hönnighausen, Lothar 35; *Regionalism in the Age of Globalism* 14, 233
Homer 22
Homer, Winslow: *The Country School* 48, *49*; *Snap the Whip* 48, *49*
Homestead, Melissa 101
horizon viii, ix–xi, xiv, 23, 46, 50–1, 55, 65, 69, 75, 92, 95, 118, 133, 156, 160, 176, 190, 194, 212, 218, 219–21
Houghton Mifflin 99, 119, 151
Howard, June: *New Essays on The Country of the Pointed Firs* 224, 233; *Publishing the Family* 28, 45, 233; "Sand in Your Mouth" 225, 233
Howe, Mark Anthony DeWolfe 100
Howells, William Dean 18, 100, 171; *A Hazard of New Fortunes* 33
Hsu, Hsuan: *Geography and the Production of Space* 21, 233
Hughes, Langston: "Let America Be America Again" 205
humor 18, 19, 30, 59, 64, 66, 105, 110, 183, 211
Hunter, Carol A. Petty 30
Hutner, Gordon xiii, 172, 225

Icelandic 38
idyll 39, 120
Igou, Brad 171
immigration 4, 156, 206
imperialism 63, 101, 126, 157, 158, 161; and nationalism 16
inauthenticity 129, 138
India 205, 207, 209
Indian Ocean 206
Indiana 15, 51, 59, 61, 74, 220
Indigenous northeast (map) *199*
Indonesia 43
Iowa Writer's Workshop 201
Ireland 18, 42, 117
Irmscher, Christoph 155
Irving, Washington 18; *Sketch-Book* 18
Islam 38
isolation 41, 69, 111, 162, 165
Ives, Charles 198

Jack Hills, Western Australia 40
Jamaica 125, 158

James, E. L.: *Fifty Shades of Grey* 155
James, Henry 24, 46, 155; "The Jolly Corner" 131, 234
Jameson, Fredric 46, 198; *The Antinomies of Realism* 23, 234; "Marxism and Historicism" **224**
Japan(ese) 123, 138, 159
Jemison, N. K.: *Fifth Season* 210
Jen, Gish: *World and Town* 204–5, 234
Jewett, Sarah Orne ix–x, xiii, xiv, 24, 26, 27, 28, 30, 39, 47, 57, 97–120, *99*, *119*, 122, 172, 173, 174, 175, 183, 184, 188, 223, 224; *Betty Leicester* 119–20, 234; *A Country Doctor* 106; *The Country of the Pointed Firs* 28, 85, 101, 103, 106, 107, 108, 118, 173, 184, 189, 224, 234; "The Courting of Sister Wisby" 104, 105; *Deephaven* 28, 100, 102, 103, 108, 112, 234; "An Everyday Girl" 100; "Fidelity" 183, 184, 185; "A Financial Failure" 26; "The Foreigner" 101; "The Gray Mills of Farley" 100, 117; "The Green Bowl" 109, 115; "Green Island" 107, 116; "From a Mournful Villager" 99; "Jenny Garrow's Lovers" 26; *The King of Folly Island* 105, 106, 234; "A Late Supper" 98, 109–15, 116, 117, 224; "Law Lane" 106; "Letters" 120; "Marsh Rosemary" 224; "Martha's Lady" 116–17; *Old Friends and New* 64, 65, 109, 234; "The Old Town of Berwick" 98, 234; "Out of the China Closet" 116; *Queen's Twin* 116, 234; "Stolen Pleasures" 100; *The Story of the Normans* 117; *Tales of New England* 99, 234; "Told in the Tavern" 26; *Transplanted Shamrocks* 99; *Uncollected Short Stories of Sarah Orne Jewett* 100, 109, 234; "A Village Shop" 101, 105–6, 224
Johanningsmeier, Charles 27; "Realism, Naturalism, and American Public Libraries" 27, 28, 234; "Welcome Guests" 28, 234
Johnson, Josephine Winslow: *Now in November* 172
Johnson, Victoria 163; *Heartland TV* 163, 174
Johnson City, Tennessee 22, 175
Johnston, Richard Malcolm (aka Philemon Perch) 64–6, 76; *Dukesborough Stories* 64; *Georgia Sketches* 64; "The Goosepond School" 26, 64–7, 69, 73, 76, 156; "How Mr. Bill Williams Took the Responsibility" 64; "A New England Sketch" 66; "Old Friends and New" 64
Jones, Gavin 33; *Failure and the American Writer* 224, 235
Jonson, Ben: "To Celia" 142
Joseph, Philip: *American Literary Regionalism in a Global* Age 21

Kaestle, Carl F. 17
Kamakawiwoʻole, Israel 36, *37*; *Facing Future* 36
Kandiyoti, Dalia: *Migrant Sites* 22, 160, 175
Kaplan, Amy 101, 171; "Nation, Region, and Empire" 21
Karem, Jeff 21, 24, 86, 175; *The Romance of Authenticity* 132, 133, 173, 174, 235
Keithan, Mary: *Michigan One-Room Schoolhouses* **50**, 235
Keller, Julia 42, 167
Kennedy, James Pendleton 19; *Swallow Barn* 19
Kennedy, Raymond 81, 223; *Romance of Eleanor Gray* 77, 85, 235
Kentucky 29, 77, 79, 93, 162, 177, 178, 186, 190
Kerouac, Jack 172
Kilauea 40
Killer Woodsman 162
King, Stephen 155, 164
Kingston, Maxine Hong 172
Klondike 126
Korea 159

Lahiri, Jhumpa 155; *Lowland* 205, 235
Lahore 212
Lai, H. M. 141
Lai, Larissa 121
landscape vii, ix, 3, 23, 58, 59, 95, 107, 110, 120, 164, 167, 178, 184, 190, 192, 193, 195, 197, 199, 200, 202, 213, 215, 216; and memory 180; of power xi, 24, 31, 206, 217; tilted 31, 44, 206, 217
Lansbury, Angela 170
[Larsson, Stieg]: *Girl with the Dragon Tattoo* 164
Latin America 5, 6
Lauck, Jon K. 21; *From Warm Center to Ragged Edge* 21
Laurence, Margaret: *A Jest of God* 77, 235; Manawaka novels 77, 209
Lazier, Benjamin 8
Lear, Bernadette 75, 76
Le Guin, Ursula x, 47, 213, 215–17; "Betrayals" 215; *Dispossessed* 210; "Forgiveness Day" 215; *Four Ways to Forgiveness* (Hainish cycle) 215, 235; Hain 215–16; *The Left Hand of Darkness* 215, 235; "A Man of the People" 216; "A Woman's Liberation" 216–17
Lee, Anthony 144
Lee, Rachel 148, 150
Lefebvre, Henri 135, 177; *The Production of Space* 44
Lendering, Jona *43*
Lennard, Katherine xiii
Levander, Caroline 155; *Where Is American Literature?* 159, 236

Levin, Janna: *How the Universe Got Its Spots* 35, 236
Lewin, Tamar 63
Lewis, Sinclair: *Main Street* 41
Library of America 100, 104
Ling, Amy 125, 126, 127, 130, 225; *Between Worlds* 130, 236; *Heath Anthology of American Literature* 130
literary history ix, x, 18, 20, 45, 47, 48, 76, 91, 96, 98, 100, 121, 133, 155, 156, 158, 159, 160, 171, 175, 177, 192, 201, 204, 205, 218, 220
Littlefield, Daniel F. 30
local color vii–x, 16–23, 25, 28–36, 42, 47, 50–2, 55, 59, 66, 68, 70–2, 79, 91, 98, 102, 103, 109, 122, 131, 151, 156, 163, 169, 172–5, 200, 201, 219, 220; *see also* local knowledge; region; regionalism
local knowledge 47, 106, 166, 181, 207, 211, 216, 217, 221; and book learning 48–96, 98, 161, 195, 197, 201, 207, 213, 220; *see also* local color; region; regionalism
local language 58, 163, 167
location and literature 1–47
Lockwood, J. Samaine: *Archives of Desire* 109, 236
Lomawaima, K. Tsianina 76: *To Remain an Indian* 72, 236
London 38, 123, 146, 155, 212, 225
Longfellow, Henry Wadsworth 151–5, 158, 212; *Belfry of Bruges* 151, 236; "The Bridge" 150–3; *Hiawatha* 151; "Paul Revere's Ride" 151
Longfellow Institute, Harvard 155, 156, 225
Los Angeles 125, 167
Louie, Andrea: *Chineseness across Borders* 137, 236
Loughran, Trish 156
Lowe, Lisa 137
Lowell, Amy 146
Lowell, James Russell 62; *Biglow Papers* 32
LOWINUS (Languages Of What Is Now the United States) 156
Luce, Henry 41
"Luck of Roaring Camp, The" 17
Lutz, Catherine 192
Lutz, Tom 174, 224; *Cosmopolitan Vistas: American Regionalism and Literary Value* 21
Lyons, Scott: *The World, the Text, and the Indian* 212–13, 236

Maastricht Treaty 4
MacLean, Alex S.: "Wheat Strips on Plateau" **214**
MacLeod, Kirsten 125
Maine 19, 28, 98, 100, 103, 108, 155, 163, 165, 170, 171, 172, 173, 174, 190, 202, 203, 204

Mandala, Susan: "Crime Fiction as Regional
     Fiction" 167
Manhattan 202, 203
Manitoba 77
Maron, Margaret 167; Deborah Knott series 166
Marshall, Catherine 47, 81–5; *Christy* 77, 81, 236;
     A Man Called Peter 81
Martin, Jay 99; *Harvests of Change* 20, 236
Martin, W. A. P. 146; *Chinese Legends and Other
     Poems* 146, 236; *Hanlin Papers* 146, 236
Massachusetts 56, 57, 85, 109
Massey, Doreen 1, 3, 218; *Space, Place and
     Gender* 1, 3, 236
Massie, Sonja 165
Mather, Cotton: *Magnalia Christi Americana* 19
Matthiessen, F. O. 98, 119
Mayor, Archer: Joe Gunther series 166, 167
McCann, Colum 155, 225; *Let the Great World
     Spin* 209, 212, 236
McCarty, Teresa L. 76; *To Remain an
     Indian* 72, 236
McClintock, Anne 101
McClurg, A. C. 128, 129, 130
McCourt, Frank 77, 80–1; *Angela's Ashes* 80,
     237; *Teacher Man* 80, 237; *'Tis* 80, 237
McCracken, Elizabeth 106, 108; *The Women of
     America* 107, 237
McGurl, Mark 197; *The Program Era* 225, 237
McHenry, Elizabeth 17
McNickle, D'Arcy x, 212; *Wind from an Enemy
     Sky* 213–15, 237
[Melville, Herman]: *Moby Dick* 210
Mendocino 171
Mengestu, Dinaw: *All Our Names* 209, 237
Meriam Report, 1928 75
Mexican-American War 157
Mexico 5
Miami 38, 163
Michigan 2, 15, 16, 24, 26, 50, 167, 220
Michigan Humanities Council 15
Middle-earth 34
Midwest 2, 15, 20, 27, 29, 163, 170, 174, 201, 209
Midwest Arts Council 15
Midwestern History Association 21
Miéville, China: *The City & the City* 213;
     Embassytown 213
Mignolo, Walter: *Local Histories/Global
     Designs* 160, 237
Miller, Caroline: *Lamb in His Bosom* 172
Miller, Joaquin 20, 225
Miller, Joshua xiii, 33; *Accented
     America* 225, 237
Miller, Rachel xiii
Milton, John 181; *Paradise Lost* 104
Minnesota 59

Mississippi 68
Missouri 172, 219, 220
Mitchell, David: *Cloud Atlas* 210
Mitchell, Margaret: *Gone with the Wind* 172
Mitford, Mary Russell: *Our Village* 18
Modern Languages Association Convention 45
modernism 1, 23, 31, 159
modernity vii, 1, 16, 30, 35, 39, 40, 41, 42, 44, 62,
     67, 75, 79, 96, 110, 117, 159, 185, 196, 206,
     208, 211, 219
Monmaney, Terence 8, 242
Montgomery, Michael 83
Moretti, Franco 26, 159
Morgan, Dr. Jay Elmer 78
Morgan, Jack 99
Moseley, Walter 167
Moses, Robert 94
Moses, Roger 95
Mott, Frank Luther 17, 64, 125
Mount Royal Cemetery, Montréal 121, **122**
Mu'allaqāt 212
multilingualism 155, 156
Mumbai 38
Murder, She Wrote 171
Murfree, Mary Noailles (aka Charles Egbert
     Craddock) 28, 29
Muslim-American 212
Muslims 38, 204, 207
mysteries 67, 108, 163, 164, 167, 168, 169, 170, 171,
     172, 198, 202; regional 35, 42, 166,
     167, 169, 170

Nabokov, Peter 7
Naipaul, V.S. x; *A Bend in the River* 206–7, 237
Nanjing 38
Narayan, R. K.: *Malgudi* 209
NASA 8, **9**, 211, 221
National Book Award 202, 225
National Book Critics Circle Award 86
National Council of American Indians 74
National Education Association 78
National Public Radio 170, 219
nationalism 93, 153, 156, 181, 205, 206; and
     imperialism 16; and knowledge 58; and
     regionalism 4
Native American literature 212, 214
Native Indians 74; *see also* American Indians
Navajo Nation 170
Nebraska 74
Nelson, Willie 161
New England x, 2, 15, 19, 20, 21, 46, 47, 51, 56, 57,
     70, 85, 102, 106, 108, 109, 113, 116, 118, 152,
     163, 174, 190, 192, 193, 197, 198, 201, 202, 204
New Hampshire 190, 192, 193, 198, 201
New Horizon spacecraft 211

New Mexico 166
New Orleans xiv, 163, 167, 190
New South Wales 211
New York 17, 24, 26, 29, 31, 38, 47, 61, 71, 80, 82,
   118, 137, 141, 146, 155, 162, 169, 171, 192, 193,
   204, 209, 212
Newton, Isaac 123
Ng, Fae Myenne 130; *Bone* 137
Ngai, Mae 134; *The Lucky Ones* 137
"No Child Left Behind" 63, 95, 96
non-standard speech 33, 163
Norris, Frank: *The Octopus* 110
North America x, 8, 14, 16, 43, 123, 125, 129, 140,
   157, 176, 197, 199, 206
North American Free Trade
   Agreement (NAFTA) 4
North Carolina 7, 66, 82
North Pole 13
Northeast 18, 20, 27, 28, 29, 58, 167, 197, *199*
Northwest Territories 40
Norton, Sara 115, 118, 173
Nurhussein, Nadia 33–4

Obama, Barack 162
Occupy movement 8
Ohio 15, 167, 169, 170, 178
Okker, Patricia 34
Oklahoma 30
Oliviere, Lucia Newell: "The Stage Driver" 26
Ono, Yoko 10
Oregon 172
Ostergren, Robert 14, 15
Ozarks 167

Pacific 18, 153, 154, 201, 210
Pakistan 209, 212
Pan Chieh-Yü (Lady P'an) 145–6
Paretsky, Sara: V. I. Warshawski series 167
Paris 108, 159, 174
Parley, Peter *see* Goodrich, Samuel Griswold
Parsons, Jr., Theophilus 113
Pawley, Christine 28
Pennsylvania 83
People's Republic of China 157
Perch, Philemon *see* Johnston, Richard Malcolm
Perkins, David: *Is Literary History Possible?* 45
Petit, Philippe 209
Philadelphia 31
Philippines 37, 126, 157
Pilgrims 41, 63
Piscataqua river 98
place: metaphors of viii, 176, 219; and time vii,
   viii, ix, xi, 16, 34, 40, 46, 118, 120, 161,
   162, 164, 174, 210, 212, 216, 218, 221;
   see also place-time

place–time x, xi, 35, 164, 168, 178, 218
Plante, David 155
Plato 103, 108, 113, 150
"Podunk" 36, 37
Podunk River 37
Poe, Edgar Allan 151
poetry 17, 20, 26, 31, 33, 36, 38, 55, 100, 113, 119,
   126, 139, 140, 141, 143, 144, 146, 147, 149, 150,
   151, 152, 153, 154, 178, 205, 208, 212
politics of knowledge 197
Port William 178, *179*, **180**
Portuguese 37, 206
Posey, Alexander 30-3, 47, 212; Fus Fixico
   letters 30–1, 33
postmodernism 159
Powell, Douglas Reichert 175, 187; *Critical
   Regionalism* 22, 238
Pratt, Richard Henry 73, 76
Pratt, Sarah MacLean: *Cape Cod Folks* 59, 232
Presbyterianism 124, 146
Price, Matthew 25
professionalization 32, 92
Protestantism 28, 124
Proust, Marcel: *In Search of Lost Time* 40
provincial realism 62
provincialism 41, 94, 116
Pryse, Marjorie 20; *Writing Out of Place*
   107, 231
Pulitzer Prize 80, 86, 172

Quakers 74, 83
"quaint" xi, 24, 33, 34, 41, 47, 99, 100, 118, 165,
   181, 207, 218
Québec 198, 203
Quigley, Sheila: *Bad Moon Rising* 167
Quimbois 108

race viii, ix, 3, 17, 19, 23, 24, 33, 67, 68, 76, 95, 101,
   117, 122, 125, 130, 131, 132, 147, 148, 149, 150,
   156, 165, 190, 205
"Race to the Top" 63, 95, 96
racism 28, 70, 71, 88, 89, 101, 118, 137, 138, 141,
   172, 175, 184–5, 193, 220
Radway, Janice: *Reading the Romance* 166, 238
Randel, William 52, 59, 61, 62, 63
Ranger, T. O.: *The Invention of Tradition* 41
Rawlings, Marjorie Kinnan 61;
   The Yearling 172
realism xi, 1, 21, 22, 23, 27, 111, 114, 131, 159, 171;
   provincial 62
Reck, Gregory 93, 95
Reck, Una Mae 93, 95
reconciliation 19, 157
Reconstruction South 19
redemption 188, 189

region viii, 20–3, 29, 30, 32, 35, 38–40, 51, 56, 59,
    77, 82, 83, 85, 99, 102, 109, 139, 157, 161, 165,
    168, 171, 172, 174, 175, 178, 190, 191, 195,
    199–201, 204, 207, 210, 219; concept of 20,
    22, 30, 40, 48, 98, 115, 161, 171, 175, 177, 189;
    definition 1–16; as field of force 177; planet
    as 217; as substantive and relational 2–3,
    14, 15, 16, 21–4, 29, 30, 39, 44, 47, 107, 115, 122,
    131, 159, 175, 177, 189, 190, 201, 204, 218; see
    also local color; local knowledge;
    regionalism
regional mysteries 35, 166, 167, 169
regionalism vii–xi, xiii, xiv, 1, 4, 6, 8, 10, 13, 16,
    19, 21, 22, 24, 27–31, 34, 35, 39, 45–8, 64, 66,
    72, 80, 85, 91, 96–9, 107, 114, 118, 120, 122,
    123, 126, 131, 132, 143, 155, 157, 159–61, 163–5,
    167, 171, 172, 174–8, 181, 186, 190, 192, 196,
    197, 200, 201, 203, 204, 208, 210–13, 218, 221,
    223–5; chronotope of 35, 47, 208, 210;
    critical 14, 16, 175; as cultural form 21, 163;
    and nationalism 4; and realism 1, 22;
    now 161–217; see also local color; local
    knowledge; region
religion ix, 14, 41, 57, 58, 67, 69, 71, 75, 85, 87, 89,
    98, 108, 109, 112–15, 119, 120, 152, 161, 183, 224
Renan, Ernest 156, 206
Renza, Louis 99
Rexroth, Kenneth 146
Riley, James Whitcomb 20
Ring, Natalie: The Problem South 157, 238
Rittig, Johann 34
Robbins, Sarah Ruffing xiii, 96
Robinson, Kim Stanley; Mars trilogy 213, 238
Robinson, Marilynne 201–2; Gilead 201, 238;
    Housekeeping 201, 238; Lila 201, 238
Robinson, Rowland 20
Robinson Crusoe 55
Rockwell, David 215
Roker, Al: Storm of the Century 203
romans champêtres (rural novels) 18
Rome 38, 114, 118, 144, 210
Rose, Mike 95, 96; Why School? 63, 238
Rosen, Jeremy 45
Ross, Harold 41
Rowling, J. K. 164; Hogwarts 209
Rushdie, Salman 155
Ryden, Kent 21, 192–3; Landscape with
    Figures 21, 238; Sum of the Parts 193, 238

sacralization of literature 113
Sagan, Carl: Cosmos 164
St. Regis, Pamela 164–5; Natural History of the
    Romance Novel 164
Saints Peter and Paul Church, North Beach, San
    Francisco 188
Salter, Joseph: The Asiatic in England 224, 225

San Francisco 38, 125, 127, 130, 133, 136, 137, 140,
    143, 148, 153, 154, 166, 171, 180, 185–8,
    188, 190, 201
Santayana, George 151
satire 30, 32, 47, 203, 204
Satterwhite, Emily 29, 30, 82, 83, 85, 212, 223
Saussure, Ferdinand de 2, 45
Scandinavia 164
"scholar-teacher" 96, 168
Schrag, Mitzi 117
Schroeder, Jonathan 23
Schuman Declaration 4
science fiction 198, 217
Scotland/Scottish 4, 10, 16, 18, 84, 124, 154, 155
Seattle 125, 130, 133, 134, 137, 139, 220
Second World War 4, 38, 178, 182, 210
Sennott, Charles 221
"sentimental education" 142–4, 148–55
Shakespeare, William 145, 147
Shanghai 38, 123
Shannon, Laurie 108
Shaw, Peter 129
Sherman, Sarah Way 104, 107, 178
Shih, David 132
Sicily 210
Sierras 20
Silber, Nina 157; The Romance of Reunion 157, 239
Silko, Leslie 132, 173
Sinbad 55
Sioux Indians 72, 74, 76, 223
slavery 33, 58, 63, 70, 87, 157, 198, 199, 207, 215–17
Smith, Zadie 155
Social Gospel 114
Society for the Study of Midwestern
    Literature 21
Solberg, S. E. 130
Sollers, Werner 34, 225
Somali immigrants 204
Sorby, Angela 94, 119, 151, 153
South America 209, 214
South Carolina 64
space-time continuum 35, 40, 44;
    see also place-time; space; time
Spanish-American War 157, 158
spirituality 7, 39, 62, 83, 89, 91, 102, 107–9, 112,
    114–16, 153, 161, 183, 186, 188, 193,
    195, 215, 224
Stabenow, Dana: Kate Shugak series 166, 167
Standard English 31–3, 91, 169, 175
Standard Time Act 1915 20
Stanford creative writing MFA program 197
"Statehouses and Sexual Harassment" 219
Steedman, Carolyn 119
Stegner, Wallace 55, 197; Beyond the Hundredth
    Meridian 182
Stein, Gertrude 174

Stevens, Gavin 162
Stevenson, Robert Louis 153–4; monument, Portsmouth Square, San Francisco *154*
Still, James 33–4; "Bare-Bones" 33; "Hit Like to 'a' Killed Me" 33; "A Master Time" 33; "The Scrape" 33; "These Goodly Things" 33
Stowe, Harriet Beecher 19–21, 25, 51, 66, 103; *Mayflower* 21, 239; *Oldtown Folks* 19; *The Pearl of Orr's Island* 19, 103, 239; "Uncle Lot'" 20, 51, 75, 239; *Uncle Tom's Cabin* 19, 156
Stribling, T. S.: *The Store* 172
Strout, Elizabeth: *The Burgess Boys* 201, 202, 204, 239; *Olive Kitteridge* 201, 202, 204, 239
Stuart, Jesse 77–80, 81, 94, 223; *The Best-Loved Short Stories of Jesse Stuart* 223, 239; *Jesse Stuart on Education* 78, 239; "The Split Cherry Tree" 79; *The Thread That Runs So True* 77–80, 239
Stürenburg, Caspar 34
Sui Sin Far *see* Eaton, Edith
Sweden/Swedish 52, 204
Swedenborg, Emanuel 113, 114
Swedenborgianism 113
Switzerland/Swiss 4, 18, 37, 59
Syria 4

Taine, Hippolyte 62
Tchen, John Kuo We 136
teachers ix, 23, 32, 47, 103, 104, 106, 107, 126, 151, 168, 170, 173, 175, 181, 182, 202, 204, 205, 207, 216, 217; and learners 91–6; and regional story-telling 48–96
teaching 48, 51, 55, 59, 68, 70–2, 75, 78, 79, 83–5, 88–90, 92, 93, 96, 97, 113, 118, 133, 192, 198
Tennessee 22, 29, 68, 82, 175
Tennyson, Alfred, Lord 140–3, 150, 151, 153, 212; *In Memoriam* 140, 142, 143, 152; "Locksley Hall" 212
Thompson, Matt 32
Ticknor and Fields 141, 151
time vii, viii, ix, x, xi, 7, 16, 20, 24, 25, 34, 46, 52, 77, 79, 83, 85, 96, 117, 118, 120, 125, 161, 162, 164, 174, 180, 183, 210, 212, 216, 218, 219, 221; local and historical 216; and place vii, viii, ix, xi, 16, 34, 40, 46, 118, 120, 161, 162, 164, 174, 210, 212, 216, 218, 221; and power 34; and space viii, 7, 24, 35, *36*, 38, 39, 40, 41, 42, 52, 79, 83, 85, 95, 96, 98, 116, 117, 118, 149, 164, 200, 206, 219; telling 35–44; zones 7, 20, 219; *see also* place-time; space-time continuum
Tokarcyzk, Olga; *Primeval and Other Times* 208
Tolkien, J. R. R. 34; Middle-earth 209
Tornatore, Giuseppe: *Cinema Paradiso* 210
Toronto xiv, 27

Totten, Gary 223
tradition x, 16, 18, 19, 33, 34, 41, 67, 83, 87, 103, 107, 124, 133, 137, 138, 139, 146, 147, 150, 152, 155, 161, 167, 168, 175, 180, 182, 185, 193, 206, 210, 215, 216, 220
transformation x, 15, 20, 61, 67, 69, 71, 80, 84, 86, 91, 94, 115, 116, 167, 190, 196, 221
translocality 31, 51, 98, 104, 109, 133, 160, 174
transnationality 34, 124, 126, 127, 205
Treaty of Guadalupe Hidalgo 206
Tsing, Anna Lowenhaupt 48, 138, 219, 220; *Friction* 42; *A Mushroom at the End of the World* 214, 218
Tuan, Yi-Fu 3, 25, 36, 42; *Space and Place: The Perspective of Experience* 35; Upright Human Body, Space and Time *36*
Tuskegee Normal School (later University) 75
Twain, Mark 18, 19, 37, 182, 224; *Huckleberry Finn* 182
Tyson, Neil DeGrasse 164

United Kingdom/Britain 4, 119, 123, 206
United Nations 43
United States vii, viii, x, 5, 6, *6*, 17, 19, 20, 34, 42, 47, 61, 94, 108, 123, 125, 130, 141, 146, 155–7, 163, 166, 172, 174, 200, 201, 204–6, 212, 217, 219, 220, 223; Civil War 16, 17, 19, 26, 52, 156, 157, 203; Congress 19, 20, 74, 76; Postal Service 82
Upper Peninsula 26, 167

Van Riper, Charles (aka Cully Gage) 26
Vanderstaay, Steven 93
Vermont 166, 167, 191, 205
Vevay County 59, 220
Victorian culture 138, 140, 146
Vietnam War 38
Vigil, Kiara xiii, 74, 76, 223
Virginia 56, 59, 65, 162, 167
Vogelius, Christa Holm 155

Wabash, Indiana 74
Wadsworth, Sarah 141
Wales 24, 42, 164
Walker, Scott (politician) 219
Warner, Michael 148
Warner, Susan: *The Wide, Wide World* 18
Warren, Kenneth: *What Was African American Literature?* 203
Washington, Booker 67
Washington, D.C. 219, 225
Washington, George 126
Watanna, Onoto *see* Eaton, Winnifred
Watts, Edward 58
Webb, Dorothy xiii, 48, 59
Weber, Clara and Carl 26

Weber, Eugen 94–5; *Peasants into Frenchmen* 94, 240
West Virginia 162, 167
Westad, Odd Arne 157
Westbrook, Perry; *Acres of Flint:* 20
"Wheat Strips on Plateau" (MacLean) **214**
White-Parks, Annette 124, 125, 130, 140, 143, 224, 225
Whitman, Walt: "Crossing Brooklyn Ferry" 202
Williams, Raymond ix, 23–5, 39, 64, 99, 177, 189, 200; *Border Country* 25, 240; *The Country and the City* 23, 39, 240; "Region and Class in the Novel" 23; *Writing in Society* 23–4, 240
Willis, Lloyd 155
Windward Islands 108
Winfrey, Oprah: Book Club 86
Winter, Kate: *The Woman in the Mountain* 26
Wisconsin 22, 24, 219
Witgen, Michael 15
Wood, Denis: *Everything Sings* 7
Woodrell, Daniel 167
Woolson, Constance Fenimore: "King David" 70

Wordsworth, William 142
world literature 155, 158–60, 206; and global village 208
World Trade Center 209
World Trade Organization 7–8
World's Fairs 133–6
Wright, Richard 133, 173; *Native Son* 133
Wu, Paul 137

Yamashita, Karen Tei; *I Hotel* 121, 130, 241
Yankton Sioux 72, 74
Yiddish 131
Yin, Xiao-huang 127, 141, 146
Yourcenar, Marguerite 43–4

Zagarell, Sandra xiii, 46, 47, 117
Zencey, Eric: "The Rootless Professors" 93, 196
Zimmerman, Jonathan: *Small Wonder* 223, 241
Zitkala-Sa 72–6, 93, 223; *American Indian Stories* 72, 228; "Impressions of an Indian Childhood" 73; "An Indian Teacher among Indians" 73, 74; "The School Days of an Indian Girl" 73; "Why I Am a Pagan" 75
Zola, Emile 159